For J.E.J.B.

The Last Dance

1936: The Year Our Lives Changed

DENYS BLAKEWAY

JOHN MURRAY

First published in Great Britain in 2010 by John Murray (Publishers)
An Hachette UK Company

First published in paperback in 2011

1

A CIP catalogue record for this title is available from the British Library

ISBN 978-0-7195-2393-9

Typeset in Bembo by Servis Filmsetting Ltd, Stockport, Cheshire

Printed and bound by Clays Ltd, St Ives plc

John Murray policy is to use papers that are natural, renewable and recyclable products and made
from wood grown in sustainable forests. The logging and manufacturing processes are expected to
conform to the environmental regulations of the country of origin.

John Murray (Publishers)
338 Euston Road
London NW1 3BH

www.johnmurray.co.uk

Denys Blakeway

...ys Blakeway is an award-winning television producer and author, special-
...g in contemporary history. He has made numerous films about the 1930s
...luding *God Bless You, Mr Chamberlain*, *The Road to War* and *Abdication, A*
...y British Coup.

Praise for *The Last Dance*:

...n absorbing presentation of a single year . . . *The Last Dance* is colourful and
...ematic. It vividly recapitulates key themes played out during the 1930s'
...nday Times

...lakeway is a respected documentary film-maker with a long record of well-
...searched films that have often broken new ground. In *The Last Dance* he
...ovides a snapshot of British society from top to bottom in this year of change
... Blakeway has new things to say about even the most familiar events . . . a
...fully written and enjoyable book' *Sunday Telegraph*

'The *Last Dance* has all the virtues of books which narrow their focus to a
limited period of time; not quite James Joyce, but something to make readers
ponder the quotidian contingency of it all. Blakeway is a witty writer . . . fair-
minded and has a keen eye for detail . . . a lively book' *The Spectator*

'Unlike many historians, [Blakeway] is prepared to think afresh, and unwilling
to trot out received opinion . . . This book stands as testimony to the value of
the cross-fertilisation of TV and the printed word' *Mail on Sunday*

'Denys Blakeway . . . has triumphed with this book, writing with humour and
sophistication about all forms of British Life' *Lady*

...nshot of one year in history is an obvious idea for a book – but I do not
...ow of another example quite like it. It is just the right length, just the right
tone and very well written' *Reader's Digest*

'Fast-paced . . . very good . . . intriguing . . . Blakeway is excellent at setting
the scene and introducing the kind of quirky evidence that helps to humanise
the story' *Herald*

Also by Denys Blakeway

Fields of Thunder: Testing Britain's Bomb (with Sue Lloyd-Roberts)
The Falklands War
The Queen's Story (with Marcus Kiggell)

Contents

'We were conscious, now and then vaguely and overcheerfully perhaps, of living on the verge of an unimaginable catastrophe.'

Peter Quennell

'As usual, I think, Oh, this will blow over. But it's odd how near the guns have got to our private life again. I can quite distinctly see them and hear a roar.'

Virginia Woolf

Introduction

L ATE IN DECEMBER 1936 the liner *Queen Mary*, pride of Britain, flagship of the greatest maritime nation on earth, sailed into a winter storm in the North Atlantic. She had been completed only six months earlier at Glasgow's Clydebank shipyards and was carrying 2,000 passengers in great luxury to New York. As the liner steamed into the storm that evening, some of the wealthy patrons of cabin class thronged the ship's ballroom high on the promenade deck, dancing to a live band while the 'thyratron' controller dimmed and raised the lights in tune with the music's changing mood. On a lower deck in the panelled tourist lounge passengers relaxed over cocktails before dinner, serenaded by the resident pianist.

The *Queen Mary* had never before encountered such ferocious weather. Battered by gale-force winds and high waves, she began to roll, leaning over to one side by as much as 45 degrees, pausing, returning to upright before heaving over 45 degrees in the opposite direction. The dance floor in the ballroom and the tourist lounge emptied as passengers groped their way to the relative comfort and safety of their staterooms. Such extreme rolling had not been anticipated. The ship's furnishings were unsecured. Sofas and armchairs slid across the polished floors of the saloons. Crockery and cutlery cascaded from the dining-room tables, clattering and smashing on the floor.

After a while loud rumbles and thuds could be heard coming from the tourist lounge. On inspection crew members discovered that the upright piano, bolted to the bulkheads, had worked itself loose. With every roll the piano was cannoning into the room's wood-panelled walls. It was too dangerous to enter the lounge to capture the rogue instrument. For two days it slid back and forth across the open space, crashing from side to side. Each time the instrument hit a bulkhead, it emitted jangles, bass booms and eerie strumming sounds, as though crying out in agonized death throes.

Nineteen thirty-six, the crucial year of the 1930s, also set sail in a spirit of optimism and ended in despair and destruction. For the majority of British people the 1930s had not been the period of gloom and darkness, 'the devil's decade', that was the general experience around the world. The trauma of the First World War cast a long shadow, but many still held to the faith that it had been the war to end all wars. The country had recovered relatively well from the slump that followed the Wall Street Crash of 1929. For those in work falling prices increased prosperity and raised living standards. Britain had been isolated in the early years of the decade from the troubling developments on the Continent. But in 1936, when Mussolini used poison gas against the tribespeople of Abyssinia, Hitler marched his forces into the Rhineland and the Spanish Civil War broke out in July, the march of world events could be ignored no longer. Fear of war and preparation for conflict came to overshadow everything.

At home, changes were also taking place that made 1936 a pivotal year, one that has justly been called 'the hinge of the decade'. If the 1930s had a dramatic unity – starting with a global depression, ending with a global war – then 1936 had its own symmetry. It began with the death of George V, continued with the troubled reign and abdication of Edward VIII and culminated in the accession in December of his brother, George VI. The story of the abdication, often told, is always compelling. Its elements of love, jealousy and family betrayal and, above all, of the human fallibility that lies behind the mask of royalty, have Shakespearean overtones and a universal significance. It is not an exaggeration to say that the abdication of Edward VIII played its part in hastening the onset of war. With the recent release of documents and the publication of previously unseen diaries and letters it is now possible to take a broader view of a crisis that reflected the strains of a changing society.

King Edward's attempts to modernize the monarchy reflected a changing country but were unacceptable to traditionalists in the

establishment. In rejecting Edward, the old guard might have succeeded in arresting his attempts at modernization, but change was
coming whether they liked it or not. Nineteen thirty-six saw the
birth of television and a continuing communications revolution,
the explosion of the suburbs, the rise of the middle classes, the growth
of consumerism and the worship of celebrity. It was the year when
some of the key ideas that would lead to the creation of the welfare
state were born. The economist John Maynard Keynes published his
world-changing *General Theory of Employment, Interest and Money*.

The roots of the Labour government's post-Second World War settlement could also be seen in the reform of maternity care that took
place that year, and in the growth of a public mood that demanded that
action be taken to remove the stain of social injustice. Although the
Jarrow marchers of 1936 may have regarded their crusade for jobs as a
failure, it turned out to be a very modern triumph of public relations.
The march brought the plight of the devastated industrial regions of
the north to millions and added to the demands that something be
done about the social injustice of the country. Many of the events and
developments that year can be seen to have been the precursors of
change that led to the modern world we know today.

The country was divided in 1936, even more than it is today, not
only by wealth and class but also by knowledge. While all were aware
of the Empire and with the development of radio millions could
follow the rise of the dictators in Europe, the way others lived at
home was often a great unknown. People from different backgrounds
lived in parallel worlds. This mutual ignorance was heightened by the
isolation of areas of extreme poverty, such as south Wales, the north-
east of England and parts of Scotland. Given the remoteness of the
poor communities, sealed from the outside world, there was little
chance for radical movements such as Communism and Fascism to
take root.

The year saw a move to end the country's lack of awareness of
much that was taking place in its own backyard and, in particular, to
publicize the life of the working classes and the plight of the unemployed. George Orwell, a former imperial policeman, went to Wigan
to report on the poverty of the northern industrial areas. John

Grierson used the emerging medium of documentary film to bring ordinary people's work to the screen. The birth of television would in time lead to the breaking down of many barriers and give the country a new sense of shared experience and self-knowledge.

For all the poverty and inequality, though, Britain in 1936 was a proud country. Most people still believed that it was the greatest nation in the world. The British Empire stretched further than ever before. A quarter of the world's population were subjects of the Crown, and the Royal Navy ruled the oceans. Schoolboys of the time could recite the superlatives of greatness – the highest, fastest, longest; most seemed to be British. The nation's supremacy, however, was a façade. Britain had paid a high cost for victory in the First World War. The conflict had sapped its strength, drained its financial reserves and knocked its self-confidence. The ideas that had sustained the imperial mission were losing their currency. For those who cared to look, the cracks were showing everywhere. India was in revolt, and the country's imperial defences were overstretched. Politicians such as Neville Chamberlain were well aware that, if war came again, Britain's claims to greatness would be finished. It was this knowledge that motivated and justified the policy of appeasement.

Nineteen thirty-six was the pivotal year for Britain between the two great conflicts, the First and Second World Wars. Until that year the prospect of another war had been unthinkable. The cataclysm of the Great War had so traumatized the nation that the cry for peace was universal. Winston Churchill's warnings of the danger of a resurgent Germany were largely disregarded. But after 1936 the clash of events could be ignored no longer. The piano hurtling from one side of the tourist lounge to the other had to be confronted.

After the storm, when calm returned to the *Queen Mary*, the crew entered the tourist lounge to inspect the damage. They found a scene of devastation. The piano lay on the floor, a steel skeleton. The room's wooden panelling had been destroyed. Splinters were strewn across the floor, mingled with fragments of the instrument's oak case and shards of its black and white keys. But the ship had to keep to its schedule. The stewards cleared away the mangled instrument, the ship's carpenter patched up the wood panelling and, in a couple of days, the tourist lounge was opened once more to passengers making the next voyage. Few noticed the damage but many were no doubt surprised to be told that there would be no dancing in the lounge or the ship's ballroom. As the year ended, the forecast was for more storms ahead.

I

The dawn of the year

'AT LAST THE sun!' Winston Churchill rejoiced. 'I thought we should never overtake it!' For two weeks, 'wandering, sun-seeking, rather disconsolate', he had tried in vain to escape the incessant rain that had dogged him through Spain and Morocco on his way south. 'I never take holidays',[1] Churchill once told a friend, but at the end of December 1935 he was in desperate need of a respite from the political difficulties and family troubles that beset him at home. His career was going nowhere, one of his daughters was infatuated with an unsuitable man, and his son was a perpetual embarrassment. Now at La Mamounia, his hotel just outside the walled city of Marrakesh, he had found the sunshine he craved and could finally relax, welcome the new year of 1936 and set to work painting and writing, away from the depressing distractions of home.

In the south of England days of torrential rain had brought floods from Devon to Kent, and in the north a mixture of frozen snow and sleet covered the ground, which by New Year's Eve had started to thaw into a grey slush. For those trapped in the British Isles, *Tatler* advised its befuddled readers not to let the bleak weather and long hours of darkness get them down: 'Wake up – Rouse yourselves – BE ALIVE. There is work to do, glory to be attained, happiness to be enjoyed.'[2] Many agreed. On New Year's Eve 'the streets of London were gay', the *Daily Mirror* reported, 'restaurants thronged with merry-makers'.[3] They had much to celebrate. Britain was at peace, and the country's economy was prospering. Victory in the First World War had extended the Empire's reach further than ever, and during the summer 500 million subjects paid homage to George V in his jubilee year. 'With hopes higher than at any time since the War,' the *Mirror* enthused, 'millions of people all over Britain welcomed 1936.'[4]

Sixty thousand revellers came to the West End that evening. The Savoy Hotel had decked out its public rooms in seasonal 'red, green, heliotrope and onyx in ordered confusion'. White-stockinged flunkeys 'with an abstract air of enjoyment on their faces'[5] walked round offering champagne to guests. In the ballroom a vast hour-glass was suspended above the dancers, the last grains of sand running through its narrow tube as the clock struck twelve, to a fanfare blown by trumpeters from the Life Guards. All things American were in vogue, and downstairs in Harry's Bar consumption was reaching record levels, with 319 martinis drunk since nine o'clock. Equally popular was the fashionable new year cocktail just imported from the USA, the 'Silent Third', made up of 'lemon juice, Cointreau, rest Scotch'. Across town at the Grosvenor House a dance band played for 1,400 guests. There was a cabaret with an American theme, 'New York 1936'. Those wanting more traditional entertainment could go to The Trocadero in Piccadilly, where George Robey, the veteran music-hall star, performed his usual blend of patter, song and *doubles entendres*, waggling of the eyebrows, all interspersed with the familiar mock telling-off of the audience, when they got the joke, 'Desist!' or 'Kindly temper your hilarity with a modicum of reserve'.

One and a half thousand miles due south, Winston Churchill was delighted with La Mamounia, his hotel facing the rose-coloured walls of the Moorish city. It was, he reported to his wife, Clementine, 'one of the best I have ever used', with its spacious suite of rooms, its balcony looking out over orange trees and olive groves, and the houses and ramparts of Marrakesh in the near distance. To the east the snow-capped peaks of the Atlas Mountains 'like a great wall' reflected the ever-changing sunlight, 'as good as any snowscape I have ever seen'. It was the perfect place for painting: clear and fresh, but warm enough to sit outside. There was time enough, too, to allow him to get on with the dictation of his current work – the life of his forebear the Duke of Marlborough – to his secretary, Violet Pearman. Churchill could not function without Mrs Pearman. She made all the arrangements for his journey, coped with his moods and last-minute changes as he hopped disconsolately from hotel to hotel across a wintry Spain and rainy North Africa, and had sacrificed her own family Christmas to be with her boss.

But he could function without his wife. Curiously for such a close and loving marriage, the couple often spent their holidays apart from each other. Clementine did not like her husband's friends, and she hated political conversation and drinking sessions late into the night. This year, at the age of fifty, she had decided to take up skiing and had gone before Christmas with her daughter Mary to the resort of Zürs, in Austria, leaving her husband to make his way south without her. 'Here we are 5,500 feet up above the clouds in the eye of the sun completely enclosed in a little valley', she wrote to him. There were few lifts in those days, and Clementine watched as the experts struggled up the mountain through the 'glistening powder-like snow' with skins on their skis. 'It takes them 1½ hours to climb up and perhaps 12 minutes to swirl down in lovely curves.'[6]

On New Year's Eve she telephoned her husband. Just to get through was a triumph at a time when international calls were a rarity, connected by operators and carried over thousands of miles of copper cable. The Churchills' brief conversation, interrupted by constant crackles and clicks, was more a gesture of love than an exchange of news. 'My beloved I have just heard yr voice on the long distance', Churchill wrote affectionately to Clementine after the call, 'It was vy Miaou Cat & I cd not hear much but it was sweet to get in touch across all these distances & foreign countries. All my wishes for yr happiness in the coming year.'[7]

Winston Churchill always travelled in luxury, and never alone. A caravan of cronies, all dissidents and bitter enemies of the Prime Minister, Stanley Baldwin, had journeyed south to enjoy the hotel's stylish blend of Art Deco and Moorish luxury with him. They were the buccaneers of the age, out of tune with the more sober old guard who ran the country. The former war leader David Lloyd George was a guest, with his wife and daughter, working on his memoirs. Like Churchill, Lloyd George was an outsider. His attempted political comeback at the recent general election had failed to capture the public's imagination. He was a spent force in British politics, embittered and antagonistic, his reputation curdled by the corruption of his last years in office. 'What a fool Baldwin is', Churchill expostulated to Clementine, 'not to gather his resources and experience to the public service.'[8] He could have been speaking of himself.

The press baron Lord Rothermere was at the hotel too, enjoying a new year break. The owner of the *Daily Mail* was, with his great rival Lord Beaverbrook, the leading press-baiter and critic of Stanley Baldwin. Rothermere had backed Oswald Mosley's Fascist movement and was a friend and admirer of Adolf Hitler and Nazi Germany. He kept in close touch with the Führer even during his holiday in Morocco and showed Churchill the letters and telegrams Hitler had sent him. Despite this close Nazi connection, his newspapers urged greater rearmament. Churchill had long accepted Rothermere as a useful member of his colourful and eclectic circle.

Another friend and loyal supporter, Frederick Lindemann, 'the Prof', was also holidaying at La Mamounia. An abrasive and fearless character (he had learned to fly in order to prove his theory of how to get out of a tailspin, and saved many lives as a result), the Prof acted as Churchill's unofficial scientific adviser. He was the opposite of his friend, being a strict teetotal vegetarian, but he had the knack – which endeared him to Churchill – of being able to explain complex scientific ideas in plain English. Lindemann regularly caused mayhem and fury in official circles by championing, with Churchill's backing, his favoured schemes. Many were crackpot, but some – such as radar – would help win the coming war.

Over a long and bibulous dinner at La Mamounia on New Year's Eve (no doubt watched over disapprovingly by the Prof) this self-appointed government-in-exile's conversation turned to new year's resolutions. Rothermere bet Churchill £2,000 that he could not give up alcohol until his sixty-second birthday the following November. It was an enormous sum of money, equivalent to £75,000 today,[9] and tempting for a man with as heavy outgoings as Churchill, but he did not take the wager, telling Clementine 'I think life would not be worth living'.[10] Given that an average wage for a worker that year was about £150 a year, the offer showed the degree of concern that Rothermere, not usually a helpful influence in his friend's life, felt about his drinking. Churchill did, however, accept a lesser bet of £600 from the press magnate, that he would not drink brandy 'or any undiluted spirits in 1936'.

Churchill's drinking was no secret in political and society circles. With his support for lost causes, his raffish friends and his overblown eloquence, Churchill was a character that 'the respectable tendency',[11] led by the homely and pipe-smoking Stanley Baldwin, Conservative leader of the coalition National Government, believed could not be trusted with power. Although when together they observed the usual courtesies, the two men detested each other. Baldwin said of Churchill: 'When Winston was born lots of fairies swooped down on his cradle gifts – imagination, eloquence, industry, ability, and then came a fairy who said "No one person has a right to so many gifts", picked him up and gave him such a shake and twist that with all these gifts he was denied judgment and wisdom.'[12]

It was a view that many shared. As the editor of *The Spectator* wrote at the time, Churchill had 'defeated himself by his own extravagance'.[13] He was in the wilderness, brooding and unpredictable, considered by most to be a magnificent but reckless liability. The year 1936 was to be a terrible one for him, with or without the fortification of brandy, and by its end almost everybody – apart, of course, from himself – would believe his career was finished.

While Churchill was sinking, Neville Chamberlain, the Chancellor of the Exchequer, was approaching his zenith. A ruthless operator, he brooked no opposition to his management of the economy. Chamberlain had first come to prominence as Lord Mayor of Birmingham, where he had embarked on an ambitious programme of slum clearance. At Westminster in the 1920s, as health minister, he continued to push forward with a wide range of social improvements. Since 1931, when he became Chancellor of the Exchequer, he had skilfully steered the country through the slump and now planned to use the country's healthy economic surplus to embark once more on reform.

No one doubted that Chamberlain was next in line to be Prime Minister. He himself was waiting impatiently to take over from

Stanley Baldwin, constantly carping at Baldwin's sloth and indolence. Early in the new year, in one of the many letters to his sisters that he used as a diary to collect his thoughts and to let off steam, Chamberlain complained: 'I saw the P.M. last night, but was totally unable to extract any opinion from him on any of the questions I wished to discuss. I never knew him worse.'[14] Chamberlain, formal and buttoned up, seldom prone to laughter, was nonetheless a man of many parts. He spent the Christmas break relaxing at home, looking after his orchids and indulging his love of Shakespeare by re-reading *Hamlet* not once but twice – 'a thing I don't remember to have done with any book before', he told his sister Ida. 'It was *Hamlet* that first attracted me to Shakespeare and now he is more absorbing and interesting than ever.'[15] Politicians in those days had what Denis Healey later called 'hinterland'.

The worst of the Depression was over. Neville Chamberlain, as Chancellor of the Exchequer, gleefully proclaimed in his 1936 budget that the recovery had been remarkable. Industrial output was up by 29 per cent, exports were up by £50 million, and unemployment was down; revenue had expanded to allow the redemption of £70 million of national debt. Chamberlain felt justified in thinking that the 'two main pillars' of his policy, cheap money and tariffs, had made a considerable contribution to the economic recovery.[16]

Life at the time, for those in work, seemed full of promise. John Prichard was eleven years old in 1936. He had recently moved with his family from the slums of east London to a modern bungalow in Bexleyheath. His father worked in the new electronics industry as a telephone engineer. 'The country itself was prosperous and happy', he remembered, anticipating the words of Harold Macmillan twenty years later, 'for many people it was an age of "you've never had it so good".' Four years of growth had fuelled a housing boom, which in turn had led to an explosion in sales of the latest gadgets. Millions, from the Prime Minister's wife, Lucy Baldwin, who installed a 'Frigidaire' in the larder at Number 10, to the new occupants of the 'Tudorbethan' semis that were marching across the southern countryside, were buying the latest consumer gadgets. Electricity powered two-thirds of the country's homes, and with the new power came light at the flick of a switch, along with fridges, cookers and vacuum cleaners. Credit, in the form of hire purchase, helped to fuel the boom. Radio was almost universal, and the BBC was about to begin the world's first scheduled television service. Outside, in the garages of the richer middle classes, a new car often gleamed.

For those in the upper classes with money – and most had plenty – life was easy. Everybody had servants (although they were harder than ever to find and keep) to manage the household, to cook, clean, do the laundry, drive and garden. Women did not go out to work after marriage, and the wealthy occupied themselves with the social round of the Season, weekend house parties, dances and charity work. For the young it was a time of increasing freedom and opportunity. Hermione, Countess of Ranfurly, was twenty-three years old in 1936:

> More and more young people owned cars and began to explore Europe. The theatre and cinema were extremely good, and dance music and lyrics excellent . . . most of us now owned a wireless and a camera. Attractive and well fitting clothes were available for those who could not afford haute couture. The young were very independent . . .[17]

But the prosperity that had brought new freedoms and ease of life existed in a bubble that many feared would soon burst. The poverty of the so-called 'special' or 'distressed' areas was a constant running sore on the face of plenty. Hunger marches, where unemployed men from these blighted regions came to London to publicize their suffering, were a frequent sight. Newsreel images of the grim but determined men tramping their way south magnified the plight of communities that were all too easily forgotten. Britain was a divided nation with a guilty conscience. Alongside such poverty the threat of future conflict hung over the country, a dark pall that it seemed nothing could blow away. The technology that had brought the very marvels of modernity that made living so easy could just as well be harnessed for war. The menace of the dictators grew ever stronger. Hitler was rearming, building a modern air force that, it was widely believed, could pulverize London in minutes. John Prichard remembered a sense of escapism that lay behind the New Year celebrations: 'the jollity was partly occasioned by people thinking enjoy ourselves now, because in another of couple of years we might be dead.'[18]

Winston Churchill was well aware of the threat. 'We are getting into the most terrible position', he warned Clementine in a letter from Morocco, 'our defences neglected, our Government less capable a machine for conducting affairs than I have ever seen.'[19] He had been out of government for seven years, in five of which his own Conservative Party had been in power, watching British politics from the sidelines with mounting anxiety. At the beginning of 1936 he was pinning his hopes on a return to office in the new post of Defence Minister, which was soon to be announced. He could then set to work on the job he considered of paramount importance: the rearming of Britain. But much stood in his way. Many mistrusted him as an unreliable flamboyant maverick. Despite having held in his time most of the great offices of state – Chancellor, Home Secretary, First Lord of the Admiralty, Secretary of State for War, for Air and for the Colonies – Churchill had learned to his frustration that no one is indispensable in politics. He lacked the steady, quiet manner and respectability that suited the spirit of the times. He had too often backed the wrong causes and opposed the right ones: most recently he had campaigned against government moves to give India some degree of independence. As the editor of *The Spectator* commented, 'it has been a crowded, an adventurous and in its way spectacular, life', but Churchill had, to his cost, 'made his reputation by sharpshooting at his own Front Bench.'[20] Now, to Churchill's surprise and fury, his son was about to do some sharpshooting of his own.

Randolph Churchill had just announced he was going to challenge the government's candidate, Malcolm MacDonald, in a January by-election. Randolph's decision to stand for the Tories against the son of the former Labour Prime Minister, Ramsay MacDonald, was hugely embarrassing – 'unfortunate and inconvenient', Churchill complained to Clementine – putting 'a spoke in my wheel'.[21] Malcolm MacDonald, like his father, had lost his seat in the general election. Baldwin wanted him back in government as a token Labour man to keep up the pretence of a coalition government. Churchill was well aware that his son's cheek might spoil his own chances of a return to office.

Clementine Churchill shared her husband's foreboding and his frustration at his impotence outside government. They both hoped that he might return to government to help Britain rearm in the face of the rising threat of Hitler. The problem was that they despised Stanley Baldwin as a mediocrity, and Clementine worried that to serve in his National Government would be a sacrifice of principle too far. 'I really would not like you to serve under Baldwin', she wrote, 'unless he really gave you a great deal of power.' Despite her reluctance to mix with Churchill's circle, she did consider coming to La Mamounia from Austria. 'The idea of joining you in Morocco attracts me very much. For one thing I miss my Pig very much; but I want to stay out here until the 21st and I suppose by then you will be thinking of moving home?'[22] Events at home, however, would soon cut short both their holidays.

For some time those close to the King had been concerned about his health. At Sandringham, where he had been celebrating Christmas, if the word 'celebrating' could apply to the monarch's gloomy family festivities, the wintry Norfolk dankness had further lowered the royal family's spirits. His eldest son, Edward, Prince of Wales (known to family and friends as David), noticed with apprehension that the King had grown 'thin and bent'. But the Prince's concern for his father was only passing. He had little thought for anything other than the object of his adoration, Wallis Simpson. He was suffering from a monomania. He cared only for her, his mistress, whom he loved with such overwhelming passion that many considered him close to insanity.

Wallis – American, divorced, remarried and totally 'unsuitable' – was the ghost at the royal Christmas party that year, casting a shadow that the King's closest friends feared was driving him to an early grave. 'After I am dead', he had prophesied to the Prime Minister, 'Edward would pull the whole throne and Empire about his ears before a year was out.'[23] The Prince and his father had long been far apart in outlook, manner and attitude. George V may have had fine qualities as a monarch, but as a father he was appalling. He was a martinet, always ready to criticize and mean with praise. He was feared rather than loved by his sons. Now he and his eldest son could barely talk to one another.

Like an addict, the Prince had to have his fix of Wallis. He bombarded her with letters, notes and gifts. He spoke to her on the telephone for hours at a time. When he left the room at Sandringham, all those present knew he was going to call her, but none reproached him. Instead there were the long silences and false jollity that make a troubled family Christmas such a trial. 'It really is terrible here', the Prince complained to Wallis, 'and so much the worst Xmas I've ever had to spend with the family.'[24]

The Prince left Sandringham as soon as he could, to spend New Year's Eve with Wallis, whose husband was conveniently away on business in Canada. Colin Buist, a former equerry, and his wife, Gladys, had invited the couple to their country-house party near Melton Mowbray. That evening they went together to the Craven Hunt fancy-dress ball, held at Edward's old stamping ground, Craven Lodge. The theme was 'pre-history'. 'Horses have a peculiar effect on their owners', Wallis sniffed, 'I've never seen the English so gay!'[25] She was not exaggerating. Pre-history was the excuse for an aristocratic bacchanalian romp reminiscent of the last days of Rome. Many of the women, in their revealing leopardskin loincloths or scanty Roman togas, captured by the unwelcome *Tatler* photographer, looked positively alarmed. Their cavemen partners in the foxtrot took advantage of the ladies and their own semi-nudity to press themselves ever closer. Mrs Peter Quennell was clearly not happy to be hugged by a bear-skinned Captain Rollo. Judging by the grimace of Lady Dorothea Head, lovely as the god Pan, she would rather not have been held close by a gap-toothed, skimpily clad and hairy-chested Mr Beatty. Lady Jersey and Captain 'Flash' Kellett sensibly sat out the dance, but the Captain's mini-skirt toga revealed too much as he sat on the sofa.

Upper-class society in 1936 was divided between a belief that standards should be maintained at all costs and a desire for sexual and marital freedom. The Prince of Wales was caught between the two. He detested the moral code of the older generation, which he regarded as a personal strait-jacket, and chafed against the view that his role as a member of the royal family demanded that he should abide by it. That week's edition of *Tatler* had examples on every page of the façade of propriety that the upper classes maintained at the time. Most egregious, perhaps, was the photograph of 'The Hon. Mrs Bryan Guinness with her sons and her sister, the Hon. Unity Freeman Mitford'.[26] Everybody in Society knew that Mrs Bryan Guinness, formerly Diana Mitford, had scandalously left her husband and was living openly as the mistress of Tom (Oswald) Mosley, the Fascist leader, but this was never spoken of in public. They knew too that Unity was infatuated with Adolf Hitler, hanging around his favourite haunts in Munich and throwing herself at him at every opportunity. But to say so publicly would have been regarded as an unwarranted breach of decorum.

For convention's sake the Prince of Wales and Wallis had to maintain a formal distance as the revellers at the pre-history Craven Ball brayed around them. Late in the night Wallis sent the Prince new year's greetings, to which he responded in the loving baby-talk he used in private with her: 'Your lovely new year message helped a boy a lot in his lonely drowsy and he was feeling sad. Give Mary an eanum [little] note for me until WE can be alone together again.' He added, perhaps hinting at his hopes for 1936, 'Oh! My Wallis I know we'll have Viel Gluck to make us *one* this year'.[27] If he was thinking of marriage, his plans were about to be dealt a catastrophic blow.

Not far from Sandringham, across the Fens in a misty and damp Cambridge, John Cornford, another star-crossed lover, was alone that New Year, pining for his love. Cornford, just twenty years old, a direct descendant of Charles Darwin, was one of the most gifted young men of his generation. A scholar of Trinity College, he had graduated with a starred First in history. Now he was at a loose end, considering whether or not to take up a graduate scholarship at the college. With his Byronic dark looks and curly black hair, he was extremely attractive to women. Margot Heinemann, who had been a Cambridge undergraduate at the same time, was the second love of his life. His first, Rachel Peters, had given birth to his baby out of wedlock, and they had lived together in a direct challenge to the conventional morality of the time.

Bourgeois values meant little to Cornford. Like so many of the intellectuals and artists of his time, he was a Marxist. Drawn to Communism by what he saw as the failure of the older generation to deal with unemployment, spurred on by the rise of Fascism, and – perhaps most importantly – motivated by a general sense of youthful rebellion, he and his fellow believers became zealots for a faith that they were certain would inevitably transform a sick society. Some, such as his acquaintance Anthony Blunt, went underground and joined the Comintern to spy for Soviet Russia. Others, like Cornford himself, were openly activist, selling newspapers at street corners, organizing demonstrations and trying to radicalize a slumbering British proletariat.

John Cornford's life was not as clear-cut as his Communist faith would have him believe. Try as he might, he found that human emotions got in the way of his political beliefs. At the beginning of 1936 it was love that clashed with commitment. As the new year approached, alone and sorrowful, he wrote a moving lyric poem to Margot, ironically entitled 'Happy New Year', which seemed to run counter to his usually ice-cold Marxist outlook:

> All last night we lay so close,
> All completeness of the heart
> The restless future will efface;
> Tomorrow night we sleep apart.

In the last verse Cornford addressed himself and his own grief at his separation from Margot. The onward rush of time could not be halted:

> Though your nerves are frozen numb,
> Your sorrow will not make time stop,
> You're not a statue but a man;
> O don't grieve, it doesn't help.

The poem expressed Cornford's agonizing inner conflict between love and the call of 'the restless future'. That year, as hard choices became inevitable with the outbreak of the Spanish Civil War, he dedicated his life to fighting Fascism.

While the solitary Cornford wrote poetry in Cambridge, all over the country thousands celebrated the New Year. In London those who could not afford the high prices charged by the West End's more classy hotels and night spots drank in pubs and thronged the streets. Others, preferring to greet the new year in a more reflective mood, went to the many churches that were open for Watch Night services.

The two worlds of revellers and faithful, temporal and spiritual, collided at St Paul's Cathedral. The churchyard was the annual gathering-place for crowds of Scots, many of them dressed in kilts, intent on celebrating Hogmanay in style. This year they were joined by thousands of Londoners, streaming up Ludgate Hill to assemble outside the floodlit cathedral under the two great Christmas trees, gifts from the King. There were foreigners too, from the different parts of the Empire, distinctive at a time when the 46 million people of Britain were almost all white. Everyone waved balloons, threw paper streamers and brandished bottles. As the crowds mixed, Cockney girls could be seen with sporrans round their necks, dancing Highland reels, or attempting to do so, to an impromptu mouth-organ accompaniment. According to the shocked *Daily Express* reporter, it was 'like a vision from *Paradise Lost*, Dante's Inferno . . . Hogarthian'. Inside the cathedral a very different scene prevailed, as worshippers kneeling in prayerful meditation tried to ignore the sounds of bedlam that floated in from outside.

The Cathedral Chapter had anticipated the problem. Encouraged by one of their canons, the modernizer and pacifist campaigner Dick Sheppard, they had reluctantly arranged for the New Year service to be relayed outside the cathedral on giant loudspeakers. But to no avail. As the clocks of the City struck twelve, the Scots launched into 'Auld Lang Syne', and the Cockney crowds responded with 'You Can't Do That There 'Ere', drowning out the mournful strains of 'Oh God Our Help in Ages Past', relayed from the cathedral. Undaunted, Dick Sheppard came out from the service, mounted a platform specially erected for the occasion and tried valiantly to lead the crowds, 10,000 strong, in community singing. The loudspeakers broke down. Sheppard, suffering from asthma, gave up the fight and, as the *Daily Mirror* reported, descended into the crowds, where his bent, cassock-clad figure and round, smiling face could be seen moving among the revellers: 'with characteristic good humour he had parried the sallies of the swaying crowds.'

Inside St Paul's, Sheppard's colleagues tut-tutted. They had no liking for this campaigning celebrity priest, whose attempts to bring the cathedral some way into the twentieth century had met with bitter resistance. This conflict epitomized the great theme of change that was to make 1936 so extraordinary: the clash between the old and the new, between British tradition and American fashion, between those who resisted modernity and those who welcomed it, between the revellers outside and the moralists within.

For campaigners such as Dick Sheppard, who sought to bridge this gap, the year 1936 was to bring seemingly impossible challenges. For politicians such as Churchill and Baldwin, faced with the threat of Hitler abroad and a tottering throne at home, the year would deliver catastrophe and success in equal measure and, in the long run, have consequences quite different from those they expected. For the Prince of Wales it would bring the crown and with it the personal turmoil of love and abdication: a crisis of kingship that would test the nation's ideas of morality and modernity to their limits. For John Cornford, the poet hero of the left, it would bring martyrdom fighting Fascism in the Spanish Civil War. It was a year when optimism turned to pessimism, and when the war that so many dreaded became, however much politicians tried to avert it, inevitable.

2

The King's life is being moved towards its close

THAT CHRISTMAS, AS the Prince of Wales had noticed, the seventy-year-old King, George V, was not his usual self. The celebrations of his Silver Jubilee the previous summer had exhausted him, and through the autumn he had grown depressed and lethargic. He had also become alarmingly shrunken and emaciated. He lost interest in his hobby, stamp-collecting. He was often breathless. His doctor, Lord Dawson of Penn, diagnosed a narrowing of the arteries, which caused him to fall asleep during the day, even at mealtimes.[1] At night he was restless, kept awake by worries. His nurse, Sister Catherine Black, had to give him oxygen to calm him.

As the autumn of 1935 turned to winter, the King's condition worsened, apparently aggravated by concerns about the international situation, particularly Italy's invasion of Abyssinia. His depression was greatly increased by the death of his sister Princess Victoria on 3 December. Most of all, though this was never spoken openly, he was anxious about his son David's love for Wallis Simpson. For a man for whom attention to public duty was an obsession, his decision to cancel the state opening of Parliament in December was a warning that all was not well. To Stanley Baldwin it seemed as though 'he was packing up his baggage and getting ready to depart'.[2]

Over the Christmas holiday the King had not taken part in the shoots at Sandringham. As his Assistant Private Secretary, Alexander 'Alec' Hardinge, anxiously told his wife, Helen, the King had preferred to follow the guns, riding Jock, his favourite grey pony.[3] This, for a man who had made it his life's mission to massacre as many pheasants as was humanly possible, was another sign that the end could not be not far off. As the guests departed Sandringham at the beginning of the new year, the Queen told her family to prepare for the worst.

Alec Hardinge returned from Sandringham to his grace-and-favour mansion at Windsor Castle for the new year. He shared his anxieties about the King's condition with his family and his mother-in-law, Lady Milner. At a time when many yearned for continuity and stability, the prospect of the King's death was deeply troubling. Hardinge was utterly loyal to the unchanging customs and traditions of the court of George V and Queen Mary. Like the King, he was an ultra-conservative, and, like the King, he was highly strung and prone to fits of bad temper.

On New Year's Day the 63-year-old Violet Milner ventured out to look at the floods, perhaps seeking respite from her son-in-law. 'Eton is almost an island', she wrote in her diary, 'it came on to rain and I came back soon.'[4] As a consolation for the grim weather, and to take their minds off the King's health, Alec Hardinge took his wife and his mother-in-law to the castle library, where they looked at the Leonardo drawings for an hour before returning home to write their thank-you letters. Violet concentrated on reading articles for *The National Review*, the monthly magazine that she edited.

By 1936 Violet, Viscountess Milner seemed a throwback to another age. She was a product of the late Victorian and Edwardian eras, when Imperial Britain was at its most confident. She came from a family of die-hard reactionaries, the Maxses, and under the influence of her father she had taken a precocious interest in literature and politics. She made friends with the artist Edward Burne-Jones and the poet Rudyard Kipling, both men of her father's circle. In 1894 she had married Lord Edward Cecil, son of the Prime Minister Lord Salisbury, and so joined a political dynasty. It was a dreadful match. The couple were unsuited temperamentally and intellectually. During the Boer War, while Edward was cooped up in besieged Mafeking, Violet stayed in Cape Town as the guest of the High Commissioner, Alfred Milner. There she fell in love with the great colonial administrator, and he with her.[5]

After the relief of Mafeking, Edward was posted in 1901 to Egypt, where Violet visited him briefly, before returning to Britain to be with her children (and nearer to Alfred). Edward conveniently died in a Swiss sanatorium at the end of the First World War, leaving her free to marry the man she adored. Their marriage was tragically brief. Milner died in 1921, but he left Violet with the imperialist inspiration of her life – 'the speech, the tradition, the spiritual heritage, the principles, the aspirations of the British race'[6] – an inspiration that by 1936 had become increasingly anachronistic. The Empire still meant a great deal to millions and was regarded by most as a force for good in the world, but its heyday was well past. Its sheer size, far from being a strength, made it exposed and vulnerable. Britain's defences were hopelessly overstretched, independence for India was becoming inevitable, and in places such as Palestine riots and disturbances were a daily occurrence.

Violet was one of a dwindling number of Conservative political hostesses: Nancy Astor, Emerald Cunard and Edith, Marchioness of Londonderry, who could still afford to entertain in the Edwardian style. She kept a town house in London where she held luncheons for fellow Empire loyalists and the leading Conservatives of the day. With her connection to the court through her son-in-law, and her links with right-wing politicians and journalists, she was a woman at the heart of the Conservative establishment. Unsurprisingly, Winston Churchill, the mistrusted outsider, was anathema to her. Despite sharing his hostility to Nazi Germany and his outspoken opposition to Indian independence, she never forgave him for the verbal pasting he had once given her husband in the House of Commons.

Violet owned a large country house in Sussex, Great Wigsell, which was close to Bateman's, home of her soul-mate, the arch-imperialist Rudyard Kipling. Just as anxieties about the King were growing, so Kipling's state of health also became a cause for alarm at the beginning of the year. It seemed that two great relics of another epoch, one the embodiment of Empire, the King–Emperor himself and the other its bard, were on the point of death. Kipling, King George's friend and contemporary (both men had been born in 1865), was an obsessive hypochondriac, but on this occasion his duodenal ulcer was real enough.

On 30 December he had celebrated his seventieth birthday, receiving numerous telegrams and letters, including a message from the ailing King. While he shared many of George V's values, above all a deeply felt conservatism, Kipling was not nearly as popular as the King. Since the First World War, in which his son had been killed, his celebrity had waned. His work had grown increasingly dense, filled with arcane spiritualism and Freemasonry. He had become a snob who enjoyed walking with the King so much that he had lost the common touch. He was also such a reactionary that he hated much of the modern world and used his position to pester ministers with warnings about the dire consequences of social reform.

At the beginning of January 1936 Kipling's domineering wife, Carrie, decided they needed a short holiday in the south of France to escape the winter in England. They set off from Sussex to Brown's Hotel in London, to prepare for the journey and deal with various family affairs, including the writer's will. Unexpectedly, Kipling fell ill on 12 January; his stomach ulcer burst and he was taken to the Middlesex Hospital for an emergency operation. Violet Milner was at work at her desk in Manchester Square. She wrote in her diary that her maid 'came in to tell me that *Rudyard Kipling was very ill indeed*'.[7]

On hearing the news, Violet rushed to Brown's to be with Carrie, and there she was slightly reassured. 'He is very ill, though not hopelessly so. I stayed with her [Carrie] for some time. I can think of nothing else.' But Kipling's condition worsened. 'Something has come adrift inside',[8] he told his surgeon. Carrie and her daughter Elsie moved into the Middlesex, where beds were made up for them. Violet meanwhile took her granddaughter Elizabeth to the pantomime. 'I was in tears most of the time, but in the dark this did not show. Rud is desperately ill.' When they left the theatre, the news vendors were shouting the news of Kipling's illness. Violet's daughter Helen Hardinge reflected that, having been 'born in 1865 when the British Empire was at the height of its fortunes and formed the most powerful community in the world, Rudyard Kipling was now, in 1936, dying with his epoch'.[9]

Kipling died just after midnight on Saturday 18 January. It was his forty-fourth wedding anniversary. Violet Milner was devastated. She had first met him nearly fifty years earlier. The following morning she wrote: 'Alas that I should outlive all those who have given me all I care for. The world is bare and empty without them. I have been so miserable all day that I have hardly known how to bear myself.' She walked about aimlessly all afternoon in her house in Manchester Square and telephoned Carrie. 'She was, as she always is, perfectly rational. I can't bear to think of her.' Then there was more bad news: 'The *King* is ill. The word anxiety has been used and his family is assembled.'[10]

Six days earlier, on Sunday 12 January, the King's doctor, Lord Dawson, alarmed by reports from Nurse Black, had driven to Sandringham, where he 'found him feeling unwell, no energy – felt life on top of him'.[11] Death in the very near future seemed inevitable, and as the King's health declined, so the apparatus of state started to gear up for the transfer of the crown to the heir, a process where public and private grief would mingle in a theatrical display of funereal pomp. For the royal family, at the centre of events, and especially for the dying monarch privacy was swept away as the rituals and mechanisms of the British constitution took over. In that January of 1936 the death of the King highlighted the changes taking place in society at large. The development of the mass media, especially radio, meant that everybody could follow the developments minute by minute. The death was not just a matter of national grief, it was an opportunity for the manipulation of opinion with the management of public relations. Even the very moment of death would be chosen by courtiers to maximize its impact. The body of the monarch became public property as he took his last breaths.

The King's wife, Queen Mary, did not object. She shared her husband's absolute belief in duty and doing the right thing, which included never letting her feelings show. She maintained an icy and dignified composure throughout this painful time. Her family was beset with tensions. All its members, including the Prince of Wales himself, dreaded the accession and the leap into the unknown that it must bring.

On Thursday 16 January the Queen sent a note to the Prince of Wales, alerting him to his father's condition. 'I think you ought to know that Papa is not very well',[12] she wrote with typical understatement, and suggested that he come to Sandringham at the weekend. Knowing his mother as he did, the Prince flew to Sandringham the next morning in his own private aeroplane. There he found his father, dressed in his faded silk Tibetan dressing gown, sitting before the fire in his bedroom. It was rumoured later that all the King could find to say to his heir was 'You look just as big a cad as ever'.[13] Certainly there had been little love between father and son, and at this moment, drugged and near death, the King seemed barely aware of the presence of his son.

That evening the first of several medical bulletins was issued to the press and pinned to the railings at Buckingham Palace. Each one was carefully composed by Lord Dawson to prepare the public by stages for the worst. It read: 'The bronchial catarrh from which His Majesty the King is suffering is not severe, but there have appeared signs of cardiac weakness which must be regarded with some disquiet.'[14] The words, printed in the morning's papers on Saturday 18 January, resonated across the country. 'Chips' Channon, the American-born socialite and Conservative MP, wrote in his diary: 'The year has, indeed, begun in gloom. The King ill – and Kipling dead.'[15] The prospect of the passing of these two titans of empire, champions of the Victorian age, when Britain had dominated the world, seemed for almost everybody, whatever their class or political outlook, to herald a new era. The controversial Bishop of Durham, Herbert Hensley Henson, may have exaggerated the power and influence of the sovereign, but he captured the national mood when he wrote in his diary:

> Two evil announcements dominate the newspapers: the King is ill, and Rudyard Kipling is dead. If, (which may Heaven avert!) His Majesty were taken away just now a formidable blow to European security would be given . . . I cannot but feel alarmed at a bulletin which talks darkly about 'cardiac trouble'.[16]

As news of the King's condition spread, crowds gathered at Buckingham Palace, waiting for further bulletins to be posted on the railings.

At Sandringham the two brothers David and Bertie, the Prince of Wales and the Duke of York, accompanied their mother on a walk in the grounds while their father lay dying in his room upstairs. The atmosphere was agonizing as this tight-lipped and emotionally repressed family made small talk, each one privately knowing, as the King's death approached, what none dared say: that the Prince of Wales was in love with a woman whom they considered totally unsuitable to be the companion, let alone lover, of the monarch. The same day the Prince had written to Wallis telling her that there was now no hope whatsoever for the King, and 'I love you more and more and need you so to be with me at this difficult time'. Using their joint pet-name, 'WE', he repeated how he longed for her, and wrote: 'You are all and everything I have in life and WE must hold each other so tight. It will all work out for us. God Bless WE. Your DAVID.'[17] It was a letter from a man looking into the abyss.

On Sunday morning he drove to London to brief Stanley Baldwin on his father's state of health, but his first priority was to see Wallis. He made straight for her flat in Bryanston Square. Baldwin was well aware of this, as the security services had long been monitoring the Prince and his lover.[18] He told his friend and confidant, the Welsh busybody Thomas 'Tom' Jones, a former deputy Cabinet Secretary, that the Prince 'had been to see the Mrs S before he came to see me . . . . The subject is never mentioned between us.'[19] Over tea at Number 10 the Prime Minister, who liked to play an avuncular role with the Prince, steered clear of the subject that was on both their minds, but he did give him a pep talk, telling him 'that the King's life was really "a dog's life", so incessant and monotonous were his official tasks'.[20]

While he did not agree with his morals, Baldwin had a fondness for the Prince of Wales.[21] In 1927 he and his wife, Lucy, had accompanied the Prince on a tour of Canada, and the two men had got to know each other well – perhaps too well. Baldwin, a God-fearing and clean-living man whose values harked back to Victorian times, had seen the Prince's womanizing and drinking at first hand. Now he faced the prospect of being the King's principal adviser, and he told Thomas Jones that he was 'distinctly nervous about him'. He hoped it was 'going to be a case of the Prince in Shakespeare's *Henry IV*, and the King in *Henry V*'.

The Prime Minister was in mourning for Kipling, who was his first cousin, and was wearing a black armband. He was put out when the Prince made no mention of this, and drew attention to it himself: 'I wonder if you know, Sir, that another great Englishman, a contemporary of your father's, died yesterday.'[22] The Prince thought that Baldwin's question showed his resentment at the King's illness putting the death of his illustrious cousin in the shade. More likely the Prime Minister took the Prince's ignorance of Kipling's death – a man of world renown, a Nobel Prize winner – as a sign of his general lack of interest in current events and ignorance of culture. He regarded Edward as an 'abnormal being, half child, half genius' and more than once remarked on the fact that he had never read a book. He politely let the Prince off the hook, saying, 'But of course, Sir, you have a great deal on your mind. I should not have expected you to know. It was Rudyard Kipling, my first cousin.'[23] After this sticky moment the atmosphere relaxed, and the two discussed the responsibilities of kingship and the tea party ended harmoniously, with Mrs Baldwin saying to the Prince 'we have faith in you', as she grasped his hand. He squeezed hers in gratitude and left.[24] Afterwards Baldwin made it plain that he had less faith in the heir to the throne than his wife did, telling Thomas Jones that it was a tragedy that Edward was not married, and that 'When I was a little boy in Worcestershire reading history books I never thought I should have to interfere between a King and his mistress'.[25]

After years at the top Stanley Baldwin was suffering from exhaustion and nervous strain. Nonetheless he was buoyed up by the prospect of dealing with this potential royal crisis. Baldwin prided himself on his friendship with Edward and thought it put him in a good position to deal with anything that might arise when the Prince became King. He felt, given this, together with his great experience and legendary ability to manage the most sensitive affairs of state, that providence itself had faced him with this role.[26] Edward would find out later that he was no match for this world-weary Prime Minister, who hid a stiletto behind the façade of fatherly friendliness.

Although he served in office three times and dominated the inter-war years, Stanley Baldwin was an unlikely Prime Minister. A cartoon by Max Beerbohm showed the young Baldwin confronting his older self and exclaiming 'Prime Minister, you. Good Lord!'[27] It was his outward character that made Baldwin seem such an improbable figure to lead the country. He gave the appearance of a comfortable insouciance, of being a man who took it easy, who relaxed by playing patience in the private sitting-room at Downing Street while his wife knitted, and who liked to keep a low profile. Once, he told Thomas Jones, when as Prime Minister he was travelling in a railway carriage, 'He was asked by an old Harrovian who saw S.B. sporting the old tie: "Were you not at Harrow in my time? What have you been doing since?"'[28] It seemed that politics was just something he had fallen into and that the job of Prime Minister had simply happened to come his way. He said he was happiest when walking in the English country-side or leaning on a fence, scratching a pig with a stick. He spoke not with the strangulated vowels of the ruling class of the time but in a plain Englishman's accent in which the traces of his native Worcestershire could be heard. This ordinary manner endeared him to the public. His broadcasts, such as his BBC tribute to King George V two days after the monarch's death, were turned into discs and sold by the thousand.

But Baldwin's outer calm marked an intense inner nervousness. As time passed, he suffered increasingly from depression and had periods of listlessness in which colleagues found it almost impossible to rouse him to action. He admitted openly to being a 'skrimshanker'. He frequently came close to breakdown and could not have continued without the support of his wife. Lucy Baldwin's diaries for 1936, a particularly testing year for the 68-year-old Prime Minister, are littered with comments such as 'Stanley rather depressed about the fatigue attacks and worried generally', 'Stanley very tired' or 'Stanley looked very tired'.[29]

Above all, Baldwin was a politician. To serve as Prime Minister three times and to control a political party for more than a decade required a supreme political ability. He was a sophisticated game-player, a tense operator who could sense the prevailing wind at

Westminster merely by sitting in the tearooms for half an hour, and could act with devastating ruthlessness if that was needed to achieve his goal. In May 1926, as Prime Minister, he had crushed the General Strike in only nine days and faced down the striking miners. Radicals on the left saw him as a reactionary oppressor of the working classes. He was regarded by his political foes on all sides as a man of guile, a Machiavelli in a morning coat.

His preference, when faced with a potential crisis, was to do nothing, in the hope that the trouble would go away. Most often it did. To the persistent irritation of Neville Chamberlain, Baldwin was a profoundly lazy man whose conservative political philosophy was to let things be, until *force majeure* prevailed. This was often successful, but when Baldwin was faced in 1936 with the challenge of a constitutional crisis and a resurgent Germany led by a cunning and dangerous fanatic, the path of least resistance was not enough. As Chamberlain complained: 'I am afraid that it is a source of weakness to have a leader who gives no lead in this particularly trying time.'[30] The Chancellor took on much of the Prime Minister's heavy burden, as Baldwin withdrew almost completely from active leadership. Chamberlain moaned to his sister that 'as I slave over my papers into the small hours I think a little bitterly of him snoozing comfortably away next door'.[31]

At Sandringham meanwhile, while the Prince of Wales was away in London seeing Baldwin, the King was approaching the twilight zone between life and death and was lapsing into incoherence. The King's friend the Archbishop of Canterbury, the Most Revd Dr Cosmo Gordon Lang, a man for whom the word 'unctuous' could have been invented, had invited himself to Sandringham, where he padded about mournfully, 'a noiseless spectre in black gaiters',[32] as an embittered Duke of Windsor would later describe him. Sensing the end, the Cabinet Secretary, Sir Maurice Hankey, decided to call the Privy Council to Sandringham to ensure that the machinery of government would continue while the King was alive but incapable.

The following morning, Monday 20 January, at midday, the Council was held in the King's bedroom. It was a pathetic occasion, miserable and undignified for the dying man. Hankey arrived at

Sandringham at eleven in the morning together with the Lord President, Ramsay MacDonald, a long-standing friend of the King, the Lord Chancellor and the Home Secretary, Sir John Simon. For half an hour the men discussed in hushed tones the appropriate legal precedents and, with the King's doctor and the Archbishop, how the special Council meeting should be conducted. A document handing the power of royal assent to his close family was drafted for the King's signature. His right arm was so weak that they feared he might not be able to sign, and they agreed that a mark would do if a signature were impossible.

The Council members then went upstairs to the King's private sitting-room, next to his bedroom, where they waited, under the beady eye of Charlotte, His Majesty's pet parrot, while Sister Catherine Black prepared the dying man for his last official duty. At 12.15 he was ready, and the three Counsellors filed into the bedroom, joined by the Archbishop and the King's long-serving Private Secretary, Lord Wigram.[33] The King had been moved from his bed and was propped up by pillows in an armchair, with the royal warrant removing his royal powers in front of him on a wooden contraption attached to the chair. His appearance, thin and debilitated, shocked the politicians.

Ramsay MacDonald read out the official warrant. The King grunted 'approved', and Lord Dawson moved forward to perch his reading glasses on his nose so that he could see the document before him. For what seemed an age he stared at it, turning it over once and muttering incoherently, before Dawson approached him and tried to make him sign it with his left hand as his right lay listless and paralysed on his leg. The King was unable to take hold of the fountain pen, saying 'I do not write with both hands' and apologizing politely for keeping his Counsellors waiting, as he was unable to concentrate.[34] Eventually Dawson was able to guide his hand sufficiently for the King to make two distinct marks, which were taken to be a 'G' and an 'R' by the relieved Privy Counsellors. According to Hankey, they 'were one and all convinced that he knew what he was doing'.[35] The Counsellors then filed out tearfully as the King, polite and dutiful to the last, smiled and nodded at them. The burden of kingship, the seemingly endless red boxes, the reading and signing, the pretence of power and obligation of duty, which his son would find so trying, were now lifted from him for ever.

For the royal family an already harrowing experience was made almost insupportable by this intrusion. 'When a King starts to die', Edward remembered, 'the whole world crowds in for the death-watch, to follow with morbid curiosity every detail in the pathetic process of mortality.'[36] He had expressly asked Baldwin the previous day, when told of the Privy Council visit, that his mother be spared the agony of having to entertain the visiting statesmen to lunch. But in her son's absence in London the Queen, with her usual stately forbearance, entertained the grandees, making polite conversation as her husband lay dying upstairs. The Prince of Wales arrived by air soon afterwards, and the politicians quickly departed.

In London that evening large numbers gathered outside Buckingham Palace, where they waited patiently for news of the King. Joyce Grenfell, later a broadcaster and comedian, went with her husband to see if there were any further bulletins. In the bitter cold the crowd, 'very silent and bewildered', their faces illuminated briefly by the flashes from press photographers, pressed around the railings. There was a wide range of onlookers from every class: 'Top hats and evening clothes, soldiers, down and outs', Grenfell noticed, and 'young men in plus fours'.[37]

Vera Brittain, the author and pacifist, walked past the Palace on her way to her home in Chelsea, as 'a snow laden wind howled through the streets'. There she overheard fragments of conversation from the edge of the crowd.

'It's very sudden.'
'Yes – it is sudden, isn't it?'
'They say he really died this afternoon.'[38]

But the King was still clinging on to life, to the consternation of his courtiers. That evening, while Wigram ordered the royal coffin,[39] Dawson 'as much courtier as physician',[40] approached the family and asked for permission, should it become necessary, to terminate his patient's life. The Queen and the Prince of Wales agreed that they did not want the King's life to be prolonged if Dawson judged the illness to be mortal.[41] While the royal family dined alone, he retired to the household dining-room, where he wrote out the final medical bulletin on a menu card perched on his knee: 'The King's life is moving peacefully towards its close', words that – broadcast on the BBC within minutes at 10.30 – resounded across the Empire and were widely praised for their dignity and poetry. But the reality was harsh: Dawson might more truthfully have written that the King's life was being moved towards its close.

It was clear that the King's weak heart was giving out, and he was fading fast, but there was no certainty as to when he might die. Some feared that he might linger on, holding the nation in awful suspense. An urgent sense grew among the attendant courtiers that his death needed to be hastened, not only to minimize the agony of the family but also to ensure that news of his passing was, in their view, properly managed. Both Dawson and Wigram had a thoroughly modern awareness of the public relations impact of the royal death and shared a horror of the news coming out in the 'vulgar' evening papers.[42] The latest deadline for the next day's morning papers was midnight, and they were determined that the news should be in them. Dawson – stage manager of the final moments – rang his wife, asking her to telephone his namesake, Geoffrey Dawson, the editor of *The Times*, and advise him to hold the presses until the last minute. Other newspapers followed suit, their copy prepared, waiting for the official signal.

Late in the evening the King gradually fell into a stupor. As he declined, the Archbishop of Canterbury was summoned to hold a short service at the bedside with the family. After some prayers and a psalm ('The Lord is My Shepherd') he glided out, and soon afterwards the Queen and her family also left the bedroom, leaving Dawson alone with Sister Black and the King. Dawson asked Sister Black to administer a lethal injection but she, objecting to euthanasia, refused. The distinguished doctor took the syringe and did it himself.

I therefore decided to determine the end and injected (myself) morphia gr.3/4 & shortly after cocaine gr.1 into the distended jugular vein: 'myself' because it was obvious that Sister B was disturbed by this procedure. In about ¼ an hour – breathing quieter – appearance more placid – physical struggle gone.[43]

Soon afterwards Queen Mary and her family returned to the bedside and witnessed the King's breathing gradually slow until it ceased altogether, the drugs inducing a gentle transition from life to death. The Queen, as ever, controlled her emotions but, just before the King's death, the Prince of Wales became hysterical, crying loudly and embracing his mother. This outburst astonished the courtiers present, who regarded him as the most estranged of the four sons. The Prince's grief was later cruelly interpreted as an expression of his 'morbid' fear of his future as King, rather than the release of natural, if pent-up emotion at the loss of a father, however remote and unloving he may have been.[44] There were suspicions that he had been hoping to relinquish his claim to the throne in favour of his brother the Duke of York, leaving him free eventually to marry Wallis. The death of his father seemed to have scotched any such plans.[45]

When calm had returned, the Queen turned to her son, half-kneeled and kissed his hand, in an act of homage to the new King, Edward VIII. This act of obeisance was embarrassing for Edward,[46] an early sign that he was ill at ease with the ancient customs of kingship. In another gesture that was seen as showing his dislike of tradition Edward ordered that the clocks be put back half an hour to normal GMT from the 'Sandringham time' of his father even before the body was cold. George V had kept this foible, to the irritation of almost everybody, in order to prolong daylight for shooting. Archbishop Lang wrote priggishly in his diary: 'After midnight he ordered all the clocks, which by long custom at Sandringham were kept half an hour in advance of real time to be put back! I wonder what other customs will be put back also!' This decision to change the clocks at the very moment of his father's death was blown up into an act of brutal disregard for the dead sovereign.

As the family grieved, Lord Wigram alerted newspapers and radio to the news of King George's death. On Fleet Street the presses rolled at last with many pre-prepared pages devoted to the life of the late

King, the borders black-edged as a mark of respect. The BBC had scooped the papers with an unprecedented news bulletin at midnight. To some of the old guard, such as Violet Milner, this development in instantaneous twenty-four-hour mass communications was unwelcome. 'Somehow this modern business of wireless', she complained in her diary, 'makes all feel more unreal, more inhuman. There are no reticences.'[47] The press, deprived of a breaking story, concentrated on analysis and background, with extra pull-out souvenir sections. Meanwhile Sir John Reith, the BBC's Presbyterian Director-General, ordered all scheduled programmes to be cancelled. Only solemn music was played, to be replaced later, to the frustration of many less loyal subjects, by the sound of a ticking clock.

Lord Dawson's management of the King's death worked well. Violet Milner was sitting in her room with the wireless firmly switched off when she heard the news from her daughter Helen Hardinge: 'Deep gloom everywhere. And my own feelings profoundly sorrowful. The loss of Rudyard Kipling beyond comforting, and now the loss of a deeply respected King.'[48] Helen told her that the King, in a final lucid moment, 'this morning . . . had asked for Clive Wigram. When he appeared the King made a great effort to rouse himself, he had something he felt he must say. "How is the Empire?" he asked and lapsed into unconsciousness. Those were his last words.' Thus was the myth of the King's final utterance born. Crafted by Lord Wigram for the popular press, it was another part of the public relations management that surrounded the King's death. As the cynical Neville Chamberlain was quick to tell his sister, what he actually said to Wigram and his fellow Privy Counsellors was: 'I am very sorry to keep you gentlemen waiting so long, but I find it very difficult to concentrate.'[49]

The death of a king in 1936, in a country where the vast majority held the institutions – especially monarchy, Church and Empire – in great respect was a cataclysmic event. It dominated everything and affected everyone, young and old, conservative and liberal, alike. Leonard Woolf, husband of the author Virginia, was woken by paper boys shouting the news in the streets at the unearthly hour of three in the morning.[50] Neville Chamberlain, lying in bed at 11 Downing

Street, heard them too and guessed what it meant.[51] In Belfast, David Strain, a young draper and diarist, came into his shop and found that the subject was 'the main topic of conversation all day'.[52] In Morocco, Winston Churchill, on hearing the news, immediately cut short his holiday and began the arduous journey home, dictating an obituary for the *News of the World* to Violet Pearman, who typed it on her knees as the train rattled on its way to the port of Tangier.

On Tuesday morning, 21 January, the body of George V was laid out by the undertakers, who had been summoned from London. Alan Lascelles, Assistant Private Secretary to the late King, went up to his bedroom to pay his last respects, 'and though like all our generation, I have seen too many dead men, none has ever had a more peaceful face'.[53] Later in the day the body was placed in a coffin (made from an oak tree felled on the estate) and the lid screwed down. In the wet and windy afternoon, as the light was fading, it was taken to the parish church of St Mary Magdalene at Sandringham. Lascelles remembered the mournful scene, as the coffin, placed on a little bier and flanked by towering Grenadier Guardsmen from the King's Company, was wheeled across the grounds, followed by the Queen and the new King. The King's piper played a lament as the procession made its way with only a torchlight to guide them.

> As we came round the corner of the shrubbery . . . we saw the lych-gate brilliantly lit, with Fuller, the Sandringham rector, standing beneath it in his surplice and hood. There was nobody else in sight. The guardsmen, with scarcely a sound, slung the coffin on their shoulders and laid it before the altar.[54]

There the coffin rested for thirty-six hours, watched over by game-keepers and foresters, before its journey from the private seclusion of Sandringham to London, where the very public rites of lying-in-state and committal would take place.

3

Recessional

I N LONDON THE new era much feared by many of the older generation, especially those in authority, was about to begin. Leaving
his mother at Sandringham, King Edward VIII set off on Monday for
his Accession Council, and to make arrangements for the lying-in-
state and the funeral. From the start he appeared to be intent on
change and modernity. He travelled to London in his aeroplane – the
first British monarch ever to do so.[1] He was hatless when he arrived
at Hendon aerodrome. This was seen as another shocking departure
from the standards of his father, a man obsessed with the importance
of correct dress.[2]

The 29-year-old poet John Betjeman captured this pivotal moment
of change, 'the final putting to sleep of the Victorian age',[3] in his
verses on the death of George V. It is one of his finest works, a
greater public poem than any of those he was to write as Poet
Laureate, and certainly better than the ramblings of John Masefield,
the nation's Laureate in 1936, on the same subject. Betjeman's last
stanza, in particular, evoked a widespread mood:

> Old men who never cheated, never doubted,
>   Communicated monthly, sit and stare
> At the new suburb stretched beyond the run-way
>   Where a young man lands hatless from the air.

While King George, with his unchanging routine and mistrust of
new fashions, represented a reassuring sense of continuity, King
Edward was the epitome of modernity. He was 'jet set before the jet
age'.[4] Many traditionalists disliked everything about him, especially
his American values, flashy clothes and the 'fast' set with whom he

mixed. They saw him as a representative of the change that was transforming much of Britain for the worse. Three years earlier J. B. Priestley had famously described 'The new post-war England . . . of arterial and by-pass roads, of filling stations and factories that look like exhibition buildings, of giant cinemas and dance halls and cafés, bungalows with tiny garages, cocktail bars, Woolworths, motor-coaches, wireless, hiking, factory girls looking like actresses, greyhound racing and dirt tracks'.[5] King Edward was well suited to this new Britain. As Chips Channon remarked, he was 'over-democratic, casual and a little common'.[6] The problem was that many in the country did not want modernity and feared the changes the new King might bring.

The same morning that Edward arrived in London the Bishop of Durham, Hensley Henson, had a breakfast meeting with Stanley Baldwin to discuss the appointment of bishops. Henson was as opposed to the rising tide of modernity as the late King, but he was an eccentric. He was drawn to controversy and had caused outrage by publicly admitting to doubts about the Virgin Birth and Resurrection of the Body.[7] To the Bishop's surprise, the Prime Minister did not cancel the meeting, despite the King's death.

After a turn in the park to steady his nerves Dr Henson joined 'the great man' at Number 10. Once the business of episcopal candidates had been disposed of, the two men quickly turned to gossip about the matter of the moment. Baldwin, Henson thought, 'was most affable, and spoke with real feeling of the King's death', getting to the nub of the problem when he told the Bishop: 'None of the sons cared much for their father. They feared him too much . . . The great question now is, How will the young man carry himself?'[8] It was a question that many were asking.

While the new King's love affair dominated conversation about him in the upper classes and political circles, most of the population were in complete ignorance of it. It was a sign of the rigid divide between classes at the time, and of the great deference paid to the royal family. To the general public the King was a hugely popular figure. He was one of the first global celebrities, loved the world over for his looks and style, and admired all the more at home for his concern for the plight of the unemployed and ex-servicemen. To those in society and the establishment he was an ambivalent figure whose behaviour caused deep anxiety and disapproval among the more conservative. Joyce Grenfell, married to a courtier, told her mother after the King's death that 'that silly little P. of W. is in no shape to take over the monarch's position . . . he's made himself so cheap with Mrs Simpson and he's lost a good deal of his popularity, I should think'.[9] All agreed that Edward was completely in thrall to Mrs Simpson. The day after the King's death Blanche 'Baffy' Dugdale, the favourite niece of a former Prime Minister, Arthur Balfour, joked in her diary: 'Much speculation rife today about Edward VIII . . . the question is being asked – who is the next Prince of Wales – Answer, Mrs Simpson!'[10]

After his breakfast meeting with the Bishop of Durham, Stanley Baldwin went to the Accession Council. More than one hundred Privy Counsellors assembled to swear allegiance to Edward VIII. The powerful Chancellor of the Exchequer, Neville Chamberlain, watched the proceedings. Dressed in a dark morning suit, his thin neck sticking out from his starched wing collar and his beaked nose combining to give him his characteristic corvine appearance, he eyed the 41-year-old King.

> His speech was not remarkable in any way and I thought he looked as uncomfortable as ever, though Austen [Chamberlain's half-brother Austen Chamberlain] says he did not fidget as much as usual. I do hope he 'pulls up his socks' and behaves himself now he has such heavy responsibilities for unless he does he will soon pull down the throne.[11]

Chamberlain and Baldwin, ever the deft politicians, while touched by the death of the King, took some comfort from the fact that his passing was also a good moment to bury some bad news. Their government was still reeling from the press revelation of its secret pact with France to allow the Italian dictator, Benito Mussolini, to carve up Abyssinia. The agreement, negotiated by the Foreign Secretary, Sir Samuel Hoare, with his French counterpart, Pierre Laval, had caused public outrage when leaked to the press. Hoare and Laval were forced to resign just before Christmas. Now, as Chamberlain told his sister, the new reign would 'still further obliterate the memory of the Hoare–Laval incident'.

Edward, unsurprisingly, felt nervous and tense at the sight of so many distinguished Privy Counsellors assembled in one place.[12] The majority were over sixty, and all had sworn an oath of allegiance to the late King, whose values they upheld. Edward sought to reassure them with a declaration that he would support constitutional government and 'follow in my father's footsteps to work as he did throughout his life for the happiness and welfare of all classes of my subjects'.[13] After the Council he left to attend to the funeral arrangements. His mother, Queen Mary, favoured cremation[14] and would have preferred a simple private ceremony. She asked that the committal take place as soon as possible. The date was set for the following Tuesday.

In the meantime the solemn ceremonial continued. On Wednesday the Proclamation of the new Sovereign was made by the Garter King of Arms at St James's Palace; similar ceremonies took place in cities throughout Great Britain and the Empire. Edward arranged for Wallis and a number of friends to watch from a window looking down on the proceedings. At the last minute, in another break with tradition, he decided to join them to watch (by convention the monarch is absent from his or her own proclamation). To insiders, this was a typically reckless act of the King. His friend the Secretary of State for War, Duff Cooper, complained: 'This is just the kind of thing I hope so much he won't do. It causes so much criticism and does so much harm. Already people are starting to talk about her and to criticize him.'[15] Newsreel cameras covering the event captured the group laughing and chatting with each other while the solemn and archaic event was taking place. The Garter King, accompanied by mace-bearers and bannered trumpeters, bellowed out the proclamation of the King–Emperor's accession. But the footage did not appear in the cinemas; it was censored.

Wallis Simpson wrote afterwards to her Aunt Bessie Merryman in the USA: 'The ceremonies have been marvellous and impressive as only this country can produce and the proclamation of Edward XVIII [*sic*] the most picturesque thing – such costumes from the middle ages, the heralds looking like a pack of cards.'[16] She was out of her depth, like many commoners who have found themselves caught up in the web of royalty. Her background, growing up in a respectable but impoverished family in provincial America, and her subsequent struggle to improve herself and get on through two difficult marriages, may have made her admirably independent, but it had also made her brittle. Duff Cooper concluded 'she is hard as nails and she doesn't love him'. Whether she loved him or not, Edward loved her more, and she now found herself in an unreal and incomprehensible situation. 'Isn't it all funny and strange too? I'm just the same however and enjoying it all as a huge game – laughing a lot inside and controlling my tongue and sense of humour on the outside.'[17] But Edward soon made it plain to her that it was not a game and that he was desperately serious about making her his wife.

When the great thunderclap of the death of the King burst on the nation, the loss of Rudyard Kipling was temporarily overshadowed. On Thursday, the day after the King's proclamation, and just before the body of George V was taken to London for the lying-in-state, Kipling's funeral took place at Westminster Abbey. It was said of Kipling's death that 'the King had sent his trumpeter before him',[18] and the solemn ceremony at the Abbey was, for many, a rehearsal for the later burial of the King. Kipling had had his own lying-in-state, his coffin, draped with a Union Jack, placed before the altar in the chapel of the Middlesex Hospital before the funeral. His body had then been cremated in a private ceremony at the Golders Green Crematorium and his ashes were carried into the Abbey by eight distinguished pall-bearers, including Stanley Baldwin,[19] and placed in an urn in Poets' Corner.

While the reputation of George V had grown in the years after he came to the throne in 1910, Kipling's had suffered a prolonged decline since the First World War. The King had successfully discarded his German heritage during the war to become a focus of patriotism. Later he steered a difficult path through the political and economic upheavals that followed the Crash of 1929. While he was revered as a figure who united the country, Kipling was seen as a source of division and, as Chips Channon commented, had 'little or no message' for the young. His obsession with imperialism was increasingly out of tune with the times. The concern for millions in 1936 was not the British Empire but the rise of the dictators on Britain's doorstep in Europe.

The obituaries mirrored this feeling that Kipling represented a world that had gone for ever and suggested that his conservatism in later life had marred his reputation. The obituarist of *The Spectator* wrote in a faintly damning piece that 'The new idealism of the twentieth century found in him nothing but an uncomprehending foe. With the social reforming current which rejuvenated British society he could make no useful contacts at all.'[20] He was seen by many as a dinosaur, 'British India's last dying groan',[21] out of touch with the times, and a poet whose veneration of imperial values in simple and conventional form had been replaced by the modernism of T. S. Eliot or the voguish leftism of W. H. Auden. But not all were critical, and some saw the qualities that today make him the author of the nation's most popular poem, 'If'. The young journalist Malcolm Muggeridge, who had recently returned to Britain from India, gave a generous assessment of Kipling in his diary, which, half a century later, would become the orthodox view: 'I read Kipling's verses all the afternoon (he died yesterday). It struck me how good the verses were, how full of genuine vitality . . . and of poetic genius.'[22] He was generous too about Kipling's unfashionable view of empire:

> If he praised Empire, it was not at all because he had not counted the cost (who has expressed better the wrongs of the common soldier?) but because, men being what they are, he saw it as one of the less despicable manifestations of their urge to over-run and dominate the environment.[23]

Such was Rudyard Kipling's declining reputation that there had been some question as to whether or not he should be honoured with a place in the pantheon of Poets' Corner. Hensley Henson, Bishop of Durham, noted in his journal how he had learned from the Dean of Westminster Abbey that there had been doubts about the suitability of placing him alongside the greats of English literature and the Dean had consulted the Provost of Eton, Monty James. James did not hesitate: 'Of course – he has been the prophet of two generations of English folk.'[24] Stanley Baldwin agreed, and was relieved that his cousin should have his place in the Abbey. The death of Kipling had depressed him, and he was hurt by the unpleasant obituaries, which had stressed political views over poetic achievement. Baldwin's friend Thomas Jones found him at the time 'much agitated and unnatural, and a large whiskey which I suspect he had swallowed . . . had not made for steadiness'.[25]

Many still venerated Kipling enough for there to be a large congregation at his funeral. In her grief Violet Milner felt detached from the whole proceedings, 'It was very unreal,' she wrote, 'the clergy all looked like private theatricals.'[26] Vera Brittain was also at the Abbey. She was completely opposed to Kipling's veneration of Empire and had come out of curiosity. She watched as the clergy and choir processed with uplifted crosses to Poets' Corner in the South Transept. After the Dean had said the committal prayer the choir softly sung a setting of Kipling's great threnody of Empire, 'Recessional', more apt than ever in 1936, when Britain's imperial commitments were overstretching the nation's limited military and financial resources:

> Far-called, our navies melt away;
> On dune and headland sinks the fire:
> Lo, all our pomp of yesterday
> Is one with Nineveh and Tyre!
> Judge of the Nations, spare us yet,
> Lest we forget – lest we forget!

The service over, Vera Brittain moved with the congregation for a closer look at Kipling's purple-draped urn, surrounded by wreaths of spring flowers and 'situated in odd companionship between the graves of Charles Dickens and Thomas Hardy'.[27] Today nobody bats an eyelid when they pass by the three stone sepulchres, which sit silently in pleasing harmony.

Although it was not said openly at the time of his death, Kipling's grief at the loss of his son Jack in the trenches of the First World War was thought to have turned his mind. A few months after the funeral Stanley Baldwin's wayward socialist son Oliver broke the silence.[28]

He alleged that Kipling had suffered an 'inferiority complex' and had forced Jack to enlist despite his poor eyesight, pulling strings and even appealing to the King to have him accepted for active service at the front.[29] He argued that Jack's death at the Battle of Loos in 1915 (which, because his body was not found, Kipling for years refused to accept) had robbed the writer of inspiration. 'All his creation went . . . all the lovely side of his nature – all the "Jungle Book" playing with children, all the love for people – went like that.'[30]

On the day of Kipling's funeral the body of George V was taken from Norfolk to London for the lying-in-state at Westminster Hall, a stone's throw from the Abbey. King Edward returned to Sandringham to accompany his father on his last journey to the capital, and as he stood in the quiet parish church contemplating the coffin resting before the altar, he thought how the late King would have preferred the simplicity of burial in the local churchyard to the full panoply of a state funeral, 'but', he reflected, 'Windsor claims the bodies of British monarchs'.[31] The King's coffin was placed on a gun carriage drawn by the Royal Horse Artillery, and in the clear cold sunshine of a winter's day the small procession set off to nearby Wolferton station. Edward and his brothers walked behind on foot, followed by Queen Mary and the Princess Royal in a carriage, and behind them the King's pony Jock, led by a groom. Alan Lascelles followed, with the estate staff and retainers. 'At the top of the road leading down to the station', he noticed, 'a single cock pheasant rocketed across the road, very high and immediately over the gun carriage.'[32] It was a victory roll by a bird that had escaped the King's guns.

At Wolferton the coffin was lifted on to the royal train, which departed for London in clouds of steam, accentuated by the frost. As the train thundered through the flat countryside to King's Cross, men and women stood bare-headed by the track, bowing their heads when it passed. Another gun carriage awaited it in London. This time, to mark the transition from the private world of Sandringham to the public pomp of the capital city of a great Empire, the Royal Standard was thrown over the coffin, and the Imperial Crown was brought from the Tower and perched precariously on top. During the slow march through the streets the jolting of the gun carriage caused the diamond- and sapphire-encrusted Maltese cross to fall off from the top of the crown and roll into the gutter. A quick-thinking Grenadier Company Sergeant Major marching behind the carriage bent down, scooped it up and put it in his pocket all in one movement, to the King's relief. He, preferring to lose the cross and keep his dignity, had resolutely marched on, but he was overheard to mutter 'Christ, What will happen next!' It was a 'a fitting motto', one MP remarked, 'for the coming reign.'[33]

News of the near disaster spread fast and was seen as a 'a most terrible omen',[34] as the diarist Harold Nicolson put it, for the new reign. Virginia Woolf, with her disinterested novelist's eye, watched the mournful little procession on its way to Westminster from amid the packed crowds in Bloomsbury's Tavistock Square. She saw the new King pass by, looking distinctly out of sorts, 'blotched & as if chipped by a stone mason: only his rather set wistful despair marked him from any shopkeeper – not an ingratiating face: bloated, roughened, as if by exposure to drink life grief & as red as a fisherboys'.[35] Thomas Jones watched 'the mournful little procession' from the window of a shop in the Strand. 'The King plodded heavily along' through the intense quiet of the streets, he noticed, 'weighed down by a thick long overcoat, looking utterly done.'[36]

In Westminster Hall the Lords and Commons had assembled, standing either side of the great catafalque which awaited the coffin. The Archbishop of Canterbury, Cosmo Lang, stood before them to receive the body, resplendent in the purple cope that a predecessor had worn at the funeral of Charles II in 1685. As Big Ben struck four o'clock, the sound of hoofs clattering over the cobbles could be heard outside. The Archbishop, flanked by the Dean of Westminster and other dignitaries, stepped forward to greet the coffin as the great doors of the Hall swung open.

Against Edward's wishes, Lang had insisted on a short service of greeting. This was another sign of the tension between them, each regarding the other across the generation gap with mutual suspicion and incomprehension. While Edward had little time for religion, the Archbishop was famed for his faith and oratory. He was a hugely ambitious man who precociously, when an undergraduate at Oxford, had practised signing himself as 'Cantuar'. He was a showman who loved the limelight – some thought a little too much. The Bishop of Durham, after listening to the Archbishop's broadcast on the late King the same day, acidly described his style as 'self-advertising sentimentalism'.[37]

During the short service in Westminster Hall, Lang struggled to retain his self-control, his voice quavering with emotion as he read the blessing. But all eyes were on the royal family. To the diarist Chips Channon the new King appeared 'boyish, sad and tired', standing with his mother (who had refused the title Queen Mother), 'erect and magnificent as ever',[38] and his three brothers. At the Queen's request the hymn 'Praise my Soul the King of Heaven' was sung by the Westminster Abbey choir, standing on the high steps at the west end of the Hall. Six huge Grenadier Guardsmen lifted the coffin on to the great catafalque, then four officers from the Household Brigade marched forward and mounted the steps to stand guard over it. They were joined, at a lower level, by the Palace of Westminster's own Gentlemen-at-Arms, holding their tall lances and dressed in their skirted red coats cuffed with blue velvet.

After the service the royal family departed, bowing and curtseying to the coffin, and the two Houses of Parliament filed by in silence (or as much silence as politicians can keep when *en masse*), their footsteps muffled by a great grey carpet that had been laid in the Hall. Then the doors were thrown open to the public. Chips Channon found the whole business 'upsets and weakens me'. His feelings were shared by Violet Milner: 'My heart is very heavy . . .', she sighed, 'the weather is wet. Bad for the devoted crowds who are pacing through Westminster Hall in their hundreds of thousands.'[39]

The lying-in-state was set to last for four days, during which time more than a million people from all walks of life filed past the coffin, just under one in forty of the entire population.[40] Sometimes the queue waiting to enter Westminster Hall stretched for three miles, snaking six abreast down the Embankment and over Vauxhall Bridge. The death of George V had struck a chord with the public that could not be explained by reverence for him alone. Reaction to his death transcended class and age boundaries and expressed a patriotism that was, in those days, almost universal. Three-quarters of those who came to pay their respects were working-class.[41] John Prichard's family shared the sense of national loss, regarding the death of the King–Emperor 'as the passing of a symbol of greatness in a world where we still thought of ourselves as a great power – the only power in the world'.[42] The country plunged into mourning. Shop windows were lined with funereal crêpe, and men and women across Britain put on black or wore black armbands on the sleeves of their coats.

Not everyone approved of this outburst of collective grief or shared the feelings of reverence for the departed King. Virginia Woolf complained to her nephew Julian Bell about the public's 'fit of grief' and its 'death trudge' around the coffin, describing the reaction to the death as 'a curious survival of barbarism, emotionalism, heraldry, ecclesiasticism, sheer sentimentality, snobbery, and some feeling for the very commonplace man who was so like ourselves'.[43] By 'ourselves', of course, Woolf meant the ordinary people of Britain. No one could have been less like the late King than she and her Bloomsbury friends. There was too a strong strand of feeling on the left that the monarchy was an outdated institution that should be abolished and that the public's grief was an over-reaction. The novelist Geoffrey Wells, already irritated by the closure of cinemas, found it all too much: 'I feel, about the King, *nothing*. A man has died. Well, what about it? – other men died also. I can't help feeling that there is an awful lot of junk about this natural sorrow stuff . . . an indulgence of the emotions.'[44]

There were some who were nervous of such a strong public expression of feeling, seeing in it some of the dangerous emotions that had fuelled the rise of totalitarian regimes in Europe. 'It would not be unimaginable that a George-culture should be started', Henson worried in his diary, 'as we are assured that a Lenin–culture has been started in Russia. The multitudes who are flocking to Westminster Hall to see the King "lying in state" are being worked up.'[45] Perhaps the Bishop was unconsciously expressing a fear of the dangerous possibilities of an over-popular monarchy, at odds with the government, a fear shared by some in the establishment when they contemplated the prospect of the new King.[46]

Edward had, as Prince of Wales, been the object of adoration the world over. While his father had symbolized the lofty ideals of a great imperial nation, he was a much more informal person, the first celebrity royal. His tours of America and the Empire made him an international figure, familiar to millions who watched the newsreels. It added to the sense of his modernity: a man whom the cameras loved, his face flashed around the world on screen and in the press, a master of public relations. He bore a striking resemblance to a later tragic and cultish member of the royal family, Diana, Princess of Wales. Like the Princess, he had charismatic appeal and charm. He too had the doe-eyed looks and was widely noticed to have the appearance of a man much younger than his forty-one years.[47] His charm, like Diana's, had something to do with an innate sadness, a sense of personal suffering that was described by one courtier as '*Weltschmerz*', an air of world sorrow. And as with her, as time passed, there was a feeling of increasing danger about Edward that was compelling: 'Edward and Diana were both guided missiles which had lost their guidance systems,' Philip Ziegler, his official biographer, noted, 'which might end up absolutely anywhere. You could only watch their parabola with terrified anticipation, waiting for the explosion'.[48]

The lying-in-state became a public event of immense significance, and many visited more than once, just for the spectacle. Violet Milner joined the slow-moving crowd as it filed silently past in two columns, either side of the stepped dais on which the catafalque rested. She marvelled at the stillness of the officers standing guard, hardly breathing, motionless as marionettes in the immensity of the shadowy Hall. From a distance 'the effect was that it was all quite small – a bibelot. But when one got near the scale became visible.'[49] Noel Coward went to the Hall and found the spectacle 'quite indescribably beautiful'. The scene was especially haunting at night, when the oak arches of the hammer-beamed Hall cast long shadows across the candle-lit stone, and the crown's diamonds glittered on the coffin, sitting in a pool of light amid the gloom. *The Times* quoted Rudyard Kipling on the lying-in-state of Edward VII: 'As they gathered in the streets without – very, very far off – so they entered the Temple, walking by fours . . . of all colours and faiths and customs under the firmament of God, from dawn till late at night.'[50] Chips Channon visited twice with society friends and remarked how 'We saw the great catafalque, the purple-draped coffin, bearing the Queen's simple wreath (changed daily), the orb sceptre and imperial crown'.[51] One of Channon's visits coincided with Queen Mary, who had insisted that the public still file by as she stood before the coffin, murmuring prayers to herself: 'I saw her well . . . Her dignity and fortitude have caught the heart of the whole nation.'[52] Throughout this year, which would see the death of her husband, the abdication of her son and the accession of her second son, the Queen would never let that mask of composure drop.

On the fourth and final day of the lying-in-state the King and his three brothers decided to pay their own silent tribute to their father and stand the midnight watch over the catafalque. Unnoticed, in full-dress uniform, they stood for twenty minutes, swords reversed, as the crowd walked past. As Edward stood, his face half-hidden in the bearskin of the Grenadier Guards, unrecognized in the cold gloom of Westminster Hall, he contemplated the shuffling feet of mourners before him passing his late father's coffin, and 'felt close to my father and all that he stood for'.[53] He may have felt a certain eerie physical sensation of closeness to the late King, but it is doubtful that he really felt any sympathy for the ideals and style of royalty that his father had stood for.

Edward wanted to modernize the institution of royalty. It was a commitment that would inevitably bring him into conflict with his court and his ministers. But for the moment his gesture of standing guard over his father's coffin was reassuring. Queen Mary was so touched by the gesture that she commissioned the artist Frank Beresford to recreate the scene. The vigil, Helen Hardinge wrote approvingly, 'had been the King's own idea entirely and it showed how priceless his imagination could have been to the country . . . It was to us then an act typical of the new King at his best, and a hopeful indication for the future.'[54] It was certainly a brilliant piece of public relations, modestly executed without prior notification of the press, but bound in the long run to reflect well on the royal family.[55] As

Prince of Wales, Edward had referred to his many PR coups rather cynically as 'stunts',[56] but he was genuinely proud of this one.

The funeral took place on Tuesday 28 January. It was the climax of what Noel Coward called 'a very strange experience for the whole country'. Once more the public packed the streets to watch as the coffin, placed again on a gun carriage with the Imperial Crown, now mended, on top. It was pulled by a company of sailors, eight abreast and twelve ranks deep, from Westminster Hall to Paddington Station, from where it would be taken by train to Windsor, for burial. It was a magnificent spectacle. Thomas Jones was watching, impressed: 'I thought the phalanx drawing the carriage which looked like a mech-anized tractor the most amazing example of time and step ever seen in London.'[57] Ahead of the coffin marched hundreds of troops from the three services, together with their bands playing funeral marches, or – in the case of the Scottish regiments – the bagpipes wailing mournful laments. They were followed by the nation's Admirals and Field Marshals in full uniform.

One million had come to pay their respects. Such was the press of crowds lining the damp and misty streets between Westminster and Paddington that the funeral cortège was delayed by two hours. At times there was scarcely room for the gun carriage to pass. In the narrow streets between Hyde Park and Paddington the sailors were forced to walk four abreast as police struggled to push back the dense press of mourners. The arrival of the gun carriage was heralded by the silencing of the already hushed crowd and the removal of thousands of hats. Not all were mournful, however. A well-known advertise-ment for the ubiquitous Lyons Corner House chain of restaurants was 'Where's George?' Somebody in the waiting throng at Trafalgar Square shouted it out and the refrain was taken up by the crowd.[58]

Behind the coffin walked the King alone, followed by his brothers, and behind them a procession of five kings and many minor princes, almost all of them descended from the great matriarch Queen Victoria. It was reported by the *Daily Worker*, probably mischie-vously, that the masseur of King Carol of Romania, who travelled with his monarch on the way to the procession to give him some last-minute treatment, had followed the King mistakenly, and walked behind him in the cortège. Victoria would no doubt have disapproved, and she would have been shocked by her great-grandson, who, as he passed the house where his lover was staying, darted a look at the window from which she was watching.[59] Queen Mary followed in a carriage, dressed in black from head to foot, with her face covered by the thick crêpe veils of German royal mourning. She was a figure from another era.[60]

At last the procession arrived at St George's Chapel, which was surrounded by a sea of wreaths of all shapes and sizes. The assembled congregation of courtiers, aristocrats, statesmen and generals sat shuffling and snuffling under the Garter banners. Their wives, wreathed in black, most of them wearing veils, were – for once - in stark contrast to the peacock gaudiness of their husbands, in their plumed and feathered hats and helmets and colourful uniforms. Winston Churchill was there, back just in time, resplendent in the uniform of a former First Lord of the Admiralty, reunited with Clementine, whose veil was so dense and all-enveloping that her face was completely concealed. Neville Chamberlain, resembling more than ever in mourning his nickname, 'the undertaker', told his sister that he was grateful for the delay as it enabled him to enjoy the spectacle.[61] It being January, many had caught chills, including the unfortunate Archbishop of Canterbury, who was suffering from one of his 'vicious catarrh colds'.[62]

The King's coffin was lifted from the gun carriage outside the Chapel, to the shrill sound of the boatswain's whistle piping 'Admiral on board' and then 'Admiral over the side'. As it was carried into the Chapel, the pipes played a final lament. After the funeral service the coffin was lowered into the vault while the Archbishop intoned 'Earth to earth, ashes to ashes, dust to dust . . .'. The new King was handed a silver salver containing some earth, which he scattered on to the coffin. At that moment, throughout Britain, there was a two-minute silence. Traffic everywhere came to a halt. Finally the Garter King of Arms proclaimed 'God Save the King!' And so began a new reign that would last almost the length of 1936, the year of change.

4

Orwell's sordid imagination

STANDING AMID THE crowds in Trafalgar Square as the coffin of the King passed by was a tall, slight man, thin-faced, with a shock of dark hair, and narrow lips edged by a pencil moustache. He was watching the public with a journalist's cool detachment, and those standing next to him, if they looked closely, would have noticed a look of disdain. It was not the outburst of public grief for the dead King that concerned Eric Blair – the writer George Orwell – but the physical degeneracy of the crowd. 'Puny limbs, sickly faces under the weeping London sky! Hardly a well built man or a decent looking woman, and not a fresh complexion anywhere !'[1] In 1936 he shared a widespread concern, even panic, about the poor physical stock of the nation. This was partly explained at the time by fashionable eugenic theory. As Orwell put it: 'The Great War carefully selected the million best men in England and slaughtered them, largely before they had time to breed.'[2] But the decline was also thought to be the by-product of another national affliction: unemployment.

Three days after the King's funeral at the end of January, George Orwell left London by train on the beginning of a journey of journalistic investigation and self-discovery. Victor Gollancz, the left-wing publisher and founder that spring of the Left Book Club, had commissioned him to write a book on Britain's ravaged industrial north, and for this purpose Orwell wanted to see the effects of unemployment and to experience the British working class 'at close quarters'.[3]

George Orwell was not the first writer to travel to the north to report on the horrors of poverty and deprivation to be found there. J. B. Priestley had journeyed around Britain two years earlier, and his best-seller, *English Journey*, drew attention to the awful conditions in towns such as Jarrow, as well as the rise of middle-class urban sprawl in the south.[4] There was a growing sense, felt especially keenly on the left, that while much was known about Britain's Empire, the experience of the working classes at home had been hidden for too long. To put this right a number of groundbreaking novels were published on the subject, one or two of them written by working-class authors who had turned to writing to fill the hours of enforced idleness and to draw attention to their plight. The most successful of these, Walter Greenwood's *Love on the Dole*, was a moving account of the suffering of an unemployed family in Salford, where the author grew up. It was a best-seller, later made into a play and a film. Photographers too, such as Bill Brandt, took a series of atmospheric portraits in 1936 of some of the most deprived towns of Britain's blighted industrial regions: the distressed areas of south Wales, the north-east of England and Clydeside. Campaigning film-makers, led by the pioneering producer John Grierson, were using the new medium of documentary in the hope of creating a new perspective on the nation.

After four years of sustained economic growth, Britain in 1936 was a wealthy nation with a conscience. The intractable problem of long-term unemployment in the depressed regions contrasted terribly with the growing prosperity elsewhere. While millions were enjoying a rise in real incomes owing to falling price levels, those who lived in the derelict industrial areas had barely enough to get by. The two nations existed in parallel. As time passed, the calls for action, for something to be done, became stronger. There was a thirst for information on which the action could be based, especially on the left.

In the first two weeks of February, when Orwell was on his journey of discovery, an exhibition was held in Charing Cross underground station about the ravaged industrial regions and the efforts being made to deal with them. There were photographs on panels, pamphlets and an accompanying BBC radio feature. Eighty thousand people visited the show. On the last day the organizer reported, 'it was not possible to put up the barriers until about 9.45 pm'.[5] It was a sign of the growing sense of unease about the 'other' Britain of poverty and deprivation. George Orwell was just one of a host of journalists, medical experts, nutritionists and economists who produced reports and studies in 1936 that were to be hugely influential in the formation of the welfare state after the war.

But Orwell was different. He scorned journalists such as Priestley for their 'middle-class writing'. He did not wish to study the poor and then go off to a comfortable hotel to rest and recuperate. He wanted to plunge into people's lives, albeit briefly, and experience at first hand the horrors of working-class life. There was in his desire to immerse himself in discomfort and squalor an urge for self-punishment which seemed to complement a sadistic streak in his character. There was also a degree of voyeurism, a tradition in English literature of slum-visiting that went back to Mayhew and Dickens, that was used polemically to alert the comfortably off to the conditions of the poor.

Britain in 1936 was still a class-bound and divided nation, split between a rapidly modernizing and growing south and the impoverished outer regions of south Wales, northern England and central Scotland. The old industries of coal, cotton and shipbuilding had been in decline for decades. After the First World War, when the demand for armaments had abruptly stopped, they all but collapsed. Their long-term decline, combined with the Crash of 1929 and the slump that followed, had devastated entire regions. Millions of men in 1936 were simply left to rot. The deep fissure that ran through the nation, dividing poor north and rich south, stagnation and growth, was as deep as at any time since the Industrial Revolution in the previous century.[6]

Neville Chamberlain, a dynamic but ruthless Chancellor, at first batted away the many pleas for help for those areas worst affected. He regarded the problems as structural and insoluble, and refused to be panicked into any short-term solutions. But in the face of overwhelming political pressure, and fearful of growing unrest, he relented. In 1934 the government passed the Special Areas Act to take some measures in four distressed regions to help the long-term unemployed.[7] Commissioners were appointed and departments created. But from the start Whitehall in-fighting and economic orthodoxy hampered their work.[8]

Orwell's journey north coincided with the publication on 4 February of John Maynard Keynes's *General Theory of Employment,*

Interest and Money. Keynes was unquestionably one of the most intelligent men of his age, as another brilliantly clever man, Bertrand Russell, recognized: 'Keynes's intellect was the sharpest and clearest that I have ever known. When I argued with him, I felt I took my life in my hands, and I seldom emerged without feeling something of a fool.'[9] He was not only an economist of genius but also a man of culture, a successful speculator and master mathematician, in all 'a magical figure'.[10]

Keynes had long been arguing against the economic orthodoxy which held that the market should be left to regulate itself, the so-called 'invisible hand' of classical theory. In particular he questioned the belief that unemployment was a problem that governments were incapable of addressing. In the *General Theory* he argued, among other things, that the state could and should play a greater part in stimulating employment by direct intervention,[11] by cutting interest rates and taxes or – most controversially – increasing spending by borrowing. His desire was to preserve capitalism, thought by so many at the time to have manifestly failed, by offering a solution to its greatest evil, unemployment. Neville Chamberlain was aware of Keynes's arguments but did not agree with them. While he had taken measures to manage the economy, keeping interest rates low, he always wanted to balance the books. When the two men met, Chamberlain was dismissive. He said that he found Keynes's ideas 'even worse than I had supposed'.[12] With some justice, he considered it impossible to borrow the sums of money the economist suggested without plunging the economy into even deeper crisis.

In the absence of Keynesian solutions large swathes of the country, from the heartlands of the first Industrial Revolution in the north to the coalmining towns and villages of south Wales, were suffering from rates of long-term unemployment of 20 per cent and more.[13] In hotspots such as the town of Jarrow, which had grown up around a single industry, there was no work at all. Unemployment peaked at 73 per cent, in contrast to rates of 4 per cent in places such as St Albans in the wealthy south.[14] As the country emerged from the slump in the early 1930s, the areas that had suffered so long from high unemployment did not see any improvement at all. To make matters worse, Chamberlain's tight public spending limits meant that, while the economy improved, the unemployed in these areas received very little benefit, and the long-term jobless were subject to the hated 'Means Test'.

It was this bleak world that Orwell intended to investigate when he went to Euston Station on 31 January and took a train to Coventry. From Coventry he set off north on foot, walking up to sixteen miles a day and occasionally taking a bus when footsore. He had little idea where he was going, trusting in providence and advice from those he stayed with on the way. At that time Orwell was a contributor to the left-wing literary journal *The Adelphi*. Its editor, Richard Rees, arranged for introductions to activists in Manchester who could guide him to the worst areas of deprivation. Orwell started his journey to the north as he intended to go on: plunging into the world of poverty, a world with which he was already familiar from his days as a tramp, which he had described in *Down and Out in Paris and London*. Walking and staying in cheap lodging-houses and doss-houses, Orwell kept a diary of his trip and often noted the physical details and smells that he encountered on the way. Richard Hoggart has described him as a 'public conscience, a conscience with an exceptionally well developed sense of smell', and nowhere did this become more evident than on the road to Wigan.[15]

On the first night in Coventry, Orwell stayed in a bed and breakfast. His hyper-sensitive nose started twitching immediately: 'very lousy . . . smell as in common lodging houses.' Alongside his susceptible nose, Orwell suffered an almost effete allergy to the ugly proletarian, which was triggered during breakfast on the first morning of his assignment: 'Half-witted servant girl with huge body, tiny head and rolls of fat at back of neck curiously recalling ham fat.'[16] Eton-educated and acutely aware of class distinctions (he described himself only half ironically as 'lower-upper-middle class'[17]), Orwell was well aware of the widespread visceral disgust that the upper and middle classes felt at the time for working people. It was at the core of his outlook and served as an inspiration for his genius, and – to his publisher's horror – he had the courage to say it loudly in 1936: 'That was what we were taught – *the lower class smell*. And here, obviously, you are at an impassable barrier. For no feeling of like or dislike is quite so fundamental as a *physical* feeling.'[18] It was a near impassable barrier that he forced himself to overcome on his journey north.

On 1 February Orwell headed for Birmingham, by foot and bus through the Midlands, rather incongruously, given the purpose of his journey, making nature notes in his diary as he went: 'Birds courting a little, cock chaffinches and bullfinches very bright and cock-partridge making mating call.' His love of the English countryside mingled with a fear that the growing wealth in the south and industrial decay in the north were combining to ruin the English landscape. It was a paradox that haunted intellectuals like him: while they wanted to see the world of poverty blown away, many hated the consequences of the new prosperity. As he walked, Orwell bemoaned what he saw, 'west of Birmingham the usual villa-civilization creeping out over the hills'. Unrestricted suburban sprawl in the wealthy west Midlands and south, bolstered by large-scale house building, was transforming the landscape. Orwell had a hatred of the modern world that he shared with contemporary authors whose political outlook he despised. Like John Betjeman and Evelyn Waugh, he detested the Americanization of culture, the concreting of the countryside and the rising dominance of the 'money culture' of finance and advertising in London. The difference was, however, that he had a visceral, if disgusted, sympathy for the poor, and blamed capitalism for their suffering.

As he passed through the Midlands that wintry February, into the more depressed potteries on the fringes of the north, his descriptions took on a Dickensian flavour as snow lay about everywhere. 'Hanley and Burslem about the most dreadful places I have seen. Labyrinths of tiny blackened houses and among them pot-banks . . . belching forth smoke'.[19] Orwell, the former Imperial policeman who had served in Burma, had never been to the north of England before; he had never seen the smoking chimneys and satanic mills of the industrial areas that had given rise to Britain's wealth and that were home to its worst oppression. Like a latter-day Engels, he experienced an epiphany, as what he saw changed him from a sceptical liberal into an unorthodox but nevertheless committed socialist, ready later in the year to fight for the cause in Spain.[20]

Three days later, half-starved and with aching feet, he arrived in

Manchester. He had spent all his money on the journey and tried to get some cash, only to find the banks were shut early. After trudging the streets in a vain attempt to find somebody who would trust him enough to cash a cheque, he eventually pawned his scarf and stayed in a doss-house. Richard Rees had sent him a letter of introduction to the Meades, a couple who lived nearby and were connected with the publishing of *The Adelphi* in Manchester, and the following day he went and introduced himself. Mr Meade, a trade unionist, put Orwell in touch with Joe 'Jerry' Kennan, an activist and unemployed coalminer in Wigan. There, on a cold Saturday in February, he arrived, 'this tall fella with a pair of flannel bags on, a fawn jacket and a mac'.[21] Orwell had found his story. *The Road to Wigan Pier*, based on the diary he kept of his experiences in Wigan, came out the following year. He would never be the same again, and the town of Wigan would never forgive him.

Central to Orwell's vision in the book is disgust: disgust at the people of Wigan, at the conditions in which they lived, at their bleak industrial surroundings and at their blighted lives. He could have visited any one of a dozen northern towns in the distressed areas and had a similar experience. It was almost an accident that he happened on Wigan. Yet because of his portrayal of it, Wigan became emblematic of what the poorer regions of the country outside the prosperous south had turned into in the 1930s – an industrial, and human, scrapyard.

Jerry Kennan took Orwell to Wigan's Market Square, where every weekend a series of political meetings took place. The slump and all the horrors that flowed from it had led to widespread but unsuccessful attempts to engage the working classes in radical action, much of which took place outside the sterile world of the coalition government in Westminster. According to Kennan that afternoon, 'There was the ILP [Independent Labour Party], there was the Communist Party, there was the National Unemployed Workers Movement and there were also various religious bodies. There was at that time seven or eight meetings going on in the Market Square.'[22] The National Unemployed Workers Movement, or NUWM, was much mistrusted by the authorities as a Communist front, but by the jobless it was widely regarded as the most effective organization working on their behalf. It had been responsible for the many hunger marches and protests against the Means Test that had helped to raise awareness of the suffering of unemployment through the years of depression. Kennan and his guest headed for the NUWM shelter – 'a dreadful ramshackle place', Orwell wrote, although he acknowledged that it was warm and welcoming. When the men there learned about his mission to discover the conditions of the unemployed, they immediately offered help with finding information and, more importantly, lodgings. To Orwell's discomfort, however, his southern origins and background could not be hidden. He wrote in his diary: 'I cannot get them to treat me precisely as an equal, however. They call me either "Sir" or "Comrade".'[23] More likely they called him the former. In 1936 class could not easily be disguised, and Orwell's public school background would have been unmistakable, however scruffy he looked after days and nights spent on the road and in lodging-houses.

Paddy Grant, the NUWM secretary, arranged for board and lodging with the Hornby family in nearby Warrington Road.[24] Orwell noted that Grant was 'in a dreadful state physically from years of underfeeding and idleness. His front teeth are almost entirely rotted away.' It was while he was staying with the Hornbys that Orwell had his first encounter with a food that would for ever after have negative associations with Wigan: tripe. In the Lancashire style, Mrs Hornby served this cheap cut of meat in 'monstrous quantities', 'cold with vinegar'. For Orwell it was 'horrible'. He cast his cold eye on the extended family plus two lodgers that were packed into the three-bedroom terraced house. Mr Hornby was one of the long-term unemployed, a jobless miner. His son, 'Our Joe', was working the night shift down the pit. He hot-bedded with the lodger, also called Joe, who was on the dole, passing the time in the local library – the haunt of thousands of unemployed, who spent their time self-improving or trying to doze without being seen. A cousin, Tom, was also lodging in the house. With the addition of their visitor from the south, the Hornbys' house was packed. Orwell calculated that the family and lodgers' total weekly income was £3 16s. 4d. – little more than £200 a year (about £7,400 in today's terms).

There were 2.13 million unemployed in 1936, thirteen per cent of the workforce.[25] The problem was not so much the number itself, which was high enough (although unemployment had come down under Neville Chamberlain's stewardship of the economy from the terrible peak of 22 per cent in 1932), as the pockets of mass long-term unemployment in places such as Wigan, where the average was 27 per cent. This was a new phenomenon, and little was known about its effects on the jobless men and their families. It was suspected that the impact on physical and mental health would be profound. On a visit to a Labour exchange the government's own Commissioner for the Special Areas, Malcolm Stewart, was shocked by what he saw:

> The ineffaceable impression given was that the men were seriously suffering from being overwrought and worn out by anxiety. Bad as is the plight of these men, there is something even worse and that is the sight of boys idling at the street corners who have never done a day's work and for whom there is little prospect of employment. They are steadily deteriorating through enforced idleness.[26]

Orwell's friend the author Jack Common, who wrote movingly in *The Adelphi* about his working-class childhood, described the effect of living on the dole at that time: 'a slow degree of bare existence which is tantamount to slow starvation'.[27]

With the publication of Keynes's *General Theory*, 1936 was the key year for advancing (but not implementing) modern economic solutions to the problem of unemployment. It was also the year in which the awful effects of long-term joblessness were first properly understood. To the government's embarrassment, a number of studies of poverty showed that there was indeed a link with poor health.[28] Orwell's publisher, Victor Gollancz, commissioned one of these studies from the Medical Officer of Health for Stockton-on-Tees, G. C. M. M'Gonigle.[29] His research showed that an appalling 94 per cent of children in County Durham schools (an area of high long-term unemployment) had signs of rickets as a result of poor diet. It was just one of a host of shameful statistics. In March the future Prime Minister Harold Macmillan, publisher and Conservative MP for Stockton, published Sir John Boyd Orr's massive study *Food Health and Income*. This was an act of rebellion by a Conservative MP representing a northern industrial constituency. The government had done its best to suppress the study, which revealed the devastating fact that 'one third of the population of this country, including all the unemployed, were unable, after paying rent, to purchase sufficient of the more expensive foods to give them an adequate diet'. Boyd Orr calculated that half the population did not eat 'up to the modern health standard'.[30]

Marguerite Patten, as a home economist, travelled around the country in 1936. She remembered the diet of the poor in the north at the time: 'they were managing on potatoes and bread and tea, and of course, with what little meat they could afford, bread and dripping, without meat it was just bread and margarine.'[31] The children of the unemployed would almost always go to school without breakfast. Boyd Orr discovered that the contrast in diets between rich and poor had a strong and demonstrable physical effect: 'the children in the higher income groups . . . are two to three inches taller than those of the lower income groups whose diet is deficient.'[32]

It was not only in the north, though, that people suffered. Rural poverty was prevalent throughout the country. Dorothy 'Dorrie' Cooper lived in the country outside the Berkshire market town of Newbury. Her father had lost his job, and the family survived on the meagre income he received for window-cleaning and the money her mother earned from taking in washing. 'My mother used to go without food so that we could eat', Dorrie recalled.[33] At the age of fourteen she went into service, working at the 'big house' in the village, where she was well fed. Often she wished she could take home scraps from the table for her family. Most poor families, whether in work or not, knew real hunger. Ted Willis, a young socialist in 1936, recalled how his mother used to go out and buy 'four pennyworth of scrag end of lamb and with that she would make a big stew which would last us two or three days'. Once Willis came home to find his mother putting a lid on the stew and taking it out of the house: 'I said "Where are you going?" She said she was taking it to Mrs Bushell, a little further down the road, and I said "But I'm hungry", and I remember she slapped my face – she said "You're hungry, but they are starving".'[34]

From every point of view it was a disgraceful state of affairs. Politicians feared revolution; priests warned of moral decay. The Church became involved. William Temple, the socialist-minded Archbishop of York, commissioned a scientific inquiry into long-term unemployment, *Men without Work*, which was to use the experiences of the jobless for twelve months up to November 1936 as its evidence. The idea behind the inquiry was broadly similar to that which had motivated Orwell's journey to Wigan: to investigate unemployment and bring the truth to a wider audience. Researchers were sent out across Britain to immerse themselves in the areas of greatest poverty, staying in the households of the jobless. But, unlike Orwell, those the Archbishop sent were specialists: economists, psychologists and social scientists. The Pilgrim Trust funded their work. Eminent academics supervised their investigations. The principal adviser was Sir William Beveridge, then Director of the London School of Economics. Beveridge suggested that they study in detail the lives of about 1,000 long-term unemployed – mostly men – and their families; their health, living conditions and physical environment.

One of the authors of *Men without Work* was a young Jewish refugee, Hans Singer. A brilliant economist, he had moved to Britain to study under his hero, John Maynard Keynes. Singer was lucky. In order to come to Britain, Jews fleeing the Nazis had to have sponsors. In his case, Cambridge University had brought him from Turkey, where he was languishing in Istanbul, having escaped from Germany. The 35-year-old Jewish professor realized it was time to leave his homeland after anti-Semitic insults became commonplace on his blackboard. At first he had responded robustly in chalk – 'will whoever wrote this at least sign his name, or else he is not only a swine but a coward'[35] – but he soon got the message and packed his bags. After two years at Cambridge, Keynes recommended him to the Archbishop of York because of his interest in unemployment, and in 1936 Singer found himself, like Orwell, coming to terms with a very different world.

On his first evening in Wigan, Orwell went as a guest of the NUWM to Wigan's Co-Operative Hall to hear Wal Hannington, a veteran activist and the head of the organization (he was another of Gollancz's authors). Hannington was also one of the founders of the

Communist Party of Great Britain, which made him an object of state suspicion and police surveillance. Stanley Baldwin, saw unemployment generally as 'fertile soil for Communism'[36] and activists such as Hannington, in particular, as a real danger to the realm. The Communist Party and the NUWM had been behind numerous strikes, sit-ins and hunger marches during the previous five years. Within the establishment there was a palpable fear of violent revolution.

Although Orwell dismissed Hannington as a 'poor speaker' who used all 'the padding and clichés of the socialist orator', he was impressed by the audience's response. 'He got the people well worked up. Was surprised by the amount of Communist feeling.' At the time the Communist Party had only 11,500 members in Britain (by comparison, the Labour Party had 400,000)[37] but its popularity and influence went much further. When Wal Hannington told his audience that, in a war between Britain and Russia, the USSR would win, he was greeted with 'loud cheers'. The Soviet Union under Stalin was revered by many, from the Labour Party's founders, Sidney and Beatrice Webb – the authors of Soviet Communism: A New Civilisation – to young Oxbridge intellectuals and working-class radicals. They believed Russia showed that there was an effective alternative to capitalism and that it had conquered the evils of unemployment and inequality. In contrast Baldwin and Chamberlain seemed hopelessly ineffective.

Orwell's lack of enthusiasm for Hannington may also have had something to do with his voice and the fact that he was from a similar background. He wrote in his diary that Hannington spoke with the wrong kind of Cockney accent ('once again, though a Communist entirely a bourgeois'[38]). Orwell, also a bourgeois, did nothing to hide his origins. He spoke in a thin, reedy voice, with the unmistakable strangulated vowels of the contemporary 'Oxford' accent, and ingenuously told Jerry Kennan of his Eton education, his previous work for imperialism with the Burmese Police and his complete ignorance of industrial areas.[39]

The next morning, 6 February, Orwell went in search of signs of poverty in the centre of Wigan, but conditions were not as bad as he had expected, although he did notice that many people wore wooden clogs, and the poorer elderly women still had shawls over their heads and wrapped around their shoulders, rather than coats and hats, as protection from the cold. Orwell had come with a journalistic mission to tell the people in the south how awful conditions were in the north. As always, this was not the full story; while many were suffering, there were others fortunate enough to have jobs and a decent living, who took civic pride in Wigan. He offended these people when he delved into the dark side of the town. That afternoon in the freezing cold he walked along the local canal, where the celebrated pier had once stood (a long-standing music-hall joke, not a 'pier' at all but a place for offloading canal cargo), and found what he was looking for. His diary description could again have come straight from Dickens: 'Frightful landscape of slag heaps and belching chimneys'.[40] The canal had frozen over, and a steamer travelled ahead of the coal barges breaking the ice, while the bargemen donned sacks to muffle themselves from the bitter wind. Here and there were stagnant pools caused by mining subsidence, frozen over 'the colour of raw umber', and 'a few rats running slowly through the snow, very tame, presumably weak with hunger'. On returning to his lodgings Orwell listened wide-eyed to Mrs Hornby's horrific tales of mining accidents. Her brother-in-law had fallen 1,200 feet down a mining shaft, bouncing from side to side as he plunged. 'Mrs H adds: "they wouldn't never have collected t'pieces only he were wearing a new suit of oilskins".'

The NUWM took Orwell on a tour of run-down housing and caravan sites so he could see some of the worst conditions. With his novelist's eye he concentrated in his diary on the look and manner of those whom he encountered rather than the facts and figures of the conditions in which they lived. That sort of research was the province of Hans Singer and his colleagues, trained economists and statisticians. Orwell was giving flesh to the dry statistical bones of their work. In one caravan he saw a woman with a face like a death's head, with 'a look of absolute intolerable misery and degradation'. Orwell reacted with horror, with the thought that she must have 'felt as I would feel if I were coated all over with dung'. He was struck too by the immutable destiny of the poor of Wigan. During the slum tour, 'passing up a horrible squalid side-alley', he saw and caught the eye of a young woman poking a stick up a blocked waste pipe. This sight, which he later creatively transposed from the 1936 diary into the celebrated vision from a train window on leaving Wigan when he came to write *The Road to Wigan Pier*, came to symbolize for him what he saw as the tragedy of the inescapable fate of the poor:

> people bred in slums can imagine nothing but the slums. For what I saw in her face was not the ignorant suffering of an animal. She knew well enough what was happening to her – understood as well as I did how dreadful a destiny it was to be kneeling there in the bitter cold, on the slimy stones of a slum backyard, poking a stick up a foul drain-pipe.[41]

How to enable people to escape that destiny was what united Orwell, the authors of the medical and nutritional reports on the unemployed, the Archbishop of York, John Maynard Keynes and his disciple Hans Singer.

Singer and his colleagues fanned out across Britain in search of raw data. For Singer, only recently arrived in the country, this presented difficulties. He had great difficulty in understanding the accents and dialects of those with whom he lived.[42] When those he stayed with referred to the Means Test officials as 'boogers', he had to ask his colleagues for a translation. He was also worried that he would be regarded as a spy because of his foreign accent. Far from being a hindrance, however, his German accent and foreign manner were an advantage. Nobody suspected he was a snooper from the hated Unemployment Assistance Board, and all trusted him with a full account of their lives. He set to work, tracing the life histories of those he lived with, examining their health records and thinking about answers to their problems.[43] It was intended to be a more scientific, less colourful approach than Orwell's method, which would lead to practical results. Although he supplied many facts and figures in *The Road to Wigan Pier*, Orwell was primarily seeking to change people through polemic and propaganda. For this reason he was happy to embellish the facts if it served his purpose.

On 15 February Orwell changed his lodgings. He explained in his diaries that the reason for the move was a 'mysterious' illness that had put Mrs Hornby in hospital. But the reality seems to have been that the house was, although poor and serving tripe, too clean and respectable for his purposes. He needed real degradation and disgust to fire him up. A local Communist, Jim Hammond, was shocked but not entirely surprised, as he remembered:

> He could have gone to any of a thousand respectable working-class houses and lodged with them or stayed right where he was. But he doesn't do that. He goes to a doss-house, just like he's down and out in Paris still. You see, when they've left the upper class, they've got to go right down into muck and start muckraking.[44]

At 22 Darlington Road Orwell found the slum he wanted.[45] The tripe shop and lodging house became the memorable centrepiece of the first chapter of *The Road to Wigan Pier*. He noted with some relish: 'Social atmosphere much as at the Hs but the house appreciably dirtier and very smelly.' There is some dispute as to the identity of the couple who ran the lodgings. Orwell called them the 'Brookers' in his book, but they appear to have been the Forrests,[46] an ex-miner, with his invalid wife who lived in a bed in the kitchen. Nine people crammed into the small house, including two aged pensioners who had fallen on hard times as a result of the Means Test.

For the long-term unemployed the only way to get assistance in 1936 was to undergo the Means Test. Introduced five years earlier by the National Government to reduce public spending, it was the most hated of all the government's measures to deal with unemployment. It aroused fierce anger against the old Labour leaders, such as Ramsay MacDonald, who had stayed on in the coalition government and were accused of treachery when it was introduced. There were petitions, strikes and riots against it. Hunger marches converged on the capital. Outside Parliament the radical left gained in strength, and there were fears of revolution.

The Means Test was particularly hated because it broke up families, driving children away from home, and forced the elderly to fend for themselves. It was applied to those who had been unemployed for more than eighteen months and were considered no longer part of the labour market. In the past they had been subjected to the Poor Law and the workhouse. Now they qualified for minimal benefit, which was paid by Treasury-funded Unemployment Assistance Boards from already over-stretched budgets. To minimize payments, the Boards demanded that claimants demonstrate their abject poverty before they could receive any money. No payments could be made if the unemployed person had savings or other assets, however small, or if other members of the family in the same household were receiving income. Thus the elderly or young received no benefits if a member of the family was working. The elderly, as Orwell discovered, were often forced as a result into lodgings, where they waited to die away from home, relying on the minimal benefit they might receive for board and lodging, and charity from the parish for anything else. For all affected it was an insult to their dignity.

Orwell shared his bedroom in Darlington Street with three other lodgers. The beds were jammed so tightly together that he, 6 feet 3 inches tall, had to sleep doubled-up to prevent himself kicking the occupant of another bed in the small of the back. All the windows were kept shut, 'and in the morning the room stank like a ferret's cage . . . the smell hit you in the face with a smack'.[47] Kay Ekevall, a former girlfriend, remembered his phobia about smells: 'I think he always exaggerated this kind of thing. I just think he had a sordid imagination.'[48] But it was Orwell's sordid imagination that enabled him to conjure up these scenes with such effect.

In *The Road to Wigan Pier*, based on his diary and published a year after his stay there, Orwell painted a vivid picture of the Forrests: their meanness, their cheating, their resentment of their lodgers and, above all, their filthy habits. Mr Forrest never washed his hands. He carried full chamber pots around the house, his thumb 'well over the rim'. He then prepared food, leaving greasy thumbprints on the buttered bread, handling it with a 'peculiarly intimate lingering manner' common, in Orwell's horrified yet gripped imagination, to all those 'with permanently dirty hands'. With the same blackened hands he would reach into the store cupboard, where black beetles apparently swarmed, to fetch the tripe sold in the shop. Mrs Forrest, meanwhile, lay bloated on a shapeless sofa in the kitchen living-room, permanently ill, Orwell believed from over-eating, and permanently moaning. Orwell's 'sordid imagination' had alighted like one of the beetles on a piece of the Forrests' decaying tripe, and the result was a cruel masterpiece of description.

Orwell built his polemic on this one unfortunate lodging-house that he had selected. He argued that these places were not unusual but 'exist in tens and hundreds of thousands; they are one of the characteristic by-products of the modern world. You cannot disregard them if you accept the civilisation that produced them. For this is part at least of what industrialism has done for us.'[49] He also argued that this kind of slum was 'fairly normal as lodging-houses in the industrial areas go, for on the whole the lodgers did not complain'.[50] To emphasize the north–south divide Orwell noted that a fellow lodger, a 'little black-haired, sharp-nosed Cockney', was the only person to protest: 'He caught my eye and suddenly divined that I was a fellow Southerner. "The filthy bloody bastards!" he said feelingly.'

In reality, of course, most northerners, whether working or jobless, kept their house clean. Miners, in particular, took great pride in keeping up standards, and many, contrary to Orwell's opinion, helped around the house when out of work. For years afterwards Orwell's assumption that the particular experience of the tripe shop could be applied generally to northerners caused understandable resentment. Sydney Smith was a seventeen-year-old unemployed youth when he met Orwell in Wigan in 1936: 'I would say that Orwell's description of the [tripe] shop was accurate, I don't think that was the correct image of Wigan by any means. Wigan people are rather proud and they were clean.'[51] Humphrey Dakin, Orwell's brother-in-law, was a northerner who lived in Leeds. The author had stayed with him during his visit to the north, and Dakin later expressed the feelings of many: 'In those days . . . life was definitely grim, you couldn't laugh everything off. But nevertheless in those sorts of places . . . there was quite a lot of cheerfulness for those who could find and see it. Even those rows and rows of squalid little houses, they look awful from the outside but in point of fact . . . were kept remarkably clean and tidy.'[52]

On Monday 23 February Jerry Kennan took Orwell down a local mine so that he could have a taste of the labour of the working classes. The writer had expected tunnels like those of the London underground, in which he could wander about. He had not bargained for the limited space in which he was forced to crawl to the coal-face, bent double for nearly a mile. For a man more than six feet tall it was agony. In places the tunnel was less than four feet high. Every now and then a large roof girder jutted across the tunnel. After 300 yards Orwell failed to duck in time and hit a beam. 'It didn't knock the helmet off; it knocked him down', Kennan reported; 'He was flat out.'[53] Once revived, he continued, doubled up and occasionally reduced to crawling. There had been a rock-fall, forcing Orwell and his guides to take a diversion to get through to the workface. The temporary tunnel was like 'an enlarged rat hole'. Soon he was feeling violent pain down his thighs, his knees giving way, and he suffered a crick in the neck. He had to ask his guides to stop and let him rest. Eventually they arrived at the working coal-face, which was little more than two feet across. Orwell was 'unquestionably exhausted'. Kennan watched him lie down on the piles of excavated coal on the floor to recover and told him, 'It's a so-and-so good job they don't want you down here for to write a book about mining'.

Orwell watched as a team of miners operated a cutting-machine to extract coal from the narrow seam, doing most of the work lying on their bellies. The machine was 'monstrous', the heat intense, and the noise must have been terrible too. After watching the 'frightful' (a favourite word of Orwell's in Wigan) scene before him for some time, this southern intellectual faced the long journey back to the cage that would take them to the surface. On the way back he was so exhausted that he 'could hardly keep going at all, and towards the end I had to stop and rest every fifty yards'.[54] The effort of bending and then rising after every beam was particularly painful. Orwell wondered ruefully whether there were any miners as tall as he, and whether they suffered as he did. The miners he did meet in the tunnel moved 'with extraordinary agility', running about on all fours 'almost like dogs'.

After Orwell emerged blinking into the welcome daylight of

Wigan, he went with Jerry Kennan for a beer in the local pub and then returned to the lodgings in Darlington Street, where he sank thankfully into a hot bath. His lodgings may have been filthy and cramped, but at least they had this one luxury. The fastidious journalist was shocked at the quantity of dirt and how difficult it was to wash it off his body. 'It had penetrated to every inch of my body in spite of my overalls and my clothes underneath those.'[55] The coal dust gave him an insight into the challenge that cleanliness posed mining families, few of whom had baths and most of whom washed in a tub in front of the fire.

The journey down the mine had been mentally and physically crushing. The sheer physical strength needed for mining, not only for the labour itself but also for getting to the coal-face, was to make a lasting impression on Orwell. Physically it took him some time to recover. Although he was obviously quite fit, able to walk sixteen miles a day without too much trouble, the two-mile journey to the coal-face left him more exhausted than he cared to admit in his diary. When Jerry Kennan's wife asked her husband anxiously the next day whether he had seen the southern visitor, 'I said, "No". Tuesday night when I came home from work, she said, "Have you seen him?" I said, "No." She says, "Don't you think you have to go and look for him?"' Kennan gave it another day, and on Wednesday evening Orwell knocked at the door: 'Believe me, Orwell was not much taller than me on the Wednesday night. Three days after being down the pits. He was stiff as a grunt.' Kennan learned that his guest had spent three days in bed recovering.[56] It may be that he secretly did what those journalists he so disdained had done and went off to find a comfortable bed in a hotel in which to recuperate.

The combination of the trip down the pit, the bleakness of Wigan and the squalor of the lodging-house had overwhelmed even this most immersive of journalists. He may have found some curious self-torturing satisfaction in plumbing the depths of working people's lives, but he admitted in his diary it was 'beginning to get on my nerves'.[57] In the house in Darlington Street nothing was cleaned or dusted, the lodgers' rooms were not tidied until late afternoon, and the degradation of Mrs Forrest prone on the kitchen sofa was overwhelmingly repulsive. 'She has a terrible habit of tearing off strips of newspaper, wiping her mouth with them and then throwing them on to the floor.'[58] One morning her husband left her unemptied chamber pot under the breakfast table.

Four days later, at the end of February, Orwell escaped Wigan by train to Liverpool, through the now familiar but no more appreciated 'monstrous scenery' of slag heaps, blackened snow and 'foul canals'. He took with him scenes that stood out vividly in his memory, and which he later wrote down in his spare but penetrating style.

> The almost bare living room of a cottage in a little mining village, where the whole family was out of work and everyone seemed to be underfed; and the big family of grown-up sons and daughters sprawling aimlessly about, all strangers alike with red hair, splendid bones and pinched faces ruined by malnutrition and idleness.[59]

On arrival in Liverpool, he collapsed with a fever that kept him in bed for days.

Meanwhile Hans Singer and his colleagues continued their studies. Their work took them to six districts scattered through England and Wales, including the bleakest parts of the distressed areas in the Rhondda (in south Wales) and County Durham, and the blighted inner city of Liverpool. They filled in their survey forms and compiled their questionnaires. They were given access to Means Test investigations, to health records and employment statistics. But, as with Orwell, they believed the key was immersion. To meet the unemployed, Singer found, was 'to be aware of depression, apathy, physical deterioration and other things', but actually to live with them gave 'the full dimension of the poverty associated with unemployment'.

Hans Singer's research concentrated on the health effects of unemployment. He found that women, in particular, suffered, often going without food so that their families could eat. When he stayed in the Rhondda, he came across countless heart-rending cases similar to those Orwell had seen. Typical were a man and his 37-year-old wife and their small boy of three. Singer visited their house and found 'a picture of extreme neglect. Poor furniture . . . I believe that she makes some efforts to keep a decent home, but her husband and brother come in drunk, and she is ill and cannot stop them.' The woman's condition was shocking: 'she looks like death, a very poor physical and social type, only two teeth, yellowish face, rags of clothing.' By contrast, however, her son 'looks well and is neatly clothed'.[60] Singer found many similar cases where women sacrificed themselves for the sake of the well-being of their children. The result was that they showed 'obvious signs of malnutrition' and that their health deteriorated: 'there was a marked increase in the number of women suffering from anaemia, neurasthenia and in . . . the occurrence of septic hands, boils and skin troubles.'[61]

The report Singer and his team compiled in 1936, *Men without Work*, was published two years later. Its principal recommendation, that the jobless should be able to participate fully in voluntary work, to give rather than to receive in order to rebalance their lives, became a reality with the outbreak of war. But it was not practicable in peacetime and did little to address the real issues. More important, perhaps, was the general impact of the findings on people's awareness of the horrors of unemployment and the particular effect on those who had commissioned the work.

Early in 1936 Sir William Beveridge had suggested the nature of the *Men without Work* study. Six years later, in December 1942, he himself would produce a report that was to serve as the basis for the Labour government's creation of the welfare state after the war and the establishment of the National Health Service in 1948. At the heart of the Beveridge Report was the stated 'assumption' that unemployment should be no higher than 3 per cent. No doubt the link between long-term unemployment and ill health, as shown by Hans Singer, had influenced him. His assumption, which became the central pillar of government policy for three decades, was made possible by the economics of Singer's sponsor, John Maynard Keynes. In 1936 a new liberal consensus was forming which, tempered by the flames of the Second World War, would sweep away the old world of hand-wringing and ineffective palliatives.

The new consensus needed a propagandist. The experience of Wigan had confirmed Orwell as a very English socialist, committed to reform, if not revolution. When he left the town, he reflected on the moral horror of the modern world, and on where the achievements of previous centuries – the Industrial Revolution, Waterloo, Empire – had led: 'to labyrinthine slums and dark back-kitchens with sickly ageing people creeping round and round them like black beetles'.[62] Although similar in sentiment to Singer, Beveridge and Keynes, he expressed himself in terms that they would never have considered using. He was a polemicist and imaginative writer who did not set out to be an objective reporter. He presented one side of the story. For the many activists who welcomed him to Wigan it was a story that needed to be told, and they were grateful. As Jerry Kennan said of the portrait of Wigan in *The Road to Wigan Pier*: 'I don't think it exaggerated the situation at all. And I think it gives a clear picture of what industrial conditions were like in 1936.'[63] Others were less grateful. Orwell's portrait of the town is resented to this day in Wigan. But he was a writer of genius who came, saw and took advantage. His epitaph for the town, as he departed, reflected the hardship of his stay: 'It is a kind of duty to see and smell such places now and again, especially smell them, lest you should forget they exist; though perhaps it is better not to stay there for too long.'

It was this haughty disregard and slightly patronizing pity, together with the vivid descriptions that came from the attraction–repulsion of a 'sordid imagination', that gave the scenes in the opening chapter of *The Road to Wigan Power* such power and influence. Orwell, by the lasting power of his writing, as much as Hans Singer, was one of those responsible for creating the consensus that gave birth to the welfare state. The poverty to which his vivid imagination was witness gave form to a world that had to be changed. Hundreds of other books about the horror of the Depression were written in the 1930s, but few have survived the test of time. Orwell the outsider, unjust, snobbish and disgusted, lives on.

5

A meeting with Herr Hitler

ON 29 JANUARY, just as George Orwell was setting off to visit the slag heaps of the north, Charles Stewart Henry Vane-Tempest-Stewart, 7th Marquess of Londonderry, boarded a Junkers JU–52 at Croydon airport and departed for Germany. Like Orwell, Lord Londonderry was on a journey of discovery, but his mission was entirely different. Much of his inherited wealth came from the coalmines of County Durham, now devastated by decline, yet he had little concern for the suffering of the northern unemployed. Londonderry was profoundly anti-Communist, feared revolution and wished to do everything he could to preserve the greatness of the British Empire. For this he believed a long-term settlement with a renascent Nazi Germany was essential. With an aristocratic contempt for elected politicians and professional diplomats, he considered he was the man best placed to bring about, as his forebear Lord Castlereagh had done a century earlier, 'peace for our time'.

Charley Londonderry was still suffering from bitterly hurt feelings. The previous October, after the general election, Stanley Baldwin had sacked him from the government, in which he had served without much distinction as a gaffe-prone and incompetent air minister and Lord Privy Seal. Shortly after his dismissal his son had come to console him and found 'A broken man', collapsed, 'a tragic sight – sitting sideways in his chair with his legs dangling over the arm'; he was holding the letter of dismissal in his hand, tears were running down his cheeks, and he was repeatedly muttering 'I've been sacked – kicked out'.[1] As so often in the cruel theatre of politics, what was blindingly obvious to others, the subject of repeated speculation in the newspapers and gossip in the tearooms and bars of Westminster, came as a terrible shock to the victim.

Charley Londonderry never forgave the Prime Minister for his sacking. 'From abject despair my father's mood turned to extreme bitterness. Baldwin became his *bête noire,* and he pursued him with undying bitterness', his son recalled.[2] Driven by burning resentment and with an extraordinary confidence in his own abilities, he set off on his diplomatic quest. He was the first of a stream of distinguished and gullible visitors invited to meet Hitler in 1936, the majority of whom came away convinced of the Nazi leader's reasonableness and desire for peace with the British Empire.

Stanley Baldwin regarded Lord Londonderry as a snob; he told the Marquess's son with characteristic frankness that his father was 'aloof and stand-offish'. To others he had a 'natural nose in the air posture'[3], and his style was reminiscent of a Regency beau, '1760 in 1936', according to Harold Nicolson.[4] He was a dandy, beautifully tailored, carrying a brown cane stick with an 'L' embossed in gold on its cork top, and he frequently wore a cravat.[5] While his manner, in the aristocratic style, was reserved and polite, he could be petulant. Churchill dismissed him as a 'half wit'.[6] But whatever others may have felt, Londonderry had great faith in himself.

In February 1936, aged fifty-seven, he believed that his visit to the Nazi leaders would restore his political fortunes. He saw himself fated by his birthright to be a player in the diplomatic game as a descendant of Lord Castlereagh, who had successfully negotiated the settlement that brought peace to Europe after Wellington's defeat of Napoleon in 1815. In 1936 the Marquess kept a diary of his journey which he used as the basis of a book, *Ourselves and Germany,*[7] in which he painted a sympathetic picture of Adolf Hitler and urged the appeasement of Nazi Germany. He proudly drew attention to his forebear's success on the first page of his book. 'History has shown us', he boasted, 'through the achievements of Castlereagh and Wellington, that the policy of restoring defeated nations was followed by beneficial results.'[8]

Londonderry was accompanied on his visit to Germany by his wife Edith ('Edie'), and his youngest daughter, the fifteen year-old Mairi.

The Londonderrys were relics of the grandeur of the Edwardian age. Their vast wealth included two country seats, Wynyard Park in County Durham, and Mount Stewart, near Belfast, 50,000 acres, extensive coalmines and a magnificent town house in Park Lane. The Marquess was a grandee at the heart of the establishment, friend of the late King, cousin of Winston Churchill and a stalwart of the Conservative Party. He had resolutely opposed the General Strike ten years earlier and had always shown extreme hostility to union militancy among mineworkers in his Durham collieries.

For more than twenty years his wife, Edie, had been the dominant Tory hostess. Her eve-of Parliament receptions at Londonderry House in November were one of the social events of the year, often attended by 2,000 or more. The guest list took up nearly two full columns of The Times.[9] Edie would stand at the top of the grand staircase, wearing a tiara and the fabulous family jewels, next to the Prime Minister of the day, greeting the guests as they arrived. Bewigged and powdered footmen looked on as the tightly packed crowds, made up of anybody of any standing in government and society, inched their way up the stairs. According to Chips Channon, her soirées were 'always glamorous'.[10] John Buchan's son William described the house as having 'the feeling of Ruritanian splendour, the gilding and the crystal'.[11]

While Charley Londonderry had numerous affairs and at least one illegitimate child, Edie had a long-running passionate friendship with Ramsay MacDonald, the Labour Prime Minister, whom she had first met in 1924 when seated next to him at Buckingham Palace. Their relationship had become closer during the second Labour government of 1929–31. She wrote frequently to MacDonald under her pet name 'Circe'. She enrolled him in her group of tame politicians, 'The Ark', and she called him 'Hamish the Hart', just as she called Winston Churchill 'Winston the Warlock' and Neville Chamberlain 'Neville the Devil'.[12] She was widely blamed by the Left for making MacDonald forget his humble roots as the illegitimate son of a farm labourer and a servant girl and betray the Labour Party, when he agreed to lead the coalition National Government in 1931 and introduced the Means Test. For a woman of her class, she was unconventional. She had been a suffragist, and believed male–female relations were now governed by 'an entirely new code of conduct and thought'. She had the figure of a snake tattooed on her left leg, which, as someone joked, when revealed as hemlines rose, caused eyebrows to rise too.[13] Baldwin thought she had 'charm, vitality and courage – priceless assets. But if allied to faulty judgement they became even greater liabilities.'[14]

In early 1936 Edie's talents were firmly in alliance with faulty judgement. She and her husband existed in a world that, if it had not actually passed away, was certainly on the way out. Chamberlain and Baldwin, the new breed of Conservative politician, might have enjoyed Edie's hospitality, but they had little time for the privileged world the Londonderrys represented. They were hard Midlands men of business who had fought their way to the top in politics. Baldwin's wealth came from iron; Chamberlain's prosperity rested on engineering. If the Londonderrys believed they could influence British foreign policy, they deceived themselves. The problem was that they deceived the Nazis too.

Shortly before the Londonderrys' departure, Hensley Henson, the Bishop of Durham, received a letter from Londonderry's son Robin, in which he referred to tensions in the family and said 'my father's retirement from the Cabinet will, I hope, have the result of a return to Wynyard. This I regard as essential. Unluckily my mother and sister both hate the place, which is most unfortunate.'[15] Wynyard Park was a stone's throw from the Bishop's Palace at Auckland in County Durham. Although the Marquess of Londonderry was the Bishop's friend and neighbour, Henson was not a man to be held back by such considerations when he felt the spirit moved him to speak his mind on issues where they disagreed. He, like Londonderry, was a reactionary on most matters. He disliked Labour politicians, detested the unions and feared and loathed Communism. But on the moral question of Fascism he was a progressive, ahead of his time, and quite opposed to the views of his neighbour. Henson was one of the few establishment figures, alongside Winston Churchill, who took a stand against the Nazis that year.

On 29 January, the same day that Charley and Edie Londonderry were beginning their tour of Germany, the Bishop started a series of outspoken attacks on Nazi anti-Semitism which drew him to national attention. 'My speech on the persecution of the Jews has made me so prominent', he wrote in his diary at the end of the month, 'that I am afraid the Jews will be disappointed when they realize how little weight the Bishop of Durham carries in any quarter.' Henson was being falsely modest. Like Londonderry, he loved the limelight that his interventions brought and never shunned controversy.

In 1936, seventy-three years old, he had a striking appearance: small, with bushy upturned eyebrows, which a friend remembered made him look 'sometimes forbidding, sometimes quizzical, sometimes like Mephistopheles'.[16] His piercing hazel eyes could fix those to whom he took exception (there were many) with a penetrating stare, but he had a ready humour and a charisma that drew people to him. He had been a Fellow of All Souls, and none doubted his intellect. Sometimes, however, his brain took him down the wrong path, as would happen later in the year, but on the rise of Hitler he was a prophet, and in his diary he dismissed Charley Londonderry as 'utterly wrong-headed'.[17]

The Junkers tri-motor plane carrying the Londonderrys to the heart of Nazi Germany stopped off at Amsterdam and Hanover to refuel on its way to Berlin. Charley Londonderry was an aviation enthusiast. As air minister he had had some responsibility for the early development of the Spitfire and Hurricane fighters and was impressed by the Junkers, 'very comfortable and not nearly so noisy as I had been led to suppose'. It was the same type of plane Hitler used for his journeys across Germany. On arrival in Berlin the Londonderrys were taken to the capital's smartest hotel, the Adlon, where officials briefed them on their programme for the next few weeks. The Nazi regime was determined to impress. It was a magnificent tour. Reichsmarschall Hermann Goering, head of the resurgent Luftwaffe, was the Londonderrys' personal host. His plane was put at their disposal. There would be visits to Luftwaffe bases and aircraft factories, aerial displays, gala dinners and concerts. The trip was set to finish with a stay in Garmisch-Partenkirchen to see the Winter Olympics (which were held six months before the main Olympics in Berlin).

The highlight of the trip was to be an intimate audience with the Führer.

For Hitler 1936 was a make-or-break year, especially in the development of his relations with Great Britain. He was determined to make a pact that would preserve the British Empire, leaving him free to dominate Europe. The Nazi leader had long hoped to reverse the traditional German enmity towards Britain, enabling him to destroy Bolshevik Russia and to settle old scores with France.[18] In *Mein Kampf* he had made clear that friendship with Britain held the key for his plans for gaining *Lebensraum*, living space, in the east. Later he said that he regarded war between Germany and Britain, racially similar, as a crime. 'When one saw the dead in the Great War', he told a British visitor, 'one was particularly pained by the sight of the English dead.' Anglo-German friendship, he said, would be the greatest achievement of his life.[19]

Hitler relied on his ambassador-at-large, Joachim von Ribbentrop, for advice on how to approach the British and bring about the longed-for alliance. It was Ribbentrop who arranged the Londonderrys' visit to Germany. Hitler and his diplomatic 'expert' were both convinced that the pro-German Edward VIII and friendly aristocrats such as the Marquess of Londonderry had great influence in government affairs, and could be used to shift British foreign policy towards lasting settlement with Germany. They simply failed to comprehend that centres of political power in Britain had changed or to understand the way that prominent figures in public life behaved. Ribbentrop even went so far as to suggest offering a substantial bribe to Churchill as the means of curbing his hostility to Germany.[20]

He and Charley Londonderry were made for each other. Both were snobs; both were widely disliked; both were regarded as stupid, vain and arrogant; both shared an archaic belief in the power of the aristocracy to change the destiny of nations.[21] Both, too, were married to powerful women, cleverer than they were, who became influential political hostesses and who managed their husbands' careers. Ribbentrop had bought his title 'von' from an impoverished aunt, using the wealth of his wife, Annalies Henkell – a member of the German sparkling wine dynasty. He, like Londonderry, had the unfortunate look of holding his nose in the air. But, despite all this – or perhaps because of it – their relationship was to end in disaster, with mutual recrimination and the ruin of one and the ghastly death of the other hanging on a rope at Nuremberg.

At that time Hitler regarded Ribbentrop as 'a genius', even though almost all those who knew him regarded him as a fool. Reinhard Spitzy, who worked as his special assistant in 1936, dismissed him as 'a combination of superficiality, stupidity, and most especially, vanity'.[22] But there was something in Hitler's more favourable judgement of the man. Ribbentrop was crafty. He had, after all, negotiated the Anglo-German naval agreement the previous year, which allowed Hitler to build a navy in contravention of the Versailles Treaty. He cultivated the upper classes of Britain, and he set up the Anglo-German Fellowship to encourage friendship between the two countries. Its members consisted of right-wing aristocrats, bankers, businessmen and retired military men. He arranged for a series of high-profile visits, such as the Londonderry tour, for a favoured few to see Germany and meet Hitler.

In early 1936 Ribbentrop felt a second, more ambitious agreement with the British was within his grasp. A new King was on the throne, who was generally believed to be sympathetic to Germany. Many in high society shared his views. The previous year Ribbentrop had dined several times at Londonderry House and at other London salons, where the leading society hostesses had lionized him, competing with each other to heap praise on the Nazis and Adolf Hitler. He had met and befriended Wallis Simpson.

At home, Ribbentrop often held Hitler spellbound with tales about Britain past and present. Ribbentrop had lived there briefly as a young man before the First World War, selling German wines. It had been a formative period in his life and had given him a conception of Britain that had petrified in his mind. As he had stood in the City, he marvelled at its greatness and 'felt the heartbeat of the world'.[23] He moved for a while to Canada, where he inveigled his way into the smart set of the Governor-General, Prince Arthur, Duke of Connaught, a son of Queen Victoria. His first brush with royalty made him a lifelong admirer of the British royal family, who, he believed, had a crucial role 'to maintain the cohesion of Empire'. He spoke English almost perfectly: his accent was 'Long Island without a trace of Teutonic flavour', according to the American-born Chips Channon.[24] Hitler shared this fascination with English royalty and aristocracy. 'He could not hear enough about England', Ribbentrop wrote, 'particularly what influential Englishmen thought.'[25] Now those aristocrats whom he admired so much were queuing up to see the wonders of Nazi Germany, and to have the honour of a meeting with Herr Hitler himself. Eventually, Ribbentrop hoped, the Prime Minister himself would be persuaded into meeting the German Chancellor.

During the Londonderrys' visit to Germany, Ribbentrop was happy to play second fiddle to Hitler's deputy, the colourful Hermann Goering. As the Marquess was a former air minister, it was considered appropriate that the head of the German air force should act as host. On 30 January Londonderry and the British air attaché visited a Luftwaffe staff college, toured an aerodrome and watched an air display by the famous Richthofen squadron, which Goering had commanded for a time during the First World War.[26]

In the evening the Londonderrys dined in the tapestried opulence of Goering's official Berlin residence. The Marquess was seated next to the Nazi's wife, Emmy, a former actress, with whom he had a stilted conversation in his limited German about her Shakespearean roles. The Prince of Hesse, a fanatical Nazi and a descendant of Queen Victoria, sat on the other side of Emmy and helped out when conversation became sticky. Meanwhile the Marchioness struck up a flirtatious and arch relationship with Goering, which she kept up in correspondence after the visit. Dinner over, the bass-baritone Rudolf Bockelmann sang an excerpt from Wagner's *Ring*. The guests were also treated to a propaganda film showing Germany's armed forces, followed by Hitler in full cry, or, as Londonderry put it, 'delivering a stirring speech'.[27]

The purpose of the day was clear: to impress on the British visitors the renewed might of the military under Hitler, particularly the air force. Londonderry needed little convincing. The evident growth of the Luftwaffe had so shocked the British government the previous year that it had been forced to introduce the first measures of rearmament, to Neville Chamberlain's lasting regret.[28] It had also embarked on a policy of seeking settlement of Germany's outstanding grievances, in the hope that this would pacify the aggressive Nazi leader. As the historian Ian Kershaw has shown, Londonderry agreed with this appeasement policy, but wanted to go further. Like many prominent Britons in 1936, he saw Germany as a bulwark against the much greater threat of Communist Russia. If a deal could be done with the Nazis that gave them mastery on the Continent, he believed, the menace from the east could be neutralized. Britain would be able to concentrate on looking after its extensive Empire, troubled as it was in so many places by rising agitation for independence. This chimed exactly with Hitler's beliefs and desires.

The only problem was that the British government at the time had not the slightest intention of negotiating a deal with Hitler that would allow Germany to become dominant in Europe. Settling outstanding grievances was one thing, but making an alliance with the Nazis at the expense of the French, Britain's closest ally, was quite simply out of the question. In London the Foreign Office was infuriated by the procession of upper-class visitors such as Charley Londonderry to Hitler's door. 'What a march of dupes', sighed a diplomat. 'Presumably nothing can be done to prevent irresponsible busybodies visiting Berlin', moaned another Foreign Office official, adding that when they returned to London their views were taken up by the pro-appeasement *Times* newspaper as propaganda for the cause.[29]

After the film show Londonderry, oblivious to political realities at home and delighted by the attention he was receiving, was shown some of Goering's priceless antiquities, 'borrowed' from Berlin's museums. He also admired a sketch drawn by Hitler when fighting in the trenches, which 'was rough but artistic'. At about 2.30 a.m. the Londonderrys returned to the Adlon, no doubt exhausted but buoyed up by the Nazis' obsequious attentions.

The next day Hermann Goering invited his guests to the Carinhall, the hunting-lodge on his Schorfheide estate, north of Berlin.

Although ostensibly a simple log cabin, it was vast in scale, resembling a set from Wagner's *Ring* at Bayreuth, in which Siegfried or Wotan might have felt at home, 'feasting, recounting the day's exploits and drinking deep after hours in the open air'.[30] Inside there was a wooden table surrounded by enormous chairs and a large open fireplace. Bearskins lay on the floor, and on the walls hunting trophies glared down at the awe-struck guests. In the cellars Goering's pets, semi-house-trained lions, padded menacingly. When the aviator and Nazi sympathizer Charles Lindbergh visited, he had watched with a mixture of wonder and embarrassment as a lioness playfully urinated over her master. Goering himself added to the Wagnerian atmosphere by indulging his love of fancy dress. He greeted the soberly tweeded Londonderrys, Lady Mairi remembered, with his huge frame clothed 'in a green hunting outfit with white sleeves, leather jacket and a feathered hat'.[31] To round off the spectacle, Goering held a hunting horn in one hand and carried a large spear in the other, purely for decoration; the waiting animals were to be killed with guns. Whether he caused awe or mirth in his British guests is not known. They diplomatically expressed nothing but respectful appreciation. The Germans had intercepted a previous British party's report of a day's sport at Carinhall. Its mockery had caused a cooling in Anglo-German relations.[32]

Goering kept a herd of bison on his estate. The party was taken down to the enclosure, the Reichsmarschall blew his horn, and some of the beasts left their grazing, lumbered up and were shot.[33] The Londonderrys, for their part, killed three deer. Tea was then served in the hunting-lodge, after which Londonderry and Goering settled down to talk about Anglo-German relations.

Although Londonderry spoke some German, Hitler's personal interpreter, Paul Schmidt, translated. He later remembered the talks as 'pleasant table conversations' rather than serious negotiation.[34] Nevertheless, Goering made it clear that the Nazis wanted further *rapprochement*. He mentioned the possibility of an air pact similar to the previous year's naval treaty between the two countries, and a return of the German colonies lost as a result of the humiliating peace terms imposed at Versailles. The two men discussed the Nazi desire for living space. Goering concluded the conversation with further boasting about the renewed strength of the Luftwaffe, no doubt with the aim of impressing on his guest the need for friendship with a mighty Germany.[35]

Over the next few days the triumphant tour continued. Londonderry held further talks with leading Nazis, including Ribbentrop, who repeated Goering's desire for an Anglo-German settlement and called for an alliance against the spread of Bolshevism.[36] The Marquess was shown more Luftwaffe bases and an aircraft engine factory. Over the weekend the family were treated to a tour of the palace of Sanssouci, in Potsdam, and went to a horse show: 'The jumping was very good over a difficult course with over twelve jumps' was Charley's somewhat jejune diary entry.[37] Finally, on Tuesday 4 February, the moment to which he had been looking forward so keenly arrived. He was to meet the Führer himself.

As Londonderry was shown into the echoing vastness of Hitler's office in the Chancellery, it was the Führer, surprisingly, and not he, who seemed nervous. The Marquess later recalled that 'Hitler was extremely embarrassed and awkward'. The party, which included Ribbentrop and the interpreter Schmidt, stood around making stilted small talk. Eventually Londonderry took the lead, sitting down unbidden, indicating with patrician condescension to his host, the former corporal, to do the same, 'a lead which he followed with gratitude'.[38] Some have interpreted Hitler's show of diffidence as a deliberate ploy, to encourage confidence in his guest and not to alienate him.[39] It is perhaps more likely that Hitler suffered from an inferiority complex and regarded the British aristocracy as the apogee of the social order. He certainly laboured under the delusion that they were powerful and influential figures in the British establishment. He enjoyed the company of those, like the Mitford sisters Unity and Diana, whom he knew well. As a radical, he also believed that he could best achieve his aims by by-passing the normal channels and dealing with important intermediaries, as he told Londonderry at the start of the conversation.[40]

Hitler talked to Londonderry for two hours, appearing restrained and rational throughout the meeting. Londonderry observed Hitler closely and noted his 'kindly' manner and his physical appearance: 'a receding chin and an impressive face'.[41] The theme of the meeting was the threat of Soviet Russia. From the outset Hitler spoke of the menace posed by Bolshevism, putting himself forward as a prophet of looming catastrophe unless something was done about the 'monstrous danger of contagion'[42] of Communism. When Londonderry pointed out that in Britain there was rather less fear of Bolshevism than in Germany, Ribbentrop insinuated himself into the conversation. He referred to a report that 'international Jews were making common cause with the Bolshevists',[43] thus conflating Nazism's greatest enemies, no doubt hoping at a stroke to play on Londonderry's fears while advancing himself in the eyes of his boss. The Führer, probably aware how badly this subject would go down in Britain, did not take the bait, and Londonderry was spared a Hitlerian tirade about the conspiracy of international Jewry.

Hitler then turned to the question of colonies, and the interview concluded with his solemn avowal that 'Germany wants to live in close friendly alliance with England'. Londonderry, Ribbentrop and Hitler then rose and stood together in front of the Führer's desk for the obligatory photograph. The three men posed unsmiling, Londonderry standing to attention immaculate in his suit, the Führer centre-stage staring into the middle distance, his 'man of destiny' posture, and Ribbentrop slightly lopsided, with a look of gravity that those who knew him well recognized for what it was: malevolent vacuity. It was a parallel diplomatic universe, each participant labouring under a delusion: Hitler and Ribbentrop that their guest was a man of real importance, and Londonderry that he could influence events at home. Such visits happened, in the cool appraisal of the British Ambassador to Berlin, 'in an idyllic and unruffled atmosphere of complete Anglo-German misunderstanding'.[44] They were profoundly damaging, leading in the long run not to friendship and peace but to hatred and war.

The Londonderrys' progress through Nazi Germany continued for the rest of the week with further receptions and meetings, culminating in a visit to Garmisch-Partenkirchen for the Winter Olympics. Charley was much impressed by Hitler's immense popularity when he witnessed the closing ceremony, at which the Führer was cheered by 100,000 people, 'one of the most remarkable demonstrations I have seen'.[45] Hitler granted the Marquess a second, much shorter meeting before he and Edie departed. They returned to London star-struck and immediately wrote letters of thanks to their hosts; Edie's breathless and effusive, and Charley's more measured and diplomatic.

Edie told Hitler that it was not enough to speak of being deeply impressed. 'I am amazed. You and Germany remind me of the book of Genesis in the Bible. Nothing else describes the position adequately.'[46] With Hermann Goering she adopted a playful and flirtatious tone, addressing him as 'Dear General der Flieger and Minister President (although I would prefer to call you "Siegfried of modern times!")'; given Goering's immense bulk, her mental image of Wagner's hero must have been unusually large. She sent him silver-framed photos of portraits of herself and her daughter Mairi painted by the fashionable Hungarian society portraitist Philip de Laszlo.

Goering reciprocated with a picture of himself, to which Edie responded teasingly 'My dear General der Flieger Siegfried', and told him how, at a political reception at Londonderry House, the photograph had been much admired. The exchange continued with a further thank-you for the thank-you, with Goering acquiescing to the by now rather heavy-handed joke, signing his letter 'Hermann Goering (Siegfried)'. Edie was using the same techniques she employed in London as a political hostess: arch and playful letters to men of influence and, to a favoured few, membership of her inner circle, The Ark. At home it had been highly effective. With Goering and Ribbentrop it was different. Although Goering had played along, Edie's style, with all its would-be irony and wit, did not fit easily with the Nazi leadership, where jokes were no laughing matter. As for Ribbentrop, who had no vestige of a sense of humour, it was completely hopeless. It was Charley, also somewhat lacking in wit, who corresponded with him.

Ribbentrop and Londonderry had talked a great deal during the visit, and the question of the Nazi attitude to the Jews was raised several times. Charley returned to the subject in his letter of thanks, voicing concern that the British did not like persecution and warning 'with the greatest diffidence' that the Nazis were taking on 'a tremendous' force which would stand in the way of what they wanted to achieve. He went on, excusing his impertinence by showing that, despite this warning, he did share Ribbentrop's outlook. 'I have no great affection for the Jews. It is possible to trace their participation in most of the international disturbances which have created so much havoc in different countries.' Edie had voiced similar sentiments in her correspondence with Goering, telling him that the British press was hostile to Nazism and 'controlled to a large extent by Jews'.[47]

In Britain in 1936 casual anti-Semitism was commonplace across most sections of society. Many people made remarks that today would be deemed quite unacceptable. Respected authors, even radicals such as George Orwell and highly cultured liberals such as the economist John Maynard Keynes, littered their writings with disparaging remarks about the Jews, as did politicians on all sides, and some senior churchmen.[48] But this was very different from the thought-through, committed and codified anti-Semitism of the Nazis, which Londonderry was politely and hesitantly warning Ribbentrop did not go down well in Britain. Unattractive though his words to the Nazi were, at least he made his mild protest. Most of the stream of distinguished visitors to Germany that year never raised the subject of anti-Semitism, preferring to keep quiet and enjoy the hospitality.

One man was not keeping quiet. While the Londonderrys were in Germany, their neighbour in County Durham, Hensley Henson, kept up his very public campaign on the subject. On 4 February the Bishop sent a rocket to *The Times* about the celebrations of the University of Heidelberg's 550th anniversary, urging a boycott. The ancient university had driven out its Jewish professors, and Jews could not be undergraduates there. 'It cannot be right', the Bishop fulminated, 'that the universities of Great Britain, which we treasure as the very citadels of sound learning, because they are vigilant guardians of intellectual freedom, should openly fraternize with the avowed and shameless enemies of both.' Henson's attacks on Nazi anti-Semitism usually brought a torrent of abusive letters from British

anti-Semites and Fascists, and this time it was no different. As well as
a private post bag, there were letters from grandees to *The Times* and
angry articles in the German press attacking his stance. But to the
Jews he was a hero. He received letters from German Jews begging
him for help in getting their children out of Germany, Jews in
America prayed for him, and in Britain he became the unofficial
champion of the Jewish cause.

The day after the letter had appeared in *The Times* Henson went
to address the congregation of the West London Synagogue. The
hall was packed with prominent British Jews, and the Bishop spoke
strongly and movingly for forty minutes against the Nazi oppression.
The day after the speech to the synagogue he received a letter from
Victor Gollancz enclosing a proof of *The Yellow Spot*, a book for his
influential Left Book Club about Nazi atrocities, asking him to write
a preface. Henson was horrified by what he read, deeming the book
'the most complete documentary record so far issued of the persecution of the Jews in Germany', and accepted Gollancz's request, as he
wrote in his diary, for 'the Jew book'.[49]

Gollancz's approach to the Bishop was highly unusual, and a canny
move. A book from a left-wing publisher with a preface by a
conservative-minded Bishop would have a broad appeal. The Bishop,
however, was privately warned to steer clear of the project. The publisher, he was told by a contact, was widely regarded as, if not a
Communist, a tool of the Bolsheviks. But Henson insisted on going
ahead: 'I did not feel I could go back on my word', he reflected in his
diary. 'Accordingly I wrote the introduction and sent it to Gollancz
. . . I seem to be driven into championing these persecuted Jews by
the logic of events.'[50] Henson's opposition to Nazism was strong and
sincere. In the privacy of his diary he showed the depth of his feeling,
denying the injunction of the sixth commandment: 'who would not
applaud that German who, in the interest of elementary morals, killed
Hitler? I should give them Christian burial without hesitation.' In
February 1936 Henson was likely to have been the only bishop in
Britain, and indeed the world, urging tyrannicide.

While the majority of the country was still deeply suspicious of
Germany in the aftermath of the First World War, millions were

terrified of another war. From the beginning appeasement was a popular policy. Many in the upper echelons of society shared Londonderry's more extreme desire that year for an anti–Bolshevist pact with Germany that would protect the British Empire. The Bishop's attacks on the Nazis provoked General Sir Ian Hamilton, hero of Gallipoli, anti-Semite and anti-Communist, and like Londonderry a member of Ribbentrop's Anglo-German Fellowship, to write what Henson called a 'very rude letter' to *The Times* a week later. Hamilton denounced the Bishop of Durham and urged the public 'not to pay the slightest attention' to what he said, as such attacks would inevitably lead to similar letters from Germany about 'the slums of Glasgow or the desolation of Durham'; the argument would escalate and 'A German would strike me with a sausage, I would throw a haggis at his head, and then the two countries would be at war – or at least a step nearer to it.'[51]

The Londonderrys shared Hamilton's sentiments and on their return to Britain in mid-February did everything they could to pass on to senior politicians the messages of friendship that they had received from Hitler and his henchmen. But no one would listen to them. It was one thing for diplomats and statesmen to visit the Führer in order to find out his intentions and gauge his sanity, but quite another for seeming sympathizers to go and conduct what appeared to be secret negotiations with the dictator.[52] Baldwin refused to see him, as did his colleagues, increasing Charley's deep feelings of rejection. Winston Churchill watched with disgust as he paraded his friendship with Hitler. He wrote him a stern warning: 'I hope you will not become too prominently identified with the pro-German view.'[53] On 20 February, Harold Nicolson, the diarist and backbencher, went to one of Edie's political receptions to meet the Marquess, 'who is just back from hobnobbing with Hitler'. Nicolson shared Churchill's sentiments: 'I do deeply disapprove of ex-Cabinet ministers trotting across to Germany at this moment.'[54] Londonderry tried in vain to get an audience with the King, and the liberal and left-wing press mocked him and his wife as naïve and willing Nazi sympathizers.

The visit was unpopular not only in British anti-Nazi circles.

Fascists were furious too that the Londonderrys had stolen their thunder. Unity Mitford wrote to her sister Diana telling her how enraged she was that the Führer attached so much importance to them. She said she had told Hitler that the Marquess and his wife were the sort of people who should be put in a concentration camp. Visits to the Führer, she remonstrated, 'should be reserved for those who have deserved it, by doing something for the cause or at any rate for really loving him'. Hitler realized that Unity was jealous and placated her with the promise of a special evening just for her and Diana, but he could not resist telling the envious Unity that he was particularly struck by the grandeur of Edie Londonderry: 'he had never seen such jewels as Lady L wore'.[55]

Undeterred, the Londonderrys continued their contacts with the Nazis. In the spring Ribbentrop made a much-publicized visit to their estate in Northern Ireland. Edie gave an interview to a newspaper, *The Sunday Sun*, in which she described her meeting with Hitler, 'a man of arresting personality – a man with wonderful farseeing eyes . . . simple, dignified, humble'. Hensley Henson was horrified. His butler 'brought me a horrible paper . . . which appears to be wholly in the Nazi interest, for it is filled with exaltations of the Nazi regime, and with accounts in the most extravagant vein of laudation of the Londonderrys'.[56]

Hitler was delighted. His campaign to win over influential friends in Britain in 1936 to achieve a long-term settlement looked, from his warped perspective, as though it might work. Leopold von Hoesch, the German Ambassador to London, cabled a report to Berlin saying 'it was unmistakable that Lord and Lady Londonderry were extraordinarily satisfied with their stay in Germany and took the most favourable impressions home with them'. Londonderry had personally told him that he would work quietly behind the scenes to make his impressions known 'in the highest quarters'.[57] Ribbentrop and his boss were further convinced that cultivating titled grandees was going to be a policy that worked. That February, reassured by a meddling and misguided Londonderry of the friendliness of the British, the German leader prepared for his next coup.

6

Night Mail

E ARLY IN MARCH 1936, shortly after Lord Londonderry's return to Britain, a group seeking to overturn the right-wing aristocrat's archaic world-view gathered to celebrate the coming-of-age of a new art form, the documentary film. They hoped it would transform the world. W. H. Auden, regarded as the finest poet of his generation, went to the Arts Theatre in Cambridge to join the production team and an audience of supporters for the première of the documentary *Night Mail*. He had worked as an assistant director and written the verse for the closing sequence of the film, in collaboration with Benjamin Britten, who had composed the music.

The Arts Theatre was the creation of John Maynard Keynes, and had just opened, on 5 February, one day after the publication of his *General Theory*. Keynes had heard much of Auden but was not impressed by his personal appearance when he met him over dinner at King's College later in the year. While he found him 'altogether delightful', Auden's hands, he reported to his wife, Lydia Lopokova, were in a filthy state. 'His fingernails are eaten to the bones with dirt and wet, one of the worst cases ever, like a preparatory schoolboy.' Try as he might to respect him as an artist, the fastidious economist could not forget the impression that the poet's hands had made on him. 'It was most disconcerting', he told her, and indicated 'something unsatisfactory in his work'.[1] Auden's shambolic manner had not impressed Harry Watt either. Watt, the director of *Night Mail* and a combative Scotsman, complained that the poet 'looked like a half-witted Swedish deckhand'.[2] To Watt's fury Auden had committed the *faux pas* of turning up late on location during the filming. There was nothing unsatisfactory, however, about Auden's work on *Night*

Mail. His poetic coda to the film rescued the documentary from plodding Post Office propaganda and helped to establish the emerging form as a new branch of the arts.

Night Mail, which followed the overnight journey of a postal sorting train from London to Glasgow, was not seen by many when first released. Documentaries were then in their infancy, finding their way with a public who loved the movies but tended to be suspicious of British-made factual films. They were often shown in cinemas before the main programme, or in newsreel theatres, sandwiched for a few days between the latest reports from Pathé, Gaumont or Movietone. To the public they often seemed dull and worthy, 'pontificating tracts'[3] with a leftist bias. There was some truth in this, but *Night Mail*, with its innovative fusing of the talents of Auden and Britten, its creative blend of poetry and music, and its scenes of men at work, was at the heart of the communications revolution taking place that year.

The driving force behind *Night Mail* was the dour but dynamic figure of John Grierson, a 35-year-old Presbyterian Scot. He had first coined the term 'documentary' when writing as a film critic in the USA in 1926.[4] Grierson made his name as a director with *Drifters*, a film in which he followed the herring fishermen in the North Sea in 1929. The documentary broke new ground and created a stir. For the first time he had shown 'workaday Britain' to the masses on the screen. His sympathetic treatment of the hard lives of the trawler crews led to the development of a new factual cinema that combined realism and humanism.[5] But since the success of his début film he had not made a single documentary, preferring to spend his time nurturing and encouraging the work of others, lobbying for the new documentary form and pursuing the government for funding.

He took a job with the Empire Marketing Board, overseeing films about the world of colonial trade. When the Board collapsed in 1933, Grierson set up the GPO (General Post Office) Film Unit, with the task of making short films about the work of the Post Office. It was an opportunity, he said, 'we grasped eagerly, for the story of communications was as good as any other'.[6]

In 1936 the Post Office was a powerful force for change in Britain.

It was the nation's largest employer, with 250,000 on the corporation's payroll.[7] It was at the forefront of the communications revolution, in control of Britain's rapidly growing telephone system as well as its postal service. The GPO was also helping to develop the new medium of television by laying the co-axial cables that would relay its signal across the country. Its head, the Postmaster-General, was the chief regulator of the BBC and a senior figure in government. Despite being a government department watched over by the Treasury, the Post Office had money to spend on publicizing its activities and saw the public relations advantage of films about its work. Under the supervision of Sir Stephen Tallents, a pioneering civil servant and PR expert, it gave its backing to Grierson to make documentaries puffing its role. But Grierson wanted to do more than simply promote the varied work of the Post Office. His overriding ambition was to use film to create a modern picture of what it meant to be British.

With this burning sense of mission, Grierson had much in common with George Orwell. Like Orwell, he was a radical and a member of the Independent Labour Party. He shared the writer's desire to bring the hidden lives of working people to a wider audience and to change the way the British saw the world. In this they were both propagandists, 'making things known that need to be known'.[8] There was, too, a shared moral purpose. Grierson saw himself as a 'sociologist, a little worried about the way the world was going'. He said that he wanted 'to create a will towards civic participation'. Both Grierson and Orwell felt that, while a great deal was known about the British Empire, very little was understood about the reality of life for millions in Britain. Grierson spoke of 'a desire to bring the citizen's eye in from the ends of the earth to the story of what was happening under his nose'.[9] It was this shortcoming that sent Orwell to Wigan and motivated Grierson to make documentaries. Both men revered what Grierson called 'the national talent for under-statement', which they expressed in their different forms in a similar direct and simple style that belied great artistry. In documentary film-making for the GPO Grierson had found a new medium in which to exploit this talent. 'It allowed', he said, 'an adventure in the arts to assume the respectability of a public service.'[10]

It was here that Grierson parted company from Orwell. The documentary producer did not share the great writer's cussed independence and mistrust of bureaucracies. In seeking to perform a public service, Grierson had no qualms about working as a civil servant for the Post Office. It was a Faustian pact. Documentaries required a great deal of money to finance the large crews, heavy equipment and studios that were then a *sine qua non* of production. The government was one of the few sources of sufficient funds, and Grierson was expert at wheedling them out. But he sold his soul in the process and was forced to make some documentaries that compromised his independence.

Also unlike Orwell, Grierson was an admirer of the achievements of central planning in Stalin's Soviet Union. He was influenced by the avant-garde Russian propaganda film-makers, with their dynamic montage (exemplified for him by films such as Eisenstein's *Battleship Potemkin*) and strong social message.[11] He wanted the British documentary movement, using government funds, to spread an essentially socialist message. 'I look on cinema as a pulpit, and use it as a propagandist; and this I put unashamedly', he once confessed. The GPO, one of the largest and most dynamic government departments, was the home from which he attempted to preach his mini-revolution.

John Grierson's ardour, together with the attraction of the new art form itself, soon created a following. He set up an office in London's Soho Square, where he was joined by a number of young artists and left-leaning intellectuals from many different disciplines – poetry, music, painting, letters and politics - including the painter William Coldstream and the Surrealist Humphrey Jennings. The GPO Film Unit was, by early 1936, a hot-house for much of the creative talent of the time, 'a powerful intellectual, experimental and left-wing environment', as one commentator called it.[12] Many connections, such as that between Britten and Auden, were made there. The attraction was both the novelty of a medium still in its infancy and the enormous open-ended potential of the films, in both artistic and political terms. To the young idealists documentaries offered a new way of connecting with the masses, talking to them and reflecting them back on the screen in a way that seemed exciting, daring and revolutionary.[13] It was a compelling new form, the purpose of which the novelist Graham Greene, then cinema critic of *The Spectator*, described as 'more than the mere communication of fact; it is interpretation, persuasion and the creative element'. In this fusion, he wrote, 'the *art* of documentary lies'.[14]

The detractors sneered at the débutant documentarists as 'the dirty jersey boys' who gathered in Soho's pubs to argue about film theory and to criticize the latest productions,[15] but the film-makers were at the cutting edge of a new means of artistic and political expression. The previous year W. H. Auden, teaching at Malvern College, had picked up the buzz and written to one of Grierson's young men, the producer Basil Wright, asking if there was any chance of a job. Wright showed the letter to John Grierson, who responded immediately with characteristic forthrightness: 'Don't be a fool. Fetch him.'[16] Auden took a pay cut, accepting £3 a week (about the average weekly wage at the time), in order to have the opportunity to work in the new medium. He moved to London, lodging with his friend William Coldstream, and set to work to learn how to make documentaries.

The 22-year-old composer Benjamin Britten had joined the Film Unit some time earlier, on a higher salary of £5 a week. To have a regular income to pursue his chosen calling was then a luxury enjoyed by few composers at the start of their careers. At the beginning of the year Britten rejoiced in his good fortune in his diary: '1936 finds me infinitely better off in all ways than it did at the beginning of 1935; it finds me earning my living – with occasionally something to spare – at the GPO Film Unit under John Grierson . . . writing music and supervising sounds for films.'[17] Harry Watt, the no-nonsense director, was introduced to Britten during the editing of *Night Mail* as a potential composer. 'Rather nervously, into our theatre came this shy, soft-spoken kid, with close-curled blond hair and a pale and sensitive face.'[18] Watt told him bluntly, 'Now I don't want any bloody highbrow stuff'. Britten knuckled down and started composing. For the newcomer it was daunting to be in the presence of the GPO's gifted and opinionated crowd of young artists and producers. He admitted in his diary to 'having a bad inferiority complex in company of brains like Basil Wright, Wystan Auden and William Coldstream'.

John Grierson was an intimidating figure to his young tyro documentarists. Newcomers were expected to kowtow in his august, puritanical presence. 'He was a god and he played up to it', Harry Watt remembered; 'He rather playacted – kicked doors open and snapped at you and all the rest of it – and we were frightened of him.'[19] Esmond Romilly, Clementine Churchill's rebellious nephew, worked for Grierson for nine months that year. He found that Grierson had assumed 'an almost superhuman position' (not uncommon to senior figures in the documentary business). Mischievously, Romilly claimed that, like Sir Oswald Mosley, the Fascist leader, Grierson insisted that he be called 'the Leader' or 'the Chief'. This was only half-true. Grierson was known as 'the Chief' and never 'the Leader'. Romilly reported that there were numerous keen young men in the Film Unit who longed 'to work all day, carrying heavy cameras or opening doors, so that they may have a chance to learn the methods of the Chief'.[20] When Grierson sat at a table with the faithful, 'all would be silent waiting for the Leader to speak. He would pick on a paragraph in the evening paper, deliver a pungent comment, and then conversation could begin.'[21] Grierson, the Scottish Presbyterian, even refused his young acolytes the right to marry. When he himself married, he kept the fact secret for a year.[22] But nearly all of those, like Harry Watt, who worked for him put up with his bullying manner and air of self-importance.

> We adored him. He had the idea, started it and had given us the chance to work on the idea of making a new kind of film . . . we were putting the British working man, the backbone of the country, onto the screen. Before that the working man was the comic relief in the ghastly British films of those days.[23]

This was the purpose behind *Night Mail*: to show ordinary people at work, to give 'the human meaning' behind the nightly journey of the Postal Special from London to Glasgow.[24] The original idea was to make a mundane information film to explain to Post Office employees how the sorting office on wheels worked. With this in mind, Grierson ordered several of his team to reconnoitre the journey and to report back, but little of the information was used.[25] It was decided to be more ambitious. Like Orwell's *Road to Wigan Pier*, *Night Mail* took considerable licence with the truth to portray a picture of the 'reality' of working life.

The budget for the production was £2,000 (equivalent to about £74,000 today), reasonable enough for a documentary. It enabled the director, Harry Watt, to use a wide variety of novel cinematic techniques. He hired a plane to take aerial shots of the Class Six engine and its twelve Royal Mail wagons steaming north at speed. The greatest innovation was the use of recording equipment to capture synchronized sound and to do so, where possible, on location. Grierson had just recruited an expert in sound recording, Alberto Cavalcanti, a Brazilian director who had been working in Paris on cheap dramas and comedies. Cavalcanti wanted the freedom to experiment with sound, which was still in its infancy, and was drawn to London. Graham Greene called him 'the first to realise the enormous possibilities in the invention and editing of sound'.[26] He did so with great success in *Night Mail*. His style – more emollient than the Chief's usual abrasiveness – and his ready willingness to teach the novice film-makers quickly endeared him to his colleagues.[27]

Harry Watt's production team on *Night Mail* was a mixture of Oxbridge artist and Cockney office worker. His two cameramen, 'Chick' Fowle and Jonah Jones, were former messenger boys who had been trained up by Grierson. The Chief used to insist that they go to the National Gallery to learn the art of lighting from the Old Masters.[28] The result was a keen understanding of the beauty of light and shade in monochrome film, which produced some glorious exterior shots of the Postal Special steaming through the British countryside. Auden acted as Watt's assistant director. He was put in charge of one or two shots, including a scene where mail bags were pushed across the platform in the dark, and acted as general dogsbody. Harry Watt made no exception for his celebrity as a poet. 'I didn't give a damn if he had written *The Ascent of F6* or whatever the hell he had written. He was just an assistant director as far as I was concerned, and that meant humping the gear and walking miles.'[29] Unsurprisingly, Auden's shambling aesthetic sensibility did not take well to being bawled out, nor did it appreciate humping spare magazines of film, cameras and tripods – the usual lot of those wishing to get a toehold in film production. To make matters worse, the equipment was very heavy, cumbersome and impractical.

The production team used British-made Newman-Sinclair cameras on location. These were large rectangular metal boxes which had to be wound up to work and could shoot only two minutes of film before the magazines needed to be changed. They were very difficult to hold steady. As a result they were usually placed on tripods, limiting the team's ability to get the action shots on location that help to bring documentaries to life. Cavalcanti's recording equipment was just as unwieldy. Synchronized sound had come to films less than ten years earlier, and was new to documentaries. The travelling microphones were hopelessly impractical on location; they picked up every piece of extraneous noise and were buffeted by the slightest breeze.

Limited by the equipment, the documentary of necessity took on the shape of a drama. Far from being an insight into the 'real' world, it was, to a large extent, recreated in the unit's studios in Blackheath. In the safety of a purpose-built film set the machinery could be relied on to work. It also did not need to be moved, which was another advantage. To give an illusion of authenticity Grierson insisted that real postal workers and railway workers be used instead of actors. They recreated their daily work of sorting the mail and directing the train in the Blackheath studio. The film was then knitted together in the cutting-room, using these drama reconstructions, stock footage of the railways and specially shot sequences from the few occasions when the team had trundled out their laborious and unwieldy gear. With the production of *Night Mail* a classic was born, but it was not what would be regarded now as an authentic documentary, more a 'drama documentary'. Indeed, if it were shown on the BBC today, those charged with policing honesty in factual programming would insist that many of the scenes be labelled 'reconstruction' or cut. This playing with reality was for some at the time as much a cause of suspicion as it is now. The journalist Arthur Calder-Marshall scoffed that 'there is nothing organic in these false-to-life, true-to-life documentaries'.[30] Like Orwell, however, Grierson was happy to play fast and loose with 'the truth' in order to get the message across. He once defined documentary as 'the creative treatment of actuality'.[31]

Reconstructing the scenes of the forty postal workers sorting half a million letters as the express train thundered north may have brought the convenience of a studio, but it created other difficulties. The postal sorters and railwaymen were ill at ease acting their parts, despite the fact that they did the same tasks night-in night-out in the 'real' sorting vans. Harry Watt solved this, to an extent, by seeking out 'the extroverts, the bullshit merchants, the boring life-and-soul-of-the-party boys — they are the natural hams but you wheedle and bully them down into some kind of naturalness'.[32] Watt, having had little experience of directing men who had never acted before, was feeling his way during the production of *Night Mail*. Some of the scenes of the sorters' repartee — 'take it away sunny boy', 'right-oh handsome!' — and the railwaymen's instructions to clear the line never came to life, despite his bullying and wheedling. At the heart of the short film is a scene where a trainee mail dropper learns how to pick up and drop a pouch of sorted mail from the train running at speed. It was hoped that the use of a real apprentice for this key scene would help, by infusing a sense of actual nervousness, but it was not really effective.

Another difficulty for the director was to recreate the swaying and jolting of a train as it ran along the line. The GPO Film Unit in Blackheath could not afford the giant springs and hydraulic motion rigs that would have been commonplace in a drama studio. Watt instructed his sorters to recreate the movement of the train as they 'worked' on the set, by swaying gently back and forth during the takes. In an attempt to enhance the feeling of movement the production team, out of shot, jiggled the lines of string hanging from the ceiling that the sorters used to tie bundles of letters. Watt claimed he was satisfied that this artifice 'worked perfectly', but the lack of authentic motion added to the stilted feel of the interior scenes.

Once Harry Watt had gathered all his rushes, including the central bag-drop sequence, he went to the cutting-room and set to work with his editor on putting together the film. The structure was relatively simple, following the narrative of the postal express's journey north. Watt had also filmed a couple of bucolic sequences in the countryside through which the train passed, and exteriors of the belching chimneys and factories of the north of England (including, by coincidence, Wigan). These were intended to give a true sense of the varied work of Britain at the time, both industrial and agricultural, all using, and united by, the central nervous system of the postal network that ran up and down the spine of the country. Out of the material the director and editor fashioned a twenty-minute rough cut which they showed to John Grierson.

Every director dreads the viewing, when he or she must show their work to the senior person in charge of the production. Many executive producers have found it impossible to resist the temptation to bully and hector, and to denigrate the efforts of those who have laboured so hard to produce their films. The Chief could be especially harsh. Nonetheless he had valuable insight. His suggestions often made the difference between failure and success. Most forgave him his brutal criticism after they had implemented his changes. *Night Mail* was a case in point. When Grierson viewed the rough cut, he expressed dissatisfaction. No doubt he disliked the feel of the stilted drama sequences and the sparse commentary to the film, which consisted of little more than facts and figures about the mail-sorting process intoned in a declamatory style. 'We've only had the machinery of getting letters from one point to the other', he complained, 'What about the people who write them and the people who get them?'[33] It was Grierson's inspiration to commission the film's assistant director to write a new experimental ending in verse. Benjamin Britten would compose the music for it. At first Watt resisted, unhappy with the extra work involved and unable to see the point of adding a coda. He objected that it would be out step with the style of the rest of the film. But when assured he would be given the extra resources he needed to complete the film in this way, he relented and set to work shooting the material that would be needed for Auden's poetry.[34]

Auden and Britten had already collaborated on a GPO film about coalminers, *Coal Face*, for which the poet had written a madrigal, 'O lurcher-loving collier, as black as night'. Auden was pleased with the results. 'We were experimenting to see whether poetry could be used in films and I think we showed it could.'[35] Now he had the greater challenge of a three-minute verse to be written both in time to the rhythm of the train and to fit the picture. There was little room in the crowded and busy Film Unit offices, and he had to perch at a desk in a passageway, 'a dark, smelly noisy corridor' at the back of the offices.[36] He shared his workplace with the messenger boys: 'fifteen-year-old Cockney kids, wild as hell, they made their tea and whistled and played cards'.[37] Auden liked the busy and informal atmosphere, which fitted with his philosophy that it was the role of the poet to be immersed in society. He wrote his verse with the aid of a stop-watch, taking completed sections to the cutting-room, where he read the lines aloud to the picture to see whether the rhythm of the words fitted the pace of the editing. Watt told him if they worked or not. If they did not quite match the film, Auden crumpled up the paper and threw it into the waste-paper basket. 'Some beautiful lines and stanzas went into oblivion in this casual, ruthless way', Watt recalled.[38]

While Auden composed his verse, Britten set about writing the music under the supervision of Alberto Cavalcanti. As ever, Watt was blunt with the young composer. 'The music has got to fit the picture, you understand, absolutely fit to a split second', he ordered. 'Also I want it to be rhythmic, to go with the beat of the train.'[39] Britten was told that he could have an orchestra of ten musicians (a luxury by today's standards). He also used a compressed air cylinder and sand-paper to help create a 'sound picture' of the pumps and pistons of a steam engine puffing and panting at speed. When he had composed the score, he recorded the music, together with the spoken words of Auden's completed verse, in the Film Unit's studio at Blackheath.

The recording was an immensely complicated business, as he wrote in his diary: 'The whole trouble, & what takes so much time is that over the music has to be spoken a verse – kind of patter – written by Auden – in strict rhythm with the music.'[40] To keep the orchestra to time Britten conducted to a 'visual metronome' of marks cut at the correct intervals in the film, which came up as flashes on the screen. It was 'a very difficult job' but one that he managed to pull off. Stuart Legg, one of the assistants on the film, read Auden's fast-paced verse 'splendidly', while Britten conducted and the orchestra played. As the pace was so fast and Auden's sentences so long, the process had to be stopped every now and then for Legg to take a breath. It was a laborious process, but the result was a brilliant fusion of spoken verse, imagery and sound. Britten's music replicated the pounding rhythm of the night mail without being too literal.

Auden's verse, 'This is the Night Mail crossing the border,/ Bringing the cheque and the postal order', was the greatest triumph, with its energy and exhilaration capturing the thrill of steam, fitting the dynamic of the film and adding a deeper meaning to the sending and receiving of letters which the rest of the film lacked. In *Night Mail* he avoided over-doing the remorseless energy of the rhythmical rhyming couplets by interspersing two lyrical stanzas of blank verse. These added a sense of pathos and meaning to the train's journey, which Britten's finely wrought music enhanced. The first of these stanzas ended:

> All Scotland waits for her:
> In the dark glens, beside the pale green sea-lochs
> Men long for news.

The film then cut hard from the pastoral scenes of the glens back to the mail train, and once more the insistent pounding verse and music took up the theme:

> Letters of thanks, letters from the banks,
> Letters of joy from the girl and boy,
> Receipted bills and invitations
> To inspect new stock or visit relations . . .

And so the list continued frenetically for another twenty lines as the express train made its final approach to Glasgow. The film ended on a philosophical note:

> And none will hear the postman's knock
> Without a quickening of the heart,
> For who can bear to feel himself forgotten?

John Grierson, the propagandist film-maker, had intended that *Night Mail* should characterize the work of the GPO, in the words of a film critic, 'as industrial enabler and social integrator . . . the social and cultural infrastructure that binds Britain together'.[41] Grierson himself said that he wanted it to reveal 'the human meaning behind the nightly journey of the Postal Special'.[42] With its first twenty minutes of recreated scenes, 'real' workers with wooden dialogue and recitation of postal statistics, the film had fulfilled Grierson's brief, albeit in a dutiful and pedestrian manner. While many who love steam may have enjoyed and may still enjoy the glorious shots of the express speeding through Britain, for others 'the film seems to struggle', as the critic of *Sight and Sound* complained.[43] In essence, some thought, it was a Soviet-style piece of propaganda which was saved from the worthy banality of Agit-prop by Grierson's last-minute intervention. The final three-minute coda that he insisted on went much further. It gave the film a sense of a shared experience and universal humanity, and made it more than a humdrum documentary. Thanks to Britten and Auden, it became a work of art.

But Auden did not find the experience of documentary-making entirely congenial. While he enjoyed the informal and unpretentious working atmosphere in Soho Square, he considered documentaries unsatisfying. He thought the laborious process of filming, recording and editing exasperating, and he disliked the unyielding demands of the medium. He also said that Grierson's mission to bring the lives of the poor to wider knowledge was patronizing.[44] After the première of *Night Mail* he resigned from the GPO Film Unit. When a former pupil wrote to him asking for his advice about working in documentaries, Auden was dismissive, replying: 'You only want to become a film director because you think it is the art of the future. It isn't. Art is the art of the future.'[45] Nonetheless he had helped to create something that many critics would come to regard as a cornerstone of Britain's single most decisive contribution to world cinema.[46] Even at the time Graham Greene recognized the work of Grierson and his colleagues; 'they have attained', he said, 'an art unattained in any other branch of cinema.'[47]

Benjamin Britten, like Auden, was never to work in documentary again after he left the GPO Film Unit later that year. During his eighteen months working with Grierson and Cavalcanti he had scored thirty-two films.[48] He and Auden later collaborated on a number of projects, but none was as successful as their venture into documentary. The discipline of composing for film had been of inestimable value to the young composer and influenced much of his later work, particularly his operas.

As with so many nascent art movements, the documentary movement was riven with disagreements and splits. After the release of *Night Mail* a bitter row broke out between Grierson and Cavalcanti. Grierson was frustrated at the inability of the new medium to break through to a mass audience and argued with colleagues about the way the form should develop.[49] *Night Mail* had had a limited showing, despite its critical success. Grierson announced to his team that the future lay with the millions who did *not* go to the cinema, in free documentary showings at exhibitions, community halls and schools. Cavalcanti and Harry Watt disagreed, preferring to try to break into commercial cinema. After much argument their view prevailed. Grierson left to pursue his dream elsewhere.

It was a tragic mistake. When war broke out, the GPO team became the Crown Film Unit. Using the skills and techniques that Grierson had pioneered, his former protégés went on to make many of the great propaganda documentaries of the Second World War.[50] The argument was, in any case, irrelevant. A few miles north of Soho Square, in the neo-Gothic edifice of Alexandra Palace, the BBC was developing a new medium that would transform the way the British would look at themselves and the world. That March the corporation's television service was only a few months from transmitting the world's first daily schedule of programmes. Although television would not take off until after the war, it was to be both the saviour and the greatest progenitor of the documentary. 'It is there that the main future . . . must lie', Graham Greene wrote.[51] In future the idealistic film-makers who wanted to follow in Grierson's footsteps and change the world would look no further than a career at the BBC.

7

The gathering storm

O N 13 FEBRUARY the diarist and MP Victor Cazalet dined with Winston Churchill at his club, Pratt's, and found him thoroughly discombobulated, 'Furious at not being in government – contemptuous of present regime, and overwhelmed with German danger – v unbalanced I thought'.[1] Many shared the view that there was something slightly unhinged about Churchill. His manner did not help. At dinners he would often sit in glum silence or – if taken up by an interest – hold forth at length to the exclusion of anybody else or any other viewpoint. 'It is like arguing with a brass band', Neville Chamberlain complained.[2]

Churchill drank heavily, despite having given up spirits since his bet with Rothermere. He was hyperactive, firing off letters night and day to a wide circle of friends, family, colleagues, informants and advisers. His knowledge of defence and the fact that he was kept informed of the latest military developments, both officially and unofficially, made him somebody the government occasionally consulted for his expertise, but whom they feared as unpredictable. As a public figure he swam against the tide of popular feeling on questions such as India and rearmament, but even so, he made waves. His word could make or break careers, give hope to lost causes and influence the cultural mood of the capital.

Early in February 1936 Lilian Baylis, the popular producer and impresario, opened a new play about Napoleon at the Old Vic. It was *St Helena,* by R. C. Sherriff,[3] who had made his name in 1928 with *Journey's End*. Sherriff had not had a success since. On the first night the play went well, with good performances and an enthusiastic audience. Sherriff felt confident that he had at last broken the jinx that had dogged his career. But 'all this wishful thinking', he remembered, 'was shattered by the notices the next morning'.[4] The reviewers denounced the play as 'wordy, tedious, totally devoid of dramatic power'.

The box office, usually thronging the day after the opening of a Baylis production, was empty. The play staggered on for a fortnight with audiences on most nights of little more than fifty, in a theatre that could seat a thousand. The producers faced a huge loss. Closure was inevitable. Then, to Sherriff's amazement 'into this dire wreckage fell the gift from heaven. It came in a letter published in *The Times*'. Winston Churchill had been to the play, slipping into the theatre unnoticed, and had enjoyed himself. Now, unbidden, on 14 February he gave it his stamp of approval. 'In my humble judgement as a life-long but still voracious reader of Napoleonic literature', he told the readers of *The Times*, 'it is a work of art of a very high order. Moreover it is an entertainment which throughout rivets the attention of the audience'. Churchill ended his letter of praise with a clever conceit on Sherriff's previous work and Napoleon's career: 'I was I think among the very first to acclaim the quality of *Journey's End*. Here is the end of the most astonishing journey ever made by mortal man.' The impact of the letter was immediate. Five hundred people came to the play that night, a thousand packed in the night after, and for seven weeks *St Helena* was a sell-out. As Sherriff wrote, 'It must have been the most complete turn-around that had ever happened to a play before.' Clearly in 1936 Churchill's political judgement was not trusted by his Tory colleagues, but the theatre-going public was more than happy to rely on his critical opinion.

Churchill had rushed to England after the death of the King and at once set about life with his usual energy. He had to work hard just to keep pace with his heavy outgoings, which included Chartwell, his country house close by the North Downs (where he had just put in a heated swimming-pool with a coal-fired boiler), a large staff of secretaries and researchers, frequent entertaining and a London base. He was, with the help of large bank loans, only just keeping afloat. He earned a great deal from his journalism. His article on George V had earned him £1,000 (a staggering £37,000 in today's terms) from the *News of the World* – twice his annual salary as a back-bench MP.[5] His massive output of books also helped, as did public speaking engagements.[6]

Churchill combined paid work with unrelenting political activity, at this time almost entirely concentrated on the Nazi menace. While others were taken up with Mussolini's conquest of Abyssinia, Churchill regarded the Italian dictator as a potential ally against his single focus of concern: Hitler. That winter and spring he devoted himself to the size and strength of German rearmament, in particular the expansion of the air force. Using his contacts in the services, as well as the information provided by his supporter and neighbour, the secret agent Desmond Morton, he gathered a dossier of facts, which he used to bombard the government with warnings, suggestions and questions. Each side accused the other of obfuscation and misrepresentation, but all were agreed that Germany was rearming rapidly. The question was by how much and what the response should be.

However irritating they found him, no one doubted Churchill's knowledge and experience of military affairs. When Charley Londonderry was sacked for incompetence, his replacement, Lord Swinton, asked for Churchill to be appointed to the Air Defence Research Committee. It was a bold move, bringing him one step closer to government, and it threatened to cause havoc. Churchill, no doubt thinking this was a sign that he might be about to get the coveted new post of defence minister, set to work with relish. Things quickly went wrong. The committee members did not appreciate his rambunctious manner and they disliked his scientific adviser, Frederick Lindemann. Churchill succeeded in having 'the Prof' put on the advisory group of scientists, where his snobbish and arrogant manner by turns alienated, enraged and divided the distinguished experts.

Many of Lindemann's ideas for air defence, which Churchill backed, were barmy. He proposed that clouds of gas or explosive dust be placed in the way of enemy bombers, and that coils of piano wire be suspended in curtains from balloons, in which the bombers would become entangled. He called for thousands of aerial mines to be strewn before the approaching enemy aircraft, suspended under

parachutes.[7] His proposals, however outlandish, called for experi-
mentation in order to be rebutted, which took up far too much of the
RAF's time and money. But Lindemann caused the greatest anger by
the way in which he used his influence with Churchill to report on
what he regarded as the committee's sloth and incompetence in dealing with the one scientific development that showed real promise:
radar.[8] On 26 February Churchill wrote to the Cabinet Secretary
deploring 'the slight and slow progress' on air defence.[9] The result
was ill feeling and bad blood, which in the view of Lindemann's
enemies hindered rather than helped the progress of this crucial
invention.[10] Churchill was unaware of the mistrust and resentment
that his interventions often aroused. His sense of the paramount
importance of his mission energized him but left his parliamentary
colleagues punch-drunk. This in turn devalued his message. People
stopped listening to him.[11]

Working for Churchill was almost impossible too. Violet Pearman,
his secretary of fourteen years, dedicated herself to him at great personal cost. During the Moroccan holiday she had had to cope with
his impetuousness – first his sudden desire to leave rainy Tangier for
Marrakesh on Christmas Day, postponed by force of circumstance to
Boxing Day, and then his indecisive reaction to the King's death.
Leaving things to the last moment made it difficult to arrange the
return. 'Mr Churchill could not make up his mind what to do . . . It
was an awful journey', Mrs Pearman complained to the travel agent
afterwards, 'so long and with so many changes.'[12] Once home, without a break herself, she plunged straight back into the hurly-burly of
life as Churchill's secretary in Britain.

Twelve-hour days often extended to fifteen hours when Churchill
dictated late into the night. He expected Violet to travel up to
London at a moment's notice, accompanying him to the House of
Commons in the Daimler, 'absorbing cigar smoke, wit and wisdom'.[13]
Often she would not get back to Chartwell until the small hours.
Unsurprisingly, Violet's health suffered. As she said, 'One gets so
stale, never having the chance to improve one's mind, even get out
of the atmosphere of the place. This state of things is deplorable, and
getting groovy is detrimental to one's work, also the health.'[14]

In March, Violet had a bad fall. Rushing downstairs from Churchill's office to answer the telephone, she caught her heel on the corner of a rug and fell heavily, landing on her backside. X-rays revealed a cracked bone at the base of her spine.[15] It was a nasty accident, brought about by the frenetic pace of work. Afterwards Churchill was kind and attentive, offering to pay for medical treatment if she lacked insurance, but his letter to her, while insisting she stay in bed until fit to be X-rayed, revealed what was really on his mind. 'Let me know when you are able to do any typing, and we will send you anything that is to be fair copied.'[16]

Such were the pressures and inconveniences of the job that Violet seriously considered resigning. But, hard as she found it, Churchill's magnetism kept her at work. Over the years she had come to know him as well as anyone, almost as well as Clementine herself. She could 'anticipate his moods, whim and fancies, and deal accordingly with crises'. Most importantly for those dealing with such characters as his, 'I am not afraid of him in the least, and can stand up for whoever or whatever is the cause of his wrath – if justice is to be done'. In short, she loved him, but her love exacted a high price, and many attributed the stroke that she suffered a few months later to the pressures of working for Winston Churchill.

Churchill himself was suffering from strain. His health was not good, and he had long bouts of biliousness. He was anxious about the prospects of his daughter Sarah, who was in the process of making a disastrous marriage to an Austrian-American entertainer, Vic Oliver, and his nerves were on edge as the prospect of the new appointment of defence minister loomed. Although he knew in his heart that he would not get the post, he still dreamed that it might be his, so convinced was he that he was the only man really experienced and capable enough for the job. But when Randolph nearly lost his deposit in the Ross and Cromarty by-election in February, the *Daily Telegraph* put it succinctly: 'another nail in the political coffin of Winston Churchill'.[17] Although there was some half-hearted lobbying on Churchill's behalf, the two praetorian guards of the 'respectable tendency', Baldwin and Chamberlain, never had the slightest intention of letting him into the Cabinet. If he became defence minister, they reasoned, what next? Prime Minister? That position was reserved for Chamberlain when Baldwin went – a departure widely expected in a few months.

Even so, Churchill remained optimistic. On 3 March he wrote to Clementine, still on her extended skiing holiday in Austria, to say that all the obvious candidates had either ruled themselves out or were in no position to apply. 'If I get it', he told her, 'I will work faithfully before God & man for Peace, and not allow pride or excitement to sway my spirit.' He added philosophically, 'If I am not wanted, we have many things to make us happy my darling beloved Clemmie.'[18] Four days later events were to take a turn that, while they would bring war closer, would make his chances of a Cabinet post even more unlikely.

On Saturday 7 March, Hugh Carlton Greene, the Berlin correspondent of the *Daily Telegraph*, went to the Reichstag to report on a special announcement to be made by Hitler. The Führer, looking pale, holding a handkerchief in a ball which he passed nervously from hand to hand, began his speech to the assembly with a familiar attack on the injustices of the Treaty of Versailles, long and tedious for the party faithful awaiting the inevitable outburst. They were not disappointed. Half-way through the speech he leaned forward over the lectern, slowing his speech for special emphasis, and intoned 'At this moment German troops are crossing the Rhine bridges and occupying the Rhineland'.[19] As one, 600 deputies rose to their feet and bellowed 'Heil', at first wildly and then in unison. Greene turned and watched General Werner von Fritsch, the commander-in-chief of the German army, for his reaction. 'The general, I noticed, was not on this occasion the very model of a calm poker-faced Prussian officer.' Quite the reverse: 'he fidgeted, he sweated, he kept polishing his monocle.'[20] Greene understood why. Hitler had taken a tremendous risk. Germany's forces were still in the early stages of rearmament. He had sent only three battalions to occupy the 30-mile strip on the right bank of the Rhine demilitarized after Germany's surrender in 1918. The French army, on the opposite side, was far superior in numbers and weaponry. If the move was militarily provocative, it was also a flagrant breach of international treaties.

Hitler was a gambler: he had pulled off a daring coup. Von Ribbentrop, expert on the habits of the English ruling classes, had advised Hitler to act over the weekend, when they would be relaxing at their country seats. The Führer's first military action was a tactical master-stroke. In Germany it was seen as the reversal of a long-standing humiliation and boosted Hitler's reputation with his sceptical generals. Abroad it caught the British and French on the hop. Although they had expected a move for some time, they had hoped that Hitler might be placated by negotiation and concessions in exchange for a permitted reoccupation of the Rhineland. Now it was too late. Hitler had crossed his Rubicon. The allies were presented with a *fait accompli*, and the last thing anybody wanted was to go to war over the issue.

The British public was in no mood for fighting. With memories of the last conflict still fresh in people's minds, there was little affection for the Germans. 'The only good German is a dead German', John Prichard's father, wounded in the trenches, used to say. But nonetheless there was widespread support for the government's cautious policy on rearmament, as shown by Baldwin's victory in the previous autumn's general election. Many also felt that Germany had been too harshly treated by the victors in the peace settlement that followed the First World War.

German intelligence told Hitler that the French would not strike back with armed force. All the signals from the British reassured him that they too would take no action. The meetings with Londonderry and other Englishmen who had come to pay court, the pro-Nazi sentiments in papers such as the *Daily Mail* and the failure to oppose Mussolini's aggression in Africa added up to a racing certainty that he would get away with his plan. Sympathy for Germany in Britain was at a high point, probably the highest at any time since the First World War, and Churchill, one of the few who might possibly have raised the alarm, kept uncharacteristically quiet.

In *The Gathering Storm*, the first volume of his Nobel Prize-winning history of the Second World War, written twelve years later, Churchill pointed to Hitler's Rhineland coup in March 1936 as the decisive moment.[21] Germany, he argued, should have been stopped by vigorous action. It was the last time that Great Britain and France could have halted the march to war. Churchill blamed Baldwin and Chamberlain for their failure to stand up to the dictator, preferring appeasement. This view came to be widely shared in the years after the war.

In reality, although Hitler no doubt could have been stopped, intervention was never on the agenda. The French had no stomach for action in 1936, as events during the war four years later would testify. In Britain all strands of opinion came together that year to oppose an armed reaction. In the House of Commons two days after Hitler's coup Harold Nicolson noted 'General mood of House is one of fear. Anything to keep out of war'.[22] Only three days before Hitler's reoccupation of the Rhineland, the Labour leader, Clement Attlee, had opposed the government's White Paper proposals for rearmament as being 'too bellicose'.[23] His foreign affairs spokesman, Hugh Dalton, said afterwards that there should be no question of any resistance to Germany's move.[24]

On the right there was widespread agreement that Hitler had merely walked into his own 'back garden' and that no action should be taken against him.[25] The newspapers strongly endorsed this view. *The Times*, under the headline 'A Chance to Rebuild', stated that Hitler should be treated as 'having recovered a status of equality' and not as an aggressor. Charley Londonderry backed this view with a letter to the paper justifying the Rhineland coup, blaming the French for seeking to encircle Germany and warning against impugning the 'good faith' of 'Herr Hitler'.[26]

The outcome was that the British huffed and puffed but did nothing. Hitler's promises of a return to the League of Nations at some point in the future and of further talks were taken at face value. The French needed little persuading to step into line and withdrew their demand that the Germans should pull out of the Rhineland before any negotiations. An emollient Ribbentrop flew to London, met with the League of Nations council and, with more empty promises, succeeded in soothing ruffled feathers.

Those who feared Germany and detested the Nazis were appalled. George Orwell, staying near Leeds on his way back to the south, went to two evening discussion groups, where he found most people gloomily saying war was now a certainty, and 'with two exceptions all pro-German'.[27] Baffy Dugdale, an arch-Zionist, attended a League of Nations union committee meeting five days later. She was shocked to hear the Dean of Chichester say that most ordinary men almost 'breathed a sigh of relief' when they heard that Hitler had entered the zone. To her horror he told her that '*at present* ninety out every hundred people feel no anger against the Germans'.[28] Public opinion, egged on by the newspapers, blamed the French for provoking Germany by making a pact with Russia, thus threatening Hitler with encirclement. Baffy's cousin by marriage Violet Milner was horrified by the attacks on France. 'The British press this morning', she wrote in her diary, 'has proved – if proof were necessary – that it is only when our allies break treaties that they are indignant. When Germany breaks them they are ready to condone her actions.' Lily-livered politicians, alongside the appeasing press, were the object of her greatest scorn: 'The Cabinet held this morning was miserable in its cowardice.'[29]

But when she went to the House of Commons on Thursday, 12 March to discuss what should be done in reply to Hitler with her friend and ally, the colonialist and National Conservative MP Edward Grigg,[30] she was stumped for an answer. Grigg, she wrote, 'was in favour of an aerial demonstration of combined fleets [of aircraft] to Berlin. I am not. I believe Germany is too strong.' Lady Milner was probably right. The Luftwaffe had grown with astonishing speed over the last three years. As ever, the question of how to deal with Hitler, if not by appeasement, posed insuperable problems. When taken to its logical conclusion, there was only one answer: war. Nobody wanted that, even though many now believed it inevitable. As Virginia Woolf wrote in her diary: 'As usual, I think, Oh, this will blow over. But it's odd how near the guns have got to our private life again. I can quite distinctly see them and hear a roar.'[31]

In his northern fastness Hensley Henson was in no doubt about the significance of Hitler's move. He wrote with foreboding in his diary on the day of the occupation. 'The clouds are gathering over Europe in deepening gloom. Is it impossible to avoid war when the fates of great nations are in the hands of theatrical bullies like Hitler and Mussolini?'[32] The darkening international situation forced him to question the very nature of his work as a bishop and even his faith, which seemed trivial in comparison with the great and terrible events of the world. 'In the midst of these fearful obsessions how can I go on talking to Confirmation candidates? Christianity seems to fade from view.' In the days that followed, Henson was appalled by what he regarded as the fatuous British reaction. 'How can one do business with these dictators who tear up treaties they sign whenever they please?'

That March, Henson was in the minority. But he was right. Meanwhile Churchill, his ally in the cause, kept silent. There were no fulminating attacks on Germany, no calls for action to stop the aggressor. When Churchill spoke in the Commons defence debate, Neville Chamberlain praised his contribution as 'constructive and helpful' – perhaps the most unusual political comment of the year.[33]

In Berlin, Hugh Greene saw the looming threat. If allowed to get away with his coup, Greene wrote in a prophetic article for the *Daily Telegraph*, Hitler would turn the Rhineland into an armed camp, swallow up Austria and turn on Czechoslovakia. Finally, Poland would be forced to surrender to German demands or face war. 'Anybody who had read Hitler's *Mein Kampf* and studied his speeches with care could have written a similar article.' The *Telegraph* did not run his article. This was unusual, as the newspaper was usually robust in its attitude to the Nazi leader, unlike *The Times*. Greene learned later that the paper's proprietor, Lord Camrose, had met Ribbentrop in London and had shown him the article. 'Ribbentrop, of course, said that it was all a lot of nonsense – and Ribbentrop was believed.'[34] It was another example of the Nazi diplomat's effectiveness in the higher echelons of British society.

Still Churchill remained silent. He never uttered the outraged sentiments about the Rhineland that he would later make the ortho-doxy. It is possible that, given his knowledge of British military preparedness ('they are *terribly* behindhand',[35] he had told Clementine on 3 March), he shared the general view that an armed response was too risky. More likely he did not want to rock the boat just when the

government was about to announce the new post of defence minister. He still harboured the hope that he might be appointed. But the
Rhineland issue destroyed any faint chance he may have had of getting the job. Chamberlain and Baldwin, masters of the black art of
political management, realized that the crisis offered 'an excellent
reason' for denying the new ministry to Churchill.[36] He was the last
person they wanted in Cabinet. His extravagant anti-German rhetoric at a time of sensitive diplomatic negotiations would be ruinous
to their developing policy of appeasement.

What they wanted instead was a quiet, dull chap who would do
what he was told. They alighted on Sir Thomas Inskip, the Attorney-
General, a mediocre lawyer who had already been promoted to the
level of his incompetence.[37] He had no expertise in defence matters.
He was best known for his vigorous opposition to the Revised Prayer
Book of 1928. The appointment was, according to Churchill's friend
the Prof, 'the most cynical thing that has been done since Caligula
appointed his horse as Consul'.[38] Or, as Chamberlain put it, Inskip
'would create no jealousies. He would excite no enthusiasm, but he
would involve us in no fresh perplexities.'[39]

For Churchill, although not wholly unexpected, it was a heavy
blow. At the time he thought it fatal to his career. With him out of
the way, the path was clear for Neville Chamberlain, impatiently
waiting in the wings, to take over as Prime Minister when Baldwin
quit in May 1937. Churchill took the knock stoically, controlling his
feelings in order to appear 'serene, indifferent, detached'. In public he
was always courteous and friendly to the Prime Minister, and especially to the Chancellor. On the very day that the pair had dealt him
the knock-out blow, 14 March, he gave a speech in Birmingham in
which he praised Chamberlain as the saviour of the country's economy.[40] Indeed, Churchill was so friendly and supportive at this time
that Chamberlain became suspicious. With his crafty political instincts
he believed he knew why, as he mused in a letter to his sister that
month: 'I feel convinced that the explanation of Winston's unexpected friendliness to the Government is that he expects a change
before long and that he is playing up for another chance with another
PM.'[41] Cynical or not, Chamberlain's suspicions were probably

correct. Churchill's ingratiating manner was most likely prompted by the realization that Chamberlain would soon be Prime Minister and needed to be cultivated. But, as so often with Churchill, it was not as simple as that.

As fate would have it, the failure of appeasement with the outbreak of war would force Chamberlain to accept Churchill into his Cabinet in September 1939. One year later, in 1940, after the disaster of the Norway campaign, the tables were turned. Churchill became war leader and graciously invited Chamberlain to join his government. Whatever the position, and wherever the two men stood on the great issues of the time, Churchill was unfailingly courteous to Chamberlain. He seemed to have always had a respect for the tragic figure he superseded. With Baldwin it was different. There was little mutual respect, and although they kept up the pretence of friendliness in public, as Chips Channon commented, Churchill was 'consumed with contempt, jealousy, indeed hatred, for Baldwin, whom he always denigrates'.[42]

The Rhineland crisis marked a turning-point. From now on the dividing lines would be clearer than ever: on the one hand those, such as Baldwin and Chamberlain, who put their faith in a policy of appeasement; on the other, Churchill and his supporters, who were convinced that there could be no deal with the German dictator. Appeasement did not mean, as was often claimed by its opponents, a lack of commitment to defence spending. It was a two-pronged policy of diplomacy and deterrence. Since 1934, Baldwin and his Chancellor had been steadily increasing defence expenditure. In March 1936 the government announced its plans to more than double spending on the RAF and to give a massive boost to the overall military budget.

The increase in defence spending was a heavy blow to Chamberlain, who announced his budget measures on the newsreels with a very modern and very theatrical flourish, taking off his glasses, leaning back in his chair and raising his eyes skyward with a sigh as he apologized for the tax increases to pay for the extra spending. 'Yes. I know. I feel exactly the same way. Each of the last four budgets was slightly better than the one before, and I was hoping that the fifth would be even better. Still. There we are! But in an arming world, we couldn't be the only great nation disarmed.'[43] It was a bitter blow to the Chancellor, a reluctant rearmer, who would have preferred to divert the money to social reform.[44]

The argument between Churchill and the government was not over the principle that Britain needed to rearm, but over how much should be spent, and how fast. The balancing act for Chamberlain in 1936 was to spare enough for the huge demands of rearmament while keeping the economy's successful revival on course. This he had done with great success, as Churchill acknowledged in his Birmingham speech: 'the credit he has now restored to our finances is now available to guard us in another sphere, the great sphere of defence'.[45] But Churchill wanted the economy put on a war footing. Chamberlain, with some justice, regarded such demands as quite unrealistic. 'If we were now to follow Winston's advice and sacrifice our commerce to the manufacture of arms', he told his sister Hilda, 'we should inflict a certain injury upon our trade from which it would take generations to recover, we should destroy the confidence which now happily exists and we should cripple the revenue.'[46] However much Churchill may have fulminated from the sidelines, the argument for seeking a diplomatic solution while carefully building up the armed forces seemed entirely rational. The only problem, as Chamberlain would learn to his cost, was that the rational approach was no way of dealing with Hitler.

The increases in defence spending, on the air force in particular, were already bearing fruit. Just two days before Hitler's troops marched into the Rhineland, on Thursday 5 March, a gleaming silver monoplane was wheeled out if its hangar at Eastleigh aerodrome, near Southampton, for its maiden flight. As it soared into the air, those watching on the ground saw a sight that in a few years time would become familiar to millions – a symbol of hope and defiance in the face of the Nazi threat. It was the Spitfire.

8

The house of things to come

THOSE WHO DESIRED an escape from the looming threat of the dictators, or indeed the travails of ordinary life, had to do no more than step off the streets of West Kensington in London and enter 'a wonderland of new ideas spread out under the canopy of a starry sky'. The *Daily Mail* Ideal Home Exhibition opened its doors, as it did every year, at Olympia, to hundreds of thousands in the last week of March. The centrepiece of the 1936 exhibition was 'The City of Beautiful Night', a recreation of a cloudless summer night in the Grand Hall: 24,000 square yards of dark velvet, set with twinkling lights, had been hung 80 feet high, as a night-time canopy over the exhibition. Stretched out in the chasm below were the floodlit pavilions and model homes of the 600 exhibitors, surrounded by terraces, from which spectators could view the cityscape beneath them. The focal point of the exhibition, spanning the 'city roadway' through the central hall, was a futuristic archway which supported a bandstand. It was built of hollow glass bricks and topped by a tall, slender glass tower, 'the entire structure glowing with a green light from some concealed source merging far up into the diffused light of the distant stars'.[1]

Betty Clark, a young girl from Walthamstow, was a regular visitor with her family to the exhibition. She came to marvel at the vision of modern domesticity on display. 'They had all the latest furniture, new houses, and there were the gardens which you paid extra to get into. They were wonderful and had rivers running through them.'[2] The organizers had created that year a suburban Xanadu, a pleasure dome in which they had done everything possible to entice and enchant the growing numbers of Britain's emerging class of aspirational consumers with the promise of dreams fulfilled under the starry night sky. Among the exhibits were: 'The Homes of the Film Stars', exactly recreating 'the favourite retreats of the world's most famous personalities'; 'How the Other Half Lives', a look into the rarely seen homes of submarine crews, a lighthouse keeper and an Oxford undergraduate; and 'The Shape of Things to Come', a vision of a future home based on the new H. G. Wells film. There was much more, from food to fashion, gadgets to gardens, to tempt the vast numbers who had recently bought a home or were thinking of doing so in the near future.

A Britain that is still familiar today was emerging in 1936, as growing areas of prosperity, mainly in the south, were transformed by a tidal wave of new building. Most of the construction was privately financed, and 1936 was the peak year, with a third of a million homes built. Large parts of the countryside were becoming suburbanized, as those who could afford to buy left the slums and pollution of inner London. The electrification of the railways and the extension of tube lines into the home counties had made commuting possible for millions. Lack of planning restrictions and the low price of agricultural land released an abundance of greenfield sites to house builders. An official regional report that March showed that the population of the suburban home counties had increased by a million in ten years, while that of inner London had declined. People were moving into Middlesex at the rate of 1,000 a week.[3] In Kent a county councillor told the *Daily Mail* that 'As fast as new houses are built there are families to occupy them'.[4]

It was these families, and those who dreamed of following them, that went to the Ideal Home Exhibition. It was extremely popular. In 1936, 600,000 crammed into Olympia's halls to enjoy the 'twelve acres of enchantment'; there were long queues for the most popular houses and exhibits, many of which cost extra to see. This show was not just a home counties affair. Visitors came by rail from all over Britain, with special excursion tickets from as far afield as Durham (32s., about £59 today), Edinburgh (for some reason cheaper at 26s., equivalent to about £48 today) and even from the Continent. For the well-off, British Airways offered its regular twin-engined

Lockheed Electra air services, twice daily from the closest continental cities to Croydon aerodrome. Many came principally to look at the show homes that stood in a specially built village inside the City of Beautiful Night.

There was a house for everyone, starting at the very bottom with the 'Next-to-Nothing Bungalow', the concept of the artist Claude Atkinson and built by him with the help of his wife, 'sewing and machining'. Atkinson created three divan beds for 6s. 6d. (£12 today), each from an old crate, 'half-inflated tyres make the mattress, syrup jars make reading lamps at the bed-head and the bolsters, pillows, and counterpanes are made from upholsterers' discarded patterns'. Armchairs, he proudly announced, were made from old tea chests, biscuit tins and – for comfort – more inner tubes. The cheese-paring artist fashioned his own ornaments out of old gramophone records, which he soaked in boiling water 'till they are pliable' and then twisted 'into vases and bowls'.[5] Although Atkinson's creation was tongue-in-cheek, many who scraped together all they had to pay for their first homes had no money left for furniture and did indeed make do with tea chests and packing cases. A large number bought their first armchairs and sofa on credit, tempted into debt by unscrupulous salesmen. Often the furniture was repossessed just before the final payment, on the grounds of a single late payment.[6] Credit, in the form of hire purchase, was not considered respectable. People went to great lengths to keep their debt a secret, despite the fact that in 1936 there was a very modern credit-fuelled boom in consumption.[7]

For the serious purchaser at the exhibition that year there was a wide range of attractive modern houses, from the 'Universal "Tile House"' for the Surrey stockbroker, at £2,100 (£77,650 today) to the all-timber £400 (£15,000) colonial home, constructed from red cedar wood and Douglas fir. This caught the eye of Randolph Churchill, commissioned by his father's friend the proprietor of the *Daily Mail*, Lord Rothermere, to write a laudatory article about the exhibition. Randolph was particularly impressed by the modernity of the timber house's interior and commented on the 'Sordo-Viso' front door 'bell': 'in the daytime it makes the lights turn on for an instant, so that whichever room you were in you would know that a visitor had called, without being startled by a deafening bell.'[8]

The exhibition celebrated modernity and its benefits. Many of the houses on show took advantage of the latest materials and mass-production techniques. The 'Olympia House', a three-bedroom semi, boasted metal-framed windows, which could be manufactured cheaply in their millions, and was built with the clean lines and curved white bays of the Art Deco style. But too overt modernity was not always trusted by conservative-minded British house-buyers. They may have liked the clinical white and curves of modernism for their kitchens and high streets, but as the exhibition recognized, they more often sought reassurance in the styles of the past for the design of their own homes. Wates, the house builders, put on show their 'Tudor House', complete with oak-timbered ceilings, gables and leaded windows, which offered the benefits of new technology under a mask of comforting tradition. It was just one of the fifty different types of mock Tudor house they were building that year on their sixteen estates in south London.[9] So popular was the 'Tudorbethan' style that it was said that there were more of this style of housing built in the inter-war years than in the entire Tudor period.[10]

Home-ownership was at the heart of government policy and backed by both parties. Neville Chamberlain saw it as a key part of the social reform to which he was committed, leading to better citizenship and the creation of what was later called 'the property-owning democracy'.[11] It had political advantages too, as people who owned their own homes tended to vote Tory. But most importantly, better housing was a step towards the ending of the slums that blighted the country. Slums were thought to contribute to immorality as large families crowded into one or two rooms, and brothers and sisters were forced to share beds. They certainly led to ill health. Most were damp, fetid and unfit for human habitation, as Orwell had discovered on his journey to Wigan. There was no proper sanitation; lavatories were almost always outside and shared, and in the poorer areas of the countryside communal earth closets were still common.[12] The close proximity of factories to housing in the inner cities and the widespread use of coal made the air often almost unbreathable.

John Prichard was eleven in 1936, enjoying the delights of suburban Bexleyheath, where his family had moved five years earlier from the docklands. The effect of the move was transforming. In the Silvertown district of east London, where he had lived before moving, pollution was so bad that men from the local soap factory would walk the local streets warning people to close their windows when the vats were opened. It was, he remembered, 'very smoky, very dirty; there were no trees, not a green thing, not a bird – no sign of life. I detested the place.'[13] The home itself was a smoky place too, with a coal-fired range with a cast-iron stove for cooking. Unsurprisingly, as a boy in this polluted inner-city environment, John suffered from asthma. The move to a new semi-rural bungalow was almost immediately beneficial to his health. 'My health was better . . . The whole place was much lighter, there wasn't a general atmosphere of gloom that you found in the docklands. There was country round about, and I liked wild flowers, the owls at night, skylarks coming out of the meadow in the day.'[14]

Education was often better in the suburbs too. John Prichard went to the village school at Bexleyheath before winning a scholarship to the local grammar school. Primary education was then traditional: 'It was excellent. I was taught a great deal of history of which present-day children know nothing. I read from authors like Robert Louis Stevenson and Walter Scott, and we learned English grammar. The only weakness was the lack of science because we did not have the apparatus.'[15] Many new secondary schools were built in the suburbs to accommodate the influx of children coming from the city. Paul Vaughan's family moved from Brixton to the fresh air of New Malden in Surrey, to a house that overlooked the recently completed Kingston by-pass. In January 1936, at the age of eleven, he went to Raynes Park County School for the spring term. The school, which had only just opened, was to make its mark on the educational system. Its headmaster, John Garrett, was a friend of W. H. Auden and invited poets of the day to speak and to read their poems to the boys. Auden wrote the school song ('Daily we sit down in form rooms/Inky hand to puzzled head'[16]) and ventured down to the new suburb to visit the school, which had been built on farmland.[17]

'There was a general atmosphere of respect for the arts and literature in the school which proved to be very important for me and my friends', Vaughan remembered. A good local school, as ever, was a motive for moving, 'part of this betterment factor that my father was after',[18] just as it was for millions of others who made the pilgrimage to the suburbs.

Betty Clark's family, like many visitors to the Ideal Home Exhibition, went to look at the affordable bungalows and semi-detached houses on display at the show. The building companies were offering them at very keen prices, so much so that they were, for the first time, within reach of those who had only lived in rented accommodation or council houses but dreamed of owning their own homes. 'There were the new houses', Betty Clark recalled from her trip to the show that year, 'which drew a lot of people. You could line up for two hours to go and see them. They gave you wonderful ideas for your own place.'[19] Many who queued up to take a look soon realized their dream. The rate of working-class owner-occupation almost doubled in the six years to 1936 and reached nearly 18 per cent.[20]

Betty Clark's father was a bus driver who was just able to afford the mortgage on a four-bedroom house in Walthamstow, at that time a much smarter area than Hackney, where the family had lived until 1936. Like so many, the family of five had squashed into a two-bedroom rented flat with a dining-room and kitchen, no bathroom and a shared outside toilet. They washed in a big copper bath in front of a coal fire in the dining-room, the family taking it in turns every Friday night. Betty was fortunate to be the youngest. 'I was first in the bath and then my brothers would follow and my parents were the last to go in, so the water was a bit grubby!'[21] The joy of moving to a house with its own bathroom with hot and cold running water and a garden in a better neighbourhood Betty never forgot: 'That was bliss, that was lovely.'

Her father could afford the mortgage not only because houses were much cheaper then (a new three-bedroom semi-detached house on show at Olympia that March would sell for about £27,000 at today's prices), but also because mortgages were for the first time readily available to most people in work and quite affordable. Ever since Britain had come off the gold standard in 1931 Neville Chamberlain's policy of cheap money had kept interest rates low. This, combined with new twenty-five-year mortgages with a 5 per cent deposit (as opposed to the previous maximum of twenty years and a 25 per cent deposit[22]), enabled people to get a mortgage to buy a three-bedroom house for about the same price as they would pay to rent a large council house. It was both economically rational and, for families like Betty Clark's, offered a chance to leap up the social spectrum: 'You were a class above everybody else if you owned your own home, and people would say "well those council people you know, they're not like us . . .".'

The Ideal Home Exhibition was officially opened by the Minister of Health, Sir Kingsley Wood, on 25 March, accompanied by Lord Rothermere's son Esmond Harmsworth, Chairman of the *Daily Mail*'s parent company. Dress was formal. The opening party wore silk top hats and tails; their wives wore dark garden-party gowns, fur stoles and an assortment of floral hats. The crowd of onlookers at the inauguration were less decorous, but − in tune with smarter times − all the men wore suits and ties, the women coats and skirts; hats were universal. After speeches Sir Kingsley and Lady Wood went on a tour of inspection of the vast exhibition. Much attention was paid to the GPO's large stand (the Post Office, thanks to the rise of the telephone, was enjoying record-breaking business and, at the time, its largest ever surplus), where the new 'Talking Clock' was on show. Wood dialled T-I-M as instructed, and listened to the clipped vowels of Ethel Cain, chosen from 15,000 telephone operators who had competed in the 'golden voice' talent competition, reciting the time. 'That's right, thank you', he said to the recorded voice before putting down the receiver, to general hilarity.

The opening of the exhibition coincided with the first sea voyage of the latest Cunard liner, RMS *Queen Mary,* on Tuesday 24 March. The construction of the great passenger vessel, saved from cancellation by a government loan, had brought many thousands of jobs to the depressed Clydebank and other areas around Glasgow. Like the Ideal Home Exhibition, the *Queen Mary*, with its great speed and luxurious interiors decorated by contemporary artists, presented an image of modernity and British technology leading the world. It was an object of immense national pride. The organizers of the exhibition sent a telegram to the ship: 'Congratulations from the Ideal Home Exhibition on land to the Ideal Home at sea – we both begin a voyage today. All success to your tests and journeyings.' The *Queen Mary* was for many in 1936 proof that Britain was still the greatest nation on earth. 'When I went to school', John Prichard remembered,

> I lived in a country with the biggest empire the world had ever seen, guarded by the largest and most powerful navy in the world . . . we had the world's biggest liner in the *Queen Mary*. The biggest and the best, you name it, it was ours. This gave the country a confidence that is now entirely lacking.[23]

A country's confidence is often expressed in numbers. The *Queen Mary*'s vital statistics were trumpeted in the media as the liner started on its maiden voyage from Glasgow to her dock in Southampton. Everything about her was, at the time, superlative: she weighed 81,000 tons, the heaviest ship afloat; at 1,020 feet she was also the longest and, with twelve decks, the tallest. The anchors weighed 16 tons apiece, the largest ever forged; the propellers, at 35 tons, were bigger by 10 tons than any built before; even the ship's three whistles were, at one ton each, audible at least 10 miles away – a record for the time.[24] But the *Queen Mary*'s greatness, which gave such a boost to the nation's pride was, like the Empire, and indeed the Royal Navy, not quite what it was cracked up to be. The ship's hull design was dated compared to that of her sleek rival the French liner *Normandie*, and she suffered from a fundamental design fault that would become apparent only during the Atlantic gales the following winter.

Britain may have been a still proud nation, but the pride was a façade in which cracks were beginning to appear. The carnage of the First World War had led to much anguished self-questioning. It had changed the country socially and transformed attitudes to work, above all to domestic service, which had for long been the principal employment for unmarried women. Since the conflict, when women had gone to work in offices, shops and factories, there had been an acute shortage of servants. Those who had left did not want to return to a life of drudgery; younger women were reluctant to follow their mothers into a job they considered demeaning. There were, however, still many thousands working in service.

For some, such as Dorrie Cooper, the plentiful food and kindness of employers made up for the heavy demands of work. At the age of seventeen in 1936, Dorrie was a scullery maid – 'the lowest of the low', as she called her position. She worked for the Aird family in a large and happy house outside the market town of Newbury, Berkshire. Work started at five in the morning and did not end until ten in the evening, with only some time off in the afternoons. 'I remember going to sleep in my clothes, I was so tired. It was tough, but you were healthy because you were on the go all the time.'[25] She earned just £13 a year (£480 today), but had all her board and lodging free.

It was little wonder that few girls and boys leaving school at the age of fourteen wanted to go into domestic service if there was other work on offer. Many of the wealthy south's servants were shipped in from the distressed areas. The rise of the middle classes with increased home ownership had exacerbated the shortage of servants, and by 1936 domestic service was in absolute decline.[26] Even the wealthy aristocracy found it difficult to find a good housemaid. Violet Milner spent most of the year in a frustrating search for a good servant, as she complained in her diary: 'interviewed house maids – impossible . . . engaged temporary housemaid . . . the maids have been hard at work clearing up after a very dirty housemaid who left yesterday.'[27]

The Ideal Home Exhibition was, in part, designed to help ease (and profit from) the burden of the moderately well-off housewife who could no longer count on the help of a cook and two housemaids. A large part of the show's 60,000 square feet that year was devoted to an array of British-made gadgets and labour-saving devices. A new industry, mainly based in London and the south-east, had grown up to manufacture them. Many of the exhibitors aggressively sold the newfangled devices. David Strain, a shopkeeper from Belfast, did not like their manner when he visited the exhibition. 'They are apt to pounce on one', he complained, 'if the slightest interest is displayed – and the whole effort is centred upon selling – not the friendly explanation which one would appreciate.'[28] Others, such as Paul Vaughan's mother, who went 'religiously' every year to the show, fell prey to the hard sell of the latest contraption. 'She was a sucker for that sort of thing. She would always get a new kind of cheese-grater or jam-making apparatus.'[29]

Many of the devices were electric-powered machines that are now considered mundane essentials. In 1936 they were marvels of new technology such as electric cookers and fridges, irons and toasters. Prominent at the exhibition that year were vacuum cleaners, once the province of the rich but now – thanks to hire purchase – available to the many. Most of those on display were British-made. One manufacturer, Vactric, took the front page of the *Daily Mail* to advertise their new models for the show: 'the airflo' upright, '20 years ahead in design and efficiency', and the 'silent Q' cylinder, 'the best in British engineering'. Both were on sale at 12 guineas (not cheap – about £465 at today's prices) or for the more affordable 3-shillings-a-week 'deferred terms' hire purchase. 'The Ideal Home', Marguerite Patten, a frequent visitor, believed, 'was opening out to people what life could be like. If you never had a vacuum cleaner, all you had to do was push it and it cleared up the dust. No more brushing!' Uptake for this dust-devouring miracle was rapid. By the beginning of the war, aided by the assiduous marketing of thousands of door-to-door salesmen, one third of households had a vacuum cleaner.[30]

Marguerite Patten, who became a pioneer celebrity cook, worked as a home economist in 1936 for the electrical industry. Part of her job was to go to the exhibition to learn about the different electrical goods on show: 'you took note of all the various appliances, and you saw a lot of different refrigerators and washers'.[31] Electricity had a dramatic effect on the quality of people's lives and seemed to open up limitless opportunities for the future. The National Grid had been completed in 1933, bringing the new power to the length and breadth of the country, freeing industries from coal and permitting enormous growth of light manufacturing around London and other major cities. It was the growth industry of the time, powering the country as its great pylons marched across the land. In 1930 only one in three houses had electric power; by 1936 that had increased to nearly two out of every three.

For those, such as Betty Clark's family, who moved into a house with electricity, the change from gas was a delight, 'switching on the lights instead of having these gas mantels that always went at the wrong time'. The new power may have been a great convenience, but for those housewives who had always relied on servants, its application had to be learned. This novel technology was a matter for women only. Men never ventured into the heat of the kitchen; modern homes were fitted with a hatch in the dining-room through which, in the absence of a maid to carry the dishes, the harassed wife could shove the evening dinner.

At a time when the future was pregnant with both opportunity and threat one of the key exhibits at the show in 1936 was a display called 'The Shape of Things to Come: A Panorama of Furniture', by Gooch's, the celebrated furniture emporium of Knightsbridge, set inside a futuristic home. It was based on the recently released Alexander Korda film *Things to Come*, the screenplay of which was written by H. G. Wells, adapting his science fiction novel of a similar name.[32] The official guide boasted that the 'Things to Come' display used 'many of the furnishings and properties from "the landmark in film history"'.[33] It was an inspired piece of publicity for the film.

Wells himself described the 'Things to Come' house in an interview for the exhibition catalogue. It had no corners or pillars, and no openings to the outside world. 'The roof curves gently over the space . . . There are no windows, but across a kind of animated frieze, a band of wall, there sweep phantom clouds and waves, clusters of flowers and the like.' Some of Wells's predictions for the future were quite accurate. The rays of the sun, he told visitors, would provide solar heating (although his idea that they would be captured to provide light 'day and night' was more far-fetched) and air-conditioning would create a dust-free interior atmosphere at a constant temperature. The house of 'Things to Come' had futuristic furniture covered with a glass and 'synthetic spun material'. Mindful of the lack of servants, there was a dining table to which meals were brought on a transparent conveyor belt.[34] On the flat top of the 10,000 square foot display there was a roof garden, where a model, looking slightly uncomfortable in an outfit of the future, rested on a sun-lounger, ready at a moment's notice to take a flying hop to the shops in the baby gyrocopter that sat beside her. Beneath her, from a stainless steel terrace, the public could glimpse the city of the future created on a giant cyclorama. This Wellsian metropolis featured airships and bridges in the sky, along which electric-powered cars drove in a frenzy of speed.

It is not surprising that the film should have inspired one of the central features of the show. Alongside the wireless, cinema was the most popular new medium of the time. Films had universal appeal across all classes and ages. A survey the year before had found that over one third of the population went to the cinema at least once a week.[35] There were about 23 million admissions across the country in 1936. Like the Ideal Home Exhibition, cinemas were places to escape and dream. They were often constructed as luxuriously carpeted palaces, exotically decorated, with commissionaires (usually resplendent in their medals from the First World War) and usherettes in uniform selling cigarettes and sweets. In 1936 these Art Deco Alhambras of entertainment were opening at the rate of three a week. John Prichard had five to choose from in nearby Erith alone, and yet more further afield. 'I went into the Granada at Woolwich the first week it opened and that was a wonder house, with the organ coming out of the pit and all the glorious oriental type décor, and a restaurant upstairs – very upmarket.'[36]

The stars of the cinema were the demi-gods and goddesses of their time. In 1936 the Ideal Home Exhibition brought eighteen of them down from their seats on cinema's Mount Olympus, Hollywood, to London's Olympia for its most popular attraction that year, 'The Homes of the Film Stars – a series of charming glimpses into the favourite rooms of well known personalities'. Naturally enough, the stars of *Things to Come* had agreed to publicize their film by allowing the interiors of their homes to be 'recreated'. The dining-room of Raymond Massey, who played the leading role, 'a mellow room, oak panelled, lighted from unseen lamps, and hospitably furnished', was placed by the side of a turquoise pond, adjacent to the floodlit glass columns that flanked the 'Things to Come' house. Across the lily-strewn reflecting pool was the bedroom of Margaretta Scott, Massey's co-star. 'It is a restful room', the *Mail*'s reporter glowed, 'green with thick-piled rugs and sycamore furnishing.'

Merle Oberon, the British star of *The Dark Angel* (for which she had been nominated for an Oscar), was happy to have the bedroom from her seaside retreat in Los Angeles displayed. She was so delighted, it was announced, that she had agreed to act as an unofficial ambassador for the exhibition, twisting the arms of her fellow Hollywood stars to let the public have a glimpse of their replica rooms. Miss Oberon had been successful in persuading American and British actors alike. Leslie Howard, the English star that year of *The Petrified Forest*, showed off his ultra-modern kitchen from his home in England, with its blue and cream colour scheme, stainless steel sinks and every possible electrical appliance. Despite its modernity, Howard's Surrey house was 'a lovely old mansion built at least 300 years ago and endowed with modern comfort without spoilation'.[37] The American sex symbol Mae West's boudoir was also on show. Unsurprisingly, the bed was the most notable feature. Another bedroom, that of the American child star Shirley Temple, 'the little sweetheart of the world', was imaginatively recreated in Olympia. 'She sleeps in a room of pastel pink and blue', the *Mail* mawkishly reported, 'beneath a ceiling of pictured starlight and with furniture of burnished silver around her. Spring flowers fill her garden and sunshine spills freely onto her playroom.'[38]

Alongside the Homes of the Film Stars was the Autograph Court, where British performers of varying degrees of fame, from the music-hall star George Robey to Miss Chili Bouchier of the silent screen, were caged for an hour at a time to sign the books of autograph hunters. They endured the crowds for the sake of charity, each signature earning sixpence for the Cinematograph Trade Benevolent Fund. The names and times of those attending were listed in the daily papers as an added draw to the crowds.[39]

A trip to the exhibition could be rounded off with a visit to the fashion display. That year a beauty pageant was held four or five times daily on the Plage-des-Modes in Brittany-by-Kensington, a mock-up of a French seaside resort, with a sandy beach, a café in the background, bathing tents and a jetty leading to a lighthouse - the catwalk for twenty-five actress-mannequins to parade the latest fashions. 'All the best frocks will be here and all the fairest fabrics', the official guides declared, 'charming young women will wear them – dance and frolic and bathe in them'. Seven hundred spectators at a time crowded into the 'shady comfort' of the temporary auditorium to see the spectacle and watch the masquerades on different themes.

When the lights dimmed, the show began with the parade of the fashionable drink of the moment, 'Human Cocktails'. It was led by the Cloverleaf, a favourite of the King and Mrs Simpson – gin, grenadine, mint, egg white and lemon – easy to identify because of the model's 'amply decorative' dress. This was followed by a humorous hint of the menace of real world with an answer to the bizarre problem 'If England had a Dictator, what would women wear?' The actress-mannequins disclosed 'in amusing fashion what manner of quaint garb they can evolve, from memories of politicians and their tastes'. No doubt much black leather and brown shirt was on show. After this came a Shakespearean fancy dress dance based on the 'Next-to-Nothing' bungalow: 'Lady Macbeth will be there in a frock that was formerly a curtain; Rosalind clad in something made from the green baize of cellarman's aprons and Juliet in drugget which she found in use as the underlay beneath the carpet.'[40] There was, as with everything on display at the show, a serious purpose behind the masquerade. Advice was given after the parade by a former editor of *Vogue,* 'to help older women to decide what to wear and what to leave to their daughters'.

The exhibition was also the setting for a formal revue, where the latest wearable clothes 'in which you would like to see yourself' were displayed, designed by top couturiers, including Norman Hartnell and Victor Stiebel. The idea was not to buy these expensive creations but to create them at home. The paper patterns that followed their designs 'so closely that you can make yourself a suit or dress in the newest style' were on sale to the amateur dressmaker. At a time when thrift was considered by many to be as much a necessity as a virtue, millions made their own clothes.

As John Prichard remembered, 'people liked to be smartly dressed'.[41] His mother made a point of always being well turned out. 'My mother's definition of a best suit was a suit that was never actually put on under any circumstances, it was just kept for best.' His father wore a suit and a bowler hat when he went out for a Sunday constitutional. 'Most people nowadays cruise about looking like they've kitted out in an Oxfam shop, but that didn't do then. You had to have smart clothes, even if you got them out once in a blue moon.' Respectability, then so crucial to a person's standing, was expressed through clothing, whatever his or her class or background.

But there was a degree of informality already creeping into society, which many suspected came from the overwhelming influence of American culture, especially the cinema. The new King, always a standard-bearer of the latest in men's fashion, had taken to appearing in public without a hat. This trend towards hatlessness caused apoplexy in some of the crustier members of the older generation. The Sheffield Advisory Committee for Juvenile Employment told of a controversial case of bare heads in its annual report that March. Two fourteen-year-old school-leavers had been offered a job with a salary of £100 a year and 'excellent prospects', with the proviso that they 'wear a hat to and from the business'. Both refused, 'striking a blow for the bare-headed brigade'.[42] Sir Walter Gilbey, the 76-year-old distiller, had mounted a one-man campaign against the hatless, calling the bare-headed brigade 'hottentots'.[43]

The suburban lifestyle that the Daily Mail Ideal Home Exhibition celebrated demanded respectability and conformity. The houses and furnishings on display were mass-produced, destined for the estates that were being constructed in bland uniformity across miles of depleted countryside. The new suburbia upset a broad coalition of opinion that did not subscribe to the *Daily Mail*'s values. The emerging countryside lobby, mainly upper-class landowners, hated the spread of housing on greenfield sites. Middle-class left-wing intellectuals despised suburban values. That March, at the same time as the exhibition, the poet W. H. Auden, having given up documentaries, went to Portugal to stay with his close friend and casual lover Christopher Isherwood. Together they were working on an experimental play, *The Ascent of F6*, a sustained attack on the values and lives of the new suburbanites.

In the play a typical suburban couple, 'Mr and Mrs A' ('A' standing, of course, for 'average'), follow the progress of the climber Michael Ransom and his team ascending a mountain. They listen to the wireless and read the newspapers to keep up with his exploits, gaining an escape from their mundane lives through his heroic achievements. When one of the climbers dies in an avalanche, Mr A announces, 'He has died to satisfy our smug suburban pride'.[44] Early in the play Mrs A is alone at home, cooking. She bemoans her empty, isolated life and the banality of her 'shop-soiled day', during which she 'dusted the six small rooms' and went to the shops.

> The delivery vans have paid their brief impersonal visits.
> I have eaten a scrappy lunch from a plate on my knee.
> I have spoken with acquaintances in the Stores . . .

Mrs A's husband arrives and asks his wife what has happened. She replies with a terrible lassitude, reciting a list of non-events, to which he responds with his own grim recitation:

> Nothing interesting to do,
> Nothing interesting to say,
> Nothing remarkable in any way;
> Then the journey home again
> In the hot suburban train
> To the tawdry new estate,
> Crumpled, grubby, dazed and late:
> Home to supper and to bed.

Paul Vaughan, a suburban schoolboy in 1936, later suspected that Auden's grim insight might well have been influenced by his visits to his new school in New Malden, where the new suburbs stretched in serried ranks for miles.[45]

Although not an active Communist, Auden at that time shared the widespread leftist view that only a cataclysmic change could bring an end to the degeneracy and *anomie* of the modern age. It was not a view shared by the millions who moved to the suburbs. Many certainly missed the sense of shared community of the old tenements and crowded housing of the cities, but none wanted a revolution to sweep away their new world of comfort and security, which the Ideal Home Exhibition celebrated.

The real concern for the new suburban dwellers, however, was not bourgeois alienation but the ever-present fear that their new houses, into which they had put everything, would be turned to worthless rubble in a conflict that seemed to come one step nearer every month. The aftermath of Hitler's move into the Rhineland continued to rumble on in the papers. Readers of the *Daily Mail* in March and April would find that the paper was full of celebrations of the dream 'to bring health and happiness to British homes', as the health minister put the purpose of the Ideal Home Exhibition. But alongside on the same page there was, as often as not, a much larger headline on the darkening situation in Europe. The 'House of Things to Come' told only one side of the story; nobody needed reminding of the other.

9

The new King struggles to modernize

A t the height of the Rhineland crisis a young German diplo-mat, Fritz Hesse, the press attaché at the London embassy, was with his Ambassador, Leopold von Hoesch, in his study, when the telephone rang. It was the King. Von Hoesch motioned to Hesse to pick up the extension and listen. The King was informal, friendly and direct. 'Is that Leo?' he asked, 'David speaking.' He continued, 'I sent for the Prime Minister and gave him a piece of my mind'. Edward VIII shared the views of millions of his subjects, and made them clear. 'I told the old so-and-so that I would abdicate if he made war. There was a frightful scene. But you needn't worry. There won't be a war!' The Ambassador was delighted. 'I've done it,' he exclaimed, 'I've outwitted them all, there won't be a war!'[1]

Fritz Hesse embellished the story when he wrote it down seven-teen years later. Nonetheless, his account contained two elements of truth: the King was fervently in favour of better relations with Nazi Germany, and the Germans regarded him as a man of influence over the British government. At the time of his father's funeral he had spoken to his first cousin Charles Edward, Duke of Saxe-Coburg-Gotha. The Duke was a fanatical Nazi who had shocked his British royal relatives by wearing an SS uniform during his stay in London. In essence, however, he was an Englishman. As Chips Channon described him: 'He speaks English perfectly, was at Eton, and is indeed English.'[2] At the end of January the Duke had sent Ribbentrop and Hitler a report of his conversation with the King. Top secret, it would have delighted its readers. The Duke informed them that he had asked the King whether he thought a summit meeting between Baldwin and Hitler would be desirable. To this the King replied with the immortal words: 'Who is King here? Baldwin or I? I myself wish to talk to Hitler, and will do so here or in Germany.'[3] The Duke reported that the King 'is resolved to concentrate the business of government upon himself' in the near future. In the meantime, he suggested that Ribbentrop should continue to handle relations on an unofficial basis, making contact whenever possible to bring the two countries together.

Edward's Nazi cousin was widely regarded as an unreliable witness who wanted to ingratiate himself with the Nazi leadership and told them what they wanted to hear.[4] But, as with the phone call to the German Ambassador, there were elements of truth within the fantasy. The King was part-German himself, spoke the language fluently and had very close family connections. He admired the Nazis' reconstruction of their demoralized and war-ravaged nation. Together with his Prime Minister and other senior ministers, aristocrats such as Charley Londonderry, many churchmen, newspaper editors and proprietors, and millions of his fellow citizens, he desired above all to avoid the carnage of another war. Like them, he saw some sort of *rapprochement* with Nazi Germany as the means to a long-lasting peace. But as his reign began, the Nazi leadership encouraged themselves – and were encouraged by his loose talk – to believe that a new chapter in the troubled history of relations between the two countries was about to open.

In the senior echelons of the British establishment the King's pro-German bias and his failure to understand the British constitution soon became cause for concern, alongside his love for a twice-married American. With the arrival of the young monarch, a shift from the staid and regular ways of King George V was inevitable. The country was changing, and Edward's informal manner and enthusiasm for modernity had been very popular. But from the beginning he faced the antagonism of the courtiers he inherited from his father.

In the days following the funeral two rival camps formed. On one side were the new King with his 'society' friends and hostesses, a handful of politicians, including Winston Churchill and Duff Cooper, the newspaper magnates Beaverbrook and Rothermere, and some loyal servants and aides. On the other side were the old guard: most of the court, many senior politicians, the Archbishop of Canterbury, the editor of *The Times* and the King's brother and heir presumptive, the Duke of York, and his wife, Elizabeth. It was a formidable array against the King.

To their disappointment but not surprise, this wayward Prince Hal did not reject his old dissolute merry-makers and turn into a kingly Henry V. Instead he continued to spend his time at the Boar's Head – in his case the Embassy Club in Mayfair – and never let go of his love, Wallis Simpson. On 12 February the American-born diarist Chips Channon went to tea with Lord Brownlow and his wife, and 'there we found assembled the 'new Court'.[5] At the centre of this new court was, of course, Mrs Simpson, 'very charming and gay and vivacious'. Official mourning was in force for six months, and she, out of deference to the King, was in black. She told Channon that 'She had not worn black stockings since she gave up the Can-Can', a remark that he thought 'typical of her breezy humour, quick and American'. For the traditionalists it was just this attitude that made Wallis Simpson so unsuitable as a companion for Edward. A reference to a risqué dance in the same breath as mourning for the late King would have been regarded as profoundly shocking and tasteless.

There is no satisfactory explanation for Wallis's hold over Edward. It was certainly mesmeric. In his eyes she could do no wrong. Those who ventured to criticize her were banished. Those who flattered her, and in 1936 there were many flatterers, were advanced at court. For some it was obvious that the King's great love, or infatuation as some dismissed it, was sexual, a 'dementia erotica'.[6] There was talk of the secret techniques of the Shanghai brothel that she had learned when living alone in China that made him her slave.[7] Others said that she supplied some want in his nature for female domination, after a childhood deprived of affection. She had a masculine look that made her attractive to lesbians,[8] and she certainly held power over Edward, as one horrified witness at a tea party recalled for Sarah Bradford, biographer of George VI:

The Prince: 'Have you got a light, darling?'
Wallis: 'Have you done your duty?'

CRAVEN LODGE   FANCY BALL

LADY URSULA MANNERS WITH MR. PARKER-
BOWLES AND MR. J. D. PLAYER

MRS. PETER QUENNELL
AND CAPTAIN ROLLO

MISS SUSAN TILNEY AND CAPTAIN THOMAS
CARTWRIGHT

SIR WESTROW HULSE AND MRS. ERIC
MARTIN SMITH

MRS.
PILKING-
TON AND

LORD
NORMAN-
TON

LORD BROWNLOW AND MRS. J. D. PLAYER

The Craven Lodge Fancy Ball was just the right kind of party to holla'
the New Year away, and though the going all round and about may be
hock deep or pretty near, the floor rode light for the fantastic toers,
and there wasn't the sign of a check from first to finish. Craven Lodge,
for those who do not know the Cut 'Em Downs, is that famous club in
Melton which is so admirably piloted by General and Mrs. John Vaughan.
As the pictures may suggest, there was a prehistoric "influence," but
no cave-man stuff was very noticeable. No one belted anyone over the
head with a stone axe or club. All Leicestershire's brightest and
bravest were on the premises and our one regret is that space forbids
the inclusion of more of them. Lady Ursula Manners, who is seen
with Mr. Parker-Bowles, was apparently none the worse for her
escape from a watery grave when out with the Belvoir a bit ago.
Captain Bill Rollo was a big success as a Neolithic Slop and Miss Susan
Tilney was a very animated mummy. Lord Normanton, snapped
dancing with Mrs. Pilkington, may have been an All White of the
Piltdown age. No one knows. Lady Dorothea Head, who is dancing
with another Early-On Tough, is a daughter of Lord and Lady
Shaftesbury, and married Captain Anthony Head last July

Photographs by Sasha

LADY DOROTHEA HEAD, MR. BEATTY AND OTHERS

New Year's Eve 1935. The theme of the Craven Lodge ball was 'pre-history',
an opportunity for the upper classes to indulge in various states of undress.
'I have never seen the English so gay', said Wallis Simpson

Three weeks into the year and King George V was dead. The country plunged into mourning. More than a million people queued for hours to walk past the late King's coffin in Westminster Hall. So profound was the national grief that the Bishop of Durham feared the growth of a 'George-culture'

'Like a mechanized tractor, the most amazing example of time and step ever seen in London': King George's funeral cortège makes its way through the silent crowds from Westminster to Paddington

The kings and princes of the royal houses of Europe follow the late monarch's coffin to its final resting place at Windsor. King Carol of Romania's masseur was said to have accidentally joined the procession. Newspaper readers tried to spot him in the next morning's editions

The Marquess of Londonderry, Adolf Hitler and Joachim von Ribbentrop.
The Marquess was one of many British politicians and aristocrats who paid court to
the Führer in 1936 in the misguided hope that a new alliance might be forged

The Prime Minister Stanley Baldwin. His carefully cultivated image
of a down-to-earth man of the people masked a cunning and ruthless
politician. In the summer of 1936 he suffered a nervous breakdown,
before recovering sufficiently to mastermind the abdication

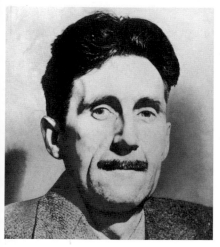

George Orwell: 'a public conscience with an exceptionally well-developed sense of smell'. In 1936 the writer and journalist went to Wigan and, disgusted by what he found, called for a fundamental change in British society

Henry 'Chips' Channon: extremely wealthy with a quick wit and piercing insight. His diary of 1936 reveals the vanities and misconceptions of Edward VIII's social circle. 'Reformers are always finally neglected, while the memoirs of the frivolous will always be eagerly read,' he observed with justifiable confidence

Neville Chamberlain: the Iron Chancellor. If he had retired or died in 1936 he would have been remembered as one of Britain's most successful peacetime ministers

Winston Churchill: in 1936 he was widely regarded as a colourful but unreliable figure who pursued lost causes to his own detriment. Later in the year his support for the King led many to believe his career was finished

The old and the new: 1936 saw a peak of house building with the construction of more than a third of a million new homes. Electricity continued its march of modernization across the country. Horse-drawn vehicles and hand-pushed milk carts would soon be a thing of the past

Two nations: a jobless man with some of his children in Ebbw Vale, south Wales. Unemployment brought terrible suffering to millions in the old industrial areas of Britain

Two nations: 'A symphony of aquamarine', Chips Channon's 'Amalienburg', an exact replica of the rococo dining room of a German palace. Chips recreated it in his Belgravia house at a cost of £6,000 (approximately £220,000 today)

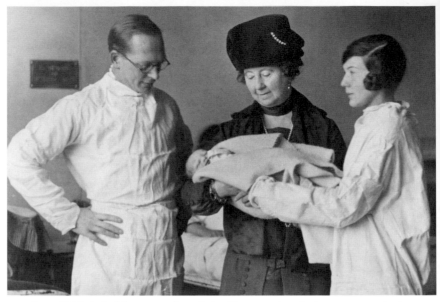

Lucy Baldwin holding a new-born baby. Her campaign for improvements in the standards of midwifery bore fruit in 1936. As the wife of a Conservative prime minister she was an unlikely pioneer of universal free health care

Edward VIII attends to his papers. The King started his reign with a burst of reforming zeal but soon tired of the business of kingship. He later admitted that he 'never had much zest for paperwork'. Another more pressing matter was on his mind

Little man gets on his haunches, puts up his hands and begs like a dog.
She then lights his cigarette. Horrible to see . . .[9]

Wallis stood for the modern: she was independent and American.
For many of the King's courtiers and ministers this meant superficiality, ignorance of the tradition and the weight of monarchy, and
above all, vulgarity. She may have come from a good Baltimore
family, but she and her compatriots were regarded with suspicion in
the Britain of 1936. The USA was perceived in conservative circles as
a rival nation exerting a baleful cultural and moral influence, as Edie
Londonderry complained in her memoirs: 'England has become
Americanised . . . the young English gentleman, or man about town,
more frequently than not tries to appear in his dress and manners as
an American tourist.'[10] She could have been speaking of Edward
himself. To people such as the Londonderrys the USA's economic
and military potential was a threat to the continuing survival of the
British Empire. The King's preference for all things that came from
North America (he even changed his official car from a Daimler to a
Canadian Buick) was a clear sign of a latent personal unreliability.
That he should be in love with an American struck at the very fabric
of the nation.

Stanley Baldwin described Wallis Simpson with a lack of generosity but some acuity as 'a third-class woman; passably good-looking;
very small and very elegant; knows exactly what to say and how to say
it. But no heart.'[11] The school of hard knocks – poverty, early marriage to a violent drunk, and being forced to make her own way across
the world after her first divorce – had made her tough, self-reliant and
quick-witted. She was out for herself alone and appeared to many
who encountered her that year as a thoroughly superficial, money-
obsessed dominatrix. But others saw her in a better light. Wallis could
be kind-hearted, as was shown by the loving letters she sent to Bessie
Merryman, her aunt. She had an easy manner and a fast wit, which
Edward and his friends found appealing. Those of a different class
who worked for her appreciated her kindness and saw a more appealing side of her character. 'All the maids spoke well of Mrs Simpson',
a kitchen maid at her London flat reported.[12] The attitude of servants

to their employer often revealed a truth about his or her personality that was masked by the conventions of upper-class society.

Perhaps Wallis's least attractive characteristic was her tight-fistedness, which seems to have grown out of her experience of poverty in childhood. Anxiety about money was a constant concern in her letters; she was always prudent and on the look-out for savings. Her chic clothes came half-price from the American couturier Mainbocher in Paris (conveniently flown to England duty-free in the King's plane, along with her strange gift to him of his favourite dish, langoustines). Even court mourning, as she told her Auntie Bessie, had its advantages: 'We all look like blackbirds. As I always wear so much black for economy I got into mourning with no expense.'[13] This thriftiness soon began to have an adverse effect on the King's first months on the throne.

The King's other American friends added to the sense of shallowness and glitz of the new court. Henry 'Chips' Channon, the Conservative MP for Southend, deserves his place in history as one of the great diarists of his age, but he was a social climber, a snob and a political lightweight. He was a naturalized British citizen (the son of a Chicago millionaire, married to a Guinness heiress) who set himself apart from the moneyed but discreet British upper classes with his conspicuous displays of wealth. The silver and blue dining-room Chips had installed in his new Belgravia home, at a cost of £6,000 (more than £220,000 today), was a replica of the Rococo confection in the Amalienburg Palace in Munich, all blues and silver: 'a symphony', as Chips put it, 'of aquamarine'. The Amalienburg, recreated for Channon by Stéphane Boudin of Paris, was an object of fascination for London society and drew gasps of admiration from the King when he visited ('he was in ecstasies'[14]), but for the traditionalists it was the height of vulgarity. Harold Nicolson summed it up:

Oh my God, how rich and powerful Lord Channon has become! . . . the dining room is entered through an orange lobby and discloses itself suddenly as a copy of the blue room at Amalienburg near Munich – baroque and rococo and what-ho and oh-no-no and all that. Very fine indeed.[15]

Emerald Cunard was probably the most influential American in the new court. She made a tremendous play for the new King and his lover, whom she regarded as a 'gold-plated passport' to social ascendancy.[16] Chips, who lived nearby, was an admirer of this vivacious and cultured hostess. 'It was in her house in Grosvenor Square that the great met the gay, that the statesmen consorted with society, and writers with the rich . . . To some it was the most consummate bliss even to cross her threshold.'

Certainly the King and Wallis frequently crossed her threshold. As one aristocratic lady disdainfully noted, Emerald Cunard 'and all her crew' were 'tumbling after' the new King and his beloved.[17] Emerald addressed Edward as 'Majesty divine', and her pursuit of the couple caused bitter resentment in society. It was rumoured that she had her eyes on a role at court, possibly Mistress of the Robes, if Wallis were to become Queen.[18] So great was the offence she provoked that someone once sent her an anonymous note: 'You old bitch, trying to make up to Mrs Simpson in order to curry favour with the King.'[19]

Into this heady brew stepped the sinister figure of Joachim von Ribbentrop. Emerald Cunard competed with her rival hostesses, such as Edie Londonderry, to entertain Ribbentrop on his frequent journeys to London. She called him a 'delicious, real live Nazi'.[20] This lionizing of Hitler's foreign affairs 'expert' was profoundly irritating to official diplomats. It was also damaging. Just as the Londonderrys' visit to Germany in February gave Hitler the mistaken idea that the aristocracy was a force in British politics, so cultivating Ribbentrop in London led to a wrong-headed impression about the influence of the King. As Harold Nicolson later put it: 'the harm that these silly selfish hostesses do is really immense. They convey to foreign envoys the impression that foreign policy is decided in their own drawing rooms.'[21]

Emerald Cunard had introduced the Nazi diplomat to the Prince of Wales and Wallis Simpson the previous year at a dinner in Grosvenor Square. Ribbentrop saw Mrs Simpson quite frequently thereafter, and by early 1936 it was gossiped that the couple were having an affair. Suspicions were aroused when the security services reported that he routinely sent her seventeen red roses. It was put about that each rose represented a time when he had slept with her. Hitler demanded to know the truth.[22] But they never had an affair. Even if the Nazi had wanted one, he would not have dared. His powerful wife, Annalies, was always a fearsome presence in his life. But Ribbentrop certainly 'used' Wallis for his own diplomatic purposes, hoping to ingratiate himself with the King.

News of Ribbentrop's keen interest in Wallis soon reached the ears of the Prime Minister. The security services were ordered to follow her, and Special Branch monitored her activities. Because the King was frequently with her, he was watched too. Nothing untoward was discovered about the loyalties of Wallis, as Stanley Baldwin confirmed in private a year later.[23] That suspicions were aroused, however, was another damaging mark against the King as his reign began.

From the start Edward faced an impenetrable barrier of fustiness and tradition. Partly this stemmed from his relative youth. At forty-one he was young when compared with the Prime Minister. Stanley Baldwin was sixty-nine. Neville Chamberlain was sixty-seven. The country was ruled by old men, whose outlook and attitudes had been shaped in the Victorian era. That they were still so dominant in Parliament was due partly to the destruction in the killing fields of Flanders of what should have been the succeeding generation. Edward, on the other hand, had served in the First World War. He shared the aspirations of his generation for a new society to be built out of the shattered world of the trenches. Frequently in letters written when he was Prince of Wales to his former lover, Freda Dudley Ward, he had spoken of his anger at the irrelevance of the pomp of monarchy, and his desire for change. 'The day for Kings and Princes is past, monarchies are out-of-date though I know it's a rotten thing for me to say and sounds Bolshevik!!'[24]

Edward was no bolshie – quite the reverse – but he did have plans for a new style of 'slimmed-down' monarchy that he felt would be more in tune with the times. The problem was that a reformed monarchy was not in tune with the majority of public feeling, which remained wedded to his father's conception of kingship.[25] There was little public support for the idea that 'the day for Kings and Princes is past'. What backing there was for reform came from liberals and the left, who were not Edward's natural allies. The majority of a conservative-minded country still wanted the King–Emperor to be a lofty figure who symbolized the greatness of the nation.

Edward's courtiers were firmly of this view. If the new King wanted to modernize, he would have to convert them to his cause. This was an impossible task. In line with tradition, his father's officials had stayed on in their posts to smooth the transition to the new reign. Naturally enough, they shared the deeply conservative views of the man whom they had served for so long. Clive Wigram, Principal Private Secretary, had been in royal service for thirty-two years. He was a dyed-in-the-wool traditionalist, who detested the 'spivvy' world of the new King and was suspicious of everything he stood for. He was soon to be replaced by Alexander 'Alec' Hardinge, who had been the late King's Assistant Private Secretary for sixteen years.

While Major Hardinge was the same age as Edward, and had served with him during the First World War in the Grenadier Guards, he was poles apart in outlook and manner. A scion of Empire, son of a Viceroy, great-grandson of a Governor-General of India, he had been brought up in the traditions of service and duty that had built Britain's domination of the world. But this upbringing had made him a prig. At Harrow he had stayed in bed rather than go on an escapade to London with other boys. He was afraid of the damage he might do to his father's reputation if the story got out. This priggishness never left him. Hardinge's loyalty to the monarchy was unquestionable. At a time when millions saw the Empire as the great achievement of the British race, he believed its very heart was the sovereign, 'the lynchpin of the intricate mechanism . . . if that lynchpin were pulled out . . . the whole system would be threatened with collapse'.[26] His duty was not to the individual but to that great institution; this led inevitably to a conflict of loyalties. With Wigram, he utterly disapproved of the new King's social life and disagreed with his desire for 'modernization' of the royal household, which he felt threatened the whole system.

Hardinge suffered from personality problems, which were put down to wounds suffered during the war. He was highly strung, an 'irascible and rigid martinet' who had little idea of managing people. His colleague the King's Assistant Private Secretary, Alan Lascelles, referred to 'his complete inability to establish friendly, or even civil, relations with his fellow men'.[27] He frequently caused offence by his intransigence and cold manner, not just to those who served under him but also to the King himself. His appointment to take over from Lord Wigram in the key role as Private Secretary was a disaster. In every way – temperamentally, politically and personally – he was unsuited to serve the man who would be his boss during the turbulent months ahead.

The third figure in this hostile entourage was Alan 'Tommy' Lascelles. Lascelles had served as Edward's Private Secretary when he was Prince of Wales but had left in 1929 in disgust at his boss's 'unbridled pursuit of wine and women'[28] and his 'callous' disregard for his father during the long tours of Empire. He came back to serve the King in 1935, and after the King's death found himself working for the man he held in contempt.

In the isolated hot-house of royalty Edward's tics and traits became magnified out of all proportion. Lascelles wrote a short memoir of 1936 in his journal.[29] Rarely has there been a more negative assessment. The King, he alleged, was venal, selfish, self-centred, ignorant, immature, ungrateful, uneducated, half-mad and sex-obsessed. 'He had no comprehension of the ordinary axioms of rational, or ethical behaviour', Lascelles thundered; 'fundamental ideas of duty, dignity and self-sacrifice had no meaning for him, and so isolated was he in the world of his own desires that I do not think he ever felt affection – absolute, objective affection – for any living being.'[30] There was unquestionably some truth in his accusations. But many princes and monarchs in the past have suffered from similar character faults. The King's grandfather, Edward VII, was a morally delinquent glutton but was able to fulfil his role well with the assistance of his staff. It is the job of the private secretaries to shepherd their unruly masters, educate them in the ways of kingship and protect them from criticism and embarrassment. Edward never had this support.

In the face of such a phalanx of fogeys in his private office it is hardly surprising that the King's desire to reform the monarchy did not get far. He had begun his reign determined to shake up the operation of the royal household. He wanted to innovate and make it more efficient and modern.[31] He embarked on a series of investigations and cost-cutting initiatives. This caused great upset. Some of his cuts appeared downright mean. He tried to reduce salaries; he discontinued allowances; he cut back the staff at Balmoral and Sandringham, 'a voracious white Elephant'.[32] He took to wandering around Buckingham Palace, unannounced, late at night or at lunchtime (he did not eat lunch, owing to an obsession with remaining slim), to the unease of his staff. The Deputy Comptroller of Supply remembered:

> He would suddenly appear in the kitchens, the cellars, and the store rooms, or other 'behind the scenes' parts of the Palace, walking round, alone, or with one equerry, on tours of inspection. It was all very informal, and quite unlike anything we had seen George V do at the Palace.[33]

Once, during one of these tours, he found an enormous room packed with candles and, as he described later, 'a troglodytish individual who seemed to sleep there'. The King was told that the occupant was a pensioner who 'helps with the candles'. Edward was infuriated. He regarded this as exploitation of the privy purse rather than, as his father might have seen it, the loyalty of a paternalist employer to an old and faithful retainer. He did his best to put a stop to such practices. He was never forgiven.[34]

There was good reason behind his desire for efficiencies. His father had allowed spending to run out of control. The royal family and court still carried on with an opulence that harked back to Edwardian times. It was out of step with the austerity that had followed the slump of the early 1930s. Edward was very conscious of the sufferings of the unemployed and of the terrible poverty in the distressed areas. But his approach to the royal household's finances was marred by the way he behaved. On the one hand, he wanted economies and imposed cuts; on the other, he was ready to waste thousands of his private fortune on his own lifestyle. Mean to his staff, he was wildly generous to Mrs Simpson. He gave her cash and showered her with jewels, spending the equivalent of millions in today's money. In the spring of 1936 alone he bought her a ruby and diamond bracelet from

Paris for £16,000 (equivalent to £600,000 now), engraved 'Hold tight 27.iii.36'.[35] When Wallis appeared at society soirées, some, unable to believe that a mere commoner could be so magnificently bejewelled, thought her glittering tiaras, necklaces and brooches were fake and no more than vulgar costume jewellery. Wallis was, according to Chips Channon, 'literally smothered'.[36] The King used his private income for these gifts. Nevertheless it gave the wrong impression and alienated his already disaffected staff still further.

Not content with bringing an axe to royal finances, the King sought to reform the monarchy itself. Edward had long hated pomp and circumstance. Courtiers noticed that he was most at ease in America, where he loved the informality and lack of snobbery.[37] His easy and relaxed style had much to do with his great public popularity. But with the old guard this style never went down well. From the moment he changed the clocks at Sandringham they were against him.

Early in the reign, when he walked in the rain from Buckingham Palace to a meeting across the road in Buckingham Gate, he was criticized for carrying an umbrella and not riding in the official car.[38] His father, he remembered, had fought 'a private war with the twentieth century', which had ended with its 'almost complete repulse'.[39] Edward's courtiers continued the battle. The most minor changes met with resistance. He tried to change the rules on how his profile should appear on stamps and coins. He struggled to streamline royal presentations. He later said that he succeeded in only two reforms: the creation of a 'King's Flight' and the ending of the rule that the Yeomen of the Guard should grow beards in the Tudor style.[40] This was an exaggeration, but only a slight one. He also managed to banish the wearing of frock coats at court, and he opened the Royal Victorian Order to women. Otherwise the great ship of royalty sailed on, unrocked by his feeble wind of change.

Just as the King started his reign with a reformer's zeal, so he set to his official duties with an initial outburst of manic energy that characterized his personality. At first he opened the red boxes and read official papers. He asked questions and attended meetings. He initialled every page of an official dispatch as though he were Prime Minister. This early attention to detail turned out to be a mistake. As time passed and energy dissipated, the lack of initials became a sign of regal indolence.[41] Edward himself later admitted that 'this interminable amount of desk work was all the more taxing' because he 'never had much zest for paper work'[42] – an understatement if ever there was one. The young Liberal MP and diarist Robert Bernays heard that that spring the King was using a small ante-room as a temporary study, where he worked in a lounge suit, and 'his papers were in the wildest disorder. He was without any sort of method and vital papers were taken out of the file and left, some in York House, some in Buckingham Palace and even, at weekends, in Fort Belvedere.'[43]

Fort Belvedere, his grace-and-favour house near Sunningdale, was next to Mrs Simpson in the King's affections. It was 'a castellated conglomeration'[44] to which he could retreat from the world, garden ferociously and, with Wallis at his side, entertain friends. The world of the court was forbidden from intruding into this crenellated hideaway. As though to emphasize its status as the King's fortress, antique cannons faced outwards from the house, ready to blast any unwanted intruders. As time passed, Edward spent more and more time at the Fort, shut away from officials, insisting that he be allowed to live his private life as he chose.

As his staff were not allowed to come to the Fort except by invitation, papers would be delivered in their red boxes only to languish there unread. Sometimes they came back marked with the tell-tale rings of a cocktail glass.[45] Often they would be returned too late to play any part in the constitutional process. Alec Hardinge was, as a result, put under intense pressure to keep things running smoothly. To make matters worse, the King – unlike his father, who was obsessively punctual and followed a strict timetable in all matters – had no schedule. He would telephone Hardinge on official business at any time of day or night, call his officials for meetings whenever it pleased him, and keep whomsoever he pleased, even the Prime Minister, waiting sometimes for an hour and more.

Once again officials became concerned about security. Special Branch was reporting that Wallis was in frequent contact with Leopold von Hoesch, the German Ambassador, as well as Ribbentrop. In

February, Lord Wigram went to Parliament to discuss the matter with Stanley Baldwin. In the cloistered secrecy of the Prime Minister's room three of the country's top civil servants, including the Cabinet Secretary, told him that 'the King is discussing all problems with Mrs Simpson and showing her state papers'. They further reported: 'the Foreign Secretary is very anxious lest the FO [Foreign Office] cypher may be compromised, as Mrs S is said to be in the pocket of the German Ambassador.' Baldwin, exhausted by the cares of office, characteristically refused to take any action. Instead Wigram spoke to the King, who reassured him that he only read the papers very late in the evening.[46] Nevertheless, officials henceforth screened papers that were sent to the King, an act unprecedented in British history.[47]

Throughout this period Wallis Simpson's husband, Ernest, was on the scene, often accompanying her to social occasions arranged by or for the King. To wear his horns so openly must have been embarrassing and humiliating. But Simpson, who was half-American, had an exaggerated reverence for royalty. In public he behaved with extraordinary composure while Edward openly fawned over his wife. Behind the scenes things were different. In early March he confronted the King. The aggrieved husband went to Edward's London apartments, York House, in St James's Palace, taking with him a friend, the finely named Bernard Rickatson-Hatt, editor-in-chief of Reuters, as witness. The meeting appears to have been so excruciating that Rickatson-Hatt at one point tried to make his excuses and leave, but Simpson held him back. He then challenged the King to declare his intentions, whereupon 'the King rose from his chair and said: "Do you really think I would be crowned without Wallis at my side?"'[48]

The fact that the King was planning to marry Wallis was beginning to dawn on his courtiers. On 28 March, Edward hosted a dinner party at Windsor Castle, to which he invited Alec Hardinge and his wife Helen, Lord and Lady Wigram, and the Simpsons. Nora Wigram had such strong moral objections to Wallis that she at first refused to go, but her husband insisted she accompany him.[49] Edward drove over from the Fort, bringing with him his party, which included an American friend of the Simpsons, Mary 'Buttercup' Raffray, no doubt considered the height of vulgarity by the old guard waiting at Windsor. Her nickname came from the flowery hats that she liked to wear. During the dinner the King and Mrs Simpson 'were in teasing mode' and shocked Helen Hardinge with 'apparently joking references to "matching" Buttercup . . . with Mr Simpson'. Buttercup and Ernest were flirting at the other end of the table. Helen Hardinge thought this a blatant and crude display of contempt for moral convention. She took it as an open indication of the way Edward intended things to go. That night, after the dinner, she became convinced that 'the King was bent on marriage'.[50] The Prime Minister was informed. But once again he took the line of least resistance, saying the problem was best left alone and that, in time, it would resolve itself.[51]

Meanwhile Wallis Simpson took the initiative. Helen Hardinge's suspicions were correct. Mary Raffray was an old schoolfriend from Baltimore who had invited herself to London for the spring. During visits to New York, Ernest and Mary had grown fond of each other. At first Wallis considered the impending visit an inconvenience, but she soon turned it to her advantage. In a letter to her Aunt Bessie she moaned about Buttercup's stay. 'I don't know what to do with her as I can't fit her night-club mind to it [the visit] and who is to take her on the town as I dine in old fogies' houses nearly every night.'[52] But then Wallis divined a useful purpose for Buttercup. 'Ernest returns next Saturday', she told her Aunt, 'and is keen about the visit as he has always loved her. I suggest her to him as a future bride.' It was meant as a joke, but it was the germ of an idea that became deadly serious. Even as she wrote to her aunt, Wallis must have seen a very convenient outcome. She would be able to divorce Ernest, on the grounds of his adultery with Mary, and – after a decent interval – marry Edward, while Ernest married Mary. It was a game of musical chairs, carefully co-ordinated by an arch-manipulator with the co-operation of all concerned. Certainly, things worked out in the short term exactly as Wallis planned. The only fly in the ointment was that Edward was King.

That spring Mary Raffray arrived, dined at Windsor and later met the 'countless old fogies', including, as Wallis told her aunt, 'von Ribbentrop, Ramsay MacDonald and poor Hoesch the German ambassador who died a few days later'.[53] In the interstices Mary and Ernest became closer, staying up to the early hours every night while Wallis went to bed. If they had not already embarked on an affair, they started one now. Wallis later told her aunt, disingenuously, that she had become suspicious. When Ernest and Mary rented a car for a holiday break, she hired a private detective. 'I then had them followed for three days and of course got the expected report.'[54] The report, together with a 'misdirected' letter, settled matters. When confronted with the evidence, Ernest announced he was in love with Mary and agreed to a separation prior to a divorce. It was the first step on the road to the abdication.

Wallis was almost embarrassed at the convenience of the outcome, an embarrassment revealed in a letter she wrote with the news to Aunt Bessie. 'Isn't it all ridiculous? Anyway, we will work it all out *beautifully* I hope.'[55] In the meantime, Ernest had some small revenge for the months of public humiliation he had endured at the hands of his wife and the King. He insisted that Mary Raffray accompany him and Wallis for the rest of her stay to 'all meals, parties, etc.'. Wallis admitted this was 'rather hard to take'.[56] Hard to take or not, she was in no position to refuse. This simplicity of the solution to the problem of herself and Ernest was played out with the exactitude of a game of solitaire, but it revealed in her a desire to manage human relations to suit her own ambitions, regardless of the desires of love.

The one person who was truly in love was the King. But it was more than love: it was an infatuation, an obsession, a madness. He could not leave Wallis alone. He came round to her London flat at every opportunity, and, when apart from her, he wrote her letters using his special baby-talk: 'Good morning my sweetheart. How is your pain? How did you sleep and did you miss eanum? A boy has overdone the drowsel but is hurrying down to a girl.'[57] In early May, as a token of his intentions and of his undying love, Edward settled a fortune on her. Wallis's money worries were over. Whether she wanted it or not, she was now set on a course that would shake the foundations of the monarchy, bring her a new husband and challenge the conventions and morality of the British in 1936.

10

The height of hypocrisy

ALTHOUGH MANY OF those in the know about Edward's affair were ready to condemn it out of hand, personal morality in 1936 was in a state of flux. George V had deliberately made the crown 'into a model of traditional family virtues'.[1] These 'virtues', however, were under threat, and not just by a King in love with a divorced and remarried woman. Edward himself made this clear to his friend Duff Cooper when they met to discuss Wallis. Taking up a chair and holding it in the air, he told his startled friend, 'Society is suspended in midair, like this chair . . . Nobody knows what is right'.[2]

Divorce, while on the increase (6 per cent of marriages ended in divorce in 1936, up from 2 per cent at the end of the First World War[3]), was frowned on in British society and still carried a stigma. To be a woman twice married, like Wallis Simpson, was considered a threat not just to respectability but also to the moral standards of the time. In his desire to carry on his relationship with her and to ignore convention Edward was a pathfinder, hoping to show a new, more tolerant way of behaving. But he was ahead of his time, fighting a losing battle against an establishment whose values were derived from the rigid rules of Victorian Britain.

To traditionalists the perceived relaxation of the conventional morality that had been dominant before the First World War was leading to a general degeneracy. The 75-year-old Professor F. J. C. Hearnshaw of London University spoke for many of the older generation when he fulminated to an audience in the summer at the Royal Empire Society that 'the age is on the decline; morals are loose; manners are bad; society is unstable'.[4] He deplored 'a lack of respect for fathers' and attacked 'the sexual freedom' of the age.

The Professor called for a return to the morality of the Victorian middle classes (and he was by no means the last to do so). Stanley Baldwin agreed. The Prime Minister told his Cabinet colleagues that since the First World War 'there has been a lowering of the public standards and of public morals'.[5]

It was the duty of the King, Baldwin believed, to uphold in public the highest standards in the face of the decline in behaviour; 'the people expect even more of the Monarchy', he said. The Prime Minister wanted the King to follow the convention of the time, as he told Duff Cooper when they discussed Edward's affair with Wallis Simpson privately. '"If she were what I call a respectable whore," he said, "he wouldn't mind", by which he meant somebody whom the Prince occasionally saw in secret but didn't spend his whole time with.'[6] Baldwin was speaking man-to-man with Cooper, a notorious adulterer, who operated by the upper-class principle that you could do almost anything within reason, so long as you were not caught. This rule – which Edward rejected with some justice as 'the height of hypocrisy'[7] – was upheld in 1936 by most members of the upper classes, from Prince George, Duke of Kent, who was bisexual and a drug-taker, to Charley Londonderry, with his numerous mistresses. If this became public, it would spell certain ruin for the individuals concerned. But in private casual sex, mistresses and homosexuality were tolerated. To the modernistic King this was the outdated morality of his grandfather Edward VII. 'Everybody could do what they liked', he complained to Duff Cooper, 'so long as they kept up appearances',[8] and for Wallis, this double standard was the epitome of all she disliked about Britain. She told her Aunt Bessie that she detested the English respect for their bourgeois morals.[9]

The Prime Minister and his wife, Lucy, seemed to be the embodiment of the middle-class values that Wallis Simpson so despised. They had been happily married for forty-four years, had five children and were regular church-goers. The Baldwins were also deeply Christian. Every morning on rising, Mrs Baldwin once told a Swedish diplomat, 'we kneel together before God and commend our day to Him, praying that some good work may be done in it by us'.[10] But the image of English ordinariness that they cultivated was only a part of the picture. In reality they were a complex couple. Their marriage was not without its share of difficulties and set-backs.

The Baldwins' son Oliver was a socialist who had sat briefly in the House of Commons on the benches opposite his father. He was also a homosexual, although this, of course, was never spoken of in public. His loving parents tolerated both his politics and his sexual orientation. They came to terms with his living openly with his lover, Johnnie Boyle, in Oxfordshire.[11] But others were not so understanding. Rudyard Kipling, who had regarded him as a 'surrogate son' after the death of his own son, John, was horrified when he learned of Oliver's 'beastliness'.[12] The author was fervently anti-gay, and from then on rejected him completely.

Attitudes to homosexuality, like those to marriage and divorce, were in a state of flux. Earlier in the year Edward and Wallis had been to the Phoenix Theatre with Sibyl Colefax and Harold Nicolson to see the opening of *Tonight at 8:30*, an evening of three witty one-act plays on contemporary themes by Noel Coward. The multi-talented author produced and directed the plays, took the main parts and sang and danced, to music that he composed. Coward's genius for light and witty comedy with sharp social insight was to Edward's taste. As a result he was frequently invited by society hostesses as a suitable guest to dine with the King and Mrs Simpson.

The fact of Coward's homosexuality, however, although widely known, was never mentioned in public. His adoring audience, the majority of them middle-class suburbanites, had no idea of his sexuality and would have been horrified if they had known it. In such circles homosexuality was hardly mentioned. It was certainly not considered a suitable subject to speak of in front of women.

Those celebrities, such as Coward or the politician and diarist Harold Nicolson, who also had numerous homosexual affairs, took great care to be discreet and to confine their activities to circles where their behaviour would be tolerated.[13] Lesbianism was also taboo, although not illegal. In 1936 male homosexuality was an offence punishable by imprisonment with hard labour. Prosecution still brought professional and social ostracism. There was also the risk of blackmail. Shortly after the First World War a Liberal politician, Lewis Harcourt, died from an overdose of a sleeping draught which he had taken rather than face exposure as a homosexual.[14] In 1931 the vengeful and sanctimonious Bend'or, Duke of Westminster (named after a race-horse), had unmasked his brother-in-law William Lygon, the 7th Earl of Beauchamp, and forced him into exile. The horrified King George V replied, 'I thought that men like that shot themselves'.[15]

Things had begun to change in some parts of society after 1918. In the artistic and literary worlds homosexuality 'came out of the closet and into the drawing room'.[16] It was practised by men and women more openly in the arts, high society, politics and journalism, and at the universities of Oxford and Cambridge. 'Everybody was queer at Oxford in those days!' the poet John Betjeman later declared about male homosexuality on the radio with wild exaggeration that nevertheless had some truth in it.[17] Waiters at The George, a fashionable Oxford restaurant, complained so much about being propositioned by undergraduates that they were replaced by waitresses.[18] Noel Annan, a contemporary at Cambridge, wrote that the feline aesthete in Evelyn Waugh's *Brideshead Revisited*, Anthony Blanche, was no caricature but a 'meticulous portrait' of the 'powdered and painted' university queens who rejoiced in outraging the respectable and baiting the beer-drinking hearties, who responded by dumping the 'pansies' in college fountains.[19]

In reality the number of openly gay undergraduates at Oxford and Cambridge was comparatively few. Most who dabbled with same-sex relationships did not flaunt their homosexuality and married soon after leaving university. But they made an impact that went far beyond their limited student experiences. Openly showing their homosexuality was a statement of rebellion. For those on the left the gay poets Auden and Isherwood were heroes. According to the journalist Goronwy Rees, a Marxist who later spied briefly for the Soviet Union, being able to admit to their homosexuality 'was very largely the particular form which the revolt of the young took at the universities at that time'.[20]

Homosexuality between consenting male adults did not become legal until the Sexual Offences Act of 1967. In the protected world of society, the arts and the universities in 1936 few suffered persecution or the agonies of concealment that they knew to be the common lot of most gay people. For those outside those privileged milieux, being homosexual was often a life of torment, loneliness and risk. In the summer that year Goronwy Rees made an appeal for a more tolerant approach to sexual freedom. 'Some forms of that freedom', he told the generally conservative readers of *The Spectator* magazine, 'may give greater prospects of human happiness and goodness than the tyranny of a rigid and conventional morality.'[21] But that tyranny still held sway for most.

David Strain was a 39-year-old Protestant who ran a successful family shop in Belfast. He lived comfortably and respectably in the suburb of Upper Galwally with his widowed mother. Strain's life mirrored the growing prosperity of millions at the time. His draper's business was doing well, and he had just bought a car and one of the new gadgets, a vacuum cleaner. He was one of thousands who had enjoyed the displays at the Ideal Home Exhibition that spring. Like millions, he went to the cinema two or three times a week to enjoy the latest features and kept in touch with world events through the newsreels and wireless. He spent his time looking after the business, going to church, where he was an elder, keeping up his house, his car and a small nearby cottage in the countryside, and – above all – searching for what he longed for most – the love of another man. David Strain kept a very personal diary that year in which he revealed a world that was usually hidden from view.

He was a romantic and thoughtful man, who loved books and music. He often went to lectures on subjects such as 'How to Look at Pictures', by Mr Horace Skipp. As he listened, he was keen to find the slightest innuendo. 'Mr Skipp struck me as being the incarnation of Oscar Wilde!' Strain wrote in his diary in February. 'He had not lectured for 10 minutes untill [*sic*] he gave a quotation from Oscar! – and then later Pater!' Strain was high-minded, influenced by the Victorian idealism and romanticism of his two heroes Walter Pater and Oscar Wilde. Like them, he worshipped young men. He saw his longing as a superior love, an ideal exemplified by Christ and his disciples.

When he went to church and heard the vicar preach on Jesus' question to Simon Peter, 'Simon lovest thou me?', the priest explained that Christ used 'the Greek word, meaning love in the spiritual sense'. For David this was a moment of insight, 'as it is really spiritual love I have been seeking for years and cannot find. I believe that spiritual love is only possible between two men, and not between man and woman because sex intervenes.'[22] His conception may have been high-minded and divorced from the physical. But the reality, as his diary reveals, was a constant longing for the friendship and love of a young man, with physical desire never far away.

Ulster at that time was the region of the United Kingdom least tolerant of homosexuality. The Presbyterian Protestants of the six counties looked on sodomy as a sin that cried to heaven for vengeance. It was a view shared by the Roman Catholic community. Those who were caught were treated with the full force of the law. Nonetheless, as David Strain's diaries show, there was an active gay scene in Belfast in 1936, with young men promoting themselves through contacts (in the case of Strain, his barber), through advertisements 'seeking friendship' in the newspapers and by hanging round in cafés and bars and on street corners. While relations with men from a similar background and class at this time would have been almost impossible, friendships and sex between older men and working-class boys took place with less risk. For the working-class youth they brought cash and were often a passing phase before marriage and respectability.[23] For the older middle-class men they gave temporary satisfaction and for some, such as David Strain, companionship.

In places such as Ulster, a world away from metropolitan London, homosexuality was as unmentionable in polite society as it had been in Victorian times. Most women knew little or nothing about it. This meant that men like Strain could cruise for boys without being obvious. He never once mentions in his diaries a great dread of discovery, or much sense of social disapproval, although he did take exception to insulting remarks about 'pansies'.

In the spring of 1936 things were not going too well for him. The kind and helpful young man John, who worked for him as a gofer at the family's draper's shop, had announced that he had been diagnosed with a weak heart. He had been ordered by his doctor to take some months off to recuperate. David was suspicious, believing the heart problem to be no more than a trumped-up excuse for John to stay at home and take advantage of the 15s. a week national health insurance that he would receive. But more than that, he had developed an unrequited love for the nineteen-year-old Catholic boy.

The fact that John was a Catholic and he a Protestant in that divided province caused some soul-searching – 'a kind of doubtfulness . . . all due to the reason of his being a Roman Catholic, & consequently being disloyal to his country'[24] – but David's attraction to the young man soon got the better of any sectarian misgivings. He longed for him to come back to work. At the same time his mind was clouded by suspicions. He felt 'a kind of rebellion rising up in me against John'; he was resentful of his absence but desperate for his return. In the meantime he spent his days on the look-out for somebody who might replace him as the object of his adoration.

On Wednesday 11 March he watched a circus procession of elephants pass the shop on their way to a performance at the Opera House. It was not the elephants that excited his attention but the youth in charge: 'the very epitome of youthful loveliness and freedom – what would I not give to have the unstinting love of such a youth!' That night, David wrote in his diary, he had a 'really wonderful dream of a most pleasing youth who expressed his love for me and kissed me – a wonderful kiss, I could have died in the glory of it, strange my kisses have been in dreams, and never from a girl!' He was quick to add that the kiss was a kiss not of lust but of love. 'I felt his lips on mine all day – really wonderful.' He telephoned the circus company to try to find the name of the young elephant trainer but dared not take it any further.[25] The reality was bleak. He could not get him out his mind, and he continued to be plagued by nagging doubts that John was a malingerer 'pandering to the doctor' to get the health insurance. In the end he could bear it no longer and decided to call on John at his home.

For a middle-class Protestant man to go into a Catholic working-class area of Belfast was most unusual, and to go into the house of an young employee almost unheard of. But the desire to see the young man was too strong for David. On Saturday 28 March he went to see John in his house off the Falls Road. It was the poorest house David had ever been in, of 'the kitchen type', its ground floor comprising only that one room. John's father opened the door, recognized the unannounced visitor and asked him in. The radio was blaring in the background. He took David upstairs, where his son John was in bed reading. 'He was quite surprised to see me. He had on his knitted pullover, and blue shirt, and evidently was conscious that he had not pyjamas or a night shirt on, because he remarked – "I put this on as I thought it would be warmer!"' David was at first suspicious. No pyjamas might be a sign of malingering, but any doubts were soon allayed. The young man was clearly unwell.

Throughout the visit John's father hovered in the bedroom 'chatting and talking', preventing any intimate conversation, save once, when he went downstairs to let his mother in. David took the opportunity of his absence to ask his employee whether he intended to return to work, to which he answered 'yes certainly'. David replied, trying to allay any suspicions that his visit might have aroused, 'I wanted to make sure of that, that is one of the reasons I came along'. John's father then returned with his mother and two sisters, who crowded into the room to see the strange visitor. After some polite talk David made his excuses and left. On the way home he reflected on the poverty of John's house. It was not at all like the other 'kitchen house' he had visited, which belonged to an odd-job man on the Shankill who looked after his father's grave, 'but then, it is a protestant house'.

The visit seems to have cleared his mind. The next few days were passed in his usual way with work, trips to the cinema and pottering about in his hut in the country. Seeing John, clearly ill in bed in the poverty of his own home, was a dose of cold reality. It compounded his loneliness. On 9 April he wrote, 'am feeling absolutely wretched and alone – John's absence has a lot to do with it, although I have added a lot to his worth in my imagination'.

Instead of fretting about John, David decided to try to find a companion by looking in the small ads of the newspaper, something he did several times that year. On Friday 10 April he arranged to meet a young man who 'wanted a friend' at the entrance to the YMCA. But when he got there, at nine in the evening, he was shocked to find a 'fellow I met some time before at the Queen's Arcade – not at all a taking kind of fellow'. Feeling 'a bit of a rotter', he walked past without stopping and took a tram home, once more, 'feeling absolutely wretched'.

David Strain's life now returned to its usual loneliness and longing. After several failed attempts to find a companion, John became once more the object of his unrequited desire. The choice he faced was the same as that for many gay men in 1936 – risk or misery – and he chose misery. At the end of May he confided in his diary:

> feeling absolutely desperate at times and wondering how I can stand it – how half my life has passed away and yet I have never known or had a moments real love . . . never one to say to me – 'I love you' or put themselves in my way as I do for others.[26]

Later in the year he became aware of the King's relationship with a divorced woman. At first he was censorious, but then he considered Edward's challenge to convention from his own point of view and concluded 'I cannot blame him'. If David were granted similar freedom, in his case to meet 'a boy I loved, and of whose love I was assured', he dreamed, 'I would give up all – even the promise of eternal life'.

David Strain was condemned to loneliness in 1936 by the fact of his homosexuality. The King came up against a wall of hostility from the establishment when he attempted to defy conventional morality. But cracks in the solid edifice were beginning to appear. In the summer William Lygon, the 7th Earl of Beauchamp, exiled for his homosexuality, was devastated by the death of his son Hugh, who had fallen from a car in Germany and fractured his skull. Lygon, grief-struck, was determined to return to the family seat, Madresfield, for the funeral. He had once before attempted to come back to his homeland but had been stopped at Dover by immigration officials, who prevented him from disembarking from the cross-Channel ferry. This time he was more fortunate. Through the intervention of the press magnate Lord Beaverbrook, the Home Secretary agreed to the lifting of the arrest warrant and Beauchamp was able to attend the funeral.[27] Later the warrant was annulled. It was a small shift, and a sign that, after the death of George V, things were beginning to change.

II

Mrs Baldwin delivers

'I'M DONE FOR, Lyd. I'm in for it. I'm going to have another. I've taken stuff to stop it and half-killed myself, but it's no good.'[1] So spoke Annie Holly in Winifred Holtby's novel *South Riding*. Mrs Holly knew that the worst was inevitable. Without access to contraception she had been unable to avoid becoming pregnant with her eighth child. It was a death sentence. Winifred Holtby's novel, published in early 1936, may have been a piece of feminist fiction, but it deliberately mirrored the real world. The high rate of maternal mortality was a national disgrace. It was the result of numerous causes, including a moral attitude to women and conception that contributed to their suffering and which had much in common with the general outlook on homosexuality that prevailed at the time. In England and Wales four women in every 1,000 lost their lives in childbirth every year.[2] (Today the rate in Britain is less than one in 10,000.[3]) Hans Singer had calculated during his researches for *Men without Work* that 3,200 such deaths in 1936 could be linked to unemployment, a shocking figure.[4] But maternal mortality was not confined to the poor alone; middle-class women suffered high rates of death too. Having a baby was a fearful prospect for all, and few people were untouched by the loss of a friend or loved one in childbirth.[5] Holtby, a feminist writer, used her last novel to draw attention to the scandal.

The rate of maternal mortality in the distressed areas of south Wales was much higher than the national average, at seven women in every thousand.[6] The reasons for this were poorly understood at the time and there was a lack of effective treatment for puerperal fever, the infection that was often the immediate cause of death. The risk of infection was often aggravated by poor hygiene. Margaret Lloyd witnessed the effects of the high rates of death suffered by pregnant women as a child growing up in Merthyr in 1936. Her grandmother, who lived next door, was a 'handywoman', a woman who attended mothers during childbirth but had no formal qualifications in midwifery. Margaret herself grew up to become a nurse and learned a great deal about the travails of childbirth from observing her grandmother at work. Without easy access to contraception, she remembered, 'many women were just too fertile. They were a machine unfortunately for giving birth. A woman would start at a good level of health. After the first child it would be quite good, the second less good, and then health deteriorated further each time.' The result of multiple childbirths was frequently chronic ill health and, too often, the early death of the mother.

Margaret Lloyd was an only child. In an area of very high unemployment she was fortunate. Her father was self-employed and paid his National Insurance contributions. As was usual, her mother stayed at home and looked after her. Margaret noticed at school that it was the children from the larger families that tended to be the poorest and have unemployed fathers: '90 per cent of large families had unemployed parents. They were means tested and not happy about it.' Although contraception was not readily available, it was becoming more widespread, thanks to the work of the Marie Stopes clinics. Whether or not contraception was accessible, however, many married couples across Britain were using some method to prevent pregnancy.[7] As a result families were declining in size, leading to widespread fears of a shrinking population. Eugenicists warned of a decline in the country's human stock, as the families with many children tended to be from the poorer working class, as Margaret Lloyd had realized.[8] One of the motivations behind Marie Stopes's publicizing of the benefits of contraception was a eugenicist belief in the necessity of limiting poor quality offspring of the working class.[9]

Despite Stopes's efforts, there were still many large families in solidly working-class towns and villages of south Wales, and across the country in the poorer districts. Margery Spring Rice, the pioneering social reformer, studied the lives of 1,250 mothers in poorer areas during the years between 1933 and 1939 for her book *Working-Class Wives*.[10] Alongside the poverty and hardship, she drew attention to the number of pregnancies the women endured. Nearly five was the average, but a third of those she studied had six or more confinements, which led to large families, despite the high rate of infant mortality (in every 1,000 births, 50.6 were dead before the age of one, compared with 5 today[11]). Only half of the poorer families she researched used any form of birth control.[12]

Lucy Thomas was a midwife living in the village of Blaencwm in the Rhondda Valley, close to Merthyr. In 1936, aged forty-six, she had twenty years' experience of walking through the valley to attend to women in labour. 'The houses had candles and the old oil lamps', she remembered later. 'People were having families then. They were having their eights, nines and tens and fifteens some of them – what was sent them, not what they ordered, like it is today.'[13] Her experience of large families was typical of the poorer parts of Britain. Margery Spring Rice found numerous examples of the hardship mothers of many children faced across the country. In east London, for example, 'Mrs E. R. of Bethnal Green' had thirteen children. She and her husband lived with eleven of them in a flat consisting of three rooms and a kitchen. Another was 'Mrs B. W. of Croydon', thirty-eight years old with a husband and nine children, all living at home in a small cottage of four rooms and a scullery. (All of those in Spring Rice's survey would have had outside lavatories, often no more than primitive ash pits.) She had 24s. a week (about £44.50 today) after paying the rent (which was 18s.), with which 'to feed, clothe and warm her family . . . She is generally twelve hours on her feet'. In Scotland a not untypical case was 'Mrs MacN. of Glasgow', who lived in one room and a kitchen with her husband, an unemployed carter, and eight children. She was thirty-seven and had been through fourteen pregnancies, which included four children who had died and two miscarriages.

> She gets up at 6 and goes to bed at 10. Her leisure consists of '15 minutes round the block with baby till he goes to sleep; 15 minutes for messages at 2pm. Club gymnasium on Tuesday, 45 minutes, and

sewing class Thursday one hour or so'. Her diet was described as mostly porridge, milk and vegetable soups.[14]

When the baby died in childbirth, Margaret Lloyd remembered, although a cause of grief, it was often a relief for the overburdened mother.[15]

Among Margaret Lloyd's neighbours in Merthyr was a family of fifteen children. The mother had died in childbirth, and the father had then married his sister-in-law, a common recourse, she remembered, of the widower with a large family.[16] If a close relative could not be found to move in and look after the children, the oldest child usually took on the role of the principal carer. This was the case with another of Margaret Lloyd's neighbours. 'My friends, there were four of them, and when the mother died the older boy went to live with an aunt and never came back home. The others just looked after themselves', she recalled. For a single child brought up by a caring mother, going round to visit this neighbour's house was a taste of freedom.

> We could do as we liked. Because there was no mother the house was pretty bare with little furniture. We children could go and play with no mother to control and no father to bother as he was at work. It was fun for us but a matter of sadness, really.

Childbirth for the poorer classes was then a basic affair. Very few women went into hospital, and doctors were rarely called on. As Margaret Lloyd said: 'You had to pay for a doctor, so if you could not afford to pay, you did not send for one.' For the vast majority there was no ante-natal care. When women became pregnant, they got on with life as far as possible until they went into labour, when they called on the services of a midwife such as Lucy Thomas or, failing that, a local 'handywoman' such as Margaret Lloyd's grandmother. Lucy Thomas would charge for her services.

> I got ten shillings for my work. You went ten days and three nights, for free on the first night. And of course, if there was anything wrong it wouldn't be long before they were fetching you! . . . If you couldn't pay I'd say: 'Never mind, pay for the next one'. That was the life, the closeness of the people.[17]

Many were unable to pay because their right to some limited maternity benefit had lapsed when their husbands lost their jobs and ceased to pay National Insurance contributions.[18] This in turn reduced the salaries of midwives and discouraged young women from entering the profession.

If the mother's resistance was low, owing to poor nutrition or general ill health, she could be too weak to fight the deadly infection that might follow childbirth.[19] Maternity nurses could do nothing in the face of puerperal fever. By the time the doctor was called, it was often too late. The risk of mothers dying following childbirth was higher in 1936 than when Queen Victoria came to the throne a century earlier.[20]

Men dominated medicine. The high levels of maternal mortality may have arisen partly because obstetrics had not been a very popular field of study in a male-dominated profession. But things were changing. In 1936 an informal coalition of left and right came together to fight for a change in the way that women of all classes were treated in childbirth. The champion of the campaign was Lucy Baldwin, the wife of the Prime Minister. Mrs Baldwin would never have regarded herself as a feminist, yet she was – in her own way – a quiet revolutionary. At Number 10 she became the first Prime Minister's wife to take an active role in national affairs, writing letters to ministers, advising her husband on Cabinet appointments and supporting him when he came close to breakdown.

Lucy Baldwin was not a follower of fashion. Like Queen Mary, she refused to move with the times, wearing a choice of outfits that was sometimes downright bizarre, a curious *mélange* of Victorian and Edwardian styles. She set these off with an idiosyncratic choice of hats. One commentator described them as 'more surrealist than Hans Arp's paintings'.[21] Mrs Baldwin was also a cricketer and joined the White Heather Club, the only all-women's team in the country.[22] When she became too old to play, she regularly attended Worcestershire matches, and went to Lord's for the Tests. For half a century she kept a journal of events in her busy life with comments, scrawled illegibly in tiny black engagement diaries.

Although poles apart from Edith Londonderry in manner and

style, Mrs Baldwin shared with the powerful political hostess an absolute determination to advance her husband in his political career.
Stanley Baldwin relied on her for the vigour and drive that he himself
so often lacked. Deeply religious, she was thought by many to be
responsible for the Prime Minister's better side.

Since 1928 she had campaigned on behalf of women in childbirth
as one of the founders of the National Birthday Trust Fund, a charity
set up by the wives of Conservative grandees to reduce the rate of
maternal mortality. Maternity in the 1930s was fraught not only with
mortal danger but with pain too. Lucy Baldwin fought to eradicate
both. Even though Queen Victoria had used chloroform after experiencing the pain of her first confinement, the medical profession had
been slow to encourage the use of anaesthetics and analgesics. Using
her position as wife of a senior politician, Mrs Baldwin had campaigned successfully for the introduction of pain relief in childbirth,
principally through gas and air machines, developed by the National
Birthday Trust, in hospitals. These modified dental anaesthetic
devices were called 'Lucy Baldwin Machines' in her honour. By 1936
most private hospitals offered this pain relief to women in labour;
so too did many municipal hospitals, which were largely attended
by working-class mothers.[23] Analgesia was spreading to home births
as well.

Lucy Thomas was the first maternity nurse to qualify in the use of
gas and air in the Rhondda. The machine was too heavy to carry, so
a local man who ran a business selling tea from his car was called
when needed.

> Old Bryan used to say: 'What number you going to? – I'll take you to
> the door' . . . And the doors were all latches – you could just lift it and
> walk in. And Bryan would say: 'But there's light by here. This is it,
> sure-to-be', and I'd reply, 'Look Bryan you can go to the top of the
> street, there'll be a light in every house until this baby's born!' And
> then they'll go to bed when they know everything is secure.[24]

Community spirit made up, in some ways, for the lack of proper
health care. It could not, however, lessen the grief and suffering
caused by the death of the mother.

The effects on the families of such deaths were always, quite naturally, disastrous. Quite apart from the grief, as one expert on childbirth wrote shortly before Lucy Baldwin's campaign got under way, there were a host of other damaging consequences. 'The unexpected loss of the mother is a tragedy to the family. It is not infrequently associated with the death of the infant for whom the maternal life has been sacrificed, and is often followed by the impaired health and nutrition of the remaining children.'[25] Despite the national tragedy that was being played out across the country, Lucy Baldwin's campaign was the object of some ridicule. Nancy Astor, the wise-cracking Conservative MP, rang up Thomas Jones 'and reproduced inimitably a peroration from Mrs B's recent speech at the Queen's Hall to the Party: "I appeal to every one of you to make it your business to be responsible for one expectant mother".' When she met the Prime Minister's wife, she announced, 'When I see the sort of children we're all having I'm for letting the mothers die'.[26] Lucy Baldwin was a formidable figure. She batted away such comments without a second thought. In public, she compared the experience of childbirth to that of the soldiers of the First World War. 'Our women daily, hourly, are "going over the top".' For a woman, giving birth was like 'going into battle – she never knows and the doctor never knows, whether she will come out alive or not'.[27]

As might be expected, in the country as a whole the rate of mortality was highest in the black spots of the distressed areas, but surprisingly the better-off suffered more than the general population. If an expectant mother was born into the professional classes, her risk of death was significantly higher than if she were the daughter of a labourer.[28] The reason, when investigated, became clear. Richer women could afford doctors, a number of whom had little training in obstetrics. The result was that they intervened too readily with forceps (perhaps not properly sterilized) at the first sign of trouble or even just to hurry on the delivery, causing the mother unnecessary injury and the risk of infection, in too many cases swiftly followed by death.[29] This problem was not new in the upper classes. Six queens of England died in childbirth out of forty-six for whom data are available, the highest rate of maternal mortality for a class or group of women ever recorded in Britain.[30]

Death was the major issue, but it was not the only problem arising from childbirth. A number of women, especially working-class mothers, suffered 'an incalculable amount of unreported and too often untreated injury and ill health . . . from pregnancy and labour'.[31] Margery Spring Rice's inquiry into the health of working-class women reflected the disastrous effects of childbirth on many women. A typical case quoted in the survey was a woman from Battersea: 'suffers from "internal trouble" (nature unspecified), which has lasted from the birth of the first child who is 10 years old; she is 31 and has had four children.' The lady suffered 'severe pains in the inside' but had not consulted a doctor, let alone a gynaecologist, and had never had any treatment. 'Such cases', the study concluded, 'can be multiplied by the dozen.'[32]

Fear of childbirth, with the possibility of awful consequences, together with a lack of contraception, prompted many women to seek an abortion when they learned that they were pregnant.[33] They did so despite the high risks to health before the availability of antibiotics and blood transfusions. They also faced the threat of imprisonment. At the time abortion was a crime under the Offences Against the Person Act of 1861. It would remain so until 1967.[34]

The medical profession was generally very censorious of those they suspected of terminating their pregnancies. Margaret Lloyd's mother was taken to hospital in 1936 when she was haemorrhaging.

> The doctor said 'You had an abortion'. He was extremely rude and treated her as if she was a criminal when she came back from the operating theatre. But the doctor then came back and apologized, saying that she had not been pregnant. She never forgot how she was treated and made to feel.[35]

Abortion was taboo. Margaret remembered that the word was never mentioned: 'It was always "miscarriage" never ever "abortion". It was never even discussed.' Nonetheless those who carried out abortions were well known and often respected in the villages for the necessary work they performed. 'People would say "Oh, she is very posh, you know how she makes her money". But not all abortionists knew what they were doing.' Many cases of maternal mortality resulted from botched abortions.[36]

In a divided society the fight to reduce maternal mortality brought together women of all classes and political outlook. It also became a focus of feminist energy. The great victory of the universal franchise had been completed in the 1920s. In 1936 women had full voting rights, they had equal rights in divorce and for the first time their access to the professions was enshrined in law. Many who had been active in the suffrage movement shifted their sights on to the question of childbirth. Edith Londonderry had been a suffragist, despite the disapproval of her rigidly conservative family. Now she backed the cause of the pregnant mother. Many other aristocratic and upper-middle-class Conservative women took up the cause. Lucy Baldwin, while never an overt feminist, used the language of feminism when she attacked men for obstructing the campaign for safer childbirth. 'Prejudice dies hard and I must say that when a man showing prejudice talks to me . . . I have a very great difficulty in preventing myself from telling him what I think. And it is a tremendous thing if a man once hears what a woman thinks of him because he so rarely does.'

Mrs Baldwin was not a figure to be trifled with. The historian Susan Williams records how she reacted when the Minister of Health proposed without a second thought that the pioneering maternity hospital Queen Charlotte's should have an all-male board. 'You know and all men ought to know that their knowledge on this subject is merely second hand', she told the minister bluntly, 'and for too long the question of maternal welfare has been shelved by them and put in the background.'[37] Thanks to her intervention, women took their rightful place on the hospital's board.

Although Lucy Baldwin insisted she was non-political, she was happy to use her influence – approaching ministers, broadcasting from Chequers and sitting on boards – to campaign for the better treatment of women in childbirth. She created a new role for the wife of the premier. Before women had the vote, the Prime Minister's consort was an invisible figure. Now Lucy Baldwin made her position the focus of a campaign on behalf of women's rights. She was a powerful and effective lobbyist, yet she managed – thanks partly to a more quiescent and deferential press, and the charitable nature of her work – to escape political controversy.

The National Birthday Trust Fund, which Lucy Baldwin had helped set up with a number of titled Conservative ladies, including Edith Londonderry, believed the best way to bring down the rate of maternal death was to improve the role of midwives and to improve the nutrition of expectant mothers. In 1934 the NBTF used its connections to set up the Joint Council of Midwifery, an unofficial body that brought together politicians and professional organizations concerned with childbirth. Its purpose was to reform the training and employment of midwives. This made sense, given evidence at the time that pointed to poverty as a major cause of maternal mortality, and given – in the case of the wealthier – the too frequent incompetent intervention of doctors. A year later the Joint Council gave its recommendations. It urged the government to set up a municipal salaried full-time service across the country, which would enable qualified midwives to attend every birth that took place in the home, regardless of the means of the mother. The Ministry of Health accepted the report and used it as a basis for legislation.

Political support had been growing for some time. Women, now half the voting population, had become a political force in their own right. Maternal mortality was a popular cause and was taken up by the government. Most important was the backing of Neville Chamberlain, who, as the keeper of the public purse, was crucial to the passage of any legislation. Like so many at the time, Chamberlain had personal experience of maternal mortality. His family had been scarred by the domestic tragedy of this all too common affliction, not once but twice. Joseph Chamberlain, his father, had lost his first wife in 1863, when she died giving birth to her first son, Austen. Joseph then married his late wife's first cousin Florence. She had four children, including Neville, in five years. She too died in childbirth, delivering her fifth child, in February 1875.

The death of two mothers had a devastating impact on the family. Joseph lost all pleasure in life, turned away from his children and buried himself in public work. Neville grew up a repressed and tight-lipped character, but the death of his mother had made him a dedicated social reformer and drove him on in politics. He entered public life, he often said, 'to improve the condition of the people'.[38] As minister of health in the 1920s he established a reputation as – in the words of his biographer Robert Self – 'the most effective social reformer of the interwar years', introducing twenty-four measures in five years to improve the conditions of the poor.[39] In 1928 he set up his own committee to look into maternal mortality, which helped lay the groundwork, alongside the National Birthday Trust Fund, for the reform that took place in 1936.[40]

In January 1936 the Prime Minister announced that a bill to establish a national midwives service, to be funded by local government, would be put before Parliament. Under the proposed Midwives Act all maternity cases would, from July 1937, be conducted by a properly qualified midwife, whether working under a local authority or a voluntary service. With the agreement of the Chancellor, the service, costing about £500,000, would be funded by central government.

The bill was largely based on the work of the Joint Council of Midwifery. It had overcome the resistance of some parts of the medical profession to get its proposals before Parliament.[41] Lucy Baldwin, as a member of the Council, had played a key role in pushing the legislation to the front of the government's programme that year. Her husband personally endorsed the bill, telling the House of Commons that maternity and midwives 'had been near his heart for many years'.[42] He urged members to push through the legislation as quickly as possible. They needed little encouragement. Conservatives responded to the call of their leader, and Labour members found the idea of a nationalized medical service in tune with their party's key pledge to provide a universal national health service. The bill also appealed to those who shared the then current obsession with the falling birth-rate and the declining physical state of the population. Arthur Greenwood, the pacifist Labour MP, brought up the eugenic advantages of improving the maternity care of mothers: 'what this nation may in future lack in numbers, it ought to be the aim of statesmanship to make up in quality. That has a very distinct bearing upon this problem of maternal well-being.'[43]

The bill became law in July 1936. In the House of Commons the campaigning independent MP Eleanor Rathbone praised all those who had campaigned for it, and 'none more than the lady who is the wife of the head of the Government, and whose unfailing and patient interest in the welfare of the mother has done so much to stimulate interest in this question'. For Lucy Baldwin it was indeed a personal triumph, but outside Parliament she received little credit. Many others had also been involved in the battle, and she did not seek the limelight.

The legislation that year was the government's sole piece of effective social reform.[44] Neville Chamberlain wanted to do more as the economy strengthened. But, as the international situation worsened, available resources had to be diverted to defence. It was a personal tragedy. He recalled on his death-bed that the demands of rearmament had robbed him of the opportunity to 'enter on a new era of social improvement'.[45] The Midwives Act was, at least, one lasting achievement.

Coincidentally, at the same time as the act was passed, the rate of maternal death had started a rapid fall. It was a decline that continued for many years, owing to the arrival of a range of drugs that were effective in treating infections such as puerperal sepsis.[46] There is no doubt that the improvement in maternity care as a result of improvements in midwifery also had an impact.[47] On a national basis the standard of care was greatly improved. Although women who could afford the fee were expected to pay 30s. for having a baby, those who could not pay received the service free of charge.

The irony was that a Conservative woman, the wife of a Tory Prime Minister, had herself been midwife to a piece of legislation that helped to give birth to the National Health Service twelve years later. There is a myth that the NHS sprang to life fully formed in 1948 with the creation of the welfare state. This is not the case. Thanks to Chamberlain's reforms of the 1920s, the foundations were already well in place. The ideas that underpinned the creation of a universal health service had evolved from the experience of the 1930s: none more so than the Midwives Act of 1936, which enshrined in law the right of mothers to maternity care. As Susan Williams has pointed out, 'It was the first time that the principles of a state medical service had been put into effect.'[48] Whether Lucy Baldwin would have approved of the socialist creation that arose in part from her fight for the universal provision of maternity care is not known. She died in 1945, when her husband's reputation was at its lowest and when her work for mothers in labour was, amid the cataclysm of the Second World War, largely forgotten.

12

The awful weight of war

LATE ONE SUMMER'S night a bent figure in clerical garb might be seen wheezing and limping past the rats and rubbish down a narrow alleyway just off St Paul's Cathedral, to his home. Since six that morning, despite his weak heart and chronic asthma, he had preached three or four sermons, taken or assisted at three services, christened a baby, twice visited the sick in Charing Cross Hospital, attended to down-and-outs in the crypt of St Martin-in-the Fields (the church next to Trafalgar Square, which he had galvanized) and broadcast on the BBC – all in one day. He carried with him a box, out of which he occasionally pulled a rubber mask that he clamped to his face, inhaling deeply to relieve his breathlessness. Once inside the empty house, he went upstairs to start writing. The light in his room was still burning at four o'clock in the morning. He was Canon Hugh Richard Lawrie Sheppard, or Dick, as he was almost universally known, the peace campaigner and one of the most charismatic, charming and dynamic personalities of his age.

More than 100,000 men had heeded Sheppard's call, made two years earlier, and pledged themselves to peace: 'We renounce war and never again directly or indirectly, will we support or sanction another.' His Peace Pledge Union, formally established in May 1936, represented the voice of absolute pacifism in the face of the looming catastrophe of another war. It was a voice which, in that year, had enormous resonance but faced insuperable difficulties. Dick Sheppard was the tragic personification of its achievement and of its failure.

Had such a diagnosis been available in 1936, Sheppard might have been seen to be suffering from a bi-polar condition. In public and among friends he was a dynamic and compelling presence. He had the gift of empathy. Vera Brittain called him, truthfully, 'one of the most popular human beings ever to tread London's pavements'.[1] Sybille Bedford, the friend and biographer of Aldous Huxley, Sheppard's associate in the peace movement, described him as 'a man overflowing with the love of his fellows, reckless in the expenditure of himself, orator, organizer, legend in his own life-time, a man who could make contact with every human he met'.[2] But in private, alone and away from the sustenance of company, Dick was prone to profound depression and agonizing self-doubt. Physically he was unequal to the stresses he imposed on his stricken body.

There was, to many of those who met him, unquestionably something saintly about him. Once, when he was returning home late from a party (he was a keen socialite), Dick stopped to look in on his church's crypt. He had converted the cellars of St Martin-in-the-Fields, where he was vicar, into a shelter for the homeless. There he found a young girl in tears. She explained that she had quarrelled with her parents, who had thrown her out of their home and having travelled from the north of England to London, she was now wandering the streets, homeless and homesick. Sensing that the situation was not hopeless, Dick scooped up the girl, took her to King's Cross and, still in evening dress, travelled with her on the last train to her northern city. The next morning the girls' astonished parents opened the door to find their daughter standing with the small, slightly bedraggled but persuasive priest. There was a reconciliation. Dick returned to London, exhausted but happy.[3]

Dick was different from most priests of the time. Informal and charismatic, he packed churches all over the country whenever he preached, and he had a huge following for his radio broadcasts. He was a modernizer who wanted to change the Church and make it less stuffy and establishmentarian. This made him enemies who mistrusted his showiness and regarded him as a self-publicist. Dick's promotion of absolute pacifism also troubled his colleagues in the Church. Many hated the way he used stunts in a political cause. When he walked the streets of London wearing sandwich boards to promote an open-air peace meeting, they were scandalized.[4] Cosmo Lang, with a churchman's casuistry, called him 'a very real and lovable problem'.[5] Dick's leadership of the peace movement was also an irritant to the National Government, wrestling as it was with the practicalities of how to deal with Hitler and Mussolini. 'These Dick Sheppard pacifists are a menace', Robert Bernays complained in his diary.[6]

Canon Dick Sheppard was without question the leading pacifist of his time. Two years before he had sent a letter to the *Manchester Guardian* and other newspapers in which he wrote that it was essential to find out whether or not 'the majority of thoughtful men in this country are convinced that war of any kind or for any cause, is not only a denial of Christianity, but a crime against humanity which is not to be permitted by civilised people'.[7] At the end of the letter he asked in a 'Peace Appeal to Men' (not women, on the rather curious basis that they were already actively involved in the peace movement and 'it seems high time . . . that men should throw their weight behind the scales of war') to send him a postcard with the simple statement 'I renounce War and never again, directly or indirectly, will I support or sanction another'.

For the first two days there was no response. On the third the village postmaster called to inquire whether there would be anybody at home to receive the postcards that had arrived.[8] Van-loads followed, crammed with sacks brimming with cards that cascaded over the floor when delivered.[9] In a few weeks 30,000 men replied, taking the pledge to renounce war. In the following months over 100,000 added their signatures. The Dick Sheppard Peace Pledge Movement was born.

Dick Sheppard was an extreme pacifist, opposed to war in all circumstances and at any cost. In 1936 his unshakable views were shared by the many thousands of men and women who took the pledge. Alongside these absolute pacifists there were also millions who opposed Britain ever going to war again on its own, placing their faith in the power of the League of Nations to stop individual nations misbehaving. Anti-war sentiment at the time crossed all class, party, gender and national lines and was almost universal.[10] In the previous year the League of Nations Union, a voluntary organization in Britain devoted to promoting the League, had organized a 'peace ballot'. The sheer numbers who called for peace in the unofficial vote showed the depth of feeling across the nation. Twelve million adult voters, nearly a quarter of the population, took part, the overwhelming majority expressing their support for the League.[11] Of these just over 5 million favoured absolute pacifism. It was little wonder that, during the 1935 general election campaign, Baldwin promised voters that there would be no great armaments.[12] He needed the pacifist vote.

As the world seemed to move inexorably towards another conflict in 1936, hatred of war, if anything, grew even stronger, energized by the worsening international situation, the development of new and terrible technologies, and by the collective memory of the First World War. That cataclysmic conflict was still fresh in the minds of all who had been through it, from the man and woman in the street, through politicians, statesmen and churchmen to the King. It had touched every family in the country and bitten into every soul. There were countless hundreds who cherished the memories of a loved one who had been killed or nursed a veteran suffering life-destroying injuries. With three-quarters of a million British men killed in the conflict, many women had been widowed and many others faced a life of spinsterhood. As one of Dick Sheppard's supporters wrote: 'In this matter I have become quite primitive. I saw the best of my family and my husband's family perish – my husband's health seriously impaired.'[13]

All believed that the country had been robbed of the flower of a generation, and all were against war. Stanley Baldwin expressed the sentiment of the nation in 1936 when he said: 'If the dead could come back to life today, there would be no war, they would never let the younger generation taste what they did . . . we are still finding and burying the bodies of those who fell twenty years ago.'[14] He was, like so many, and as his son said, 'rather obsessed' with the First World War and the obligations on those who were left.[15] His colleague Neville Chamberlain, who had also been too old to fight, had lost his cousin and closest friend Norman at the Battle of Cambrai in 1917. This death devastated him, turning him for ever against war and driving his desire for appeasement.

The anti-war movement was a broad church and extended even to Winston Churchill. In 1936 – cynically jumping, some thought, on the back of a populist bandwagon – he made common cause (while always arguing for rearmament) with the pacifists who supported a strengthened League of Nations.[16] He joined pressure groups and attended rallies. He wrote a speech for the King in July describing 'the awful weight of war with all its horrors'.[17]

Edward VIII was completely in tune with the sentiment that Churchill had expressed for him. In the First World War he had come as close to the trenches as the authorities would allow. His frustration that he was not permitted to go into battle with his comrades remained with him long afterwards, a lingering source of guilt and resentment. For years he worked for the welfare of ex-servicemen. Shortly before becoming King he had personally endorsed a British Legion visit of British veterans of the First World War to Nazi Germany in the hope of furthering understanding and reconciliation. His father criticized him for it, but the cause of peace was more important to Edward than royal reticence.

For Dick Sheppard too the First World War was the most important motivating force behind his pacifism. In 1914 he had served briefly as a hospital chaplain in France, where he witnessed the death and suffering of the ordinary soldiers at first hand. On his thirty-fourth birthday, shortly after arriving in France, he knelt beside a dying man whose wife was expecting a baby: 'he died thanking God that if the child was a boy, he would never have to go through the hell of war.' Sheppard wrote that the young soldier had believed his sacrifice was made in a just cause: the war to end all wars. 'Innumerable others also believed it and died, as he died, at least happy in the thought that their sons would be spared Calvary.'[18] It seemed unthinkable to the British in 1936 that, only eighteen years after the end of the First World War, another generation would be forced to pick up the cross once more.

But the unthinkable was unfolding in front of them in 1936. Hitler's daring move into the Rhineland that March was a blow for those who put their faith in international treaties and the League of Nations to preserve peace. Many considered Mussolini's aggression, with his dreams of a new Roman Empire in Africa, even more alarming. The League had been powerless to prevent the Fascist dictator's attack on Abyssinia and could only respond with condemnation and the threat of sanctions. The British and French governments had no desire to push Italy into Hitler's camp and at first secretly proposed to appease Mussolini by handing him a large part of Abyssinia. The offer was withdrawn after it was leaked to the press and led to a public outcry. The allies then shuffled back to the League, agreeing to impose half-hearted sanctions. The British refused point-blank to do the two things that would have been effective against Mussolini: to close the Suez Canal to Italian shipping and to cut his access to oil.

To the Foreign Office and anti-Nazi politicians the prospect of a Hitler–Mussolini pact in Europe was far worse than the Italian occupation of a far-off country in Africa. While Churchill fulminated against Hitler, he kept quiet about Mussolini. All sides of the political spectrum agreed that Italy had to be appeased. Then, in the spring of 1936, after a faltering Italian military campaign against the spear-carrying but determined Abyssinian army, Mussolini resorted to barbarism to gain victory.

In February and March 1936 the British press carried several stories that the Italian air force had used mustard gas bombs against the Abyssinian population. At first the Foreign Office dismissed the reports as hearsay, but on 3 April *The Times* reported that the Red Cross confirmed that it had treated numerous victims of gas attacks. In March, British medical teams said that they too had cared for patients with gas injuries. The newspaper quoted the Emperor of Abyssinia, Haile Selassie: 'he cannot sleep at night for misery at the screaming and groaning of his fighting men and country people who have been burned inside and out by gas.'[19]

The Italian air force had bombed indiscriminately, attacking hospitals and Red Cross facilities. Three types of gas were used: yperite, arsine and phosgene, all banned under the 1925 Geneva Protocols, to which Italy was a signatory. The effects of these weapons were abominable, as one of the Abyssinian military chiefs, Ras Imru, described how 'a hundred or so of my men who had been splashed with the mysterious fluid began to scream in agony as blisters broke out on their bare feet, their hands, their faces.' The victims were not only Abyssinian soldiers; the Italians bombed peasants tending their cattle at water-holes, and attacked nearby villages. When the victims rushed to water to cool their burns, they 'fell contorted on the banks and writhed in agony that lasted for hours until they died'.[20]

When news of the Italian atrocities reached Britain, the reaction was one of horror. *The Spectator* denounced 'the unspeakable brutality against defenceless negroes of an instrument diabolical in its capacity for inflicting agony and disablement'.[21] But, given the mood of the time, there was no stomach for confronting Italy. Instead the majority put its faith in collective action by the League of Nations, which – deprived of teeth by Britain and France – could only stand on the sidelines impotently wringing its collective hands.

In frustration Dick Sheppard rang Kingsley Martin, the editor of the *New Statesman*, to propose that a 'peace army' should assemble at the headquarters of the League of Nations in Geneva to protest against the Italians. Martin dismissed this as futile. He suggested instead that the peace army go to Rome, posing as tourists before revealing themselves as protesters outside the Duce's palazzo. Nothing came of that idea either.[22] The Peace Movement may have had many members, but in the face of a determined dictator such as Mussolini it had no practical solutions. 'Dear Lord,' wailed Dick Sheppard, 'what *can* be done?'[23]

On Saturday 9 May a triumphant Duce announced the fall of the Abyssinian capital, Addis Ababa, to cheering crowds in Rome. The author and journalist Rose Macaulay was visiting Italy at the time. She was quick to condemn Mussolini but, like many of her fellow pacifists in Britain, expressed guilty relief that there was no war. She called the outcome 'peace with ignominy',[24] ironically pre-figuring Neville Chamberlain's words after the Munich agreement with Hitler two years later.

Meanwhile the fugitive Emperor of Abyssinia, the Negus Haile Selassie, arrived in Britain on 3 June. The government reluctantly granted him asylum. It was a small concession to a ruler for whom the British had done nothing at all in the face of unprovoked aggression by a fellow member of the League of Nations. A diminutive figure, as though from another age, the Negus was an object of curiosity to the public, and of embarrassment to the British government. The King refused to pay him a courtesy visit and sent his brother the Duke of Gloucester instead. When Edward was told that meeting the deposed ruler would be a popular move, he responded 'Popular with whom? Certainly not the Italians.'[25] He agreed that nothing should be done to drive Mussolini into Hitler's arms. In the face of the overwhelming tide of appeasement the Bishop of Durham lamented, 'A larger view sees no hope of lasting peace in such a pusillanimous condonation of tyranny'.[26]

The country may have had no stomach for war, but conflict appeared to be approaching inexorably. The bombing of Abyssinian tribespeople with chemical weapons provoked fear as much as outrage. Gas, a weapon of mass destruction before the coming of nuclear and biological weapons, had been used to lethal effect in the trenches. Many veterans of the First World War still bore the scars. Now it had been deployed against civilians. It was a terrible omen. In *The Times* a Red Cross official described how peasants in an Abyssinian village had been blinded by chlorine, and warned:

> Whither? To-day a few thousand peasants in Wallo will be groping their way down the dark years because of a dictator, whose name they have never heard of, but whose decree of ruthlessness has put out their eyes. Wallo is a long way from Charing Cross – yes, but not for aeroplanes. Whither to-morrow?

Aeroplanes had entered the collective imagination as potent and ambiguous symbols of modernity. Streamlined for speed, their sleek designs influenced the shape of everything from vacuum cleaners to wirelesses. They were at once symbols of advance, of high-speed travel and mass communication but also of the potential annihilation of civilization. The bomber, with all its destructive force, as Stanley Baldwin said, 'will always get through'.[27]

The possibility of an air war that would deliver gas and high explosives to the densely populated cities of Britain, leaving nothing but death and rubble, was a ghastly prospect. The Abyssinian crisis reinforced this pessimism. Reacting to Mussolini's indiscriminate bombing of civilians, Baldwin warned that in a future conflict 'there is to be no limited liability about it for any party that goes into it. It will be every man, woman, and child.' The use of gas added to the sense of foreboding. If Mussolini had used the weapon in Abyssinia, what might happen in Europe? Baldwin voiced the fears of millions when he said, 'Europe, with its cities more densely populated than Abyssinia, may suffer far more, but it is not only that . . . the next war will be the end of civilization in Europe.'[28] The term 'total war' was coined to describe the nature of modern warfare, where the front line would extend into people's homes, bringing destruction and death.

That spring the eleven-year-old schoolboy Paul Vaughan had been to see *Things to Come*, the film that had been publicized at the Ideal Home Exhibition. For an intelligent and impressionable boy the film, with its all too credible vision of a mass bombing raid, 'was a great factor in our fear of war'.[29] At London Films' studios at Denham in Middlesex, the film's producer, Alexander Korda, constructed a huge and realistic set of Wells's 'Everytown' for the opening scenes. It was a contemporary city centre, modelled on London, with a St Paul's Cathedral-like dome towering over the centre, and a large interchange similar to Piccadilly Circus, complete with underground station.

The film opens with crowds out Christmas shopping in the department store of Everytown's West End. Scenes of carol-singing and festivity are juxtaposed with newspaper billboards announcing the coming of war. Soon an air raid begins. Set to the composer Arthur Bliss's pounding militaristic score, the crowds scramble for gas masks, trampling each other as they rush down narrow stairways to the shelter of the tube. Loudspeakers ring out with instructions to take cover, and mobile anti-aircraft guns move into position. As the guns start firing, the bombs fall from unseen aeroplanes. Buildings collapse, cars are overturned, clouds of gas asphyxiate those who survive the blasts and stretcher-bearers in gas masks carry away the dead and injured. In seconds nothing is left but rubble and death. But the war continues; soldiers march forwards, tanks attack and thousands upon thousands of bombers appear over the white cliffs of Dover to continue their raids. Paul Vaughan remembered: 'this rigid pattern of aeroplanes moving across the sky, absolutely in the same relationship with each other. It was enough to scare us.'[30] Britain is left utterly destroyed. Civilization is at an end, and the survivors, plagued by a sickness brought on by chemical weapons, are left at the mercy of a self-appointed bully and mini-dictator, 'the boss'. The film ends with a vision of a Utopian future, on which the Ideal Home Exhibition focused. In Wells's dream bungling politicians are replaced in 2036 by technocrats and scientists who bring a shining world of peace and harmony.

When Hitler saw the scenes of the total destruction of a British city by bombers, he was apparently so impressed that he ordered Goering to show it to all subordinates in the Luftwaffe.[31] Mussolini was less pleased; he took exception to the actor Ralph Richardson's parodying of him as 'the boss' and banned the film. For British audiences *Things to Come* reinforced a general view of an almost inevitable war bringing the end of civilization. John Prichard used to go into school and say to his friends '"Hello cannon fodder!" because that's what we thought we were'.[32] This view had become so widespread in 1936 that Stanley Baldwin called it 'a truism'. The public were gripped by what the historian Richard Overy has called a 'war psychosis', which dominated the public mood.[33] Some believed that society was so sick that war was the only way to cleanse it of its injustices.

George Orwell's novel *Keep the Aspidistra Flying* was published later in the year. Its penniless hero, Gordon Comstock, reflected the mood of alienation from a world of materialism and militarism then prevalent on the left: 'the sense of disintegration, of decay, that is endemic in our time, was strong upon him.' He fantasizes about the destruction of the hated 'money culture' of the new consumerism:

> In imagination he saw them coming now; squadron after squadron, innumerable, darkening the sky like clouds of gnats. With his tongue not quite against his teeth he made a buzzing, bluebottle-on-the-window-pane sound to represent the humming of the aeroplanes. It was a sound which, at the moment, he ardently desired to hear.[34]

The prospect of the total annihilation of human society and culture by bombers was based on an unrealistic and exaggerated view of their capabilities. But peddling this pessimism had its political advantages and was exploited for all its worth by a surprising coalition of pacifists, statesmen and air marshals. The RAF talked up the danger of the bomber to gain the lion's share of the increased defence spending. Politicians of all shades used the threat to justify their policies. Pacifists such as Dick Sheppard spoke in the starkest terms so as to mobilize support and motivate the peace movement.

Later that year Dick Sheppard sent Herbert Hensley Henson, the Bishop of Durham, a pamphlet written by his fellow pacifist the philosopher Bertrand Russell. In the pamphlet Russell had drawn a horrifying picture of the next war and concluded that complete pacifism was the only way forward. The Bishop was sceptical: 'Probably he exaggerates the destructive effect of the new devices for destroying life and property, and underrates the moral resources of the community. In any case his counsels are base, pusillanimous and intolerable.'[35] Few people at the time shared Henson's view that the anti-war cause was 'base, pusillanimous and intolerable'. Even Winston Churchill was prepared to share a platform with the head-in-the-clouds, teetotal Labour MP Philip Noel-Baker,[36] in the joint enterprise of strengthening the League of Nations. But as the months passed and the international picture darkened, the anti-war movement became increasingly divided.

In the spring of 1936 Dick Sheppard changed his movement's name from the Dick Sheppard Peace Pledge Movement to the more simple Peace Pledge Union, saying that his own name 'stank in his nostrils'.[37] Although he was hugely popular, a charismatic preacher and radio broadcaster, Sheppard was criticized as 'self-advertising'. George Bernard Shaw described him as 'an actor! WHAT an actor!'[38] He had an essentially contradictory nature. In public he was always the confident extrovert. In private, he was a self-doubting tortured figure, prone to depression. For some time his marriage had been troubled. His wife, Alison, found that living with a man who was loved by all he met and who loved all he met, who was crippled both physically and mentally, was an unbearable burden. In these final agonizing but exhilarating months of his life she left him to bear the burden on his own.

At first Sheppard tried to put the Peace Pledge Union on a proper footing. He rented an office, opened a bookshop and set up branches throughout the country. On 22 May the Union's formal launch was celebrated with a march from Trafalgar Square to the Albert Hall for a packed prayer meeting. Despite his asthma and weak heart, Sheppard travelled the country speaking wherever and whenever he was invited, to halls overflowing with pacifists. He never stayed the night, preferring to travel home by the last train, and often collapsed exhausted and breathless in the early hours at his lodgings close by St Paul's Cathedral. Sometimes he did not make it home at all but would admit himself instead to Charing Cross Hospital for treatment, before resuming the never-ending round of talks, sermons, services, mass meetings and processions. It was clear that he had taken on too much, and as a result the Union did not run smoothly. 'The thing is all so big and at times so critical', Sheppard admitted in a letter to a fellow pacifist, 'I have been overwhelmed with work which means I have not been on the spot so much as I should have been.'[39]

He became depressed by the lack of support from his fellow Anglicans. Appealing on the radio for aid to the Abyssinian evacuees, he let his feelings get the better of him: 'I cannot understand why professing Christians lack an overwhelming sense of mission – unless they do not believe in their religion.'[40] Such outbursts drew criticism from fellow churchmen. The BBC insisted that he did not preach pacifism on the airwaves. He was called a crank. But to millions he was the living embodiment of their most fervent belief: that war was wrong and had to be stopped.

Dick Sheppard's pacifist motivation was absolutist and, some thought, simplistic. He held that resort to arms was contrary to the teaching of Jesus, and that war was therefore wrong. Like many, he believed that vested interests, 'mental and financial', lay behind the impulse to fight. Although his own pacifism sprang from faith, the movement was open to all, whether believer or atheist. The basis of his own belief, as he confessed in a letter that May to one of his backers, was a little woolly: 'I am blowed if I know exactly where I stand. I am mostly Quaker these days, but Jesus Christ, Man or God (I have never wished to define him) is the hero I would wish to follow.'[41]

For the formal announcement of the Peace Pledge, Dick Sheppard canvassed support from a diverse range of prominent pacifists, few of whom were Christians, 'to help dispel the idea that we are merely emotional and religious'.[42] He recruited a menagerie of sponsors made up of a cross-section of British intellectuals, writers, spiritualists, poets and politicians, who proved very difficult, if not impossible, to corral. Prominent among the celebrities was the tall, slim, stooping and bespectacled novelist Aldous Huxley, once the bright young satirist of *Brave New World*, now an earnest student of geopolitics and mysticism. The militant atheist and former conscientious objector Bertrand Russell also joined. George Lansbury, the former Labour leader, whose Christian pacifism had led him to resign from the party the previous autumn, also became a sponsor. Earlier in the year Lansbury had visited Hitler dressed in his peace campaigner's uniform of woolly jumper, crumpled trousers and sandals, shocking the Führer's entourage.[43] Several well-known writers also committed themselves to the cause of absolute pacifism, including A. A. Milne, the creator of Winnie the Pooh, and the wartime poet Siegfried Sassoon. Old soldiers whose experience of battle had turned them against war were represented by the former soldier turned preacher of peace Brigadier-General Frank Crozier.

Dick Sheppard had at first addressed his appeal to men alone. In 1936, under feminist pressure, he opened the Peace Pledge Union to women and recruited the influential novelist Storm Jameson as a sponsor. Later, Rose Macaulay joined after meeting him at the Union's offices in July. In common with most people who encountered Sheppard, the usually acerbic Macaulay was smitten by his charm. 'I think I have never met a clergyman so genuinely and pleasantly interested in people and their affairs', she told her sister; 'I was there an hour, and alone, but must go again some time, he says and finish discussing Peace.'[44]

Discussing peace was the problem. With such a disparate and strong-minded group of sponsors, producing a coherent manifesto, other than a general statement of pacifism and a hatred of war, was next to impossible. Sheppard became increasingly frustrated as each one of his big beasts wandered into the forest on its own path of eccentric rumination. He would listen and with his preternatural charm would take on the hue of the person speaking. Rose Macaulay remembered him as 'chameleon-like . . . turning a little redder when with communists . . . doubting with the doubtful, certain with the convinced, seeing everyone's point of view at once'.[45] Occasionally a pacifist pontificator would become too much for him to bear. After two hours of attention to one of the grandees, he burst out to a sympathetic friend, 'You know, he's only *just* not a bore!'[46] Sheppard was not an intellectual; 'I've no brains, Middleton', he told his friend and supporter John Middleton Murry.[47] He was, as a result, often at the mercy of the thinkers who came to the cause.

Aldous Huxley was perhaps the most influential intellectual behind the movement that summer. His pacifism was the culmination of a long spiritual journey from humanism to the idea of a spiritual reality of God, 'regarded, and if possible experienced as a psychological fact, present at least potentially in every human being'.[48] He specifically rejected Dick Sheppard's Christian belief in an exclusive deity, arguing that it inevitably led to war.[49] This was hardly a good start. Such was Dick's tolerance, however, that the two men co-existed peaceably despite this fundamental difference in outlook.

Huxley was much influenced by his close friend the author and spiritualist Gerald Heard. This opened him and the Peace Pledge Union to the charge of crankiness. Heard believed it was possible to transform human nature. Influenced by Gandhi and Indian spiritualism, he urged that young men be trained to form an army of non-violent resisters by a programme of meditation and physical exercise.[50] Huxley enthusiastically took up the idea. With Heard he set up the Peace Pledge Union's 'Research and Thinking Committee'. In the summer he produced a pamphlet, *What Are You Going to do About It?*, in which he urged pacifists not just to commit to the pacifist cause but to undergo a wholesale change of lifestyle. He subtitled the essay 'The Case for Constructive Peace', arguing that pacifism should embrace personal morality.

There are men who profess to be pacifists in international politics, but who are tyrants in their families, bullying employers, ruthless and unscrupulous competitors. Such men are not only hypocrites; they are also fools. Constructive Peace must be first of all a personal ethic, a way of life for individuals.[51]

Huxley and Heard's crony Richard Gregg, an American psychologist, put out a pamphlet under the Peace Pledge Union's banner, entitled *Training for Peace: A Programme for Peace Workers*, which put forward a programme that would lead, eventually, to a pacifist consciousness.[52] He counselled group exercises to 'build the pacifist personality', community singing for eleven minutes, a brief period of manual work (knitting for women, spinning for men), a thirty-minute silence during which 'thoughts relevant to pacifism to be written on a piece of paper' and folk dancing to encourage 'harmony of mind'.[53] It was not surprising that some in the movement found this regime, together with Huxley's call for a new ethic, a misguided response to the threat of the Fascist dictators.[54]

The problem was the very nature of pacifism. It had few concrete responses to offer to the looming prospect of war. In the early days of Dick Sheppard's peace movement the idea had been floated of a group of pacifists marching between enemy lines when fighting started but that soon proved unrealistic. In March the idea of demonstrating in Rome had come to nothing. In the summer it was proposed that Sheppard should travel to Germany to preach peace to the Nazis. This too was rejected when concerns were raised about the Gestapo. Instead, he wrote a letter to Hitler, which he also sent to *The Times*. But after George Lansbury's visit earlier that year the German dictator seemed to have had enough of British pacifists. He did not reply. To the concern of many, in the absence of effective action Huxley was the man with ideas. His influence grew stronger, just as the movement seemed to be weakening. Although he hid it, Sheppard became increasingly depressed: 'There are cranks who run in and out of every forward movement, and they get dreadfully in the way', he lamented.[55]

Sheppard was also caught up in a struggle within the broader anti-war movement. As absolute pacifists, his supporters came into conflict with the members of the League of Nations Union, who supported the use of force as a last resort. On a blazing Saturday that June the feminist author and anti-war campaigner Vera Brittain made her way to Dorchester to take part in a Peace Pledge Union rally for peace. *Testament of Youth*, her memoir of personal loss and public service in the First World War, was an international best-seller. Hundreds of thousands in Britain and America empathized with her grief at the death of her fiancé, brother and two friends in the trenches. They were moved by her vivid descriptions of the suffering of the wounded and dying from both sides whom she had nursed. She was much in demand as a speaker. Brittain was a mercurial character, self-centred and demanding. For years she had managed a *ménage à trois* with her husband, the aspirant politician George Catlin, and her great friend since university, the author Winifred Holtby. Holtby's death in September had left her grief-stricken and self-questioning.

After the success of *Testament of Youth* the public saw Vera as a mouthpiece of the revulsion that was felt against war and the general longing for peace. For some time Dick Sheppard had been wooing her as an ideal sponsor of the Peace Pledge Union, but without success. As an active supporter of the League of Nations she had not accepted absolute pacifism. She had turned down several invitations to appear as a public speaker on his platform.[56] Eventually she relented to his repeated requests to speak, agreeing to take part in the mass rally at Dorchester.

The rally was to take place at the ancient Roman amphitheatre of Maumbury Rings, just outside Dorchester. Local branches of the Peace Pledge Union from all over the south and south-west were due to attend. The other speakers, alongside Dick Sheppard, included the celebrated Methodist orator Donald Soper and George Lansbury. As the day approached, Vera's misgivings grew. She was intimidated by the stature of those sharing the platform and was concerned about the speech she had prepared.

In the scorching heat of the summer's day 10,000 pacifists gathered on the grassy stepped embankments of the amphitheatre, some carrying flags and banners, others holding parasols, almost all wearing sensibly brimmed hats. Vera, impeccably turned out as ever, wore a light cotton dress and jacket, with a matching picture hat which she sported jauntily at an angle. The speakers took cover from the beating sun under a large striped umbrella.[57] Later Vera remembered how Dick, as he listened to the speeches, 'inhaled oxygen from a rubber apparatus which he carried to relieve his chronic asthma'.

The speeches got under way, and the voices of the speakers were relayed to the crowd through powerful loudspeakers. The audience was the largest that had ever assembled in Britain for a peace rally. Sheppard, Lansbury and Soper were motivated by their Christian faith, and the atmosphere took on something of the spirit of an evangelical rally. Vera's misgivings turned to panic. She had prepared a 'customary little speech in support of collective security'. Her text was political; those of her fellow speakers 'sprang from the love of God'.[58] She threw away her prepared speech and improvised instead, quoting Bunyan and recalling a visit she had recently made to the memorial town of Verdun, where she had met French First World War veterans. It was, for the thousands of pacifist pilgrims, the biggest disappointment of the afternoon.

Vera was not immediately taken with Dick Sheppard. With her sharp eye for appearances, she noted that he 'even in his canonicals did not look impressive'. Nor did she find him handsome. He was short, balding, broadening in middle age and had a round, lined face, which, when he smiled, gave him the look of a leprechaun. But she was soon drawn to his personality. In the dining car of the train on the way back to London, Dick worked his charm. He had been warned that Vera had a tendency to 'belligerence'[59] (like many pacifists, she relished a good fight) and immediately set about putting her at ease. To the evident shock of a strait-laced female passenger, Dick threw off his coat and rolled up his sleeves, and, looking like 'a tipsy cricketer going home at the end of a too enjoyable afternoon', started telling 'racy' stories as he put the serious business of pacifism behind him. The usually prickly Vera was captivated. Her journey to absolute pacifism had begun.

After the day in Dorchester, Vera and Dick exchanged polite letters of mutual thanks. A few days later she wrote again, asking for the opportunity to talk things over with him.[60] For a while she retained her loyalty to the League of Nations Union and went to a number of their meetings, where, to her horror, members of Dick Sheppard's Peace Pledge Union turned up to heckle her, revealing the deep split that was opening up in the anti-war movement. As she fended off the barracking pacifists, Vera came to an understanding. Only a spiritual revolution bringing about the conversion of humanity to a different ethical plane would suffice. 'For what Dick Sheppard and his friends offered to their fellows was not . . . a policy but a principle – the revolutionary principle put forward and still rejected by the majority of mankind, in the Sermon on the Mount.'[61]

Sheppard's idealism and charm had worked their magic; he had won another convert. A few months later Vera rejected the League and became a sponsor of the Peace Pledge Union. Earlier she reflected to herself, 'I fear War more than Fascism . . . I am sure you can't use Satan to cast out Satan.'[62] How to oppose the evil of the dictators was the dilemma of the time, and her solution, alongside Dick Sheppard's, was to accept that 'though my country go down before the invader, it will find in non-violent resistance to evil the final answer to occupation and war. By accepting crucifixion my nation and I will return through suffering to a new security.'[63] With the benefit of hindsight the idea of accepting crucifixion at the hands of the Nazis seems hopelessly naïve. At the time many thought so too, as Vera's husband, George Catlin, gently pointed out in a letter: 'In measurable time you will not convert to it the majority of this great nation and therefore (whatever one's private view) it will not, as a public fact, avert war.'[64]

Just as Vera Brittain was embarking on the journey to absolute pacifism, others were going in the opposite direction. That summer an event took place that was to shake the remaining few optimists, if there were any left that troubled year, out of their complacency. On 17 July 1936 a group of army officers launched an abortive coup against the Spanish government. It was the trigger of a Civil War that would foreshadow the much greater conflict that was to start in three years' time. For Dick Sheppard and his supporters in the Peace Pledge Union the Spanish war was another sign of the pacifists' impotence in the face of the shifting and clashing tectonic plates of history. Dick tried once more to intervene in the process, proposing to fly to meet General Franco to intercede on behalf of the besieged people of Madrid. The Foreign Office put a stop to the plan.[65]

As the earthquake of world war approached, the Peace Pledge Union could only pass motions, quarrel with its rivals, send letters, organize deputations and pray. The Union became increasingly fractious, depending on Dick to smooth over the frequent rows. While on the surface he retained his 'muscular-jocular Christian manner' (as Huxley, on the point of departure, acidly described it[66]), in private he became more despondent. He rejected his wife's offer of reconciliation. Alone at home, 'the loneliest man in London',[67] his thoughts turned towards the grave. Ill health and depression combined to make him morbidly pessimistic. When his friend Ellis Roberts asked him what he had to look forward to, he replied, 'I have death'.[68] Three times that year he collapsed while taking part in pacifist meetings. His end, alone in his garret in the narrow alleyway by St Paul's, was not far off. Active to the last, he pushed himself beyond endurance. Dick Sheppard died, aged fifty-seven, on 31 October 1937.

13

History forming in our hands

O<small>N</small> W<small>EDNESDAY</small> 1 July, a blisteringly hot summer's day in London, the artist and showman Salvador Dalí arrived at the New Burlington Galleries in the West End to deliver a lecture on Surrealism. He was dressed in a deep-sea diving-suit. In one hand he held a billiard cue, and in the other a dog's leash, to which two white wolfhounds were attached. On his belt was a jewelled dagger, and plasticine hands were stuck on to his diving-suit.[1]

Dalí's lecture was one of a series held that summer at the London galleries as part of the hugely successful International Surrealist Exhibition. Many of the thousands of visitors had come because of the lurid publicity and hostile comment that the show had attracted. Dalí, the supreme showman of Surrealism, was to give the final exposition of the movement's aims and purposes. His talk was entitled 'Paranoia, The Pre-Raphaelites, Harpo Marx and Phantoms' or 'Authentic Paranoiac Phantasies'. The diving-suit was intended to illustrate how Surrealists plumbed the depths of the subconscious to express hidden feelings and desires by means of paintings, poetry and *actes gratuits*.

The diving-suit had been rented by Lord Berners, the eccentric author, painter and composer, and Dalí's great friend. It was an authentic heavy-duty deep-sea costume, topped by a large round steel helmet. The rental company telephoned to ask how deep the artist was planning to dive, to which Berners replied, quick as a flash, 'To the depth of his subconscious'.[2] When Dalí put on the suit, the mechanic from the diving company bolted the helmet on tight, as though for a real submersion. Dalí's entrance, leaning on friends, his suit's lead-soled shoes clanking, accompanied by the panting dogs, caused 'exactly the right sensation'[3] among the audience. The sensation soon turned to alarm. The Spanish Surrealist managed, with exertion, to get to his seat behind the microphone when he realized that his helmet made it impossible to breathe, let alone deliver the speech. Dripping with perspiration, and on the point of suffocation, Dalí 'made the most energetic gestures [he] could to have the helmet of the diving suit removed'. Sensing an emergency at last, the organizers rushed to help. 'They tried to open a slit between the helmet and the suit with a billiard cue so that I would be able to breathe. Finally they brought a hammer and began to strike the bolts energetically to make them turn. At each blow I thought I would faint', Dalí later wrote. The audience, naturally enough, believed that this was all part of the show and started applauding. As all efforts to remove the helmet failed, David Gascoyne, the prime mover behind the exhibition, rushed out into the West End in search of a pair of pliers. He returned to remove the bolts just in time. Dalí emerged, breathless but alive and triumphant: 'Everyone was impressed by my really deathly pallor, which constituted the accurate gauge of that Dalinian dramatic element which never fails to attend my most trivial acts and undertakings.'[4]

Dalí's stunt with the diving-suit was typical of the artist, who tended to trivialize the art form of which he was the most famous exponent. For the organizers of the exhibition the show was a serious attempt to bring to the British public a revolutionary and radical art movement that explored and released the hidden desires and pathologies of the unconscious. But in 1936 it was Paris, not London, that was the powerhouse of contemporary art and the home of the Surrealist movement. Herbert Read, one of the stellar cast of poets, artists and critics behind the exhibition, wrote an essay, 'Why the English Have no Taste', in which he tried to explain why there had been so little British interest in Surrealism since its birth on the Continent in the 1920s. 'I do not say that the English have bad taste – that, perhaps, might be said of other nations', he wrote with English superciliousness, 'but simply that they do not exercise those faculties of sensibility and selection which make for good taste. Our condition is neutral – an immense indifference to questions of art.'[5]

The success of the Surrealist exhibition in London did not come from a new-found British taste for connoisseurship. Many of the thousands who attended did so merely out of curiosity, or to mock the artists and their attempts to explore and release the unconscious. Some went solely to be scandalized. The public gaped at the lips turned by Dalí into a large pink sofa and gawped at his telephones with lobster hand-sets. They scratched their heads when faced with 'found objects' – everyday artefacts such as freak branches or stones that, when taken out of context, were meant to express the subliminal – and they recoiled from the shocking, exemplified by the documentary film-maker Humphrey Jennings's *The Minotaur*, which portrayed Lord Kitchener wearing a red fez, with a child upside down in miniature on his chest. When a woman complained that the image was 'a slander on the memory of a great British soldier', Jennings responded, with the arrogance of an artist, foreshadowing post-modernism: 'I am not interested in other people's views . . . To a surrealist, everything is anonymous and everything in the world is material to create imagery.'[6]

The exhibition's notoriety was the work of the organizers. The private view, on Thursday 11 June, needed no advance publicity to draw the newspaper diarists. The William Hickey column in the *Daily Express* reported that Sheila Legg, one of the curators, wandered round the New Burlington Galleries dressed in white satin, her head and face entirely hidden by red roses. 'She had meant to wear long white rubber gloves, couldn't find any; she had meant to carry a pork chop, carried instead a human leg stuffed with roses.' The composer William Walton arrived with a red herring 'freshly procured from a fish shop', which he hung on a three-dimensional composition. 'Aesthetes remarked how right the herring was, professors and critics sniffed at it, surprised but reverential.' The *Daily Mirror* reported that there was a white pair of shoes, surrounded by white crinkly paper, entitled *My Nurse*. 'There are dozens of gorgeous jokes like this', its critic continued, 'You can see a *Poached Lion's Head* or a *Garden Aeroplane Trap*, or, if you care to, *Marks and Spencer in a Japanese Garden*'.[7] Dylan Thomas added to the atmosphere of hilarity by wandering round offering people cups of boiled string and asking them if they took sugar.

Many of the works by British artists were either derivative or – as in the case of Henry Moore's sculptures – not Surrealist at all. Continental genius produced most of the great art on show. There were a number of fine works by Pablo Picasso, Alberto Giacometti and René Magritte, but in 1936 the more serious critics and art lovers were not impressed even by these. Raymond Mortimer, writing in *The Listener*, dismissed the superficiality of the show. 'Most of the exhibits . . . have nothing to recommend them except this ability to surprise – for about one minute.'[8] The art historian and closet Marxist Anthony Blunt, writing in *The Spectator*, rejected Surrealism as a revolutionary art form, arguing that, insofar as the works were clari-fications of the subconscious, they were no more than 'works of medicine'.[9]

The negative views of the critics and the mirth of the newspapers could not dampen the success of the exhibition. The crowds it drew and the notice it garnered marked for André Breton, the prophet of Surrealism, the high-water mark of the movement. For London it was the first of the great exhibitions that would, after the interval of the war, pave the way to the capital's eventual equality with New York and Paris in the art world.

There was also a more profound sense that visitors and participants in the exhibition could not fail to feel: deep-seated anxiety. Many of the works, with their images of warped reality, uncomfortable juxta-position and dream-like dissolution, conjured up a feeling of unease. The critic Peter Quennell described a pervasive consciousness 'that we were . . . vaguely and over-cheerfully perhaps living on the verge of an unimaginable catastrophe'. René Magritte's work *On the Threshold of Liberty* was one of many paintings in the exhibition that captured this mood, with its curious but haunting image of a howitzer field-gun placed in a multifaceted interior, pointed at a panel with a naked torso of a woman. It seemed to speak of threat and vulnerability, of an uncertain future, which was bound to end with the firing of the gun.

The anarchist poet Herbert Read, in his introduction to the exhi-bition, described this sentiment with a terrible clarity. His was the prophetic expression of an outlook that Auden called 'the clutch of crisis and the bloody hour',[10] that had become almost universal among thinking people in 1936:

> in a few days the face of the world may change. Bugles blow, klaxons screech, an immense machine begins to move and we find ourselves segregated, regimented, drafted into armies and navies and workshops. Bull-necked demagogues inject a poisonous propaganda into our minds and then the storm of steel breaks above us; our bodies become so much manure for an acid soil; and our ideas, our aspirations, the whole structure of our civilisation, becomes a history which the future may not even record.[11]

The 'storm of steel' seemed to be breaking even as the Surrealist exhibition came to a close. The revolt in Spain on 17 July by a group of army officers against the leftist Popular Front government was the start of a brutal Civil War that was to last three years and cost thousands of lives. It attracted many thousands of volunteers from fifty-three countries around the world.[12] In Britain broad public opinion was at first bemused by the conflict, as news of atrocities by both sides was reported in the press. The Fascists bombed civilians and killed hostages; the loyalists burned down churches and shot priests. According to John Prichard, 'people's views were ambivalent. It was seen as a war of communism against fascism, and so people didn't know which side to stick up for.'[13]

The more politically committed were divided, polarized at first between the right, who tended to support the rebel forces led by General Francisco Franco, and a broad spectrum of liberal and left-wing opinion, who backed the loyalist Republican forces. It was much more than a simple division between left and right, however. For many, especially young idealists, artists and writers, and members of the Communist Party, the Spanish Civil War came to be seen as a titanic struggle, which the sculptor and volunteer Jason Gurney called 'a movement comparable with the great Christian crusades of medieval times'.[14]

The outbreak of the Civil War had an electrifying effect on the British organizers of the International Surrealist Exhibition. Surrealism, as a revolutionary movement, had historical ties to Communism. Its founder and high priest, André Breton, was a Trotskyist, and many of its members were Communists. Shortly after the start of the war, the nineteen-year-old Surrealist poet and rescuer of the suffocating Dalí, David Gascoyne, joined the Party and went to Spain. He wrote in his journal, 'there is no longer any honest alternative for me than direct action in the direction of Communism'.[15] Two of his fellow organizers, Roland Penrose and Humphrey Jennings, went too, to help with propaganda. It was not only the exhibition's organizers who became active proselytizers for the Republican cause. Many of the exhibitors became involved too, including the sculptor Henry Moore and the young painter Julian Trevelyan, who spoke for his generation when he wrote: 'Until the Spanish War started in 1936, there was an air of gentle frivolity about our life in London . . . for the next three years our thoughts and consciences were turned to Spain.'[16]

It may have been in reality a battle between Spaniards, the complex origins of which went deep into the Spanish past, but for those young radicals watching from Britain it was the first act in a drama that could, unless the Fascists were stopped, lead to the cataclysm of world war that all dreaded, but which seemed inevitable. James Albrighton, a Communist medical student from Salisbury, came to the view that 'unless we took action by not allowing the Fascists, and Nazis, to take control of Spain, then it would only be a matter of time . . . before they would unleash the same action in Europe'.[17] He left to fight in Spain in the autumn.

The revolt against Spain's chaotic government began with a rebellion of military garrisons in Morocco and the Canary Islands, which quickly spread to the mainland. Not all the Spanish military joined the rebels, and the forces were at first evenly matched. The coup leaders desperately needed the assistance of the élite Army of Africa, made up of battle-hardened Moorish soldiers, commanded by General Franco, which was trapped on the wrong side of the Strait of Gibraltar. In early August, Hitler intervened, ordering his air force to bring them over to Spain. The rebels, hugely strengthened by Franco's African columns, advanced north towards Madrid, threatening the capital. In desperation the Republican government called for help from abroad.

Spurred on by their own government's strict neutrality and longing to have a crack at Fascism, British men and women of the left rallied to the cause. They tended to be young intellectuals, often with a poetic or artistic bent. Idealism, combined with a desire for adventure, took them to Spain. All wanted to fight Fascism, but their motivations were various: some saw the conflict in terms of democracy against totalitarianism, others as a chance to stop the advance of Hitler and Mussolini and to prevent the development of 'a world war in embryo'. Jason Gurney wrote that 'the war became a microcosm of all the ideological divisions of the time – freedom and repression, constitutional and arbitrary authority, nationalism and internationalism, the people and the aristocracy, Catholicism and Marxism . . . everybody saw Spain as the epitome of the particular conflict with which they were concerned'.[18]

Many of the first to go to Spain were no doubt motivated by their politics, but also moved by a spirit of romantic adventure. In the early days of the conflict, those who wanted to fight had to make their own arrangements. The Communist Party became more actively involved in recruitment when, later in the autumn, the International Brigades were formed. For this reason the pioneers were often from middle-class backgrounds; young men and women who could pay for their own passage and travel independently. But there were many from other backgrounds and walks of life. What all found when they arrived on the battlefield was too often a sordid reality of disunity, inefficiency and poor equipment. Many would end up either disillusioned or dead.

One of the first to go was David Marshall. A nineteen-year-old from Middlesbrough, he was the son of solidly working-class parents. His father was a gardener, and his mother was in service at a local hall. Both were highly literate and wanted the best for their son: 'a decent job with a pension', as they often said to him. After finishing at elementary school David won a scholarship to the local Grammar. He left, aged sixteen, and joined the Civil Service as a clerk. Two years later he packed in his secure job, lured by the chance of fighting Fascism. After forging his father's signature on a letter of permission in order to get a passport, and telling his parents he was visiting his sweetheart in Tyneside for two weeks, he set off for Spain in early August.

David was not a member of the Communist Party when he left, but at school his liberal education had broadened his horizons. 'In sixth form our literature master had been gassed [in the First World War], and he was the most important and widening influence on us. He introduced us to George Bernard Shaw . . . and I began to nick books from the store, and the first one I nicked was Keats' 1820 poems which I took to Spain with me.'[19] The heady combination of Shavian iconoclasm and Romantic poetry was one motivating force for the studious young man. Another was reading about the Russian Revolution. Alongside books, radio was also opening up new horizons to young men such as David Marshall in a world that was already shrinking. He remembered 'listening with greed to all the South American music that was played, and so my interest was in the revolutionary aspects that came across'. His particular favourite was the Mexican ballad that became one of the themes tunes of the Spanish Civil War, 'La Cucaracha'.

Underlying his decision to throw in steady work and seek out the battle was a consciousness of the disjunction between his upbringing and his education. The son of poor working people, brought up in the harsh reality of the depressed north-east, his education had broadened his mind to the possibility of change and created a desire for escape.

One day I bought *The Times*. Now *The Times* was bloody tuppence, nobody really afforded that. And I remember reading a very short paragraph about an inch long, which just said there is no doubt that if the Spanish Republican government wins the war a socialist state will be set up. And really that was the trigger – I thought Christ, here's a way out.

While David Marshall was not a Party member when he left for Spain, most of those departing in the summer were committed Communists. Among them there were many young Marxists who often came from solidly middle-class backgrounds, converts to a rigid ideology that seemed to offer certainty in a world of encircling doubt and darkness. Many were intellectuals, artists and writers. The poet John Cornford was the most celebrated of the early martyrs for the cause. He appeared in every way the archetype of the young poet hero. His rugged, sultry looks, sculpted features and curly black hair were reminiscent of an earlier freedom fighter, Lord Byron. Cornford's first name, never used, was Rupert, after the soldier–poet Rupert Brooke, who died of blood poisoning on the way to fight at Gallipoli in 1915.[20] Cornford came from a family of Cambridge intellectuals. His great-grandfather was Charles Darwin; his father Francis, a clergyman, was a classicist at Trinity and his mother Frances, a fine Georgian poet with whom he had an intense and sometimes fraught relationship. While at school at Stowe he wrote precociously advanced poetry, and came under the influence of W. H. Auden and Robert Graves. Noel Annan, a fellow history student at the school, remembered him, 'sitting in the classroom slumped at his desk, contemptuous of the level of discussion, waiting only for the end of term when he could win a major scholarship to Trinity'.[21]

If, to borrow Stanley Baldwin's characterization of Churchill that year,[22] the good fairy had given Cornford all the gifts bar one, the one he was denied was charm. The lightness and grace of that elusive quality were not much in evidence in him, or indeed in many of the earnest young radicals of his generation. Faced with the perceived failure of the capitalist system after the crash of 1929, the collapse of the Labour Party two years later in the face of the economic depression and the refusal of the National Government to confront Fascism, they turned to Marxism and Communist Russia for answers. For many, joining the Communist Party was an act of rebellion. Few actually had read the works of Karl Marx or understood his dialectical theory. They embraced Communism because they saw it as the solution to the many injustices of the world and the only way to avert war. As A. L. Rowse, another brilliant if priggish young historian and poet, wrote on 31 July, 'there is no hope whatever of peace so long as the existing economic and political order maintains its hold, so long as the rule of the upper classes lasts'.[23] Many gifted students at Oxford and Cambridge joined the Party; a number of them did so covertly, to serve the cause as spies for the Comintern.

But Cornford was different from most. Esmond Romilly, a public-school rebel who cycled to Spain later in the year to join the fight, classed him as a 'real Communist'. To fit this category, 'you had to be a serious person, a rigid disciplinarian, a member of the Communist Party'.[24] Cornford exuded a deep commitment and a steely belief in the onward march of history. With characteristic precociousness he had converted to Marxism at school before his arrival at Cambridge and wrote technical letters from Stowe to his mother about the theory of capital when he was sixteen.[25] He had been particularly moved by the plight of the unemployed in the distressed areas and by the sight of the hunger marchers as they made their way to London.[26] After winning a scholarship to Trinity he spent a year filling in time at the London School of Economics, during which time he came under the influence of Harold Laski, the prominent Marxist intellectual. By the time that Civil War came to Spain, though only twenty, he had been an active Communist for more than five years.

Not all of the first wave of volunteers were men. The Spanish Communist militias, to the shock of many in Britain, were actively recruiting women to fight in the front line. Felicia Browne was thirty-two when she answered the call to arms and left for Spain in August.[27] Like Cornford, she came from a reasonably well-off, middle-class family. Her mother, Edith Johnstone, was an actress and singer, who played in the original Gilbert and Sullivan productions and later in plays by J. M. Barrie. Her father ran the family commercial marketing and advertising business. When Felicia was a child, her parents separated, and the children were cared for by a fearsome nanny, Mrs Coleman, 'Coley'. It was not a happy time. Inwardly, a teacher wrote, 'she was a volcano'.[28] Felicia later wrote: 'I know well what it is to drown in the well-upholstered family household as I endured such a condition for some years, unwillingly.'[29] In the First World War Harold, her eldest brother, was shot down and killed flying over the Somme.

Felicia grew up as a 'rather plain dumpy young woman' who wore large round horn-rimmed spectacles and a black hat.[30] She was known for her kindness and generosity, a humane character who could be 'painfully truthful and honest' and who was 'completely without guile, duplicity or vanity'. Above all, she was gifted: she could draw and sculpt, and could turn her hand to any craft with success. Her directness and her honesty meant that she was her own fiercest critic. Little of her work survives because she destroyed anything that she believed to be below standard.[31] 'Her distrust of herself, her too great humility concerning her own work', a teacher and friend wrote, held back her development.[32]

Like Cornford, Browne had the potential to be a fine artist. She trained at the Slade School of Fine Art under the great teacher Henry Tonks. Her later work showed his influence in its ability to capture in watercolour the grace and movement of animals, and its natural fluency when handling the human figure. She came to love 'the strange and elaborate cosmogenies'[33] of Dante and Kafka, whose work she illustrated. In 1928 Felicia went to Berlin, where she stayed for several years, studying stone and metalwork. For some time she lived with unemployed craftsmen and experienced the poverty of their lives. She used her private income to support some of them.[34] These experiences, together with witnessing the brutality of the Nazis, led to her conversion to Communism. On her return to Britain in 1933 she joined the Party. Like Cornford, her political commitment seems to have imbued her with a deep seriousness. She was also depressive, finding it hard to reconcile her own personal wealth and bourgeois upbringing with her political radicalism. She revealed her sense of isolation and solitariness in a self-portrait from the time. Painted from above, in shades of grey watercolour wash, she looks up, arms folded, peering at the viewer with a deep, mournful look of inquiry, her lips turned down, a sense of fatalism enhanced by the monochrome hues of the portrait. She also learned Russian and took up ju-jitsu. A friend drily remembered 'seeing this rather fat young woman being flung down by a tiny little Chinese man'.[35]

Felicia became an active Communist, attending meetings and selling newspapers on street corners. She wanted to escape her bourgeois roots and immerse herself in the lives of working people. This led to an inner tension that she found hard to reconcile, as a fellow artist later wrote: 'She had most of the best human characteristics, but she conceived her own variety rather as a source of opposition than of enjoyment.' She wrote a number of revealing letters to her friend Elizabeth Watson, which were later discovered by Tom Buchanan, historian of the British response to the Spanish Civil War. Unsure of herself as an artist, she took a job working ten- and eleven-hour days in a teashop – 'a long and tedious job', she told Watson – but asserted nonetheless that she 'would not be in any other job in the world because so much is to be done getting the girls to fight (and it will be a fight) to change unspeakable conditions'. Even to her comrades this was a tragic waste of her talents. Instead of helping the cause with her art, she undertook menial tasks, 'mainly spuds and floors, and tried to organize her fellow workers into a union'. Her continuing contacts with German friends and fellow Communists drew her to the attention of Special Branch and MI5, who intercepted her letters and phone calls.

Although Felicia was an active member of the Artists International Association – a Communist front for painters – she always put her political commitment before her art. There were long periods where she neither painted nor sculpted. She tried to justify her lack of creativity to Elizabeth Watson, also a Communist artist, by emphasizing the importance of her political and union work.

> You say I am escaping and evading things by not painting or making sculpture . . . If painting and sculpture were more valid and more urgent to me than the earthquake which is happening in the revolution, or if these two were reconciled so that the demands of one didn't conflict (in time, even, and concentration) with the demands of the other, I should paint and make sculpture.[36]

That August the two worlds of art and action came together for her in the earthquake of the Spanish Civil War.

At the end of June 1936 John Cornford, aged twenty, had just finished his first degree at Cambridge, and was considering what to do next. His time at the university had been taken up with political activism and hard study. The Party's injunction 'A Communist student is a good student' was one that he had followed assiduously. Noel Annan, also an undergraduate at Cambridge, remembered seeing him, 'his handsome Moorish face, a cigarette hanging from his lip, his shoulders hunched, as he slouched past marshalling the ranks of a demo at Cambridge. He emitted power, energy and conviction. He did not set out to charm: his mission was to convince.'[37] Another remembered him as an 'extremely clever, forceful, merciless, rather inhuman boy'.[38] He graduated with a starred double first in history and the offer of the prestigious Earl of Derby Research Scholarship at Trinity.

In the world of student politics there was little time for the gaiety, wit and douceur of Oxbridge, which Evelyn Waugh called in *Brideshead Revisited* 'the enclosed and enchanted garden'. John affected the ragged clothes of poverty, took part in student rallies for peace, recruited fellow students to the Party and instructed his friends to infiltrate the Cambridge Union,[39] the university's debating society. As ever, leftist student politics were a thicket of alliances and plots, a youthful stage where the real world of Communism's doctrinal struggles, splits and somersaults could be played out in microcosm.

Cornford's ultra-orthodoxy led him to make some strange bed-fellows. At the Union he proposed the motion, 'That this House, regarding Parliamentary institutions as an obstacle to progress, deplores the failure of Guy Fawkes',[40] giving a well-received speech on the shortcomings of Parliament and the need for a workers' revo-lution. He was seconded by another Trinity student, Peter Kemp, who supported the motion but for completely different reasons – that the institution be abolished in favour of the monarchy and aristoc-racy. A year later the two young men would be fighting on opposite sides in Spain. Kemp became one of a handful of British volunteers for the Francoist cause in the Civil War.

Although he took little part in the social life of Cambridge, devot-ing himself fourteen hours a day to politics and study, John did have time for two intense relationships. In London he met and fell in love with Rachel (Ray) Peters. Ray was a fellow Communist, older than him by a couple of years, and from a Welsh working-class background. For two years John gave the relationship all the intense commitment one might expect from this driven young man. He installed Ray in a flat in Cambridge, where, defying convention, the couple lived to-gether, John dividing his time between her and his studies and politics

at Trinity. To his parents, pillars of the Cambridge liberal establishment though they were, this was something of an embarrassment.
People gossiped; he was said to be keeping a Russian mistress.[41]

Together, intensely physical, passionately political, they made an
arresting couple. The portrait photographer Lettice Ramsey asked
them to pose for her.[42] John was happy to oblige. The result was a
striking image of political commitment and romantic love that
became a pin-up for the engaged leftist students of the time. Taken
in profile, Ray who, like her lover, was dark and curly-haired, stares
ahead with a heroic readiness to take whatever the future may hold,
while John broods beside her, brow furrowed, eyes downcast, a
tragic yet protective figure.[43]

Shortly afterwards, in a further defiance of polite society, Ray gave
birth to a son, James. For a while the pair lived together with the
baby in Cambridge, but the relationship did not last. John fell in love
with another Cambridge undergraduate, Margot Heinemann, also a
Party member, but – unlike Ray – from a middle-class background
and more intellectually in tune with Cornford. With the easy brutality of a revolutionary, John dispatched Ray and took up with
Margot.

Just as with Felicia Browne, the political struggle came before anything else. He had almost given up writing poetry at the time, but he
made an exception with a poem about the break-up, entitled 'Sad
Poem', the last verse of which seemed to echo his political outlook:

> Though Parting's as cruel as the surgeon's knife,
> It's better than the ingrown canker, the rotten leaf.
> All that I know is that I have got to leave.
> There's new fighting in me to get at the air,
> And I can't stop its mouth with the rags of old love.
> Clean wounds are easiest to bear.

Cornford was completely taken up with the orthodoxy of
Communism. Loyalty to the doctrines of Stalinist Russia meant, in
1936, buying in to the show trials, terror and mass-murder. He did so
with equanimity. Of the assassination of one of Stalin's henchmen,
he wrote:

Everything dying keeps a hungry grip on life.
Nothing is ever born without screaming and blood.[44]

Violence, as Noel Annan remembered,[45] was much in the air at the time, despite the almost universal protestations against war. A contemporary remembered Cornford 'telling, with genuine relish, a story of Béla Kun machine-gunning five thousand prisoners during a forced retreat in the Russian Civil War: he told it not in a spirit of sadism, but of appreciation of an act of political necessity firmly carried out.'[46]

David Marshall had little of Cornford's passionate intensity when he arrived in mid-August 1936 at Portbou in Catalonia, on the Spanish side of the border with France. He was soon, however, taken up with the revolutionary spirit. At first he was refused entry, as he had no Party membership documents or Trades Union Card with which to satisfy the border guards of his socialist credentials. In the suspicious world of revolutionary Spain he was suspected of being a spy. After an Italian anti-Fascist vouched for him as no more than 'a typical Englishman', he was allowed through. Straight away he joined the anti-Fascist Militia of Catalonia and left for Barcelona, where he joined the Spanish Communist Party and became a member of the Tom Mann Centuria, a group made up of foreign volunteers. For a young man from a narrow background in the grim industrial wasteland of the north-east of England, the first experiences of Spain at war were an invigorating liberation.

He encountered for the first time an engaged and intelligent discussion of politics in a completely new setting. 'I was on the continent – nobody travelled to the continent from the working class in those days. All these immense influences, the colour, the light, the sheer intoxication of the air, it went to my head.'[47] At this early stage in the Civil War there was a good deal of political education for volunteers but no formal military training. To harden up the new recruits, David and his comrades were taken to the morgue to see the victims of fighting and to the railway station. 'If you ever want to be anti-war,' he recalled forty years later, 'watch the troop train going out – all the tears, the partings, the chucking of paper parcels through windows. Dreadful experience'.

Felicia Browne's journey to Spain was, if anything, more haphazard. She had set off on a driving holiday in her own car through France before the outbreak, with the intention of ending up in Barcelona.[48] She went with a friend and fellow Communist, the Hungarian-born photographer Edith Bone. The 47-year-old Bone was fifteen years older, a feisty personality, whom Felicia came to find a burden. Before reaching Dover it turned out that she was not to be trusted at the wheel. 'I have never before seen anyone go berserk through driving a car', Felicia told Elizabeth Watson.[49] The security services monitored the couple as they left Dover on 11 July in their rickety two-seater Austin coupé, with Bone at the wheel and Felicia dressed in a 'grey costume and a black beret'.[50] The couple arrived in Barcelona in late July just as the military rebellion was taking place. The city was in turmoil. In order to crush the uprising the Republican government had enlisted the help of the popular militias, mainly groups of anarchist and socialist men and women. After putting down the revolt, the militias moved out to attack the Fascists who had captured the cities of Huesca and Zaragoza to the west, in neighbouring Aragón.

Edith Bone, unsurprisingly, had 'murdered' the car on arriving in Barcelona, Felicia reported, 'meeting a lorry coming round a corner on the hill. No-one was hurt'.[51] Felicia went to the British Consul to inform him of the accident. He warned her not to go outdoors. If she did, he said, 'and you meet any of *those fellows* with guns just do this' (he clenched his fist delicately) 'and smile nicely'.[52] Most likely she was already doing so. Edith, meanwhile, had taken up with the journalist Claud Cockburn, photographing alongside him as he reported for the *Daily Worker*. Felicia was left to explore the streets of Barcelona on her own, using a press pass they had arranged for her. Mopping-up operations were continuing in the city, and Felicia dodged the fighting as best she could:

> guns and firing all over the place. I landed (unexpectedly, not know-
> ing my way about) on the edge of the battlefield Plaza Catalunya at
> 11am on Sunday, terrific firing going on. There was no-one in place
> except one cop . . . who whistled frantically from the other side of the
> boulevard, and then disappeared in a doorway, shouting to me not to

move. Between the firing, you could hear the wind going through the trees, peaceful as hell.[53]

As order was restored in the city, Felicia wandered around in a state of depression and indecision. She tried to join the militia but was rejected, not because of her sex but because there were not enough guns to go round for the volunteers.[54] After an abortive attempt to get to the front she returned to Barcelona. She was disconsolate, incapable it seemed of finding a way to help the cause or, for that matter, of doing anything else. 'There seems no prospect of exploring, painting or getting anywhere beyond this monstrous city', she lamented, 'where for a foreigner existence is suspended for the time being.'[55] But she was determined to join the struggle. On 3 August her persistence at last paid off. The *Daily Express*'s correspondent Sidney Smith went with her to the office of the PSUC, the Communist militia. He reported that she had demanded to fight on the Zaragoza front, saying, 'I am a member of the London Communists and can fight as well as any man'. The Communists accepted her immediately and ordered her to the garrison to be equipped. Smith went to say goodbye to her at the garrison gates. 'I am not at all afraid,' she told him, 'I am fighting for a different country, but the same cause.'[56] Faced with the full force of a committed English Communist, and desperate for volunteers, the Spanish welcomed her to their ranks. She was one of the first of the British volunteers, totally lacking in any military training or experience.

Five days later John Cornford arrived in the revolutionary city. His decision to come to Spain had been almost as impulsive as David Marshall's departure or Felicia Browne's enlistment. He had been planning to spend a month with Margot Heinemann in the south of France before travelling to a peace conference in Brussels. But the prospect of experiencing a workers' state in Catalonia, together with the chance of fighting Fascism, proved irresistible. He cancelled his holiday plans and made his way to Barcelona. Later he wrote to his father apologizing for the hasty departure: 'the idea suddenly occurred to me to go to Spain for a few days. I expected at the time the fighting would be over very soon; so in a tremendous hurry I got a letter of introduction from the *News Chronicle* and set out.'[57]

His plans were vague and unformed, his knowledge of the background to the Civil War limited, but here at last was the chance for action. There was another motivation too. John was at a loose end. He had failed to get a job in Birmingham, where Margot was working, and the idea of continuing his education at Cambridge, where the research scholarship was open to him, did not appeal. Spain, in every way, was the answer to his dilemma as he explained to Margot, when he wrote to her to apologize for letting her down. 'You know the political reasons. There is a subjective one as well. From the age of seventeen I was in a kind of way tied down, and envied my contemporaries a good deal their freedom to bum about. And it was partly because I felt myself for the first time independent that I came out here. But I promise this is the last time I shall leave you unnecessarily.'[58] John's father suspected one of the reasons behind John's decision to go to Spain was the need to get away from his complicated private life, as he put it, to 'escape from the hot entanglements of personal responsibilities'.[59]

When he arrived in Barcelona, the city was still in a ferment. Everywhere there were men with rifles slung over their shoulders. Others patrolled the streets at top speed in 'requisitioned' cars, guns poking out of the windows. The revolutionaries had taken over department stores, hotels, government offices and stations. There was no formal Republican government. Barcelona and the surrounding region of Catalonia were ruled by a collective rabble of leftist groups identified by their initials, sprayed in paint on every available surface. The middle classes had fled the city, leaving their valuables to be plundered by the red and black flag-waving anarchists. John plunged into this super-heated atmosphere with all the passion of a revolutionary. He told Margot:

> in Barcelona one can understand physically what the dictatorship of the proletariat means. All the Fascist press has been taken over. The rule is in the hands of the militia committees. There is a real terror against the Fascists. But that doesn't alter the fact that the place is free and conscious all the time of its freedom.

David Marshall was in the city at the same time as John Cornford. Although the two young men never met, they shared a romantic enthusiasm for the revolutionary spirit they found there. Neither had tasted battle, and both in their innocence were taken up with the sense of fervour, even gaiety. David walked through the streets, marvelling. 'The entire working class was in control! And it was well organized too. We went to canteens where you could eat at any time for free. The feeling was one of great happy comradeship.' In the evenings he strolled with his new friends down the city's boulevards, 'these would be stacked with stalls, with soft drinks and sticky sweets and cakes, big stalls laden with bright foliage and everlasting flowers, and crowds of young people in line, linking arms, swinging along and singing'. From a street-seller he bought a badge, a red star with hammer and sickle. For a young man who had been no further than Tyneside this first experience of revolution was little more than a glorious first holiday abroad. At the time the volunteers were doing no more than play-acting. 'It was a favourite sport to go riding round the town on a lorry, sitting on the wing, holding a rifle – a favourite revolutionary pose. Bit precarious.'

John Cornford, the true Communist, soon tired of the fiesta spirit of revolutionary Barcelona. Frustrated by the lack of action, he set off on 12 August with a couple of journalists to find the front in Aragón, 200 miles to the west of Barcelona. After an arduous journey through the hot and dusty yellow plains of the Spanish summer, lurching round corners and plunging into the deep ravines, the party arrived the next day at Leciñena,[60] a small town high on the plain of Aragón, close to the front and rebel-held Zaragoza. They made their way to the headquarters of the Partido Obrero Unificación Marxista (POUM), or Workers' Party of Marxist Unification.

POUM, an anti-Stalinist revolutionary organization, was considered by those who followed Moscow's Stalinist line to be a 'wrecking' Trotskyist organization. That John Cornford should have thrown his hand in with a proscribed group was out of character for such a doctrinaire party loyalist. But a sense of urgency, together with the romance of battle, seems to have pushed him into the arms of the renegades. That evening a column of POUM militias shambled into town, having spent five days on duty as an advance guard. According to John, it was a sight 'more picturesque than military. There was not the slightest sign of military discipline.'[61]

After a harangue from their leader, the company, together with their visitors, retired to the tavern for some refreshment. One of the militia men took out an accordion, his comrades joined in, singing 'La Cucaracha' and other rebel songs. A female camp follower stepped forward, dancing as the men sang.[62] In the heat of the Spanish summer, no doubt intoxicated by the romance of the atmosphere as well as by the wine, John Cornford made up his mind. When his two companions returned to Barcelona the following day, 14 August, he stayed in Leciñena, a lone Stalinist militiaman amid a chaotic band of Trotskyist revolutionaries, unable to speak a word of their language.

Back in Barcelona, Felicia Browne was also learning how to be a soldier. There were no arms or uniforms, 'so everybody looks like pirates', she joked.[63] To add to the sense of a rag-tag army, the barracks in which she stayed were 'v. filthy indeed', but the 'enormous cubic women' who dealt with the catering met with her approval. Her first duties were as a sentry, guarding the commandant's HQ for two-and-a-quarter hours. 'Tough work when you don't understand the language, so you prevent the chief from entering his own office, and let in all the louts.' Three Jewish tailors from Stepney joined her, having cycled from London to join up. One of them was assigned with Felicia to a machine-gun unit.

Around 19 August, after six days as a soldier, Felicia was sent to the small town of Tardienta, a strategic railway junction close to the front line, and only 15 miles or so due north of Leciñena, where John Cornford was based. Tardienta was the headquarters of a pro-government force that included two battalions of regulars, some shock troops and Felicia's militia. There were also many foreign volunteers, she reported: 'Germans, Italians, French, Belgians, a half-Czech/half-English girl and one lone Englishman from Stepney.' The town was 5 miles or so from the enemy, although there was no conventional front line; instead there was a large no man's land, into which small commando groups from the opposing forces would now and then venture to skirmish.

Fascist-held Huesca, 10 miles to the north, was the target. For the moment small groups, 'Storm Troops', were harrying the Fascist enemy and attacking the trains that were supplying Zaragoza to the south. Felicia had spent three days in Tardienta, evidently frustrated and at a loose end, when she fell into conversation with a French volunteer, Georges Brinkman. When he told her that he was a member of one of the Storm Troops, she immediately asked to join. Brinkman asked his Captain if he would accept a woman into the troop, and he responded, 'If she wants to, she can come with us'.[64]

At two o'clock in the afternoon of 22 August she set off from Tardienta by car with Brinkman and the troop of volunteer fighters. Unfamiliar with any sort of gun, she did not carry a weapon. Her role was to act as look-out during an operation to blow up a rebel munitions train. She must have seemed an improbable soldier, her only uniform a tin helmet, her lack of military experience all too obvious. Her commando group drove as far as they could to the front line, then walked some seven miles to the railway to set the explosives that were meant to destroy the train.

On their return they came into contact with a party of Fascists. The group was heavily outnumbered. In the ensuing fire-fight an Italian volunteer was hit in the foot. His comrades succeeded in dragging him behind some cover. Felicia rushed forward to give him first aid, but, as Brinkman remembered, 'when she reached him, the Fascists directed their united fire against the two of them. With several wounds in the breast and one in the back, Felicia, our brave fighter in the cause of Freedom, sank dead to the ground. The other comrade also lost his life.'[65] Under the accurate fire of the Fascists the comrades were unable to bring the bodies back with them and instead fled with what they could gather of their personal possessions. Felicia's sketchbook was flown back to Britain.

Felicia was the first British volunteer to die in the Spanish Civil War. Her death was not widely covered, except in the *Daily Worker*, which paid tribute to her courage and commitment, and her difficult personal life: 'she had her own troubles . . . yet these never daunted her.'[66] She was an isolated figure, out of her depth in a conflict into which she had fallen almost by accident. There was a carelessness about her death, which gave it a terrible sense of waste. She had the potential, as the anonymous Marxist author of the introduction to her Memorial Exhibition catalogue wrote, 'to represent the very best type of the new woman'.[67] But, the writer asserted, in the harsh tones of the dogmatist, she was held back by her background: 'the kind of upbringing to which she was automatically subjected and the forces with which she had to compete in a society where commercial values are pre-eminent, seriously and unnecessarily delayed her in harmonising all the remarkable powers within her.'[68] There was truth in the words of the obituarist. In 1936 Felicia prefigured the sort of independence of action and spirit that women would achieve in the decades that followed. She courageously challenged convention. But, as a pathfinder for the modern age, she found the journey solitary and difficult. She fell victim to a doctrinaire ideology. Her bourgeois background seems to have overwhelmed her with a sense of guilt, even self-loathing, which drove her on to sacrifice her life. Perhaps, if she had survived, the disillusionment that some on the left came to feel after experiencing the Civil War in Spain would have affected her too, and she would have been freed from the agonies of contradiction that beset her short life.

Fifteen miles to the south John Cornford was going through his own dark night as he sought to come to terms with his impulsive decision to join the militia at Leciñena. On his first day he was assigned to sentry duty on the nearby hills, close to the key targets of rebel-held Zaragoza and Huesca. None of his fellow guards could speak any English. His only communication was in broken French with a young Catalan volunteer. In the baking sun on the yellow sandstone hill there was 'nothing at all to do' except watch, wait and write. One or two aeroplanes droned overhead. There was the occasional crack of a rifle shot, and the odd burst of machine-gun fire, but otherwise nothing to distract him from his own morbid introspection.

On 16 August he started a revealing 'Diary Letter' to Margot Heinemann in which he admitted to her that he had enlisted. Perhaps for the first time in his life John Cornford was being tested. From beneath the cold carapace of political commitment there emerged briefly a tenderness that transcended his usual Marxist dogmatism. His words to Margot from the hilltop, as he faced mortal combat for the first time, have a sincerity that came from the heart: 'I love you with all my strength and all my will and my whole body. Loving you has been the most perfect experience, and in a way, the biggest achievement of my life.' He promised once more that he would never again leave her unnecessarily. 'Maybe that the Party will send me, but after this I will always be with you when I have the chance.'[69] He admitted to feeling depressed. The sun was so hot during the day that it made him 'almost ill'. He was unable to eat. At night he was cold. He had nothing to protect him when it rained other than a blanket, and had to lie on the bare stones. He not only felt 'utterly lonely' but also 'a bit useless'.

John had joined a suspect military organization that was proscribed by his beloved Party. He had nothing to do. He did not know how to fight. Stuck on a barren hilltop with a bunch of men with whom he could not speak, he was deprived of the warrior's great comfort and support: comradeship. It was a Sunday, and the bells of the ominously named enemy-held village of Perdiguera rang out across the valley 'very slow and mournful across the distance'. The tolling dragged him down still further.

The next morning he came down from the hilltop to rejoin the column. Things were better within the larger group, as he could speak in English to the German comrades, and engage in the political dialogue he loved. On Tuesday the men were ordered into the village plaza and told to prepare for an attack on Perdiguera. Breathlessly John scribbled in his letter to Margot: 'Going into action. Thank God for something to do at last. I shall fight like a Communist if not a soldier. All my love. *Salute.*'

Although the attack turned out to be a fiasco, it had a transformative effect. From a homesick depressive John emerged as a man of action: 'having joined in, I am in whether I like it or not. And I like it.' He certainly looked an extraordinary sight: a mixture of a clean-cut British ex-public-school boy and Mexican revolutionary. He was dressed in a pair of heavy black corduroy trousers which had been 'expropriated' from the bourgeoisie, a blue sports shirt, an alpaca coat, rope-soled sandals and 'an infinitely battered old sombrero'. Over one shoulder he carried an ancient German Mauser rifle, over the other a blanket. A big tin mug was stuck in his belt.[70] Some of his comrades were dressed in a uniform of blue or brown overalls and blue shorts. This informality was mirrored by the style of command. The men elected their officers, and there were no shouted orders. Saluting was forbidden.

The assault on Perdiguera began on Wednesday, four days after John's enlistment. To his astonishment he realized no one was in command when the attack began. Each section of the force was firing at random. There was no plan. Having, like all public-school boys of the time, undergone some military training with the cadet corps, John had a little understanding of what should be done. 'It seemed clear to me that we should attack to the right, because there was the enemy machine gun which was holding up our counter-attack. But no such thing . . . All this time I hadn't the faintest idea who was winning or losing.' In fact, John's side was losing. As he fired his Mauser at random at doors and windows, a formation of Fascist planes flew over and bombed the men on the other side of the village, causing them to flee. The attack had failed.

That night John and his fellow militias withdrew to an abandoned monastery along the road to Huesca, possibly in preparation for another attack.[71] For the next two weeks he took part in a number of minor actions on this front line, close to where Felicia Browne had died. He became relatively battle-hardened and grew closer to the German volunteers. They taught him their language and argued about politics. Having fled Nazi Germany, they had lost everything; as John wrote, they 'have been through enough to break most people, and remain strong and cheerful and humorous. If anything is revolutionary it is these comrades.'[72] Yet, by supporting Stalin's enemy, Trotsky, they stood in direct opposition to the Party he loved. Paradoxically, as he debated with his new comrades, this made John even more of a die-hard loyalist. 'Even when I can put forward no rational argument, I feel that to cut adrift from the Party is the beginning of political suicide.'[73]

David Marshall, just as John Cornford and Felicia Browne had done, became increasingly frustrated by the lack of action as the days passed in Barcelona. 'We were feeling the shame of being idle', he recalled. To his relief, at the end of August he and his group, the Tom Mann Centuria, were sent to Albacete, 150 miles south-east of Madrid. There they were given some rudimentary training as part of the newly forming International Brigades, before being sent into action in the defence of Madrid. With the reality of battle looming, he discovered 'there was a great feeling of tension and a different kind of excitement to that in Barcelona'. David's first taste of battle was to be his last, and – as with so many experiences of the British volunteers – 'it was a bit of a shambles'. Although he had never used a rifle before, he was ordered to advance on a Fascist-held building at the top of a hill, the Sierra de Los Angeles, a strategic post that overlooked Madrid in the distance. 'We were firing at the windows of this building in a controlled way. We felt bloody exposed.' David had taken shelter in a shallow furrow as the enemy returned fire, 'and then this marksman got into me, and I heard the bullets hitting the ground around me, and then he hit me in the leg. Didn't hurt, was like a red hot blow. My foot leapt up and hit me in the backside.'

Without any proper training, his short experience of actual combat had been a disaster. After his wound had healed, he sought and received permission to return home. 'I was a bit demoralised, you know, a bit frightened. My reactions to the actualities of war were a bit serious, as they are to everybody.' What had started as a glorious adventure for an innocent abroad ended in violence and shock. David Marshall was fortunate. Although a casualty, he survived. Most of those fighting with him went on to die in the bloody battles of the autumn and winter. He went back to Middlesbrough still an idealist, but a young man who had learned some hard lessons in a very short time.

John Cornford was still in Aragón. There was little fighting at the end of August and beginning of September. His principal duty at this time was to take part in the guarding of the defectors who came over from the Fascist lines.[74] During this time he made notes for the essay on the situation in Catalonia that he planned to write on his return home. Most importantly, he found time for poetry. The personal journey from misery and loneliness to the exhilaration of commitment and combat were distilled in three poems that he wrote in September 1936. He must have written them in his mind, perhaps while on sentry duty, and then pencilled them into his notebook. There were few alterations.[75] For a young man of twenty they have an astonishing maturity. The first, composed during a night-time guard duty on 2 September and then copied into a notebook is entitled 'Full Moon at Tierz: Before the Storming of Huesca'. The poem's penultimate verse is a fine statement that encapsulates why so many British radicals saw Spain as the first battle in a looming revolutionary fight against not only Fascism but also the capitalist forces that had brought the lasting poverty and unemployment of the Depression:

> England is silent under the same moon,
> From Clydeside to the gutted pits of Wales,
> The innocent mask conceals that soon
> Here, too, our freedom's swaying in the scales.
> O understand before too late
> Freedom was never held without a fight.[76]

'Full Moon at Tierz' was composed before an expected attack on Huesca. It never took place. Instead, five days later, on 7 September, John wrote in his diary, 'Asleep! By the shit house. Beginning of the sickness.'[77] Hoping that by ignoring his stomach cramps they would disappear, he volunteered for guard duty. The next day, however, the pains had got much worse. He had a high fever and bad diarrhoea. His commander decided that he should go to hospital. As he lay on the stretcher, his German comrades came to say goodbye. He would never see them again. He was carried on a truck to a nearby militia first aid post, and from there to hospital at Lerida. On 12 September, his thirty-seventh day in Spain,[78] he was back in Barcelona, ill and exhausted. He and the POUM commander had decided that he should return to Britain, recruit a band of volunteers and come back to Spain in three weeks' time. Shortly before he departed for England he wrote a final poem, 'A Letter from Aragon', which had its roots in his experiences at the front but also carried a message from a Spanish anarchists to his comrades at home:

> Tell the workers of England
> This was a war not of our own making,
> We did not seek it.
> But if ever the Fascists again rule Barcelona
> It will be as a heap of ruins with us workers beneath it.[79]

It was a stirring rallying-cry, which many would heed to their cost. Those who followed in Cornford's footsteps and came to fight in Spain suffered an appalling casualty rate. Of about 2,400 British volunteers in the International Brigades some 1,700 were wounded and 500 killed.[80] John Cornford was ready to make the sacrifice. His father wrote movingly of his unwavering and deadly commitment:

> I see a boat slipping out of the harbour & breasting the first waves beyond the bar. The youth at the helm is so confident that he has made the sheet fast; and while one hand is firm on the tiller, the other holds a book, from which he glances up only now & then to set his course closer to the wind that is driving him into the heart of the storm.[81]

14

Eternal gossip around the situation

A WORLD AWAY from the savage Civil War in Spain, London society was going about its usual round of the summer season, or at least attempting to do so, in the face of a royal crisis at home and conflict abroad. At home the death of George V still cast its shadow. The new King, in compulsory mourning for six months, had not attended the Derby to see the Aga Khan's horse Mahmoud, an outsider, streak home in a record time of 2 minutes 33.8 seconds.[1] It was not a popular victory. Robert Bernays reported that, because so few had bet on the horse, 'hardly anyone cheered him'.[2] Not that the King would have much cared: he cared for nothing at this time except Wallis Simpson.

In the absence of the King, the season's round of house-parties, débutantes' coming-out dances and balls continued, one following the other in a haze of chiffon and champagne. June was the month, according to *Tatler*, 'of roses, of sunshine, of large hats, sunshades and intensive entertaining'.[3] The same small and wealthy section of society met each other time after time, discussed the same topics (more often than not the King) and became thoroughly overtired. There were so many coming-out parties for débutantes in Belgravia that it was quite possible to enter the wrong one by mistake, as Hermione Llewellyn (later Countess of Ranfurly) discovered to her cost: 'On one dreadful evening when I arrived innocently and cheerfully at the wrong party, a furious host picked me up and flung me out on the street, ruining my dress and hair-do, and grazing my face.'[4] Some of the debs' parties were so crowded that the guests 'seemed to be standing in a solid mass, unable to move despite the encouraging efforts of a first rate band'.[5] There were cocktail parties too. Sibyl Colefax held a gathering with Countess Munster in her interior decorating shop in Bruton Street. It was specially timed to end before the start of the opera, so that guests could go to Covent Garden, where Kirsten Flagstad was stunning packed houses with her interpretation of Isolde in Wagner's *Tristan*.

Grand parties in the few remaining great houses were still tremendous affairs, redolent of the days of sumptuous entertaining of the Edwardian era. A number were cancelled that year out of respect for the late King. But, *Tatler* reported, 'Lady Astor's dance is marked with a red letter on the social engagement lists of all who've been lucky enough to receive invitations'. On Tuesday 16 June, Nancy Astor held a ball at Cliveden that topped the season in its lavishness, style and the sheer number of guests: one thousand thronged the vast golden ballroom. Her niece Joyce Grenfell was there and 'never enjoyed a party so much before in my life. It was fun from the word go.'[6]

Nancy Astor had used the wealth of her husband, the second Viscount Astor, to turn Cliveden, her Italianate palace on the banks of the Thames, into one of the key social and political salons of post-First World War Britain. The Cliveden set, as a coterie of her pro-appeasement guests later became known, included the editor of *The Times*, Geoffrey Dawson, and Baldwin's confidant Thomas Jones. Nancy had taken over the Conservative seat of Plymouth Sutton from her husband in 1919 and was notorious for her sharp sense of humour. Many thought her wit had declined with age, and she was now plain rude or, as Lucy Baldwin had discovered with her misjudged joke about maternal mortality, embarrassing.

For the ball that June all political machinations were put aside, as Nancy, in pale blue satin and wearing a crown tiara greeted her guests. 'Everyone was there, the whole caboodle', Joyce Grenfell enthused. Huge sprays of laburnum, taken from the gardens, bathed the ballroom with the scent of vanilla and tinged it with a golden aura. After dinner of clear soup, cutlets and lobster encased in aspic,[7] the dance orchestra started at 10.30, and guests took to the floor for polkas, waltzes and the quick-step. Joyce Grenfell was 'never off the dance floor . . . I almost wore my shoes through'.[8] At four in the morning 'Aunt Nancy made us stop . . . we had eggs and bacon after the music had finished and we all agreed it was the world's best party. And on champagne cup and lemonade!' Nancy, a Christian Scientist, was strictly teetotal. Those unable to survive the evening without a drink had to take quick nips from a hip-flask, hiding behind a palm.

The King loved to dance, and mourning for his late father was, though he never admitted it, a trial. It did not, however, prevent him attending numerous private dinner parties, many of them arranged by the dominant hostesses of the time. Now that an understanding of sorts had been reached with Ernest Simpson, Wallis was able to accompany the King unhindered by a husband. The affair was kept out of the press as far as possible, though it was by now common knowledge among wide swathes of the upper and middle classes, who only needed to glance at the court circular, with its frequent references to 'Mrs Ernest Simpson', to grasp what was going on.

By the summer cracks were beginning to appear in the façade of silence. *Cavalcade*, a self-styled British news magazine which boasted that it was 'Accurate Brisk Complete', cheekily challenged the newspapers' self-censorship. In July it produced a five-column profile of Mrs Simpson, but it did not go so far as to state that she was having a relationship with the King. A few weeks later the magazine mischievously reported that the Japanese Imperial government, noticing that foreign newspaper reports of the King and Wallis were cut out of British editions, requested that the same be done for the Emperor. Such reports caused acute embarrassment.

While Edward's love affair was open season for the upper classes, it was widely held that the mass of ordinary people should not know. If they did, respect for the lynch-pin of the social order that bound society together might collapse. Revolution could follow. One hostess, *Cavalcade* reported, 'fines any one of her guests 5 shillings every time the King's non-state activities are mentioned in front of a servant'.[9] Sibyl Colefax, London's most indefatigable people-collector, told her friend Bernard Berenson in a letter early that summer that the affair was the only subject of conversation: 'eternal gossip around the situation – and all the gossip is false – but its perpetual repetition is dangerous and foolish.'[10]

Sibyl Colefax's loyal but dull husband, Arthur, a patent lawyer, had died suddenly in February, forcing the hostess to make economies and downsize. That summer she sold her mansion on the King's Road, Argyll House, and moved to a terraced house in Westminster. Although she still grieved for her husband, feeling, she wrote, 'a curious underworld of grey sorrow',[11] she had no intention of letting this get in the way of her great *métier*: socializing. Before moving out of Argyll House she arranged one last dinner party. It was tó be her swan-song, a triumphant finale to years of the most assiduous networking.

The guest of honour was King Edward VIII, accompanied, of course, by Mrs Simpson. Those invited with him were an eclectic cross-section of London society. Included were: Winston Churchill; Harold Nicolson and Robert Bruce Lockhart, both diarists and diners-out; the art historian Kenneth Clark and his wife, Jane; Lord Berners, waspish and witty ('brush pen and keyboard are all mediums familiar to him', gushed *Tatler*); the lesbian Princesse de Polignac; the socialite Daisy Fellowes; and Robert Vansittart, head of the Foreign Office. Sibyl Colefax's lion-hunting had stretched across the Atlantic: the all-powerful Wall Street banker Tom Lamont, head of the mighty J. P. Morgan, graced Argyll House with his taciturn presence. To round it off with a dash of high culture, Sibyl invited Arthur Rubinstein, then a young pianist, famous as an interpreter of Chopin. Before the dinner Sibyl telephoned Berners, saying, 'Gerald, I particularly want you to meet Arthur'. He replied, 'But I thought Arthur was dead'. 'Oh not my Arthur,' she exclaimed, 'Arthur Rubinstein'.

That evening Argyll House was at its harmonious best. As a professional interior decorator, Sibyl Colefax had an eye for tasteful, soft pastel colours combined with restrained classic furnishing. Her business, Colefax and Fowler, set up as a result of financial disaster following the Crash, had defined the look of the 1930s interior. As the guests arrived in the warmth of the evening, 'the great double doors stood open, and they could see the garden in the distance, spreading lawns and what Sibyl called a sea of green trees'.[12] The scent of jasmine wafted in through the garden doors. Chinese lanterns hung from the trees, their glowing orbs lending a faint light as the guests talked together in anticipation of the arrival of the King. Half an hour later Edward arrived with Wallis Simpson, and the guests went into dinner almost immediately. It was a sign of the new informal style that the King had come without an equerry or an aide-de-camp.

During dinner Edward talked to Robert Bruce Lockhart about international affairs, repeating that 'he was in favour of coming to some square deal with Germany'. He admitted this was difficult, but said 'he hoped to be able to use his position in the right direction'.[13] If the die-hard anti-German diplomat Sir Robert Vansittart overheard this, he tactfully made no comment. The King turned to the dour Tom Lamont to talk of conditions in America and, as Nicolson noted, he impressed him 'very deeply with his wide knowledge and intelli-gence'[14] – knowledge perhaps garnered from discussion with Wallis. Harold Nicolson was one of the few who believed that Mrs Simpson had been a good influence on her lover: 'There is no doubt about it that he has infinitely improved since the old Prince of Wales days. He seems almost completely to have lost his nervousness and shyness, and his charm and good manners are more apparent than ever.'[15]

After dinner the company retired to the drawing-room. More guests drifted in, some from a late sitting at the House of Commons, others, such as Noel Coward, from the theatre. Arthur Rubinstein, small and highly coiffed with tightly knit curls, stepped forward to take his place at the piano. The guests gathered round, the older ones reclining on chairs and sofas, while the young perched on stools or took their places on the floor, where Sibyl Colefax joined the society beauty Diana Cooper, daughter of the Duke of Rutland, as Nicolson waspishly noted: 'to give a sense of informality and youth to the occa-sion. But Sibyl, poor sweet, is not good at young abandon. She looked incongruous on the floor as if someone had laid an inkstand there.'[16] Rubinstein started to play. Nicolson's sharp eye continued to rove round the room. He watched as the Princesse de Polignac wan-dered in and sat on a stool close to the piano, evidently keen to show her appreciation of the maestro at work: 'I have seldom seen a woman sit so firmly: there was determination in every line of her bum', he wrote. Others were less entranced. The King, whose musical taste was for something light and modern, and whose favourite instrument was the bagpipes, quickly tired of Chopin. According to Kenneth Clark, he had been expecting some easy listening, the barcarolle from *Les Contes d'Hoffman*. On hearing the first piece, a barcarolle by Chopin, the King, bewildered and irritated, muttered, 'That isn't the one we like'.[17] Rubinstein then played a prelude. This was too much. The King stood up, crossed the room, saying with royal command, 'We enjoyed that very much, Mr Rubinstein'.

He then made to leave. Seeing her party was heading for disaster, Sibyl Colefax was on the verge of tears. Rubinstein, 'filled with anger and humiliation', retired with Kenneth Clark to an adjacent room for a consoling whisky and soda. Sibyl turned in desperation to Lord Berners, begging him to 'play something'. He refused, saying that he had come as a guest rather than as a performer, to which she shrieked, 'I'll never ask you here again'. With practised disdain he replied, 'I rather think you will'.[18]

It was now 10.15, and the King was at the front door, on the point of departure. At that moment, with perfect timing, Winston Churchill arrived from the House of Commons, delaying him with some friendly greetings. Just then the notes of a familiar song could be heard from the drawing-room. Noel Coward, 'like the kind man he was had put his artistic scruples in his pocket in order to save his friend's evening',[19] and had started on 'Mad Dogs and Englishmen'. The King and Wallis came back; he was 'bucked up and looked quite amused'.[20] Coward continued with 'Don't Put your Daughter on the Stage, Mrs Worthington'. The evening was saved. They stayed till one.[21]

The six months of court mourning came to an end that summer, and the King and Mrs Simpson were everywhere to be seen. To the dismay of the old guard, Wallis's name appeared with increasing frequency in the court circular. She dined with Edward and she was seen at Ascot without the King, who was still in mourning. On 16 July she attended the Presentation of Colours to three regiments of the Brigade of Guards.

The scene that sunny summer's morning in Hyde Park summed up the gulf between the old and new, tradition and modernity, that was dividing the royal family and fracturing the court, and which, when made public, would split the country. Two viewing stands had been erected: one for the royal family and another, directly adjoining, for the King's friends. Edward had invited Chips Channon, one of his most loyal supporters. Channon observed the proceedings with his customary mixture of amused detachment and social insight. He went with Diana Cooper, who arrived in a War Office car supplied by her husband, the Secretary of State for War. On arrival Channon sat with what he called 'the new court', typified by Emerald Cunard, the pro-Nazi American hostess. She, dressed in an inappropriate sable coat, was sitting beside Wallis Simpson. In the next-door stand he saw the royal party: Queen Mary and Elizabeth, Duchess of York, with her two daughters.

The two sides eyed each other uncomfortably as they waited for the martial display to begin. In the royal pavilion Queen Mary and the Duchess sat with formidable poise, the epitome of royal respectability. Princesses Elizabeth and Margaret, the public's favourites were, as usual, dressed identically in hats, short coats and skirts, with sensible shoes. The Yorks represented the ideal modern, nuclear family, as Marguerite Patten remembered. 'They were a picture book family, with the two enchanting little girls, they were the lovely sort of family that everybody would like.'[22]

The two girls were taking a keen interest in the proceedings under the watchful eye of Marion Crawford, 'Crawfie', their nanny, oblivious of the unspoken tension of the adults in their group. Only a few feet away but divided by an unbridgeable chasm, a group of Anglo-American socialites, a cocktail of wealth, fashion and self-conscious modernity, chatted and gossiped as they waited for the ceremony to begin. To the Queen and the Duchess they posed a deadly threat to the survival of the monarchy itself. Elizabeth had recently written a pointed letter to the court doctor, Lord Dawson, thanking him for his care when she was unwell and bemoaning the change of atmosphere at court. 'Though outwardly one's life goes on the same,' she confessed, 'yet everything is different – especially spiritually, and mentally. I don't know if it is the result of being ill but I mind things that I don't like more than before.'[23] It was a clear – if coded – signal of a profound difference in outlook from the King.

When the six Guards battalions marched into the park, Channon's eye turned to the ceremonial. 'It was London at its very best, London well-dressed, London in high summer, the grey sky, the green of the trees, and then the sun coming out at the right royal moment, the bayonets glistening, and the horses . . . the Waterloo-ness of it all.'[24] The two royal brothers, the King and the Duke of York, took the salute on horseback before dismounting to present the new Colours and make short speeches. The Duke's address was, as usual, an agony for all concerned. All silently urged him on, praying that he would get through without too much of a stammer. The King's speech, written for him by Winston Churchill, caught the mood of the moment with its acknowledgment of the horror of war. 'Humanity cries out for peace', he declaimed in his light voice with its curious accent: posh, Cockney and American all rolled into one.

On his way to the House of Commons after the ceremony Chips noticed with shock a newspaper placard: 'The King Shot At'. In Westminster he soon discovered, to his relief, that a deranged Irish journalist, George McMahon, had not in fact fired at the King but had pointed a loaded revolver at him. A sharp-eyed special constable had seen the gun, grabbed McMahon's arm and dislodged the pistol from his hand. It clattered under Edward's horse as he passed. The crowd immediately set upon the would-be assassin, who had to be rescued from lynching by a posse of police, who manhandled him above their shoulders to safety.

Edward had felt a split-second of terror when he saw the pointed gun; 'for one moment I braced myself for the blast that never came', he recalled. He turned to the General on his right and said, 'I don't know what that thing was; but, if it had gone off, it would have made a nasty mess of us' and rode on as if nothing had happened.[25] This display of *sang froid* increased the King's already enormous popularity. Even his most critical courtiers had to admit through gritted teeth that the episode showed strength of character and that at all events he was not, as some had thought, a coward.[26]

But what good his courage did him in the eyes of the court was soon undone. Five days later, to mark the end of the season, 600 débutantes who had received their 'Command' cards from Lord

Cromer, the Lord Chamberlain, began the lengthy and elaborate process of putting on dresses, arranging their hair, applying make-up and practising curtseys for 'presentation' at court. It was part of the process of coming out, marking the end of childhood and the emergence into 'society' of the aristocratic young woman.

These archaic presentation ceremonies had not taken place since the death of King George, in recognition of the six-month period of court mourning that followed his passing. In order to make up for the backlog, it was decided to hold two garden receptions at Buckingham Palace at which the débutantes could be presented. Most would have preferred the usual glittering evening courts held in the magnificent Throne Room, where the young women dressed in all their finery, ostrich feathers, train, long gloves and were accompanied by their male escorts in full dress uniform. The Gentlemen of the Household wore the court dress of knee-breeches, silk stockings and buckled shoes.[27] Instead, as *Tatler* moaned, 'the lot of those making presentations will not be a happy one! If it is fine they will be given seats "so far as it is possible" (Oh, cautious Lord Cromer!).'[28]

It was the first time that a presentation court of this nature had been held in the open air. The gold-fringed shamiana, a crimson canopy supported on hammered silver posts, which King George had brought home from his Indian Durbar in 1911, was put up to provide shelter for Edward and other members of the royal family from rain or sun. The débutantes, their chaperones and escorts were not so lucky. They had to crowd behind a roped-off enclosure opposite the royal dais. Many were forced to crane their necks for a sight of the proceedings.

On Tuesday 21 July the Mall was jammed with the Daimlers, Rolls-Royces and Bentleys of the upper classes. Their occupants sat primly in their finery, staring straight ahead like waxworks as the public ogled, enjoying the sight of the trapped débutantes. Most of the young women, according to the *Daily Express*, 'wore a big hat, a frilly frock, ground length, invariably in organdie, high puffed sleeves and a ribbon sash'.[29] One or two dared to buck the trend and wore short skirts, as though going to a cocktail party. To King Edward the presentation ceremony was just the sort of ancient ritual that he wished to abolish as he modernized the monarchy. To the girls and their families it was an ancient rite of passage imbued with as much meaning and significance as a tribal ritual in New Guinea. The King dismissed it at his peril.

Proceedings began faultlessly, with all the precision of the Buckingham Palace ceremonial assembly line. As Lord Cromer, the Lord Chamberlain, read out a name, a young woman, part of a long line stretching across the great lawn, walked forward and made a much-practised curtsey to the King. He was seated beneath the Durbar canopy on a gilded and ornate large chair brought out from the Throne Room. Each time the débutante curtseyed, he nodded slightly. She then rose and walked on, just as another stepped forward. Far to the King's left, out of his sight, hundreds of the young ladies, penned in a large enclosure, waited to be summoned to the presentation queue.

As the seemingly endless line of débutantes went through this repetitive action, Edward appeared increasingly bored and fidgety. He glanced around, hardly bothering to acknowledge those paying obeisance to him. Behind him, the Duchess of York could be seen gossiping animatedly with her jolly brother-law, the Duke of Kent, and his wife, the beautiful Princess Marina. About half-way through the proceedings, to the King's evident relief but to the dismay of the girls and their families, grey clouds gathered over London. Spots of rain began to fall on the assembled crowd.

It was the perfect excuse to call a halt. Glancing up at the menacing sky, Edward summoned the Lord Chamberlain and the Prime Minister, who was also present, consulted them as though it was an important matter of state and ordered the ceremony to cease. He then retired hastily, and no doubt thankfully, to the shelter of the palace. The contingency plan of continuing the presentation in the State Ball Room was also abandoned. The distraught young women, holding their hats and clutching their dresses, were left to run for the cover of the Palace chestnut trees, where they huddled in bedraggled clumps, like a fine herbaceous border laid waste by a summer thunderstorm. Others made for the refreshment tents, which quickly became overcrowded and stuffy. Those who defied their parents to wear short skirts were vindicated.

It was not the rain, or the ruined dresses, that the débutantes and their families minded. It was the fact that the ceremony had been peremptorily cancelled, and there was therefore no chance of being presented to the King. Those who had missed the opportunity to go forward and curtsey had to make do with a card from the Lord Chamberlain acknowledging their presence at the presentation. It was a trivial matter. The presentation at court was a ceremony that the modernizing King was right to wish to reform, as its later abolition confirmed. But the manner of its cancellation, as with so many of his changes, was cack-handed. It made him enemies just at a time when, as the Simpson affair simmered dangerously, he needed as many friends as possible.

One of his most loyal supporters over the summer of 1936 was the diarist Chips Channon, who had by now made himself a lynchpin of the new court. As an American and a *nouveau riche*, Channon was drawn to Wallis Simpson and the King. He wrote in his diary in July:

> The Simpson scandal is growing and she, poor Wallis, looks unhappy. The world is closing in around her, the flatterers, the sycophants, and the malicious. It is a curious social juxtaposition that casts me in the role of Defender of the King. But I do, and very strongly in society.[30]

As the King's champion, Channon was at his social peak that summer. He and his wife, Lady Honor, the Guinness heiress, were invited everywhere during the season. They spent weekend after weekend at the great country houses, tramping the luxurious treadmill of entertainment so furiously that, as the end approached, he became jaded. 'What a bore weekends are, forty-eight hours social crucifixion',[31] he groaned like the bored young Gaston in *GiGi*.

Chips's social apotheosis had come on 17 July, the day after the Presentation of the Colours, when Queen Mary graced the Channons' house in Belgrave Square with an afternoon visit. No doubt the Queen had been told by her son, after he had dined there a month earlier, of the fabulous decoration of the house. At 3.25 sharp the green royal Daimler dew up outside no. 5, where Chips and Lady Honor were waiting on the specially laid red carpet. Honor curtseyed deeply and Chips bowed low and then ushered the Queen into the house. A 'minute detailed examination' of the interior followed. Queen Mary was notorious for her partiality to other people's precious knick-knacks and furnishings. Chips's heart was in his mouth as she looked around, 'revealing her very great knowledge and flair for pictures, furniture and bibelots'; but fortunately nothing was singled out for the special praise that indicated a desire for the object in question, or – if it were – Chips was not playing ball.

The Queen, stately as ever, was still in mourning, dressed in black, and, as it was summer, she carried a matching parasol. 'But here were no weeds, no crepe,' Chips was relieved to see, and she referred several times to the late King as 'my husband'. The party admired the Rex Whistler fresco in the drawing-room, before they were led into the *pièce de resistance*, the 'Amalienburg' dining-room. 'I have never known such praise', Chips exulted. 'She felt the walls in her black gloved fingers and she patted the stove, and examined the Dresden pieces. We were there quite twenty minutes.' After the Amalienburg, and a quick tour of the nursery, where baby Paul pinched the royal nose and tugged the Queenly ear-rings (HM not so stiff and formal after all), the Queen and Chips squeezed into the lift and 'shot down' to the basement, where the host proudly showed his guest 'the cloakroom and "loos" which we have arranged so gaily'. Chips had momentarily forgotten that this was where he had hung his portraits of George III and George IV. Had he made a *faux pas*? Fortunately not. 'Ah', Queen Mary laughed, 'What a place to keep the family.' After lemonade and cake the Queen took her leave. The visit, Chips wrote 'was a *riotous* success, and one felt it'.

An outsider, it is said, sees most of the game, and few outsiders were more acute observers of the social scene than Chips, wealthy, bisexual and American-born. He wrote as an interloper, looking on at the game as a wry observer, possibly the sharpest of his generation. Although a Conservative MP (taking over the seat of Southend from the Guinness family), he rarely dared make a speech in the House and had little ambition for office; he rose no higher than Parliamentary Private Secretary.[32] Nonetheless he knew that he was destined for immortality. On 7 July that summer, writing his diary in the House of Commons library, he noticed the fiery leader of the Independent Labour Party, Jimmy Maxton, sitting opposite him, and mused: 'in what different paths our lives lie, and yet I wonder, shall I not be known when he is forgotten? Reformers are always finally neglected, while the memoirs of the frivolous will always be eagerly read.'[33]

Channon shared the foibles and fantasies of a number of his aristo-cratic and royal friends, as well as his political colleagues. He was anti-Semitic and pro-Nazi, he supported Franco in Spain, and he was happy to be cultivated by Hitler's diplomat, Joachim von Ribbentrop. He first met Ribbentrop at dinner in late May that year, dining with the American hostess Laura Corrigan, another of London's many misguided Nazi-promoting hostesses. The encounter was not a success. Chips was put off by Ribbentrop's over-hearty handshake and dismissed him grandly as a man who looks like 'the captain of someone's yacht, square, breezy and with a sea-going look'. He took an instant dislike to Frau von Ribbentrop because of her lack of make-up and 'appalling khaki coloured clothes' and he pondered in his diary about German men: 'is it because their women are so unattractive that the race is largely homosexual?'

With the Berlin Olympics approaching in early August, Joachim von Ribbentrop had come over to London with a fistful of invi-tations to the games, which he distributed among such aristocrats, politicians and newspaper magnates as he considered useful to the cause. Channon must have realized what was on offer; his manner to the German diplomat underwent a marked change in the space of a few days.

He bumped into him again a week after their first unhappy meeting. This time things went with a swing. He took him to a night-club, where Ribbentrop, now looking like 'a jolly commercial traveller', laughed a lot with his host (not an experience usually associated with the sour-faced emissary). At the end of the evening Ribbentrop proffered the hoped-for invitation on behalf of the Führer, which was accepted 'gleefully'.[34] Later, when told of a friend's earlier visit to Berlin and how 'he was received by Ribbentrop, Hitler, and escorted everywhere by stormtroopers', Chips wrote breathlessly that 'Honor and I can now hardly wait to go'. Not all in the upper-class circles in which Channon moved took up the invitations so lavishly handed out by Hitler's personal emissary, and, as the ever-sensitive Channon noticed, 'Harold Nicolson and Lady Colefax disapprove of our journey, and so I felt, though they have not said so, do the truculent Coopers'.[35] The 'truculent Coopers' were Duff Cooper, and his wife, Diana.

On Friday 1 August, Sir Philip Sassoon, Under-Secretary of State for Air in the National Government, invited the Channons to join him and the Coopers for the weekend at Port Lympne. Other guests included the pro-appeasement Lord Aberconway with his wife, Christabel, and the Conservative MP Victor Cazalet, another diarist and a friend of the royal family. The weekend turned out to be an unpleasant affair, as Chips's diary revealed, reflecting the divisions in British society over Nazi Germany and the ugly side of upper-class attitudes to the Jews.

Although the great country house had been in decline since its heyday in the Edwardian era, in 1936 a number still thrived, entertaining in the grand style. Lympne was one of them. There the enormously rich and brilliant Sir Philip, cousin of Siegfried the war poet, art collector and scion of the two great Jewish merchant and banking families, the Sassoons and the Rothschilds, specialized in the political house party and spent his fortune developing the exterior of his new house and on works of art for the interior.

He had built Lympne shortly before the First World War. It was constructed of small red bricks in the Dutch Colonial style. The interior was intended to resemble an opulent Roman villa with marble columns, a great curving stone staircase and an intricately patterned tiled hall. Outside, Sassoon had created a white marble patio in the Moorish style, overlooking grounds that swept down to the sea, with vast herbaceous borders tended by twenty gardeners. When the Channons visited in early August, the borders were in all their glory, an explosion of colour.[36] It was enough to make even Chips envious. Although fabulously rich himself, he was not in the same league as his host. He, perhaps not for the best of motives, found Sassoon and his house too cosmopolitan and 'foreign' for his taste, expressing his opinion of it with typical acerbity as 'a triumph of beautiful bad taste and Babylonian luxury, with terraces and flowery gardens, and jade green pools and swimming baths and rooms done up in silver and blue and orange. A strange hydro for this strangest of sinister men.'[37]

The Channons arrived for the weekend house party with the garden designer Norah Lindsay. As their car approached the great house, they met Philip Sassoon in the drive. Sassoon waved a welcome to his guests and walked on without engaging them in conversation. 'Very Jewish of him', Norah remarked.[38] This undertone of anti-Semitism persisted as the house party got under way. Chips had been to stay at Sir Philip's other magnificent country house, Trent, in Hertfordshire, the year before, and there he had played golf on the estate's course and enjoyed his host's magnificent hospitality. He had noticed then, however, that 'the servants are casual, indeed almost rude; but, this too, often happens in a rich Jew's establishment'.

He returned to the theme at Lympne, complaining about the obsequious but second-rate servants to Duff Cooper, who was working at a jigsaw puzzle (a ubiquitous pastime at country house parties, and often a haven for the shy or bored). 'Yes, one sees who has the upper hand here', Duff laughed. Chips continued the coded anti-Semitic theme with his wife. 'The house is large and luxurious and frankly ugly. Honor said it was like a Spanish brothel.' An example, perhaps, of the pot calling the kettle black. Chips went on to sneer about his bedroom, 'the so-called Alhambra suite looking on to a sort of courtyard, attractive but uncomfortable'.

That evening, after dinner in the lapis lazuli dining-room (a rival to the 'Amalienburg'), the women departed, leaving the men to talk politics. Inevitably, the subject of Nazi Germany arose, 'with Philip and Duff attacking the Nazis with a violence born of personal prejudice',[39] understandable given that one was Jewish and the other had fought in the trenches and was an ardent Francophile. Characteristically, Channon kept his views to himself, but what he thought was clear. Afterwards a fellow guest, a young RAF 'flying boy', came up to him and whispered, 'Is Duff Cooper off his rocker, or what?' Less than four years later, no doubt, the flying boy would be piloting a Spitfire against the Luftwaffe.

Two days later the subject of the Nazis came up again. Max Aitken, the playboy son of the newspaper magnate Lord Beaverbrook, had just flown in from Berlin, where he had been bedazzled by the display of Nazi power that heralded the Olympic Games. It was too much for Victor Cazalet, who 'tactlessly flew at him and a dreadful discussion ensued during which everyone lost their temper'.[40] That summer of 1936 no one could avoid the question of Germany, which, like Spain, divided not just dinner tables but also the heart of government, media and all sections of society. After the success of the Rhineland it was Hitler's hope that the Olympics would be a propaganda coup that would tip the balance of British opinion in his favour.

The next day the Channons left for Berlin, already converted. It had been a thoroughly unsatisfactory weekend, as Chips noted in his diary, still harping on about the servants. 'The whole affair is second rate, even the lavish lapis dining room, and especially the white coated footmen who will wait on one at tea, always a bad sign.'[41]

Just as the Channons departed for the Olympics, the King was preparing for his summer holiday. He had arranged with Lady Yule, the film financier and Britain's most wealthy woman, to charter her massive 1,500 ton steam yacht the *Nahlin*. The plan was to cruise with a party of friends – including, needless to say, Wallis – through the Adriatic, passing along the Dalmatian coast before venturing into the eastern Mediterranean to visit Greece and Turkey.

The yacht was specially fitted out for a King. All the books were taken out of the library ('not wanted on voyage'), the shelving was removed, and the large space converted into a state room, so that he might have a place in which to attend to official business and relax with Wallis in private. A dance floor was laid in the lounge, and Edward's favourite records placed by the gramophone, ready for use. A powerful wireless doubled as a communications hub for the King's daily official dispatches and, in the evening, a means of tuning in to the dance orchestras of the BBC. Quantities of food and drink were carried on board, along with a large trunk containing 3,000 golf balls for Edward to practise driving into the sea, 'partly because it would give him exercise, and partly because he liked to see them splash into the water',[42] as Helen Hardinge, by no means an impartial witness, acidly commented. The King's luggage was stamped 'The Duke of Lancaster', the traditional title used by the monarch when travelling incognito.

The *Nahlin* steamed out of Portsmouth at the beginning of August. On board was a crew of fifty-eight, including a team of valets and maids, to attend to the twelve guests' every need. The elegant yacht, with its high prow and stern and distinctive raked orange-yellow funnel, sailed through the choppy waters of the Bay of Biscay without His Majesty and his party. Not a good sailor, he had decided to travel with his guests by train to Venice.

Before Edward left, he decided, on the spur of the moment, to say goodbye to his mother at Sandringham. He summoned his blue and scarlet bi-plane and flew from Windsor to Sandringham, where he greeted Queen Mary, who was strolling in the gardens. Eight thousand day-trippers who had also been permitted to wander in the grounds 'gaped when they saw the King, hatless, walking along the garden paths with the Queen'.[43] In a romantic gesture Edward stopped and plucked a rose from the border for his mother, who took it smiling and, a little later, went over to a group of visitors and handed it to a girl. The King stayed for lunch and tea and then flew back to Fort Belvedere. The trip was typical of his informality and spontaneity. It was also one of the last times that he would see his mother in circumstances not clouded by crisis.

Two days later he flew to France to join his guests for the train journey south to join the *Nahlin*. His guests were the usual mix of the new and the old, the conventional and the more modern-minded. They included the ever-popular Duff and Diana Cooper, Helen Fitzgerald (sister of Lord Beaverbrook, and a dead-ringer for Wallis), Perry Brownlow, loyal Lord-in-Waiting, and his wife, and a disapproving faction from the Palace: Sir John Aird, an equerry, and Tommy Lascelles, Edward's most bitter critic at court.

The King had wished to sail from Venice. At the last moment, however, Anthony Eden, the Foreign Secretary, intervened to insist that at all costs he avoid Italy. Any visit to a Fascist country, he feared, might be seen as a propaganda coup for Mussolini. To Edward's intense irritation, in order to by-pass Italy, 'I subjected myself to an indescribable night journey by train into Yugoslavia with a clanking and jolting such as I had never before experienced'.[44] Given that the train was the royal Pullman laid on by his friend Prince Paul, the Prince Regent of Yugoslavia, this criticism was perhaps a case of the prince and the pea.

On 10 August, Edward boarded the *Nahlin* at the small Yugoslav fishing village of Sibenik. The yacht then started its leisurely cruise down the coast, stopping every now and then to allow the host and his guests to explore a picturesque town or village. It was escorted by two destroyers of the Royal Navy's Mediterranean fleet. The warships' purpose, apart from providing security, was for the King's Messengers to pick up and deliver the red dispatch boxes, to which he was meant to attend in his private state room. While at sea, the party behaved as they might at a country house party. They idled away the hours with games and gossip, drank dry martinis, clover leafs and whisky sours, listened to the wireless and danced, and filled in time toying with a jigsaw of a shapely nude perched on a cushion, which had been put out on the quarter deck.[45] For a man addicted to exercise, the King found an outlet in rowing the *Nahlin*'s skiffs around the Royal Navy escorts, joking with the sailors 'I am reviewing the Fleet!'[46] His private detectives followed, rowed by a red-faced rating, panting as he laboured over the oars to keep up with his super-fit sovereign.

The King's hopes that his alias, 'The Duke of Lancaster', would give him the cover of anonymity during the holiday were disappointed from the moment he arrived in Yugoslavia. Whenever he and Wallis disembarked, crowds gathered, jostling to catch sight of the couple. Some cried, 'Vive le roi', others 'Vive l'amour'.[47] At Dubrovnik the mayor issued a proclamation forbidding the townsfolk to stare. It only made them ogle more.[48] Edward was used to crowds. What he did not like was the intrusive presence of numerous American journalists and photographers, who pursued him everywhere.[49] While the British press was generally keeping mum on the matter by mutual agreement, there was no such restraint in the USA, where lurid stories of the relationship with Wallis were beginning to appear.

In Britain too cracks continued to show in the wall of deferential silence. *Cavalcade*, in its August editions, carried numerous photographs of 'The Duke of Lancaster' with his friend 'Mrs Ernest Simpson'. On the cover of one edition she could be seen placing a steadying hand on the King's forearm as he clambered from a tender, with the caption 'The motor-boat arrived at Paradise Island'. The implications were all too clear.

The cruise continued southwards. The King, under instructions from the Foreign Office, paid courtesy visits to various Balkan dignitaries and met King George of the Hellenes in Corfu. The British Ambassador to Greece was impressed by the contemporary note that the couple struck, as he mused in a dispatch to London, wondering 'whether this union, however queer and generally unsuitable to the state, may not in the long run turn out be more in harmony with the spirit of the new age than anything that wisdom could have contrived'.[50]

Despite being on board a yacht costing £300,000 (equivalent to about £11 million today), with every conceivable luxury, close proximity, as so often on holiday, led to tensions and scratchiness among the party. To everyone's relief, the cruise ended in Istanbul. Any pretence of the visit being private was ignored by the Turks, who placed a huge 'Welcome' in electric light bulbs in the garden of Topkapi overlooking the Golden Horn, where the *Nahlin* docked.

The King and Wallis travelled back overland, stopping briefly in Vienna, where Edward had his hearing tested and met the Austrian President. They stayed at the Hotel Bristol, which boasted a large steam room. Helen Hardinge noted primly: 'with his chauffeur and six detectives in attendance, the King stripped down and wandered naked round the steam-room, to the astonishment of the rather proper Austrian bathers who were there.'[51] Always ready to find fault, the carping wife of the King's Private Secretary was quite wrong about this. Austrians, like their German neighbours, consider it thoroughly indecent to enter a steam room clothed.

15

The Berlin Olympics

O<small>N</small> S<small>ATURDAY</small> 1 August 1936, at precisely four o'clock in the afternoon, Adolf Hitler entered the Berlin Olympic Stadium through the Marathon Gate. As the trumpeters standing on the towers above him blew the Olympic fanfare, the crowd of 125,000 spectators rose as one, their arms stretched out in the Fascist salute, a forest of jagged spikes. Soon their voices drowned out the music with their united roars of 'Heil Hitler'. Outside, waiting to take part in the march past of athletes, Dorothy Tyler, a sixteen-year-old high-jumper in the British team, could hear the crowd: 'there was an absolute hysterical shouting, yelling and cheers', she recalled.[1] It was pure propaganda, a spectacle that Hitler and his devoted young architect Albert Speer had honed at countless party rallies and assemblies of the Nazi faithful. Politics and sport had never before been joined so successfully to such a malign purpose.

The Führer strode the long distance into the vast sunken oval stadium, leading the International Olympic Committee members and organizers, who were dressed, incongruously beside the uniformed German leader, in morning suits, carrying silk top hats. On his way Hitler paused once to take a small bouquet of flowers from a five-year-old girl, who first saluted, then curtseyed, still holding her arm outstretched in a precarious movement. The Führer, always keen to display his love of children, gently pushed down the girl's arm and took the flowers before resuming his purposeful march to his seat on the south side of the stadium.[2]

Once the shouts of 'Heil' had subsided, the Olympic orchestra, conducted by Richard Strauss, and accompanied by a 10,000-strong chorus, burst forth with 'Deutschland, Deutschland über Alles', followed by the Nazi party anthem, the 'Horst Wessel' song. The crowd joined the singing, before falling quiet for the chorus's rendition of the Olympic hymn. Then the great Olympic bell, hung at the top of the tower that dominated the entrance to the stadium complex, started to toll. The flags of the fifty-one competing nations were slowly raised. Overhead the sinister cigar-shaped airship the *Hindenburg*, the largest Zeppelin ever built, nosed round in circles above the stadium.

Seated among the thousands of Hitler-worshipping Germans were a large number of influential British spectators, guests of Joachim von Ribbentrop. Many of them were Nazi sympathizers or admirers. 'From London alone', Ribbentrop wrote, 'I expected something like a friendly invasion. Lord Monsell . . . had accepted, and so had Lord Rothermere and Lord Beaverbrook, together with other newspapermen; all our personal friends had been asked.'[3] Only four days before the opening ceremony Hitler had announced the appointment of Ribbentrop as Germany's Ambassador to Britain following the sudden death of Leopold von Hoesch. The new role for the Fuhrer's special diplomat was a sign of the importance he attached to the possibility of an alliance with Britain, which, he hoped, would leave him free to dominate Europe and expand eastwards.[4]

Although some suspected Ribbentrop of having poisoned Hoesch to get the job, in reality he was ambivalent about his new post. While he wanted to ingratiate himself still further with Hitler by forging the alliance, he feared the position would lose him influence in Berlin. He was happiest when based in the capital, as during the Olympics, plotting against his arch-rivals Goebbels and Goering, and entertaining on the grand scale.

The opening ceremony continued its orderly progress with the parade, at 4.15, of the athletes. The teams, led by Greece, honoured as the founding country, had been waiting outside on the Maifeld, a vast expanse of green with a 400-metre track adjoining the Olympic Park, and were now waiting at the mouth of the stadium. The whole affair was a marvel of Teutonic efficiency, as everything from the immaculate facilities to the very precise official directions for the Ceremony testified: '4.14 p.m. At the command "Participants, march!", the nations enter the Stadium, the spacing between the different nations being regulated at the mouth of the tunnel. A space of 5 metres should be maintained between the placard carrier and the flag-bearer.'[5]

On passing the German Chancellor, each team was ordered to salute according to the custom of its country.[6] This proved controversial. The French team, swept up by the occasion, chose to follow the Greeks in giving Hitler the 'Olympic salute', raising the right arm and stretching it at full length to the right. The difference between this gesture and the Nazi greeting, which required the arm to be stretched straight ahead, was academic to the crowd who responded with a vast chorus of 'Heil's and raised arms. Hitler too raised his forearm in response, his lips pursed and head tilted in a characteristic moue of appreciation. *The Spectator*'s correspondent found that 'there was something deeply moving in the passionate response of the German crowd'.[7] By contrast the British team members, who followed the French, had diplomatically decided to make a modest 'eyes right' when they passed the saluting platform. Unlike the French, they were greeted with lukewarm applause. Dorothy Tyler, with her team-mates, considered the 'eyes right' was the appropriate Olympic gesture. 'We didn't think much of the others; their salute had more to do with politics than the Olympics.'[8]

Von Ribbentrop was fighting his diplomatic battle on all fronts to gain an alliance with Britain. The Olympics were the means of entertaining and influencing a wide range of British luminaries in an impressive if unofficial setting. But the new Ambassador also had dreams of progress on an official level, hoping for a meeting between the Führer and the British Prime Minister. On this front, however, he was making little progress. Despite his best efforts, Anglo-German relations had not moved forward since Hitler's march into the Rhineland in the spring. The Führer considered the British Foreign Secretary's latest response to his coup, a list of questions designed to elicit his future intentions, as the height of impertinence, and angrily tossed it aside without a further glance. Anthony Eden was still waiting for a response. None would come. Government-level discussions were in stasis.

In private there had been numerous contacts as Ribbentrop

shuttled back and forth between the capitals, with his fistful of invitations, wining and dining the inconsequential and the self-important, and wheeling a succession of grandees into the Chancellery to meet Herr Hitler. He had continued his prolonged but fruitless talks with Lord Londonderry, staying with him over the Whitsun holiday at his Ulster seat, Mount Stewart, where he was reported to have been involved in a boating accident, and had to be fished out of Strangford Lough with a boat hook.[9]

Ribbentrop's primary goal remained the summit between the Führer and the Prime Minister. To this end he now cultivated Stanley Baldwin's close friend Thomas Jones. In May he invited the former civil servant to Germany for talks with Hitler. The Führer met Jones in his Munich flat, where he reiterated his desire for an alliance with Britain and 'his great desire to meet Mr Baldwin'.[10] Jones replied that Baldwin was a 'shy and modest statesman who had never entirely got over his astonishment at finding himself Prime Minister', to which Hitler, progenitor of the Leadership principle and believer in his own manifest destiny, had interrupted, smiling and saying disingenuously, 'I also'. When the meeting ended, he gave Jones a gift for Baldwin: his three Nuremberg speeches (on 'Liberty', 'Art' and 'Nationhood'). What the modest Mr Baldwin made of them is not known, although Jones assured Hitler that the Prime Minister would particularly like the oration on art, as he was 'acutely sensitive to all forms of beauty'. Thomas Jones returned to Britain and delivered his message to 10 Downing Street. Stanley Baldwin listened intently, interjecting once: 'Go on, this is like an Oppenheimer [sic] story.' (E.Phillips Oppenheim was a popular author of thrillers.) When Jones had finished, Baldwin invited him to Chequers to 'talk this out'.

The Prime Minister was exhausted physically and mentally, close to a nervous breakdown. Approaching his sixty-ninth birthday, he was overwhelmed with the cares of office, sleeping badly and taking French phosphorus pills, a remedy of the time for depression. He was increasingly reliant on his wife, 'the missus', the all-powerful Lucy, for guidance. When Jones came to Chequers at the weekend to repeat the account of his visit to Hitler, Baldwin said to him: 'My wife and I are one. I want you to tell her the story of your last weekend.' He then busied himself with a game of patience, and Lucy sat and listened to Jones, who recounted the conversation once more 'with gusto'.[11] As he spoke, Jones tried all the while to divert Baldwin from his cards, but without success. After he had told his story there was a discussion between all three, during which Mrs Baldwin appears to have taken the lead. Any idea of shuttle diplomacy was dismissed: 'S. B. did not fly and did not like the sea.' Perhaps, she suggested instead, it would be better to wait for the summer holidays, when 'S. B. could go by car to some mountainous rendezvous?' (by which she meant their holiday retreat of Aix-les-Bains, close to the French Alps). There the conversation ended. 'Then some more Malvern water, and to bed', as Jones put it.

The Prime Minister was so exhausted that his wife, now acting almost as a proxy premier, was convinced that the idea of a meeting with Hitler was quite out of the question. She had an ally in Anthony Eden, who was becoming increasingly resentful of the amount of unofficial diplomacy that was taking place, complaining of 'a Cabinet of twenty Foreign Secretaries'.[12] He vetoed any idea of a meeting with Hitler for fear of upsetting the French, Britain's most important ally. A Prime Ministerial summit with Hitler would have to wait another two years until Baldwin's successor, Neville Chamberlain, boldly ventured into the lion's den – only to emerge so badly mauled that his reputation would never recover.

As Lucy Baldwin noted in her diary throughout the summer, her husband was growing ever more depressed.[13] Over four days in succession in June she wrote: 'Stan tired'; 'Stanley seemed tired & depressed more than usual'; 'Stan very tired'; 'Stan looked very tired.'[14] At weekends he stayed in bed until teatime. The annual trip to his beloved Aix-les-Bains was cancelled on Foreign Office advice because of the danger of the Civil War in Spain, and 'undesirable characters about',[15] and on the very day the Olympics began, 1 August, the eminent surgeon to Kings and Prime Ministers, Lord Dawson of Penn, examined him and ordered three months complete rest. Baldwin obeyed. He sank back from politics and the world, 'tired out, with no desire to move',[16] taking a retreat from which he was not to emerge until October.

Meanwhile, in the Olympic Stadium that Saturday afternoon the opening ceremonies continued in the presence of a leader who was, in every essential, the reverse of Stanley Baldwin. Once the march past of the competing nations was over, each team lined up behind its national flag in deep columns on the arena, facing Hitler and the International Olympic Committee, who were in the reviewing stand. After an official speech of welcome, the Führer, who had assumed the role 'Patron of the Games', stepped forward and announced: 'I proclaim the games at Berlin in celebration of the XIth Olympiad of the modern era open.'

The trumpets blared out once more. In the distance eleven canons, marking the XIth Olympiad, roared and the Olympic flag was raised above the ramparts of the brownstone coliseum. Three thousand doves were released, circled round the stadium and flew off. At the same moment the lone figure of an athlete in white singlet and shorts appeared high on the east end of the stadium. In his right hand he held aloft the Olympic torch. The steel torch, hammered from a Krupps ingot, had been carried by 3,075 bearers the 3,075 kilometres from Olympia in Greece, where it had been lit by the rays of the sun in a specially designed helio-furnace. The carrying of the torch and the lighting of the flame were new, another masterpiece of presentation created by the Germans as they sought to marry the lofty ideals of ancient Greece with their own half-baked and perverted racist ideology.

Carrying the torch high, the young German ran down the southern track and then bounded up the long, wide steps at the opposite end of the stadium to the black steel tripod brazier, where he lit the Olympic flame. It was a piece of pure theatre. The huge crowd, mesmerized, rose again in unison, their right arms held high once more in salute, roaring out their 'Heil's in recognition not only of the Games but also of a Germany renascent on the world stage.

All was not over, however. The final ritual of the opening ceremony was the swearing of the Olympic oath. A German weightlifter, Rudolf Ismayr, intoned the pledge before the crowd, the assembled athletes following his words, their right arms raised in affirmation. They promised to respect the regulations, and swore to participate 'in the true spirit of sportsmanship for the honour of our country and for the glory of sport'.[17] Ismayr was meant to hold the Olympic flag as he read out the oath. Perhaps by mistake, but more likely intentionally, he grasped the Nazi swastika.

For Nazi Germany the Games were a triumph from beginning to end. The nation put on an unrivalled spectacle and dominated in almost every sporting event. But the laurels were not theirs alone. The USA showed its supremacy over the track and field, with one man, Jesse Owens, outshining all the others. Owens captured four gold medals. In the first week alone he won the 100 metres and 200 metres and set an Olympic record for the long jump. A 22-year-old African-American from Cleveland, Ohio, he was the second-oldest of a family of nine children: hardly the sort of pure-bred Aryan that the Nazi leadership wished to win. On Wednesday 5 August, after Owens's triumph in the 200 metres, the Nazi propaganda minister, Joseph Goebbels complained in his diary: 'We Germans win a gold medal, the Americans get three, two of which are won by niggers. This is a scandal. White humanity should be ashamed of itself.'[18] The white humanity in the stadium, to Goebbels's irritation, far from feeling ashamed, cheered Owens's victories with as much fervour as they did the German athletes: 'O-vens, O-vens', they chanted. *The Spectator*'s correspondent reported that the host nation had 'fallen completely under the spell of the American negro . . . who is already the hero of these Games'. Owens, he wrote, 'made his opponents look almost ridiculous, not only by the speed but by the sheer beauty of his running. No athletic art has ever been so perfectly concealed.'[19]

The myth has grown up that Hitler, so disturbed by the popular clamour for Owens, deliberately snubbed the black runner. In fact, Hitler was requested by the Olympic organizers not to greet individual medal winners, other than those from Germany, to avoid unintended slights when he was absent.[20] It was a convenient request with which he was happy to comply, especially as it enabled him to avoid being photographed shaking the hand of a black man. The success of the USA's athletes was the only factor to take away from the total dominance, indeed possession, of the 1936 Olympics by Germany.

Nazi racism was deliberately muted during the Games. The threat of British and American boycotts had forced the Germans to allow Jews to take part, including Jewish competitors from Germany itself (one of whom, Helene Mayer, a fencer, even gave the Hitler salute on the victory podium after winning a silver medal). Signs forbidding Jews from public spaces were taken down, and the outrageous anti-Semitic propaganda of *Der Stürmer* (the Nazi propaganda newspaper edited by the odious Julius Streicher) was removed from the streets. Nineteen thirty-six has been called the year of 'the Olympic pause', a time when Hitler, showcasing Nazi achievements, sought respectability on the world stage. Prejudice and brutal oppression continued, but behind the scenes, out of public sight. As a result, many of the stream of visitors from Britain were gulled into a naïve admiration for all things German. Chips Channon was one of them.

The Channons arrived at Berlin's smart new Tempelhof airport on 5 August. They were met by a gloomy Baron von Geyr, who had been appointed their personal aide-de-camp for the duration of the trip. To Chips's delight a stormtrooper was at the wheel of the 'grand' car that was to speed them around Berlin for the next ten days, taking them from party to party, with an occasional enforced interlude at the Games, which Chips, like many of the British visitors, found dull. Athletics in Britain, dominated by Oxford and Cambridge and starved of funds,[21] were not popular at the time. The result was a lacklustre performance in Berlin. The focus of interest for many of the visitors, like Chips, was not sport but diplomacy and socializing.

Channon was not the first, nor by any means the last, MP to be on the freeloading trip of a lifetime, but he made the most of it with more than usual gusto. He and Honor were given a 'magnificent suite of rooms' at the luxury Eden Hotel and were ferried from place to place to meet Nazi bigwigs at parties, receptions and galas. At first sight it may seem surprising that such a minor figure on the political scene should be treated like a high functionary. Ribbentrop's blind faith, however, in the influence of aristocracy and royalty over British foreign policy was so great that Chips, as a member of the inner circle of Edward VIII, had an importance in German eyes that he did not merit. The lionizing of Channon was typical of the fundamental misunderstanding of Britain that was at the root of Nazi foreign policy in 1936.

On Thursday 6 August Chips and Honor paid their first visit to the Olympic Stadium to watch the athletics, 'which bored us'. They were slightly more interested by the arrival of Hermann Goering, 'a large rotund figure, dressed in a white uniform', and later of Hitler himself. The Führer failed to impress: 'he looked exactly like his caricature – brown uniform, Charlie Chaplin moustache, square stocky figure'. Chips claimed he had been more stimulated by his encounter with the Pope sixteen years earlier.

On this day, as on every day, Germany dominated the games. The final Nazi gold medal tally of forty-six was higher than all other nations. Each time there was a win, Channon noted, the national anthem of the victor's country was played. As Germany was frequently victorious, 'not only Deutschland über Alles was bellowed, but also the Horst Wessel song, the Nazi anthem, which I thought had a rather a good lilt'. While Chips's light wit and feline insight were ideally suited to the gossipy bantering of the British upper-class drawing-room, when faced with the hardcore world of Fascism, he could only flutter around the surface, bedazzled.

The majority of the British in Berlin that month who were not athletes were, if not outright Fascist sympathizers, at least friendly to the Nazi regime. Among them was a delegation from the Anglo-German Fellowship: a group of aristocrats, businessmen, politicians and ex-servicemen who had come together to try to change British policy. Hitler himself entertained them in the Chancellery. There were also numerous right-wing MPs, including the aviator the Marquess of Clydesdale, who would become Duke of Hamilton in 1940, and was, like Channon, enjoying a junket.[22]

The Führer had invited his personal guests, the Mitford sisters, Diana and Unity, British torch-bearers for Nazism and Hitler-groupies. Like the Channons, the sisters found the games themselves dull and preferred to slip away from their official seats to enjoy themselves elsewhere.[23] Three years earlier Diana had left her husband, Bryan Guinness, to live openly with Sir Oswald Mosley, the British

Fascist leader. Now, in August, she was on a secret mission to Germany to raise funds from the Nazis for the British Union of Fascists. She also intended to make arrangements to marry Mosley at a secret ceremony in Berlin in the autumn.

Diana and Unity stayed with Josef Goebbels in his large villa over-looking the Wannsee lake, close to Berlin. There was something about the two sisters' manner – their sense of humour and clever repartee – which attracted the Nazi leadership. At first slightly in awe, Goebbels found that 'The two English girls are actually very nice'. On the evening of 2 August he stayed up late chatting to his guests. Diana and Unity imported the manners and mores of the upper-class English world in which they had grown up. They taught Goebbels and his wife, Magda, party games, laughed and joked, and spoke reverently of the Führer.[24] Diana got on particularly well with Magda.

As aristocratic British women, they were not only the objects of the respect and reverence that the Nazis felt for the British aristoc-racy. Like court jesters, they could also make jokes and tease Goebbels and Goering – or even Hitler himself – without causing offence or earning hostility. The Führer delighted in their detached manners and indolent directness. He was fascinated by their gossipy comments on British politicians and aristocrats. For their part, Diana and Unity sincerely believed that Hitler's National Socialism, if applied to Britain, could bring an end to mass unemployment and poverty: 'his ideas, if they had prevailed at the time, would have saved a great deal of suffering', Diana later said.[25] She found the Führer easy to talk to, quite different from his public image. She and her sister were delighted by his humour: 'he was very clever at imitations, a sign that somebody is very observant; he could take people off in a very clever way . . . Mussolini, for example.'

While Unity had made no secret of her obsession with Hitler, hanging round outside his favourite tea-house in Munich in 1934 until she attracted his attention and staying near him ever since, Diana was more discreet in her admiration. To publicize her close links with the Nazis would have harmed the purpose of her visit, which was to gain more Nazi financial support for Oswald Mosley's

British Union of Fascists. (The BUF had to steer clear of public links with Hitler, given his increasing unpopularity in Britain.) Two months earlier she had succeeded in wheedling £10,000 from the Führer, but Mosley considered this insufficient and sent her back for more.[26] In the event, despite her best efforts to charm her host, Hitler rejected her request for money when Goebbels mentioned it to him. 'He was very sticky about it', Diana complained.[27] He did, however, later agree to help her with the necessary arrangements for her secret marriage to Mosley, planned for 6 October.[28]

Although almost all those invited to the Olympics by Hitler and Ribbentrop were sympathetic to the Nazi regime, there was one influential figure who was not: Sir Robert Vansittart. Of all the figures that Ribbentrop cultivated, this senior diplomat was possibly the sole British visitor to the Berlin Olympics of any real significance. He was also the most hostile. 'Van', as he was widely known, had come to Berlin with firm preconceptions about Nazi Germany which he shared with his brother-in-law, the British Ambassador, Sir Eric Phipps. He was to leave with them unchanged. His prejudice (he readily accepted it was a prejudice) had arisen from visits to Germany during the height of anti-British feeling during the Boer War. It had been reinforced by the loss of his brother at Ypres in the First World War. Vansittart's views had much in common with those of Winston Churchill. Like Churchill, his opposition to appeasement would cost him dear, but in 1936 his views still counted.

As the most senior British diplomat in the 1930s, Vansittart liked to put forward the idea that 'original German sin' in international relations was the cause of all Europe's woes. With the rise of the Nazis he prophesied that 'the present regime in Germany will, on past and present form, loose off another European war just as soon as it feels strong enough'. He described the Hitler regime as 'very crude people, who have very few ideas in their noddles but brute force and militarism'.[29] He proposed a two-prong policy to deal with Hitler: building up arms and diplomacy. He had come to Berlin to try the latter. Chips Channon bumped into him at a banquet at the Opera House, hoping to find some signs that the Games had neutralized his prejudice. He was encouraged by their conversation. The British diplomat 'admitted to being impressed by the Nazi regime, and the way it had transformed Berlin and rejuvenated the country'. But being impressed was one thing; changing policy on the basis of a fleeting visit was quite another.

Vansittart was the most important guest at Ribbentrop's reception at his house in the wealthy suburb of Dahlem on 11 August. The news of Ribbentrop's appointment as Ambassador to London was the subject of much gossip, with some speculating that it was a downward move in the byzantine world of Nazi power politics. Chips's antennae were tingling, sensitive to the slightest vibration as he arrived at the party.[30] 'We were led up to the Ribbentrops, who were busy thanking people for their congratulations on his appointment . . . No-one quite knows why he has been selected. Is it because his power is waning? Have the machinations of his jealous colleagues led to this dignified banishment?' The party was intended to reverse any impression of a decline in Ribbentrop's fortunes. Chips himself was unaware that he too was seen as a pawn in the game of diplomatic chess, which was intended to end with the capture of the British King.

Eleven years later, as he waited in his cell for the verdict from the judges at Nuremberg, Ribbentrop dreamed of his glory days before the war, and of that splendid party in 1936. Annalies, his sparkling-wine heiress wife, had put up a huge marquee for the 600 guests. He remembered wistfully how she 'turned our garden into a veritable little fairground . . . at night it all looked like fairyland: the beautiful lawn, of which we had always been proud, the swimming pool covered with water lilies, the gorgeous rhododendrons, and the festively laid tables. My wife had surpassed herself.'[31] Goering and his wife were among the guests, no doubt observing everything with a critical eye in preparation for their rival extravaganza two day later. The diminutive, bespectacled figure of the security chief, Heinrich Himmler, could be seen among the guests, along with numerous British MPs, including Kenneth Lindsay, who bearded Hitler's deputy, Rudolf Hess, asking him why he had said Edward VIII was the only person who could maintain peace in Europe.[32] The moon-faced Unity Mitford was there too, without her more attractive sister, a solitary youthful hanger-on among the elder statesmen, diplomats and senior Nazis.

After dinner a popular Hungarian violinist entertained the guests, and there was dancing on the tennis court, specially covered for the occasion in coconut matting – not the ideal flooring for the evening's waltzes, foxtrots and quicksteps. The party went on into the early hours. Ribbentrop was encouraged to see that the Vansittarts stayed the longest: 'they danced a lot and seemed very happy – was this a good omen? Could it be that Sir Robert did not find Berlin so repulsive after all?'[33] His hopes were soon to be dashed. When he and the British diplomat talked later, they found no common ground: 'I felt from the start I was addressing a wall', the Nazi complained. 'Never was a conversation so barren.'

While the diplomatic dance went on in the marquees and banqueting halls of Berlin, the games continued in the cratered splendour of the Olympic Stadium. The German sporting juggernaut forged its way to the top of the league table in front of the 'Heiling' masses. Everywhere in the packed city of Berlin houses and streets were festooned with double banners – the Olympic flag with its multicoloured interlocking rings, and the red German flag emblazoned with a black swastika on a white circle. For the British athletes, many of whom had never left their country before, it was an exhilarating time. The sixteen-year-old Dorothy Tyler was not allowed out of her Olympic quarters without a chaperone. 'It was a happy experience. Sixteen in those days was considered very young, one was a child really. We were taken shopping, and were greeted "Guten Morgen, Heil Hitler" wherever we went. Some of our team replied "Good Morning, Hail King Edward!"'[34]

The Olympic Games were not the focus of attention in Britain that they are today. Dorothy Tyler found that 'people were more interested in the fact that we were visiting Germany and seeing Hitler than they were in our taking part in the Games'. The British performance was fairly lacklustre; with little training and half-hearted national support, few of the athletes shone. Tyler was one of the exceptions, winning silver in the high-jump competition. Another success was in the 4 × 400 metre relay, in which the British athletes beat the dominant American and German teams into second and third places. One of the four-man team, Godfrey Rampling, a 27-year-old Royal Artillery officer, had the run of his life. 'I never felt so good as that day', he recalled; 'I seemed to float around the track passing people without effort.'[35] When he picked up the baton from his team-mate Freddy Wolff, the Americans were in the lead. After his lap, the British were five yards ahead. Harold Abrahams, the great runner who won gold in the 100 yards in the 1924 Olympics, called Rampling's performance 'the most glorious heaven-sent quarter-mile I have ever seen'.[36] The victory of their team in the 4 × 400 metre relay, however, caused only a momentary ripple of interest among the British visitors; the attention of the grandee or tourist, journalist or spectator, was firmly fixed on the spectacle of German power, modernity and national unity that was playing out before them.

In the militaristic culture of Nazi Germany men in uniform with swastika armlets were omnipresent on the streets, keeping an eye on security and stepping forward unasked to assist the bewildered visitor. Futuristic booths of glass and steel were placed all over Berlin to provide information in different languages for the many visitors. Results of the competitions were called out in German to the slow-moving crowds on the streets from strategically placed loudspeakers. The sports were also televised by men in white coats operating futuristic box-like machines with huge telescopic lenses, perched on silver mounts. This was more a test than a broadcast, as few Germans had a television. To make up for the lack of sets, eighteen receivers were set up in halls around Berlin and at the Olympic village.[37] The screens were small, and the reception poor, but it was another sign of Germany's technological lead.

For truly effective propaganda that lasted long after the Games were over, Goebbels had commissioned the master documentary maker Leni Riefenstahl to make a film of the Olympics. She combined her genius for visualization (already put to use in her film *Triumph of the Will*) with an overbearing manner. Few – not even Goebbels himself – dared say no to her. She was given unparalleled access to the best angles and vantage points. High platforms were built for her, underwater cameras placed in the swimming-pools, trenches dug in the pristine turf for low angles of high-jumps, blimps floated above the stadium for unrivalled top shots. The result, after a year of editing, was the two-part epic *Olympia*, a massive hit in Germany. A disturbing work of genius – part celebration of human athleticism, part paean to Nazi Germany – it was not shown in Britain until after the war. Those who saw it realized immediately that in the modern field of propaganda Germany was, as in so much else, in the lead.

E. A. Montague, of *The Spectator*, noticed in Germany's approach a fundamental change in the spirit of games from previous Olympiads. It was a change that heralded a new era in the politicization of sport. 'This is not an Olympic festival as that has been understood in the past', he told his readers. 'Germany has taken the Olympic Games under her patronage.' Symbolizing this takeover of the spirit of international sport, a large German eagle carved in stone was placed over the entrance of the Olympic village, its claws clasping the five rings. It was an image of supremacy repeated throughout the country in 1936.

The battle of the receptions continued. Hitler joined the fray, giving a formal dinner in honour of Sir Robert Vansittart. It took place in the Chancellery, in the vast State Dining-Room, where three tables, bearing golden candelabra, were shaped in a horseshoe for the 150 guests. The Führer himself had overseen the design of the pillared Banqueting Hall, which boasted one large Gobelins tapestry on the cream-coloured wall, and a ceiling of blue and gold squares.[38] Before dinner the British guests were shown into an ante-room, where they were introduced to the Führer. Most, such as Lord Clydesdale, had been selected from the aristocracy and represented British sporting institutions and the Anglo-German Fellowship. Lord Rennell was particularly impressed, and wrote to *The Times* on his return of the 'good taste' with which the German Chancellor, 'that remarkable man of vision . . . had shown his perceptive feeling in the remodelling of his official residence'.[39] Hitler was an autodidact. He had not travelled and knew little of the world other than his native Austria and adopted Germany. But in 1936 he must have gained a thorough knowledge of the style and manner of the upper-class Briton. Few foreign leaders can have willingly entertained so many Old Etonians in so short a time to so little effect.

After dinner Hitler invited Lady Vansittart for a private tête-à-tête in his study.[40] He told her that he had watched *The Lives of a Bengal Lancer* five times. The film, made in 1935 and starring Gary Cooper, purported to show how the British defended the Indian Empire. Hitler explained that he wanted to learn from the film the secrets of British Imperial power – how, as he later said, a ruling class in India 'with two hundred and fifty thousand men in all, including fifty thousand soldiers, govern four hundred million Indians'.[41] It was his firm – if bizarre – belief, shared and encouraged by Ribbentrop, that the British aristocracy, topped by the monarchy, provided the answer to the conundrum. 'With the German army and the English navy', he once told Unity Mitford, 'we could rule the world.'[42]

Hitler may have been impressed by the British Empire, but there was little to admire in the British sporting achievement at the XIth Olympiad. At the end of the Games, Germany far exceeded the nearest rival, the USA, with eighty-nine medals, thirty-three of them gold. Great Britain trailed behind, tenth in the league, with a paltry fourteen medals, only four of which were gold.[43] There was, inevitably, a debate at home about the reasons for the failure even before the games had finished. Some argued that Britain's weak performance reflected a national decline in fitness, something that had long been troubling the authorities.[44] But the truth, as ever, was a question of resources.

The British, rigidly adhering to the Olympic ideal of amateurism, could not possibly compete on equal terms with the Germans. Hitler had ordered the construction of the Haus des Deutschen Sports to prepare for the Games. It was a massive modern complex, where the athletes could live and train full-time, with indoor and outdoor Olympic-size pools, a gymnasium, a special boxing area and running tracks.[45] By contrast, the British had to train in their spare time, without the benefit of the masseurs, specialists and individual trainers who were on hand to attend to the Germans' every need. One leading member of the British team who asked his employer for permission to attend the Games was refused, on the grounds that he had already taken his quota of annual leave.[46] Gold medallist Godfrey Rampling's training consisted of 'just running around the cricket ground twice a week at my army camp, or running up and down in short bursts'.[47] Dorothy Tyler, the young high-jumper, was one of the few to train actively during the games, by taking advantage of the sports field next to her team's quarters: the field was almost always empty. The surprise was not how badly Great Britain performed, but that any medals were won at all.

Off the sporting field Goering emerged the victor of the dinner parties with a banquet on 13 August that, as an awe-struck Channon remarked, rivalled not just the court of Louis XIV but that of Nero himself.[48] The dinner, for some 800 guests, was held in the gardens of his official ministry residence. Spotlights mounted on neighbouring buildings and lamps in trees illuminated the scene, as the guests, dazzled by the splendour of the setting, took their seats. To his delight, Channon was placed at a table with the pro-Nazi Duke and Duchess of Brunswick, members of the German Imperial family and relatives of the House of Windsor. Joining them were the two sons of the Duke of Hamilton, Lord Clydesdale and Lord Geordie Douglas-Hamilton. Clydesdale, a keen amateur boxer as well as an aviator, was internationally renowned for flying over Everest in a bi-plane in 1933. Goering had invited him on the strength of this feat. To the Nazis he represented the highest form of racial specimen: Nordic, blond, blue-eyed, athletic and aristocratic. Hitler's deputy, Rudolf Hess, also a keen aviator, had already marked out Clydesdale as a man of influence. It was to him he flew on his solo peace mission four years later, when Britain and Germany were at war. It has been a source of much incredulity that Hess should have sought out this minor figure on the British scene, but his choice would have appeared entirely rational to the Nazi hierarchy.

To mark Goering's role as head of the Luftwaffe, Ernst Udet, a fellow ace from the First World War, performed aerobatics in his glider over the heads of the guests while it was still light enough to see. At ground level, when darkness fell, a troupe of ballet dancers performed in the moonlight, 'the loveliest coup-d'oeil imaginable'.

Chips's fellow guests agreed that 'Goering had indeed eclipsed Ribbentrop'. But there was more to come. Suddenly, without warning, the end of the gardens, shrouded in darkness during dinner, was brilliantly lit by hidden floodlights to reveal a full-size amusement park. As the lights came on, 'a procession of white horses, donkeys and peasants, appeared from nowhere'. Chips was entranced: 'It was fantastic, roundabouts, cafes with beer and champagne, peasants dancing and "schuplattling", vast women carrying pretzels and beer, a ship, a beerhouse, crowds of gay laughing people.'[49] It was the height of kitsch, a cross between a scene from *Die Meistersinger* and the Munich Oktoberfest. The astonished guests were led into the Nazi theme park, where they wandered, dazed and amazed, until it was time to dance. Goebbels and Ribbentrop could only look on 'in despair with jealousy'. Before the Channons departed, they were given a tour of Goering's private quarters, 'unimpressive except for their size'. Although Chips found the fat Nazi charming and child-like in his vanity, he was not completely taken in, recognizing 'a strong pagan streak, a touch of the arena' in his jovial but sinister host.

Three days later, on 16 August, the XIth Olympiad came to an end with the closing ceremonies. Although more muted than the opening, the closing was nonetheless spectacular. There was no march past of competitors, only a parade of representative individuals carrying the banners and flags of their nations. Once again they were led by Greece. The flag-carrying athletes marched the length of the arena, filled to capacity, before coming to a halt beneath the Olympic flame, which flickered brightly in the darkness in its steel brazier. The President of the International Olympic Committee then stepped forward to call on the youth of the world to assemble in four years' time, ironically enough in Tokyo. After the President had spoken, the Olympic flag was slowly lowered from its high mast, distant cannons boomed a farewell salute and the Olympic flame was slowly extinguished.[50] Hitler rose from his seat as the crowds stood, all saluted in unison and sang with one voice once more 'Deutschland, Deutschland über Alles'. As Channon wrote: 'the Olympic Games, the great German display of power, and bid for recognition, were over.'

What had been a triumph for Germany was viewed with disquiet in London. Those, such as Chips Channon or Lord Rennell, who returned singing the praises of Nazi Germany, failed to persuade the majority. Other distinguished guests followed in their footsteps to attend the September Nuremberg party rally and to pay homage to Hitler, 'the greatest German of the age', as David Lloyd George called him after his visit. But such views did not represent the majority. While many, if not most, appear to have felt sympathy for the claim that Germany had been too harshly treated after the First World War and condoned Hitler's move into the Rhineland, very few in Britain admired Fascism at home or abroad.[51]

The diarist and MP Harold Nicolson stayed with Channon one month after the Games, and found to his disgust that he and his wife had fallen under the 'champagne-like' influence of Ribbentrop. He heard them arguing 'that we should let gallant little Germany glut her fill of the reds in the East and keep decadent France quiet while she does so'. Nicolson told Channon flatly 'that this may be expedient but . . . it is wrong'. He then gave the American-born Channon a short but stirring homily on British values and German faults: 'We represent a certain type of civilised mind, and . . . we are sinning against the light if we betray that type. We stand for tolerance, truth, liberty and good humour. They stand for violence, oppression, untruthfulness and bitterness.'[52] The problem was that 'they' – the Nazis – seemed to be in the ascendant. Lord Decies, who had just returned from the Games, wrote a letter to *The Times* full of foreboding:

> I left Berlin with the impression that a new race of energetic, virile young people had sprung up in Germany. They appeared to be ready to go anywhere under the orders of the Führer – a nation fully armed, equipped with the best of war material, and an air force second to none.[53]

This was the true lesson of the Berlin Olympics of 1936.

16

They shall not pass

AFTER THE OLYMPICS were over, the Mitford sisters, Diana and Unity, stayed in Germany in order to attend the annual Parteitag at Nuremberg, as Hitler's 'Ehrengaste', or honoured guests. The German leader also invited them to the Wagner festival at Bayreuth, where they enjoyed *Die Meistersinger* and were photographed for the newspapers with their 'darling storms', the SS men who guarded the Führer. During her stay Diana reported to her lover, Sir Oswald Mosley, that Hitler had rejected her request for more secret funds. This was yet another blow for Mosley, the leader of the British Union of Fascists. His movement had failed to prosper in the years since he founded it in October 1932. It had not won a single parliamentary seat and, after violence at a rally at Olympia in June 1934, membership had declined to a paltry 5,000. By the autumn of 1936, however, thanks to a national campaign and changed tactics, the number joining was on the increase once more and had climbed back to 10,000.[1]

Mosley, who was rich, clever and charismatic – 'England's most brilliant misfit'[2] – shamelessly copied Mussolini and Hitler. He adopted their uniforms, policies and style of speech-making. To some extent this plagiarism worked: thousands came just to hear him and see the spectacle of his rallies. He claimed Fascism was 'the only alternative to destructive Communism' and adopted a mesmerizing stare, which his son called 'his lighthouse trick'.[3] It gave him an air of fanaticism that some found funny but which many thought frightening, vain and repellent. While the mainstream regarded him as a cynical opportunist, he inspired great loyalty in his supporters.

Everywhere Mosley spoke, leftist agitators followed to heckle, often at great personal risk. They were usually set upon and beaten by the Fascist stewards. Mosley turned increasingly to the anti-Semitism of Hitler to energize the movement and gain the working-class support he needed. He encouraged the Fascist movement's newspapers, *Blackshirt* and *Action*, to publish crude anti-Jewish propaganda, mimicking the obscenities of Julius Streicher's *Der Stürmer*. In speeches he blamed Jewish City financiers for Britain's economic problems. This sinister tactic seemed to be working.

In the spring George Orwell had gone to one of Mosley's rallies, held in a theatre in Barnsley. Several hundred men and women, mostly working-class Labour voters, turned up to hear 'the Leader'. On duty were about 100 of Mosley's followers, the blackshirts, so-called because of the uniform they wore. Orwell dismissed them as 'weedy looking specimens' but, to his dismay, found that Mosley was 'a very good speaker' and turned the audience from booing at the beginning to loud applause at the end. He 'bamboozled' the audience by speaking from a socialist viewpoint, and condemned the treachery of previous governments. Orwell rejected the speech as the 'usual claptrap'. Mosley rounded on the Jews, blaming them for everything, including the international situation: 'We fought Germany in a British quarrel; we are not going to fight them in a Jewish one.' Anybody who interjected or barracked was pounced on. Orwell was particularly shocked when one man who tried to ask a question found 'several Blackshirts throwing themselves upon him and raining blows on him while he was still sitting down'. A woman was hit on the head with a trumpet and taken to hospital.[4]

Later in the summer Rose Macaulay went to report on a full-scale BUF rally at the Royal Albert Hall. After the audience had been warmed up with rousing songs, Mosley entered the hall, heralded by a procession of banners, drum rolls and a fanfare, lit by a single spotlight. 'Between massed ranks of his frenzied approvers, the Leader proceeded up the hall to the platform, wearing an air of exalted uplift. He then spoke for two hours, during which he once again attacked the Jews, vowing to expel them from Britain. 'At every reference to British Jews, Sir Oswald appeared to experience a considerable and painful excitement; he cried out, he gestured, he pointed . . . The

Fascist part of the audience, answering hysteria with hysteria, responded with frenzied applause.' Macaulay became alarmed at the thought of what members of the audience might be roused to: 'One felt, woe to any Jew who should that night cross the path of the applauding mob.'[5]

Bill Fishman, a fifteen-year-old Jewish East Ender, took the risk and went to Mosley's rallies in London to find out for himself what the Leader was like. He stood at the back, 'probably out of cowardice as much as anything', and watched the build-up to the speech, the crowd of 'black shirted warriors' chanting the letters M–O–S–L–E–Y in unison before their idol stood up. 'He got up, arms akimbo, very handsome, very dignified, and came over not like his fellow dictators – but rational in his arguments and reached his crescendo very slowly.' By the end of the rally the blackshirts had been roused to a frenzy, calling out 'Hail Mosley! Perish Judah! Down with the Jews!' For Fishman this was the moment when 'it hit me in the chest: Mosley personified all that was evil.'[6]

The East End of London, with its large Jewish community, was a particular focus for Mosley and his thugs. He was stirring up racial antagonism in this impoverished area by blaming the Jews for the high rates of unemployment, rent increases and poor wages. In 1936 about 330,000 Jewish people lived in Britain,[7] less than one per cent of the population. About half of them lived in the East End, most of them concentrated in a densely populated area centred on Brick Lane.[8] Bill Fishman grew up there. During the years of the Depression the area had suffered particularly badly. 'For months on end our fathers walked the streets; the feeling of despair and depression was a common sentiment to the people of East London', Fishman recalled. It was a pocket of poverty as bad as anything in the distressed areas of south Wales and the north, with 'the eternal slums, the litter, the filth, the futility of it all'.[9]

Many, like Fishman, were second-generation, the children of parents who had been forced to flee the pogroms of Eastern Europe for the sanctuary of Britain. Most of the older generation spoke only Yiddish and lived in an enclosed community of crowded tenements, synagogues, baths and kosher butchers. They tended to work in the clothing and furniture trades.[10] They were an obvious target for the Jew-baiters of the BUF, who regularly smashed the windows of Jewish grocery shops, chalked anti-Semitic graffiti on walls and shouted racist insults during street meetings ('the Yids, the Yids, We've got to get rid of the Yids'[11]) as they marched through Jewish areas. That summer, to the fury of the anti-Fascists, the more abusive the blackshirts became, the more the police appeared to protect them from their victims. In September there was particular anger in the East End over two incidents. Fascist thugs threw a Jewish boy through a plate-glass window, blinding him.[12] Later, to the community's horror, a Jewish girl was caught in White Horse Lane and strapped to an advertisement hoarding in the attitude of the crucifixion.[13] Neither incident led to a prosecution.

Young Jews did not take these attacks with the forbearance of many of their parents and the official bodies that represented them. They wanted to fight back. Joyce Goodman was a twelve-year-old living in the East End: 'If you were a Jewish kid and you stood there listening to them belting out their message of hate, you learned to hate back.'[14] Even though they were British-born and British-educated, young Jews such as Joyce felt alienated and stigmatized by the anti-Semitism that flourished in British society. They saw Germany, boosted by the success of the Olympics, and the Civil War in Spain, and feared that the contagion would spread to Britain. Many became Communists, seeing the Party as the most vigorous opponent of Fascism. Others joined the Labour Party (although it was much less active in the fight), while some formed street gangs in self-defence.[15] When, in the summer of 1936, the BUF announced that it would celebrate its fourth anniversary with a mass march through east London on Sunday 4 October, a coalition formed to confront Mosley. The battle lines were drawn.

The prospect of a deliberately provocative march into the heart of the Jewish East End caused widespread concern. There had already been violence at a number of regional rallies. On 12 July six black-shirts at a rally were knocked unconscious by men wielding iron bars. Mosley's car window was shattered by a bullet as he drove away. At other meetings across the country anti-Fascists pelted the rally-goers with bricks and stones. Many were injured. At a rally on 27 September outside Leeds, attended by 30,000 people,[16] the Leader himself was showered with missiles. The prospect of another demonstration and counter-demonstration in the capital, with all the inevitable violence, led many to call for a ban on Mosley's demonstration, planned for 4 October. Labour MPs and the mayors of London's boroughs pleaded with the Home Secretary to halt the march. A petition of 100,000 signatures was presented to him, but to no avail. Mosley was allowed to go ahead.

The coalition of Communists, leftists and young Jewish activists set to work organizing the opposition. The older generation of Jews was dead-set against them. The Jewish Board of Deputies urged people to stay away. The *Jewish Chronicle* told readers in the East End to remain indoors and pull down the shutters. But their advice was ignored. The leaders of the Jewish community had lost control of their people. Labour too urged its members to keep off the streets; the party newspaper, the *Daily Herald*, argued with typical pusil-lanimity that the best way to defeat Fascism was to ignore it.[17] Even the Communist Party at first kept quiet. No official body wanted to be seen to be encouraging action that would inevitably lead to violence and law-breaking.

For most, taking to the streets to stop Mosley's march was a spon-taneous expression of hatred of Fascism. Spain was the constant refrain. For Charlie Goodman, an East End Jew who was not a member of the Communist Party, it was the motivating factor: 'it was not a question of a punch-up between the Jews and the fascists . . . in my case it meant the continuation of the struggle in Spain.'[18] Those planning to take part in the counter-demonstration were by no means all Jews or Communists. The bleak turn of events abroad was a mobilizing force for thousands with a liberal view of the world, whatever their race or party affiliation, and halting Mosley in the East End had a wider significance, as Harold Smith, an eighteen-year-old office worker and activist, remembered: 'we were young, enthusiastic, Spain was on, Hitler was on the march, it was a British contribution to stop Fascism.'[19]

Two East End Communists, Joe Jacobs and Phil Piratin,[20] planned

the unofficial fightback. The first task was to find out the route of the
march. They knew that the BUF was planning to assemble at Royal
Mint Street, on the fringes of the City, before marching east towards
Whitechapel, stopping to hold four meetings with Leader speeches at
various stops along the way. There were numerous side-streets that
might be chosen, but the most obvious routes were either down
Cable Street or up Leman Street, before turning right at Gardiner's
Corner and heading east down Commercial Road. Piratin arranged
for his flying squads of cyclists and motor-bike riders to be stationed
on both routes, ready to race back to HQ at his house in Stepney with
news of which way had been chosen. Piratin also had informers in the
police and spies in the BUF itself. A week before the demonstration
he arranged a meeting in his house for a group of 'aryan-looking'[21]
Party members, who would be able to pass themselves off as Fascists
during the march and keep an eye out for any changes to the route. A
young medical student, Hugh Faulkner, took Piratin aside after the
meeting and told him, 'I think I can get into Mosley's mob to offer
medical aid'. The offer was taken up.

On Sunday 4 October, in the early afternoon, 3,000 blackshirts,
men and women, assembled in Royal Mint Street, close to the
Tower of London, to await their leader. They stood in rank, as
though on parade. All were wearing the uniform of the British Union
of Fascists. At first the demonstration was peaceful enough. There
was a diversion when a man holding a red flag gave the clenched fist
salute from a rooftop. A few people shouted rather mild insults: 'Go
to Germany' and 'Down with Fascism'.[22] They were greeted with
the usual riposte: 'We must get rid of the Yids.' As anticipation of the
imminent arrival of the Leader grew, so did the heat of the exchanges.
When Ronald Webb, a young member of the BUF, arrived at the
scene, 'there was a mob outside screaming their heads off, and I had
butterflies in my stomach, I do not mind admitting'. Many of the
anti-Fascists were shouting 'They shall not pass', the war cry of
the Spanish Republicans defending Madrid.

There were cheers and raised-arm salutes when Mosley arrived in
an open car. He was wearing the new uniform of the Party, a medley
of Italian and German Fascist chic, 'a black military-cut jacket, grey

riding breeches and jackboots, a black peaked cap, and a red and white armband indicative of "action within the circle of unity"', as *The Times* reported. He was soon to pay a heavy price for the introduction of this overtly military style of dress. Mosley was driven up and down the lines of his supporters, exchanging more salutes in the Fascist style. He then stepped from his car and began an inspection on foot.

At the same time Hugh Faulkner approached the assembled blackshirts, who were penned behind rows of police. He was dressed as a doctor, wearing his best suit, a borrowed black hat and an empty medical bag. Faulkner went up to the police and said 'Doctor' very firmly to them. They allowed him through.

> I found myself in the middle of the Fascists and caught sight of a member who worked in my hospital. On the spur of the moment I said 'I've finally made up my mind, I want to come in with you'. He was such a clot he immediately accepted this . . . he was absolutely delighted and almost immediately showed me a duplicate sign of the route.

Armed with this latest intelligence, Faulkner ran off to telephone the plan of the march to Piratin and his fellow organizers. Meanwhile, vast crowds had assembled, ready to do battle with the Fascists. They had already built barricades and were being held back by the police.

The Cable Street riot was not a battle between the blackshirt supporters of Oswald Mosley and his opponents; it was a battle between the police and the anti-Fascists. The first set-to took place at Leman Street, on Gardiner's Corner, where Phil Piratin had placed trams to block the entrance to Commercial Road. The tram-drivers' union, not usually militant, had agreed to help on this occasion. The drivers had simply driven to their pre-assigned positions in Leman Street and Commercial Road and left their trams, to Piratin's delight. 'In those days you could not move the trams because the tram driver took a little thing out and put it in his pocket and walked away and you could not move them. Beautiful.'

When Harold Smith arrived at Gardiner's Corner at midday he found a sea of people. 'It was like the Cup Final, we were cheering, we were singing, and saying "Move along there, move along there".'[23] By now an estimated 310,000 people had turned up to stop the Fascist march.[24] Although Communists under Phil Piratin had been the principal unofficial organizers of the opposition, it was not a Communist demonstration. The Party in 1936 had only 11,000 members. But it was able to mobilize far greater support across a wide section of British society from all backgrounds and faiths. Bill Fishman walked to Gardiner's Corner from his home near Brick Lane. As he passed through a tenement block he came across an old Jewish woman sitting on a box. He remembered her shocking appearance: 'her bald head and wig all askew, she was swinging back and forwards and moaning. I tapped her on the shoulder and said "Granny, don't worry". And she said, "Oh, I have seen it in Poland, and it is coming here".' For Fishman, and thousands of others, this was the motivating fear.

The police set to work to clear a path through the demonstrators so that Mosley and his supporters could gain access to Commercial Road, down which they planned to march. They used a combination of brute force and mounted police, first moving forward on foot with batons and staves – long metal rods encased in leather – and then charging with the horses. The crowd, according to Yvonne Kapp, a Communist writer who had arrived by tube at Aldgate and walked to Gardiner's Court, had been 'pacific' and 'good humoured' up to this point, milling around and chanting 'they shall not pass'. But now the police's repeated charges terrified her with their brutality. People everywhere were bleeding from head wounds caused by 'the flailing weapons wielded by powerful men on horseback'.[25]

Joyce Goodman may have been only twelve but had decided with a friend to heed the calls chalked on walls urging people to come to fight the Fascists. It was a terrifying experience. As the police horses charged, 'women were falling under the horses hooves – there was blood everywhere – you can imagine how terrifying this was'.[26] The two twelve-year-olds huddled together for protection. At first the anti-Fascist demonstrators resisted passively, refusing to move, but they soon started to fight back. Many had experienced years of running battles with the Fascists at other Mosley rallies and at street corner meetings. They tried to force the police off their horses. Some threw marbles and ball bearings under the hoofs, others pricked the horses with hat pins, causing them to rear up, hoofs flailing. Many marchers were kicked and injured.

The wounded were carried into side-streets to be given first aid. Yvonne Kapp took shelter with them. She found that the narrow alleys had been rendered impassable by the occupants of the tenement buildings above, who had thrown down every glass bottle they could lay their hands on to prevent the police and horses getting through. 'The mingled odours of camphor, vinegar, vanilla essence, eucalyptus, kerosene, cough syrup, ammonia, brilliantine, lime juice, turpentine, alcohol and methylated spirit filled the air.'[27] Crowds had also gathered in the side-lanes to prevent any passage to the police.

After several baton charges and more forays by the mounted police it became clear to Sir Philip Game, the Commissioner of the Police, that there was no way Mosley and his blackshirts could pass through Gardiner's Corner to Commercial Road, the route of the planned march. 'Short of mayhem and murder', Yvonne Kapp remembered proudly, 'no force could have broken up that tight packed, solid press of people standing there, a human barricade, in stoic and apparently immovable strength.'[28]

The police decided on an alternative route: Cable Street. Thanks to Hugh Faulkner's intelligence, Piratin was aware of the change and ordered his flying squads to barricade the street. Charlie Goodman rushed down to join the action. Cable Street, close to the docks, was lined in those days with ships' chandlers, lock-ups and warehouses. Goodman and his comrades forced open the garages, pulled out carts and overturned them in the street. They raided a builder's merchant for planks and bricks: 'one fellow who was very sympathetic drove his lorry out and we overturned it and made barricades.'[29] Soon afterwards the police charged the demonstrators. As at Gardiner's Court, they were unable to make headway. They retreated to regroup, and, as they did so, Goodman looked up and saw women in the tenement blocks 'throwing everything they could lay their hands on – boiling water, kitchen oil, fat, urine, lumps of shit'. The police retreated from the infernal pelting, some taking shelter in the sheds and lock-ups that lined the street. The women came after them, banging and kicking at the doors until the unfortunate officers could take no more. They came out with their hands in the air. This was a novel situation for many of the rioters, more used to being on the receiving end of the truncheon. 'What could we do? We'd never ever thought of a copper surrendering – we took their helmets and told them to shove off!'[30] Cable Street remained impassable.

Charlie Goodman returned to Gardiner's Corner, where the mêlée was still in full swing. He climbed a lamppost and taunted the police as they tried to get him down, 'Come on you yellow bellies'. He was now a marked man. When he descended, he rejoined the fray, intervening to stop an officer beating a woman with a truncheon, punching him in the face. Goodman was promptly arrested and taken to the police station at Leman Street. It was time for revenge: 'they tipped me up like a battering ram, charged me in through the charge room door, opened it with my head, knocked me down; one was kneeling on me the others were bashing me up with truncheons, calling me "yellow bastard" and "dirty Jew" and that sort of thing.'[31]

More than a hundred were hurt in the riot. The police arrested eighty-three anti-Fascists during the disturbances and packed them into the cells at Leman Street.[32] At about six in the evening the news that all had been waiting for came through: the march through the East End had been cancelled at the orders of the Police Commissioner, after consulting the Home Secretary. For Charlie Goodman and his comrades it was a moment of jubilation. 'Everybody shouted, and cheering and banging away . . . it was a right carry on.' There was less elation when he was sentenced the next day to four months' hard labour.

There was despair among Mosley's followers in the BUF. They had waited with the Leader for several hours, 'kettled' by the police in Royal Mint Street, until the disturbances were over, when they were allowed to disperse. They then marched 'in orderly fashion' to their headquarters in Westminster. The setback was significant, not because the march had been stopped but, as with the Olympia rally two years before, because of the violence that it had triggered.

For the left, by contrast, the Battle of Cable Street was a tremendous victory. It brought together for a brief moment a fractured movement that had long been divided on the major issues of the time. It also united different races and classes, as Goodman remembered: 'the most amazing thing was to see a silk-coated religious Orthodox Jew standing next to an Irish docker with a grappling iron.' For many it was an inspiration that went far beyond the confines of the East End. A number, men such as Frank Lesser, took such pride in having succeeded in stopping the Fascist march that they were motivated to fight Franco: 'it seemed to me that the fight against Fascism had to be fought in England, it had to be fought, and I went to fight it a year later in Spain too.'[33] But the authorities saw it very differently.

Eight days after the riot the Home Secretary, the steely-cold Sir John Simon, produced a memorandum for the Cabinet that showed the degree of concern that he and his colleagues felt. They faced an almost complete breakdown of law and order on the streets of London. The police had not been able to control the demonstration, nor had the Fascists been able to march, as was their right. More clashes were likely as Communists, buoyed up by success, took to the streets again to prevent further Mosley rallies and demonstrations. The stopping of the march at Cable Street was a blatant denial of free speech to the BUF, as well as a victory over the legitimate authorities. As Mosley complained, 'We were prevented from doing what we had done before, marching through London where we had tremendous support and would certainly have won a parliamentary seat'.[34]

Surprisingly, however, those who had beaten back the police and stopped the BUF in its tracks were not the subject of Sir John's wrath. Instead he singled out Mosley and his blackshirts for their provocative behaviour and drew attention in particular to their uniform. There was something essentially un-British about a political party dressing up and strutting around in military style. The Home Secretary spoke of the intense resentment that it caused in the country at large, with 'the assumption of authority by a private army'.[35] That was bad enough. What was worse was Mosley's aping the anti-democratic regimes in Europe, where 'the wearing of black or brown uniforms led to the overthrow of popular liberties . . . Sir Oswald makes no secret of his desire to follow the German and Italian examples.'[36] Simon told the Cabinet that the men and women who dressed as blackshirts looked much smarter than when wearing their everyday clothes. He thought this added to the appeal of the Fascists among poorer people. There was only one course of action: uniforms had to be stopped.

Banning uniforms was not the only measure needed to prevent a repeat of the disturbances. Like many Home Secretaries faced with a threat to security, Sir John Simon threw in a restriction of liberty for good measure. He told the Cabinet that the onward thrust of modernity had made the police's job impossible. Thousands of people could now be summoned at short notice by radio and newspaper; they could travel quickly by public transport, and they could be harangued by demagogues using loudspeakers. These developments, combined with the European crisis and the 'hysterical fear that an anti-Jew agitation might gain the mastery in this country', meant that the authorities had to be able to stop demonstrations in future, if they feared they might lead to disorder.

The Cabinet agreed. Despite the limitation on freedom of speech and assembly, a public order bill went before Parliament less than a month later. It banned the wearing of military uniforms and gave the police the power to stop processions. It was rushed into law. A coalition of all sides of the House of Commons came together to stop Mosley, united in hatred of his use of the blackshirt as a political tool and in loathing of him as a politician. It was a thoroughly partial bill. Its practical purpose may have been to prevent the recurrence of violence on the scale of the Battle of Cable Street, but its political effect was to cripple the BUF. Denied their uniforms, prevented at the whim of the police from marching, their movement went into steep decline. Mosley may have had a following outside Parliament, but he had few friends at Westminster. 'The British government', he said, had 'surrendered to red terror.'[37]

On 5 October, the day after the failed march, Oswald Mosley, still reeling from the disaster at Cable Street, flew to Germany on a secret mission. It was a matter of the heart. He was to marry the Mitford daughter Diana Guinness, in a ceremony to be held in the inner sanctum of the Nazi Party, the Reich Chancellery. It was a privilege extended to few, but Diana had used all her charm, together with

Unity's influence, to cajole her friend Josef Goebbels into persuading Hitler and making the necessary arrangements.

Mosley was a notorious womanizer. He had first met the 21-year-old Diana in the summer of 1931. He was married at the time to Cynthia Curzon (the daughter of Lord Curzon, the late Viceroy of India), and had three children by her. He soon began an affair with Diana, considered the most beautiful of the celebrated Mitford sisters. In the spirit of upper-class mores at the time this caused little scandal. Oswald Mosley had never allowed his private life to interfere with his politics. When he was a Labour MP, he commented: 'I vote Labour but sleep Tory.'[38] But when Diana announced she was leaving her husband, Bryan Guinness, to become Mosley's mistress, society was scandalized and her family devastated.

In May 1933 Mosley's wife, Lady Cynthia, was taken ill with acute appendicitis, which developed into peritonitis. She died at the age of thirty-four, leaving Mosley free to marry Diana once a decent interval had elapsed. He installed her in an isolated country house in Staffordshire, keeping any plans to marry secret. The reason for this, he said, was to prevent her being damaged by the animosity and violence that his political activities aroused.

But secrecy was necessary for many other reasons. Diana could continue her confidential fund-raising missions to Germany for the BUF as 'Mrs Guinness', and she could, with Unity's help, open up contacts with Hitler. More importantly, if her marriage to Mosley became public knowledge, the British Fascists and their leader would be profoundly damaged. Diana's fondness for Nazi Germany was well known. She and Unity were frequently the subject of British press reports detailing their latest escapades in Nazi Germany. Such was the mistrust of the Nazis that open friendship with Hitler would have finished any remaining chances of Mosley winning wide public support in Britain. The Führer, too, had reasons for wanting to keep the union confidential. In 1936 he wanted good relations with respectable British politicians. Any links with the BUF would have ruled those out of the question. He deliberately kept apart from his British emulator. For political reasons in Britain and Germany the marriage had to be secret.

By the autumn of 1936, with the help of Josef Goebbels and his wife, Magda, Diana had completed the legal formalities for marriage in Germany. By sealing the union in Berlin the couple would be shielded from prying British eyes and the press (usefully for them, under state control in Germany). They would also cement British Fascism's secret liaison with Hitler. Although Mosley had met the Führer only once before, Diana knew him well. Like her sister Unity, she learned German so that she could converse with him, and, like Unity, she got on very well with him.

Two weeks before the wedding Hitler personally welcomed her to the Parteitag. He was looking in 'blooming health', she reported excitedly to Unity. When he met her, 'he made his beloved *surprised* face, and then he patted my hand', saying how delighted he was that she had come to Nuremberg for the party gathering. They laughed and joked together about her brother Tom, how the one-time 'lackey of the Jews had almost become a National Socialist'. Hitler sent Unity his love, 'and darling everything is arranged for the 6th'.[39] Diana had managed to persuade the Führer to take the day off for the wedding ceremony. She had also ensured that Ribbentrop, who had wanted to come, would be excluded from the festivities.

On Tuesday 6 October the Mitford sisters were staying once more with Goebbels and his wife (Magda, Diana reported, was being 'an angel'), in their Villa Schwanenwerder. At about 11.30 in the morning they set off with Magda in Unity's car to pick up Oswald, who was in a Berlin hotel. The incongruous party then made its way to the propaganda minister's official residence, close to Hitler's Chancellery, where the wedding was to take place. Diana was dressed in a yellow silk tunic dress. Her witnesses were her sister and Magda Goebbels. Mosley was accompanied by two supporters from Britain.

At 2.30 that autumnal afternoon Hitler walked across the leaf-strewn gardens from his quarters in the Chancellery to join the wedding party in the Goebbels' official residence for the short ceremony. Diana caught sight of her hero as he approached: 'the blick [sight] out of Magda's window of the Führer walking across the sunny garden of the Reichskanzlerei was the happiest moment of my life', she told Unity afterwards. 'I felt everything was perfect, the

Kit [her nickname for Mosley], you, the Führer, the weather, my dress, Magda . . .'.[40] Both Hitler and Mosley had given Diana orchids and, when the ceremony was over, Hitler presented the bride with his gift. 'It was a huge photograph in a silver frame with an eagle, in a rather nice red box', she remembered.[41] Afterwards the party returned to the Goebbels' villa for a late lunch. It was the 'loveliest day' for her. But she announced it was also 'the most terrible'.

Oswald Mosley, exhausted and depressed by his defeat at Cable Street, was not in the mood for a wedding, and especially not his own wedding where his intended seemed more in love with the Führer than with himself. Hitler had succeeded in everything in which he had failed, including street battles with his opponents. His presence, and his bride's wide-eyed hero-worship of him, were more than Mosley could stomach. He could not understand German and could only look on as they talked and laughed together. He became petulant; 'his awful childish behaviour', Diana reported to Unity, upset her and spoiled the day. 'He tried to say everything he could to wound me. He succeeded in a way because I had been so happy and excited.' The newly-weds eventually patched up their quarrel and that evening went with 20,000 others to the Sportpalast to listen to Hitler make a speech. Diana thought it 'wonderful. The perfect ending to the day when I blotted out of my mind the sad part.'[42]

Although the wedding in Berlin had the advantage of secrecy, in the long term it proved to be a disaster almost as great as the Battle of Cable Street. When the story of the marriage broke in 1938 with the birth of their first child, the link with Hitler was damaging to Mosley, as expected. Worse was to follow. After the outbreak of war the Nazi connection served as justification for the couple's imprisonment. Diana came to wish she had never met Hitler. 'I was held for three and a half years. I missed the whole little childhood of two of my sons, and a large part of the childhood of the other two.' By that time, however, there was no sympathy for Diana and Oswald Mosley, such was the hatred for Nazi Germany. Nor was there much compassion for Diana's sister Unity when she arrived at Dover with a bullet in her head, having attempted suicide on the outbreak of war.

17

The Jarrow march: tragedy and triumph

JUST AFTER 10.30 in the morning on a brisk autumnal day, Monday 5 October, 200 men left the derelict north-eastern town of Jarrow and started their 300-mile march to London. They were on their way to Parliament to draw attention to the desperate plight of their town. The brass band of Palmer's, the bankrupt local shipbuilders, led the procession through the crowds: almost the entire town had come to bid farewell to the men. The Mayor, Alderman J. W. Thompson, resplendent in robes, cocked hat and chain of office (forged as an anchor chain in recognition of the town's shipbuilding heritage), walked behind the band. The diminutive Ellen Wilkinson – 'Red Ellen', as she was known, the town's feisty but troubled MP – walked beside him.

Children ran alongside as the men made their way in an orderly column behind the dignitaries, marching in time to the beat of a kettledrum, their shabby clothes spruced up by their wives, their waterproof capes carried over their shoulders 'bandolier fashion' like Republican fighters in Spain.[1] They were thin from years of under-nourishment. More than half the marchers had served in the First World War. The oldest, a 62-year-old, was a veteran of the Boer War. The men's military training showed in the tight discipline of their marching: four abreast, silver and blue banners proudly held at the front. 'They marched as well as the Durham Light Infantry', one of the organizers proudly commented.[2] All were unemployed. They carried with them a petition, signed by 11,000, to present to the House of Commons. It read: 'Your petitioners humbly pray that His Majesty's Government at this honourable House will realize the urgent need that work should be provided for the town without delay.'

The Jarrow march (or 'Jarrow Crusade', as its leader, Councillor David Riley, called it) was one of many such demonstrations that took place during the years of the slump. The Communist-backed National Unemployed Workers Movement (NUWM) had organized six hunger marches across Britain in the 1930s. Some had been marred by violence, but the Jarrow march was a peaceful demonstration, without a single complaint from the police during the four weeks it took to get to London. It was smaller in scale than the NUWM marches, and took place when the worst of the slump was over, but afterwards it became fixed in the collective memory as a symbol of the Depression and of the economic failure of the 1930s.

The march captured the public imagination for a host of reasons. It was a triumph of modern media management: two local reporters, who quickly lost any sense of impartiality, were embedded with the marchers. The national papers took up the story. The newsreels, watched by millions of cinema-goers, covered it too. By publicly declaring the crusade as non-political and making a show of rejecting Communism, its leaders consciously appealed to the influential middle classes. The march was, in its own way, a thoroughly modern affair, but for those who took part it was, in the short term, marred by bitterness, betrayal and failure.

The Jarrow Crusade also came to prominence because the marchers came from a single place. It was the stage on which an awful narrative, with all the unities of time, place and action of a Greek tragedy, was played out. Of all the deprivation and suffering that affected the old industrial towns of the distressed areas of Britain, Jarrow, a town of 35,000 on the south bank of the Tyne, could claim to be one of the worst. After the collapse of its single shipbuilder, Palmer's, in 1932 it was left on the scrapheap, without any major source of employment. 'Palmer's was Jarrow, and Jarrow was Palmer's', it used to be said. Like many similar northern towns that suffered particularly badly during the Depression, it was a one-company town, without a company. Soon three-quarters of the town's workforce were on the dole. Ellen Wilkinson described it as 'utterly stagnant'.[3]

In a town where most of the men were out of work, wives and daughters were often the family's sole breadwinners. This could be humiliating for men in a society where women usually looked after the home. Jean Clark had a job in the council offices while her father walked the streets looking for work. 'It was hard on the family to watch a rather loved father. Week by week, you could see him getting a little bit more morose, trying to keep cheerful, going out, stopping out all day.'[4] It was hopeless to look for a job. Some of the men would walk to Newcastle and back as a way of passing the empty hours.

J. B. Priestley had visited Jarrow in 1933 on his *English Journey*. He was horrified by what he found. 'There is no escape anywhere in Jarrow from its prevailing misery, for it is entirely a working-class town.' One out of every two shops was closed. Of the 8,000 skilled manual workers in the town, only 100 had jobs. Wherever Priestley went, he found men hanging about, idle. 'The whole town looked as if it had entered a perpetual penniless bleak Sabbath', he wrote, horrified. 'The men wore the drawn masks of prisoners of war. A stranger from a distant civilisation, observing the condition of the place and its people, would have arrived at once at the conclusion that Jarrow had deeply offended some celestial emperor and was now being punished.'[5]

Three years later, in 1936, the documentary photographer Bill Brandt came to Jarrow to record the misery of the town. His grainy images of men at street corners, with boarded-up shops behind them, and women hanging out the washing between the grimy back-to-backs, became emblematic of the suffering caused by the slump. Early in 1936 hopes for the blighted town had been raised by the prospect of a new high-capacity steel mill on the old shipyard site, capable of making 350,000 tons of cheap steel a year.[6] But the plan was stymied by the British Iron and Steel Federation, which considered that a modern plant, with its new, rationalized process of production, would threaten to undercut the price of steel they produced from their old-fashioned factories. Jarrow sent 'deputation after deputation' to London to beg the President of the Board of Trade, Sir Walter Runciman, to intervene so that the plant could be built. He refused.

Runciman was himself from the north-east, but he occupied a

very different world from the people of Jarrow. He was part of the
local plutocracy, alongside other dynasties such as the Londonderrys.[7]
His family wealth came from ship-owning. Despite his local connections, he was detached from the plight of those on whom his wealth
had depended. Ellen Wilkinson called him 'one of England's minor
disasters. For him nothing can ever be done about anything.'[8]
However, Runciman was only following government policy which
forbade direct intervention to help industry, lest it upset the working
of the market. But the coldness with which he dismissed appeals for
help only increased the feelings of hurt and betrayal of Jarrow's
townsfolk. 'Icily correct, icily polite, apparently completely indifferent to the woes of others',[9] Wilkinson described him when he
declared to the final, desperate deputation that 'Jarrow must work out
its own salvation'. With these seven heartless words Runciman
'kindled the town' and started the crusade.

There had been sustained growth in the national economy since
1933, but the revival had passed Jarrow by. The town was at the
heart of one of the country's pockets of poverty and deprivation,
the so-called 'special' or 'distressed' areas. These regions of deprivation were isolated from the rest of the country, out of sight and
mind of the millions who were benefiting from the new prosperity. But they were not helpless. As Ellen Wilkinson discovered,
in a tight-knit community such as Jarrow, where almost all are
workless, 'the highly skilled man, the ambitious young foreman,
the keenest trade-unionists provide the leadership for the unemployed'.[10] One such man came forward to lead the march to
London: David Riley, the Council leader. A hefty Irishman with
an iron will,[11] Riley insisted that it should be a 'crusade' for jobs
rather than a hunger march. Behind this powerful and motivated
man was Bill Thompson, the Mayor of Jarrow, a Labour man
whose master-stroke it was that the march should not be political
and that it had the backing of all parties. The Council met in
solemn session to approve the crusade. An appeal for signatures for
the petition and funds was made under the Mayor's name.
Thompson used his civic role to gain the support of Conservative
town councils along the route of the march.

Such was the enthusiasm for the idea that 1,200 men volunteered, from whom 200 were chosen, vetted for their fitness by the borough medical officer.[12] Many older men were rejected, despite pleading to be allowed to join the march. One man of sixty wrote to Ellen Wilkinson: 'I have suffered all that a man may suffer. Nothing that can happen on the road between here and London can be worse.'[13] She turned him down, and, in the event, something did happen that was worse. He died while the marchers were on their journey.

A degree of fitness was necessary. Although the men were to average a relatively undemanding 12 miles a day, they were expected to sleep on the bare boards of schools, drill halls and church institutes. They walked in all weathers. Food was provided *en route* by a travelling field kitchen, lent by the Boy Scouts, to supplement any hospitality they might receive. A second-hand bus, bought for £100 from the Northern Bus Company, who guaranteed to buy it back for the same price, trundled ahead, carrying the kitchen, the men's kit and blankets and a clerk from the Borough Council, Sam Rowan. It was his duty to account for the money spent and to arrange accommodation and meeting-places at the overnight stops.

Not a penny was wasted in getting the men ready for their four-week march. Jean Clark was one of the many women who helped them prepare. 'Each man had to have a kit bag. The cheapest way of doing this was to cut up calico . . . and the wives sewed them up.' The marchers were provided with socks bought wholesale and medicated inner soles for the shoes. 'We got everything for rock bottom prices, free if we could.' Tea, of course, was an essential. Here too money was saved, as Jean remembered: 'Oh golly! The tea bags – out came the sewing machine, umpteen tea bags made and plenty of kettles supplied!'[14] Each marcher received 1s. 6d. pocket-money and two penny stamps for weekly letters home. Every day there was a hand-out of cigarettes (then considered an essential) – forty a day per man.[15] An unemployed barber marched with them, offering haircuts and shaves to keep the men looking presentable. To ensure good health two medical students, members of the Inter-Hospital Socialist Society, accompanied the marchers in relays, travelling in a car packed with first aid equipment. One of the students told a local reporter why he was volunteering.

> Anything we can do to help Jarrow and the other distressed areas we shall do. I have seen people dying of poverty and tuberculosis as a result of unemployment. It is one thing to read the health statistics, but it is another thing entirely when you have these people dying under your care.[16]

A public meeting was to be held every night of the march, when the leaders would relate some of the medical statistics of Jarrow. These included the infant mortality and tuberculosis death rates (which were both nearly double the national rate), the malnutrition and the overcrowding of the slums. This was the awful litany of the distressed areas, a tale of suffering that the government seemed incapable of alleviating. As one marcher said, Jarrow was a 'filthy, dirty, falling down, consumptive area'.[17] Ritchie Calder, a *News Chronicle* journalist who reported on the march, remembered the near-starvation of the citizens: 'You saw the face of hunger. You were seeing the face of hunger in your own streets.'[18]

The idea of the march as a crusade was reinforced at the start of the march by a service of blessing. Before the men set off, they went to Jarrow's Christ Church, accompanied by their womenfolk, many with shawls covering their heads. Dr James Gordon, the suffragan Bishop, presided. Ten other priests, representing all the town's varied denominations, joined his call for God's backing for the marchers and prayed for the uplifting of the unemployed. The congregation was wryly amused when the Revd Harvie Clarke, Rector of Jarrow, also prayed for the leaders of the National Government.[19] After the service the marchers set off to the beat of the kettledrum with Mayor Thompson's injunction ringing in their ears: 'Remember you are going to London for Jarrow, and we depend on you to maintain the credit of the town.'

When Bishop Henson of Durham learned that his colleagues had led the blessing of the crusaders, he was apoplectic. Only the previous week Dr Gordon had assured him 'that he had decided to have nothing to do with what he considered an unwise & certainly futile demonstration'.[20] He had also shown the Bishop, his superior, a letter that he planned to send, declining the invitation to take part in the service. Now, to Henson's shock, he had publicly given it his blessing.

The Bishop of Durham may have had all the instincts of a liberal when confronting Fascism, but when faced with anything that smacked of trade unionism or leftist agitation, he was a die-hard reactionary. Perhaps sensing an impending thunderbolt, Gordon's junior, the wily Rector of Jarrow, stepped in quickly to dissociate himself from the service, despite having taken part in it, and blamed Dr Gordon, telling Henson that 'reasonable people . . . in Jarrow were opposed to it'. This was hardly a Christian act. The Bishop of Durham excused him but ordered the hapless Gordon to write a letter to *The Times* repudiating his role in the service of blessing and recanting his support for the march.

Henson was not alone in expressing disapproval of the march. The Labour Party (together with the TUC) was fearful of the taint of Communism that went with hunger marches and instructed local branches to reject requests for help from the crusaders as they passed. Some members at the Party conference in Edinburgh that October attacked Ellen Wilkinson. One delegate, Lucy Middleton, criticized her for sending hungry and ill-clad men on a march to London. She advocated making propaganda films about the distressed areas instead. This 'stab in the back'[21] by the Labour Party was a far greater betrayal than the Bishop of Jarrow's letter, and one that would rankle for years to come. Paradoxically, it was Conservative councils who most often held out the hand of friendship to the crusaders. Following Thompson's request, and joint letters from the town's Conservative and Labour agents, they offered food and lodging at every Tory-controlled town and village through which the men passed.

During the first days of the march the men tramped through the distressed area of the north-east. In County Durham they saw more of the poverty with which they were familiar at home. There were the slag heaps and derelict villages of the under-worked coalfields, whose communities were so poor that they could offer little to their fellow unemployed as they marched past. Some in these poorer socialist areas were unfriendly, if not hostile, to the marchers, object-ing to their non-partisan stance, which many felt was a betrayal of socialist principle. Others simply believed that unemployment was a cross to bear and that the march was a waste of time.[22]

But as the crusaders headed south, they came into more prosper-ous areas, where the welcome was warmer. At one early stop they were given ham sandwiches and scones at the local miners' institute. One of the men took the ham from the sandwich, placed it in an envelope and posted it home. He told his companions that his family had not eaten meat for six weeks.[23] The journalist Ritchie Calder was shocked that some men were sick, unused to such quantities of food − 'one of the most tragic things, because they couldn't take a square meal'.[24] As the days passed, the combination of three good meals a day, unheard of at home, and exercise led to an improvement in the men's health. Some received medical treatment from the accompa-nying students for conditions from which they had suffered for years.[25] For many the march had the qualities of a holiday; with something to do and a sense of purpose, instead of loafing about idle, morale rose quickly.

At wealthy Harrogate there were tales of £5 notes handed from Rolls-Royces,[26] a banner was unfurled welcoming the 'Jarrow Workers' and the townspeople raised the money for the compulsory dog licence for Paddy, the black labrador who had attached himself to the march outside Jarrow. At Leeds the Lord Mayor and the President of the Conservative Party gave the crusaders a 'sumptuous meal' of roast beef and Yorkshire pudding, washed down with a bottle of beer. Even Paddy ate out of a silver tureen. 'I found out', Ellen Wilkinson wrote, 'what a difference a white table-cloth and a paper serviette can make to one's outlook on life.'[27] Some of the marchers had never experienced such luxuries before in their lives.[28]

The redoubtable Ellen Wilkinson, the force behind the crusade, did not walk the whole way with the marchers. There were many other calls on her time, not least addressing the Party conference on their behalf. Like the peace campaigner Dick Sheppard, she suffered from asthma, and, like him, she yo-yoed between exuberance and depression. She also never refused any request and overworked herself until she became ill. Ellen was a true radical, one of the small band of women MPs in the House of Commons with a national reputation. Sarah Burton, the fiery heroine of Winifred Holtby's posthumous best-seller *South Riding*, was based on her.

Ellen was a member of the Labour Party's maverick partner the Independent Labour Party and described herself as a 'revolutionary socialist'. She supported diverse causes, from women's rights to independence for India. She was a friend of Nehru and Gandhi.[29] Ellen came from a modest background in Manchester. She never married, but she had a number of affairs, including a long-lasting relationship with Herbert Morrison, Labour MP and leader of the London County Council. He was much less of a radical than the 4 feet 10 inch 'pocket Pasionaria', as Ellen was affectionately called in the British press, after the female orator who was at the time rousing Spanish loyalists in the Civil War.

Ellen had needed a great deal of persuasion not to raise the issue of politics during the march. But she kept quiet on that score, and the marchers gained and held support in Tory citadels by carefully eschewing any sign of Communist sympathy. David Riley insisted on the removal of socialist banners that appeared along the route. One marcher was sent home for 'communistic beliefs' and another was threatened with expulsion.[30] It was an effective policy. While other marches were ignored, the crusade received widespread friendly media attention. Some newsmen clubbed together to buy mouthorgans for the men. A harmonica band was formed to accompany the lone drummer keeping time at the head of the procession. Instead of political songs, the men marched to tunes reminiscent of the First World War: 'Tipperary', 'Keep the Home Fires Burning' and 'The Swanee River'. With typical British sentimentality the dog Paddy became a national pet and featured on front pages as the Jarrow Crusade became a running national story. 'There could be no doubt', the *Manchester Guardian* reported breathlessly from the north, 'that the march was a bounding success – the organisation seems well-nigh perfect.'[31] The government became alarmed.

The Cabinet met on Wednesday 14 October. Marches and protests were high on the agenda, second only to the disturbances in the East End at Cable Street. It was not only the men from Jarrow who concerned the politicians. Two other marches were heading for the capital at the same time. One was a contingent of 250 blind men campaigning for better treatment of the sightless, and the other a deputation from the NUWM demonstrating against the Means Test. The prospect of more revolutionaries fighting in the streets with the police after the debacle at Cable Street was more than the politicians could stomach. Action was needed. The problem was that there was little that could be done to stop the marches. To the Cabinet's frustration, the legislation giving the police powers to ban demonstrations was weeks away from enactment.

Stanley Baldwin, recovered after two months' rest from his physical and mental collapse of the summer, was in the chair. He called on the Home Secretary to report on the situation. Sir John Simon first briefed on Cable Street, then he told his colleagues that nothing could be done to prevent 'orderly bands of demonstrators' marching where they pleased.[32] He suggested action be taken to minimize the risk of violence, and that newspapers should be informed of the futility of the marches. Baldwin agreed that selected journalists should be briefed so as to counter the favourable publicity given to the marchers. No deputations would be received by ministers. Finally, the Cabinet issued a statement in which the government turned its back on the men of Jarrow. It said that the marches 'were altogether undesirable' and 'are liable to cause unnecessary hardship to those taking part in them'. In a parliamentary democracy, it argued, 'processions to London cannot claim to have any constitutional influence on policy'. For this reason no minister would meet any deputations of the marchers.[33]

This Downing Street declaration was another snub. The Labour Party had already turned its back on the Jarrow Crusade at the annual Party conference. The National Government's public hostility was not so unexpected and consequently less hurtful. It did not damage the Jarrow cause. It may have actually helped it, giving it yet more publicity. The government's own supporters were, curiously, the people most angered by the statement.

When the press release was issued, the Jarrow marchers were about to leave Sheffield, where, once again, they had received support from Tories. The Conservative Party's local secretary and chief agent, Major E. G. Whittaker, wished the men luck on their journey. He then startled them with a fulminating attack on his own Conservative-dominated government: 'We are told that you will not be received by the Powers-That-Be. To the devil with that. Your march is a good thing, in my opinion, and whether my head office likes it or not, I don't care.' The Major's words were a sign that the crusade had captured the hearts of middle England.

In 1934, in response to public pressure, the government had set up a Commission for the Special Areas to take action to alleviate the suffering in places bypassed by the emerging prosperity. Malcolm Stewart, a businessman with enlightened views on employment, was appointed Commissioner. He was hampered from the start by Treasury limits on his spending powers, and he could only tinker at the edges. Many of his schemes, such as cookery lessons for women to help domestic budgets go further, or physical exercise classes for men grown flabby on the dole, were mere window-dressing. Others, such as food hand-outs for pregnant mothers, or the resettlement of the workless in southern smallholdings, were the patronizing projects of the influential.[34]

Stewart wanted to do much more and was at draggers drawn with the unbending Chancellor, Neville Chamberlain, who regarded most of the Commission's schemes as 'piffling',[35] which they were, thanks to his own parsimony. On 9 October, Stewart announced 'with great reluctance' his decision to depart at the end of the year, citing 'personal reasons'. The popular verdict was that he was resigning his job because the Chancellor had frustrated his ability to help the Special Areas.[36] He wrote a final report which caused outrage at the Treasury. It was a Keynesian manifesto, calling on central government actively to help industry to relocate to the impoverished areas of Britain, through a system of cheap loans and reduced council rates. He also criticized the treatment of Jarrow, saying that its future had been 'sacrificed to secure profits' of the steel industry elsewhere.[37]

Chamberlain, under tremendous political pressure, not least

because of the popularity of the Jarrow march, was forced to yield. The following year he introduced a new act of Parliament for the distressed areas: the Special Areas (Amendment Act) 1937. For the first time he promised regional planning with some directed investment. But the legislation was too late to be of any help for Jarrow, or any other Special Area. It was only through the desperate need for armaments and, later, the application of the new Keynesian economics after the Second World War that they would recover.

Chamberlain believed the only effective solution for the distressed areas was internal migration. 'When all is said and done', he told his sister with a degree of fatalism, 'there must remain a large number of people for whom we can find no work . . . who must either move or stagnate there for the rest of their lives.'[38] He encouraged the unemployed in the north and south Wales – in the words of a future Tory minister – to 'get on their bikes' and move to areas where jobs were plentiful.

During the Jarrow march several men did take up offers of jobs in the more prosperous south and relocate. Nineteen thirty-six was the year of greatest movement in a decade of internal migration: 43,506 people were officially recorded as transferring to employment in other areas at the behest of their labour exchanges, and 10,025 families upped sticks and moved to find work.[39] Movement on this scale led to the growth of the north–south divide, as towns like Jarrow lost significant numbers of younger workers to the booming industries around London and Birmingham.

On Saturday 17 October the crusaders left Sheffield, heading for Chesterfield, 12 miles to the south. They had no reason to shake the dust from their feet. To Bishop Henson's increasing irritation, his episcopal colleagues were flocking to the cause. Dr Leonard Burrows, Bishop of Sheffield, had received a carefully worded joint letter from the agents of Jarrow Conservative and Labour parties appealing for his attendance at the marcher's public rally. 'The Crusade', they told him, 'is organised on strictly NON-POLITICAL lines . . . At each stopping place, we have received the active support of the leaders of religious thought.'[40] The Bishop readily agreed, giving the men his blessing and a donation of £5 (equivalent to £185 today) and commenting that 'all governments are like wheelbarrows, useful instruments but they need to be pushed'.[41]

Sam Rowan, travelling ahead in the bus, did his best to ensure the marchers were as comfortable as possible. He secured the stopping places for lunch in fields next to the road from farmers, who received a talk on the problems of the unemployed in exchange. When he reached the overnight halt, he would inspect the men's sleeping quarters. Sometimes they were no more than a derelict school or the old workhouse. Rowan objected to the latter. 'We are not two hundred tramps', he remonstrated, 'we are two hundred unemployed men.' Immediately the marchers were relocated by a penitent town council.[42]

The reception in Chesterfield was markedly different from the one in Sheffield. The Labour town council turned down all pleas for assistance, forcing the marchers to turn to local businessmen and Conservatives for food and blankets. 'They weighed in', Ellen Wilkinson remembered of the local Tories, 'with hot meals and a place to sleep.' A clear pattern was emerging of Conservative welcoming and Labour shunning – or at the most a guarded welcome from nervous individual members of the Labour Party. This pattern would continue until the very end of the journey, to the enduring bitterness of all those who took part.

Each day of the march followed the same routine. The marchers rose at 6.30 a.m., having slept in their clothes, huddled together on bare floors. Washing was only possible when local bath-houses were opened; otherwise the men made do with a hasty shave in a shared basin. Morning parade was at 8.45, and the crusade set off on the road at 9.00, with the men carrying their two banners, which they unfurled as they approached villages and towns. In army style the marchers were divided into ten platoons of twenty, each with its own commander. The march marshal, the bowler-hatted David Riley, led the way, followed by the mouth-organ band; behind them tramped the men. They marched to the British military timetable, fifty minutes on, followed by ten minutes' rest. Lunch at midday was provided by the field kitchen. In fine weather 'stew, tinned fruit, hot tea . . . and the greatest of blessings a long stretch out for a sleep on the grass'.

When it rained, the men stood about in the rain under their capes eating sandwiches 'with always the blessing of hot strong tea'.[43] The weather made all the difference to their morale. When it was fine, they strode their daily 12 miles with ease; when the wind howled around them and blew rain in their faces, each step was purgatory. Their boots soon wore out and much time was spent repairing them. At Nottingham, where they arrived on 20 October, manufacturers and the local Co-op kitted them out with new boots, trousers and 'nearly 200 sets of underwear'.[44]

Ellen Wilkinson re-joined the marchers at Loughborough on Thursday 22 October. She declared, to their surprise and concern, that she would march the rest of the way to London, more than 110 miles. It was a rash gesture typical of her exuberance. Small and slight, Ellen was no match for the men, who had grown march-fit over the previous two weeks. The first day she held them up. The second, on arrival at Market Harborough, she collapsed. The assistant Bishop of Leicester came to her rescue and took her in to recover at his home. For the rest of the march she joined the crusaders at intervals, marching only some of the way with them.

The Bishop of Durham continued to fulminate. While he and Ellen Wilkinson may have been in complete sympathy on the question of Hitler and Nazi Germany, he regarded her support of the marchers as dangerous and exploitative. On Thursday 22 October, after breakfast, Henson retired to his study to write a letter to *The Times*, which caused him some self-questioning reflection in his diary: 'I am doubtful of my wisdom, yet I am troubled at the persistent way in which an apology is being pressed upon the public for a proceeding which is neither reasonable nor wholly sincere.'[45] The Bishop distrusted the marchers' motives, suspecting them of subversion. He feared insurrection, as he told the readers of *The Times*. 'The policy of marches is, in my view, a revolutionary policy. It involves substituting for the provisions of the Constitution the method of organized mob pressure.' If such marches became more widespread, he warned, 'it may bring us before the winter is out into grave public confusion and danger'.[46] Henson was right to be doubtful of the wisdom of his letter. His views reflected those of the government, but few others shared his outlook. The Jarrow marchers had won their place in the hearts of the people. They were not going to be displaced by the forebodings of a maverick prelate.

The Spectator, not usually liberal in its views, firmly rejected Henson's warning. 'Whatever the march is, it is – pace the Bishop of Durham – in no way a "revolutionary act"; the title to petition Parliament is an ancient, a valuable, a well recognised right. The march itself is to be welcomed.'[47] The Economist agreed, arguing that it was hypocritical to attack the marchers as unconstitutional when vested interests had worked behind the scenes to deny the town a new steelworks. Many more letters followed Henson's to The Times. Almost all agreed that the Bishop was wrong to refer to the crusaders as revolutionaries, even if they agreed with him that the march was a mistake. The newspaper itself praised the men of Jarrow for their 'wholesome and poignant' demonstration and called for government action.[48]

While the marchers were winning widespread support, the government was working hard behind the scenes to counter their favourable publicity. The Cabinet had agreed on 14 October that, if marches could not be stopped, they could at least be briefed against. One or two newspapers fell into line, accusing Ellen Wilkinson of exploiting her constituents and using the crusade for political ends. The Bedford Press struck a sour note, calling the marchers a 'pathetic procession' after they had left Luton. It parroted the government line that marches were 'ill advised and that they serve no good purpose'. It was clear, however, that the media battle was lost when Lord Rothermere's Daily Mail gave the crusade its backing.[49] The government would have to find other ways to limit the immense political damage the march was doing.

At last the marchers approached London. Only three had dropped out. They arrived on Friday 30 October at Hendon, where the Mayor invited them to dinner at the White Hart Hotel in Edgware. They were treated to tomato soup, steak and kidney pudding with vegetables, and apple pie. Given their meagre diet at home and the grinding poverty of the dole, it was not surprising that many were dreading their return to Jarrow. That evening they bedded down, as so often, on the bare boards of a school hall. The next morning they set off for the last day's march to their lodgings in the East End, from where they would deliver the petition to Westminster after the State Opening of Parliament.

What they hoped would be a triumphant climax to the days of hard slog turned into something of a let-down, marred by rain and the political shenanigans of Westminster. But they set off cheerfully enough on the last leg of the journey, despite the downpour. Ellen Wilkinson, with the aid of a walking stick, headed the procession alongside the Mayor of Jarrow, who had come down to be with the men when they handed in their petition. The crusaders, as usual, marched briskly in military style. They all wore flat caps, put on their mackintosh capes, sang along to the mouth-organ band and kept time to the beat of their drum. Soon they were soaked to the skin.

As they passed along the Edgware Road, they unfurled their banners. Hundreds of people had turned out to see them pass by. According to *The Times* reporter, 'the men were frequently greeted with shouts of "Good luck!" and – from the North Country people who had turned out to meet them – cries of "Good old Tyneside".[50] A woman bystander handed the men a dozen packets of cigarettes. The reporter from the *Shields Gazette*, Selwyn Waller, one of those who had been embedded with the marchers, gave – as might be expected of a journalist wholly converted to the cause – a colourful description: 'We were received with no less enthusiasm than the Crusaders of the middle ages. Women wiped their eyes and men on the pavements waved a salute as the column swung trimly along the busy streets.' Such was the fame of the mouth-organ band, he reported, that the men had received a number of approaches to make 'gramophone records of their marching songs'.[51] As they approached central London, friends and relatives, part of the northern diaspora, joined the march.

There were others who tried to attach themselves but were given the cold shoulder. A group of thirty unemployed men had marched in the rain overnight from Bethnal Green to show solidarity.[52] David Riley curtly refused to let them accompany the crusaders on the final leg. Despite his best efforts, however, about a hundred communists attached themselves to the end of the procession and embarrassed Riley by singing the 'Red Flag' and the 'Internationale' as they approached a soup kitchen in Garrick Street.[53] It was a stark contrast to the usual 'Tipperary' and 'The Minstrel Boy'.

That afternoon the men reached their lodgings in Stepney, in the East End. Ever conscious of the danger of the taint of extremism, security cards were issued to each of the marchers. David Riley had been warned that both Communists and Fascists wanted to take advantage of the popular feeling for the crusade. He feared that agitators might infiltrate their night shelter and insinuate themselves among the marchers,[54] inflaming buried political sentiments. At this late stage it may have seemed like paranoia, but Riley was rightly convinced that the success of the march hinged on its apolitical nature.

The crusaders spent four days in London. On Sunday 1 November they held an open-air rally in Hyde Park. Ellen Wilkinson and David Riley led speakers in describing the suffering of the town of Jarrow, much as they had done at countless public meetings on their way south. Riley made a powerful appeal for action. 'We want the right to work: we do not ask for charity. Something must be done, and we shall not stop until something is done.'[55]

After a day's rest the crusaders went to the Mall to watch King Edward in the State Coach pass on the way to the State Opening of Parliament. No doubt to the King's relief, given his dislike of pomp and ceremony, but to the marchers' disappointment, the procession was cancelled because of the rain. The men had to make do with a glimpse of the official Daimler as it sped by. That evening they held their final public meeting in the Farringdon Street Memorial Hall. It was intended to be the culmination of the crusade and the final moment when the plight of Jarrow would be brought before a sympathetic audience of influential Londoners. They had hoped that some people of note, at least of the stature of the Lord Mayor of London or the London Labour leader, Herbert Morrison, might address the gathering. In the event none volunteered, no doubt following the instructions of their political masters.

At the last minute Canon Dick Sheppard, saintly as ever, agreed to fill in as the keynote speaker, followed by the usual contributions from Ellen Wilkinson, the Mayor of Jarrow and some of the marchers. In small print on the handbills announcing the meeting the name of Sir John Jarvis MP appeared, announcing he would attend 'if his engagements permit'.[56] His presence, and the announcement he would make, were part of a canny political move on behalf of the National Government that would, in the short term, blow the Jarrow marchers out of the water.

Jarvis was a home counties political bigwig and entrepreneur. He was a Surrey MP and philanthropist, but with a long connection with Jarrow. In 1936, before the days of centralized regional planning and direct state intervention, it fell to charities to fill the gap. It was a tradition that went back centuries and, during the Depression, had been revived as a measure to help the distressed areas. There were sixty schemes where prosperous southerners 'adopted' impoverished towns and villages affected by long-term unemployment.[57] Sir John had set up one of the largest, the County of Surrey Scheme, to provide aid for Jarrow. It attracted the interest of local schools, who helped raise money: £40,000 was collected, a vast sum (equivalent to £1.5 million today). With this money, together with his own substantial contribution, Sir John had established two businesses in the town: furniture-making and ship-breaking on the site of the Palmer's yard. He spent £100,000 in bringing the old passenger liner the *Olympia* to be scrapped there. He claimed such philanthropy was much better than doing nothing. It had created a number of jobs, as he proudly announced three days before the start of the crusade. The unemployment rate had declined to 50 per cent, and he promised that more investment would be forthcoming.[58]

Sir John aroused mixed feelings in Jarrow. Some suspected ulterior motives. Ellen Wilkinson took him to task in the Letters column of *The Times*.[59] She later described him bitingly as 'the type of rich man who, with the very best of intentions, desires to be fairy-godfather to what he assumes to be a derelict town of down-and-outs'.[60] There was, she realized, a political as well as a financial motive for his good works. The Conservative Party was facing wipe-out in a region devastated by economic malaise. The good works of a prominent

Tory in the north-east had electoral advantages. With the projected increases in armament spending, the skills and plant of a defunct shipyard also had profitable potential.

Dick Sheppard opened the meeting with a moving, if bland, speech to the Memorial Hall, which was only half-full. The marchers followed with their well-rehearsed rhetoric. Then Jarvis dropped his bombshell. He announced that he was negotiating for a new steel tubes mill on the site of Palmer's shipyard. Hundreds of new jobs would be brought to Jarrow by the new plant, which would make cases for shells needed as part of the rearmament programme. 'While you have been marching,' Sir John told the flabbergasted crusaders, 'I have been busy. I have found new methods abroad for the production of steel. It is an ideal industry for Jarrow.'[61]

At a stroke his announcement deflated the marchers. They did not know how to respond. There was a note of harrumphing in the Mayor's cautious welcome of Sir John's plans. 'I have been called a doubting Thomas but I say now, as I said when the steelworks were mooted – I shall believe it when I see the chimney smoking.'[62] In fact, as Matt Perry, the historian of the crusade, has shown, the scheme was cooked up in discussions with the Board of Trade, under Sir Walter Runciman, the man who had so cruelly told the town to 'work out its own salvation'.[63] The projected tube works saved the government's face at a time of acute embarrassment. It also had the potential of being a nice little earner. As it turned out, when it opened a year later, it employed only 200 skilled and semi-skilled men, a tiny number compared with the 8,000 who had lost their jobs with the closure of the shipyards. But it served its purpose. The political sting, so carefully gathered by the crusaders, was drawn by the crafty work of Sir John. As Ellen Wilkinson saw it, 'the newspapers next morning gave the impression that a rich Santa Claus had suddenly appeared to solve all Jarrow's problems at one stroke'.[64] No doubt feeling dispirited by the poor showing at their final meeting, and bemused by Sir John's dramatic intervention, the men retired to their quarters before the next day's finale, the presentation of the petition. Here too, things turned out in an unexpected fashion.

The following morning, smart in their suits specially bought for the occasion with funds raised during the march, the crusaders went to the House of Commons. They were expecting to deliver their petition. In the morning Ellen Wilkinson gave them a guided tour of the Palace of Westminster. After lunch, before going to the House to hand over the casket with its signatures, she packed the majority of the men on to a River Thames pleasure-boat for a sight-seeing cruise. It was a deception, cooked up with Sir John Jarvis, who paid for the trip, to avoid any ugly scenes. Stanley Baldwin, with the backing of Neville Chamberlain, had refused to allow the men to come to the bar of the House to deliver the petition in person. Only a few were permitted to watch from the Strangers' Gallery.

While the crusaders took in the sights, the business of handing over the petition took place on the floor of the Commons. Ellen Wilkinson went through the formal procedure, placing Jarrow's petition in its oak casket in a bag behind the Speaker's chair. She then read tearfully from the town's moving appeal to Parliament: 'The town cannot be left derelict, and therefore your petitioners humbly pray that His Majesty's Government and this honourable House will realize the urgent need that work for the town should be provided without delay.'[65]

When the men returned for tea in the House, they were astonished to learn that the petition had been presented in their absence. Ellen Wilkinson wrote that they 'were rather disappointed', a classic understatement. For many the exclusion from the key ceremony symbolized the failure of the crusade, as one of the marchers remembered years later: 'We got turned down. We got a cup of tea, they gave us a cup of tea. When we got turned down in the House of Commons, that was it . . . you knew you were finished.'[66]

The last days in London made a sad finale for the Jarrow crusaders. First trumped by the cleverly stage-managed announcement of a new steelworks, then excluded from the petition ceremony, they were out of their depths in the sophisticated world of Westminster. Their dignity may have captured the hearts of the nation, but it was not sufficient to change the ways of politicians. Ellen Wilkinson straddled both Jarrow and London. It cannot have been easy for her. Her management of the men at the end of their long journey smacked of manipulation, but political necessity required her to handle them carefully. Years later, when Minister of Education in Clement Attlee's Labour government, she found that the expediency demanded of politicians in power compromised her ideals too greatly. She committed suicide with an overdose of barbiturates in 1947, aged fifty-five.

The crusaders' return to Jarrow by train took a mere five and a half hours. Leeds City Council, who had treated the men with such generosity early in their journey, had raised the money for their train fares home. Any sense of failure at the government's snub evaporated, in the short term at least, when they arrived home. Jarrow went mad, greeting their men as conquering heroes returning from the wars. Those who witnessed the surging crowds, the cheering and screaming, the sobs of fainting women, were reminded of the jubilation that greeted the peace celebrations eighteen years earlier, at the end of the First World War.[67]

Crowds collected outside the station some time before the crusaders' train was due. It seemed as though all Jarrow had come out to greet their heroes, oblivious of the bitter wind blowing from the North Sea. It was 5 November. Rockets flared in the sky, adding to the mood of jubilation. Soon so many had gathered at the station that they were barred from the platforms. Only some families and officials were allowed forward to form an orderly reception party.

At 6.46 on the dot the arrival of the train was announced by the thunderous detonation of fog warning signals. The headlamp of the steam engine glared through the smoke, and the train, bedecked with the silver and blue banners of the marchers, pulled into the station. Families and officials swarmed forward to greet the men as the crowds cheered outside. After some moments milling around, David Riley blew his whistle, and 'the discipline instilled by a month's concerted effort along the road to London reasserted itself'.[68] The men retreated to a waiting-room to collect themselves before reappearing in marching order.

The station's doors were thrown open, and the cheering crowd rushed to greet their crusaders, swamping them with hugs, kisses, handshakes and pats on the back. The police gave up their attempts to control the crowd. Any hopes of a formal march to the Town Hall quickly evaporated in the crush of people. Palmer's Band, which was to lead the procession, was overwhelmed. Men and women passed out in the crush and were dragged away to recover.

Ellen Wilkinson's diminutive figure was nowhere to be seen. 'Then the cry went up', the *Shields Gazette* reported, '"Where's Ellen?" It was taken up on all sides until the town rang with it. "Here I am", Mrs Wilkinson's strong voice replied from somewhere in the darkness.' She was nearly trampled as well-wishers pushed forward. 'Men seized her hands, women smothered her with kisses, children hugged her.' The marchers, too, were embraced by the crowds. Many gave way to emotion at the warmth of the welcome and stood with tears in their eyes. Only 'Geordie' Smith, veteran of the Boer War and, at sixty-two, the oldest man on the march, seemed unmoved, 'as befitted an old campaigner who still retained memories of the scenes which followed the relief of Mafeking'.[69]

Slowly order was restored. To renewed cheers the throng made its way, pushing and jostling in the darkness, to the Town Hall. Several ministers of the Church had gathered at the Hall's porch to bless the returning heroes. There was no sign of the Bishop of Jarrow. He had tactfully stayed away, having disassociated himself from the march with the treacherous letter to *The Times*. The speeches began, with the speakers struggling to make themselves heard above the buzz of the crowd. From time to time they were interrupted as the police carried limp bodies of unconscious women into the side-streets for first aid.

The speakers put a brave face on the apparent failure of the crusade. The goal of the march was to overturn the decision of the government, working in league with the steel industry and the banks, not to put up a new steelworks in Jarrow. That had not happened. Stony-hearted Westminster had ignored Jarrow's petition. But Ellen Wilkinson told the people of Jarrow not to be downcast. 'Do not think the march is the end. It is not. It is only the beginning.' David Riley sought consolation in the impact of the march: 'The credit goes to all the lads, who have done their job magnificently. They have aroused a sympathy throughout the country which compels the

Government to act.' This was not entirely wishful thinking. The Jarrow Crusade may not have achieved its main aim, but it did strike at the conscience of the country, and in the longer term it earned a place in history.

It was a triumph of public relations. Millions followed its progress through favourable reports in the press and in the newsreels. Marguerite Patten remembered the reaction at her local London cinema. 'We'd seen a picture in the newspaper, and we realized that they were absolutely desperate, not a hope of a job. But when you saw their faces at the cinema I can almost remember the gasp that went round.'[70]

By rejecting politics and appealing to sympathy the march touched the hearts of many for whom the talk of the distressed areas had meant nothing. With its military discipline, and containing in its ranks many veterans of the First World War, it harked back to that conflict, evoking in the bystander feelings of compassion and guilt: Britain, it was painfully clear, had not built a land fit for heroes.

Over the years that followed, the crusade came to have a deeper significance. It was, as Ellen Wilkinson said at the time, 'only the beginning', but not in the way she meant. The Jarrow Crusade was one of the foundations of a new consensus that was emerging, and which would solidify during the Second World War. The country came to agree almost unanimously that such extremes of poverty should never be allowed to exist again. A new very British idea of social justice was emerging and a collective opinion forming that would eventually give rise to the welfare state.

18

Something must be done

ON 26 OCTOBER Joachim von Ribbentrop marched into the German Embassy in London for the first time as Ambassador to inspect his staff. He resented being there: Berlin was the place for an ambitious Nazi. In the ruthless power-politics of the Third Reich absence from the centre could spell political ruin – or worse. But he was on a mission, personally entrusted to him by the Führer, to make an alliance with Britain, and to do so using the friendly influence of the King. Unfortunately for him, there were two obstacles to his assignment: first, Edward VIII had in fact almost no standing in the councils of state; and second, his mind was concerned with another matter to the exclusion of everything else, a matter that would lead, in six weeks' time, to a constitutional crisis and his abdication.

When the new German Ambassador arrived at Victoria Station, he gave a Nazi salute lasting half a minute before haranguing the waiting press corps on the need for an Anglo-German alliance against Communism.[1] This breach of protocol was badly received in the next day's papers, not auguring well for Ribbentrop's time in London. On reaching the German Embassy in Carlton House Terrace, Ribbentrop ordered his staff to form a large semicircle and walked slowly round, giving each an ominous glare, before saluting with a smart 'Heil Hitler', which he expected to be promptly returned. After a short speech in praise of the Führer he rounded off the meeting with a communal shout of 'Sieg Heil'.

In London's political and society circles the Nazi diplomat, once the man of the moment, was losing his lustre. The free trips to Germany and meetings with Adolf Hitler dished out to anybody who asked were becoming less sought-after as the international scene darkened. No less significantly, the man's personality was being revealed in its full awfulness. Thomas Jones, who had accompanied Lloyd George on his ill-advised trip to meet Hitler the month before, received the Ribbentrop treatment when they talked – or rather when Ribbentrop addressed him – 'speaking with the most intense seriousness, unrelieved by any human or light touch whatsoever'.[2] The subject was almost always the Jewish-Bolshevik conspiracy, with the need for Germany and Britain to stand together against it. People came to realize that Ribbentrop was a crashing bore, with no light or shade about him at all. The problem was compounded by the Nazi diplomat's cadaverous appearance. This was not altogether his fault: he lacked a kidney and suffered permanent pains from war wounds, a disability which did nothing to lighten his spirits.

The Ribbentrops temporarily closed the Embassy for redecoration, turning its Regency splendour into a smart, if bland, interior that resembled a transatlantic liner. They moved the offices to temporary accommodation and rented a house (bizarrely enough from Neville Chamberlain) in Eaton Square. Once ensconced, Ribbentrop set about his mission to have a serious conversation with Edward VIII. His ability to do so was hampered not just by the King's attention being elsewhere but also by his own office's chaos. Reinhard Spitzy was a young Austrian SS officer attached to Ribbentrop's staff. His job was to act as his chief's 'shadow', on call at any time of day or night to answer the Ambassador's whims. In the morning, Spitzy remembered, the ill-tempered Ambassador would lie in his bath ordering people to be brought from Berlin and 'from all over Germany, accepted or rejected, appointed or dismissed', all the while dictating to a nervous secretary cowering behind a half-open door.[3] When necessary, a white telephone was brought to him in the bath, down which he would bellow demands and insults to his colleagues. On the rare occasions when the Führer called he would immediately stand up, phone in one hand, and give the Nazi salute, covered in soap suds. It was fortunate that the prudish Hitler could not see him. As the day progressed, meetings would be set up, and others cancelled, appointments missed, diplomatic gaffes made and social clangers dropped. Ribbentrop became known as 'Herr Brickendrop'. Society hostesses teased him to his face.[4]

Part of Ribbentrop's difficulties stemmed from his lack of ability. He was simply not up to the job. Spitzy recalled how he would often plan to write a diplomatic dispatch to Hitler, drawing up numerous drafts which he spread out all over the floor. Most would end up in the fire by the evening.[5] With such incompetence combined with bad management, the probability of an alliance with Britain grew less likely by the day. To Ribbentrop the fault lay not with his own diplomatic disabilities but with the King. Soon after his arrival in London, Ribbentrop presented his credentials to the monarch in Buckingham Palace. It was a formal ceremony, with Anthony Eden, the Foreign Secretary, in attendance. There was no opportunity for the sort of private conversation the Ambassador wanted; in the weeks that followed he met him on a few occasions at large social functions. 'A real conversation with the King', Ribbentrop remembered ruefully, 'which friends wanted to bring about confidentially, never materialized; something unforeseen always intervened.'[6] On such a missed opportunity, Ribbentrop believed, the fate of the world rested.

For the King the problems of Anglo-German relations were of little significance in his complex life. He certainly wanted friendship with Germany. He was ready to use what little influence he had in that direction. However, he had other things on his mind. Since his return from cruising the Mediterranean in August the crisis in his personal life had worsened. Not only had the Prime Minister approached him, begging him to stop the affair with Wallis, but his private office was in revolt on the issue and his close family was openly against him.

In September, following royal tradition, King Edward had travelled up to the castle of Balmoral for a brief holiday, but he broke with royal convention by failing to ask Cabinet ministers and other grandees to join him. Instead, he invited some of London's 'fast' set to a house party with him. They included the Buists, with whom Edward and Wallis had celebrated the new year, the Mountbattens, the Duke and Duchess of Kent, and Wallis's close American friends from her days in China, Herman Rogers and his wife, Katherine.

Although Edward loved to dress up in a kilt and have a 'blaw' on the bagpipes, he was no upholder of the great and austere tradition of 'Balmorality', which, since the castle's reconstruction by Queen Victoria and Prince Albert, had come to define the essence of the British royal family. Balmorality, among other things, celebrated the great Scottish outdoors. Field sports were sacrosanct. But Edward did not like field sports. Tramping through bogs and over heather in freezing rain was not his idea of fun. He preferred a round of golf to stalking a deer or casting a fly. Nor was he interested in upholding the quasi-feudal relationship with the ghillies and retainers who had loyally run the estate since the days of Queen Victoria and John Brown. As for Wallis Simpson, Balmoral was a Scottish theme park from hell: always cold, draughty and decorated in an invented Scottish style that even Walter Scott might have found over the top. When she first entered the home that generations of royals had come to consider as their 'highland paradise', she screamed, 'this tartan's gotta go.'[7]

The tradition of Balmorality was not dead, however. Albert and Elizabeth, the Duke and Duchess of York, with their two daughters, were staying on the estate at Birkhall, about six miles away from the castle. There they set up what appeared to Edward as a rival court, maintaining the ultra-conservative traditions of George V, in every way different from the cocktails and cinema shows that were being enjoyed by the party down the road. The Duke and Duchess made a point of inviting the Archbishop of Canterbury, an annual visitor in the days of the old King, as the Duchess told him, so that 'the links with Balmoral may not be wholly broken'.[8] Cosmo Lang was, if not in heaven, then at least in ecstasy. He described in his diary how, after tea on the second day of his visit, the Yorks' children, Elizabeth and Margaret Rose, came down from the nursery: 'They sang some action-songs most charmingly. It was strange to think of the destiny which may be waiting the little Elizabeth, at present Second from the Throne! She and her lively little sister are certainly most entrancing children.'[9]

Within a few weeks Elizabeth would be first from the throne. A

Dick Sheppard, the most effective preacher of his day and 'a man who could make contact with every human he met'. His pacifist message inspired millions, but he was tortured by self-doubt and physical disability

Débutantes learn to curtsey in preparation for their presentation to the King at Buckingham Palace. The event would end in disappointment and count as a further black mark against Edward VIII

Loyalist republican militias at the start of the Spanish Civil War in July 1936. One idealistic British volunteer remembered 'it was a sport to go riding round the town on a lorry, sitting on the wing, holding a rifle – a favourite revolutionary pose.' He would soon experience the horror of war

Above: John Cornford with Ray Peters, mother of his child. The epitome of the romantic revolutionary, he was driven to martyrdom in Spain by the fervour of his Communist faith

Right: Felicia Browne – a self-portrait. The artist was the first British volunteer to die in action in the Spanish Civil War

A mass hypnosis: German spectators in the Olympic stadium greet their Führer at the opening ceremony in August. The games were a propaganda triumph for the Nazis and convinced many gullible British visitors of Germany's greatness under Adolf Hitler

The touch that said it all. Edward VIII and Wallis Simpson
during their Mediterranean cruise

'This tartan's gotta go', commented Wallis Simpson during her visit to Balmoral.
The Highland holiday and the beginning of divorce proceedings against Simpson's
husband convinced the establishment that the time had come for action.
Two months later, in December, King Edward abdicated

Hitler groupies Unity Mitford and her sister Diana Guinness, with Diana's children. The sisters went to the Olympics, stayed with Joseph Goebbels, flirted with the Führer and made arrangements for Diana's marriage to Sir Oswald Mosley, the British Fascist leader

Oswald Mosley greets his blackshirts before attempting to march through the East End of London on 4 October. The militaristic style of his new uniform and the violence he provoked that day prompted the government to take firm action. He would never again pose a threat to public order

The Jarrow marchers step out on their way to London in October. 'They marched as well as the Durham Light Infantry', one of the organizers remembered with pride. Although in the short term the crusade failed to bring jobs to Jarrow, it succeeded in publicizing the plight of the jobless to millions

The *Queen Mary* on her maiden voyage. At the time the largest passenger liner ever built, for many the ship was a symbol of continuing British greatness. But she had a fundamental design fault that only became apparent during the winter storms in the Atlantic

The fat lady sings for the BBC and a communications
revolution is born. The world's first scheduled television
service started in November

The ruins of the Crystal Palace still smouldering after the fire at the beginning of
December. Its destruction symbolized for many the final passing of the Victorian
epoch and the dawn of a new and frightening age

tacit recognition of this possibility was growing at court and in Parliament. Edward must have been aware of it. He was put out that his brother was entertaining his father's ex-courtiers in what seemed a deliberate snub,[10] but this did not make him any the keener to carry out his royal duties when Wallis was there to distract him. While at Balmoral he refused to open the newly completed Royal Infirmary at Aberdeen, on a trumped-up excuse of court mourning (which had ended on 20 July), sending his brother instead. What offended was not his absence but the fact that he was seen on the very day driving himself to Ballater station to pick up Wallis from the station, badly disguised by a pair of driving goggles. 'This has shocked the Scotch and British bourgeoisie', Harold Nicolson noted in his diary, adding ominously that 'there is seething criticism which may develop into actual discontent'.

During the Balmoral holiday the King invited the Yorks to dinner. This, their only direct contact during the Highland retreat, turned into a clash between two alpha-females. On arrival at the Castle, in a clear breach of protocol, Wallis Simpson rather than the King advanced to the *porte-cochère* to greet the Duchess of York. It was a deliberate assertion of power. Wallis was to be treated as the hostess and partner of the King and not as a mere fellow guest. Elizabeth would have none of it. Striding past Wallis, with her head held high, she announced to the world at large, 'I have come to dine with the King'.[11] It was a defining gesture: the old world of Balmorality rejecting the parvenu modernity of the King's American mistress. From then on it was war.

For the forces of reaction it was time for action. Alec Hardinge, without consulting his employer, went to see the Duke and Duchess in mid-October, as soon as soon as they had returned to London. He told them what they had been dreading but half-expecting. He had learned that Mrs Simpson was planning divorce proceedings against her husband later in the month, opening the way for her marriage to the King. Hardinge explained to the Duke that this would not be tolerated by the Prime Minister and his Cabinet. Edward would face a choice: to renounce the woman he loved or to abdicate. There was no question as to which way he would go. Prince Albert was appalled by what Hardinge told him. Significantly, however, he did not step back from the prospect of kingship. Hardinge returned to Baldwin and told him, in the utmost secrecy, that the first step in the process of removing the King – if it were to become necessary – was satisfactorily completed. The successor was primed and ready.

The news of the impending divorce added to the sense of crisis surrounding the King's affairs. While the American press trumpeted the story, the British newspapers kept silent. Anticipating that the divorce proceedings could be the trigger for sensational and damaging reports, Edward begged his friend Lord Beaverbrook, proprietor of the *Daily Express*, to muzzle the media.[12] The press magnate agreed, arranging through the Newspaper Proprietors' Association for the silence to be maintained. The divorce proceedings would be reported as normal, without any reference to the King. It was an extraordinary piece of self-censorship, and one that made the gentlemen of the press a little queasy. As *The Spectator* asked after the affair was over, where was 'the point at which loyal reticence becomes a conspiracy of silence'?[13] Churchill believed that 'the voluntary muzzling of the British Press for so many months gave the worst forms of rumour and gossip their chance'.[14]

With divorce a certainty, Stanley Baldwin was at last forced into action. After over two months' repose, staying in the stately homes of friends in England and Wales, he was well rested and had recovered from his breakdown. He told Neville Chamberlain that he felt as well as he had done at 'any time during the last few years'[15] and – to Chamberlain's horror – that he was ready to stay on as Prime Minister until the coronation the following year. Chamberlain, rather gleefully, thought that this might not now be the case.

A certain Lady (who shall be nameless except that her initials are Mrs S-) intends on Friday next to begin proceedings for the purpose of obtaining a divorce from her husband. SB will be informed that the most alarming consequences would or might ensure & that it his duty to stop it.

Feeling, as he admitted to his sister, 'bloody minded', Chamberlain added that 'what effect that will have on his health remains to be seen'.

But Chamberlain had misjudged the Prime Minister. Although Baldwin had been reluctant to confront the problem of the 'King's matter', he was well suited to handling such a delicate business. His manipulative skills, masked by his homely manner, had been honed over nearly three decades of wheeler-dealing in the House of Commons. He was a master power-broker. King Edward, naïve and infatuated, was no match for this avuncular but ruthless politician.

On 20 October Baldwin presented himself at Fort Belvedere, crunching up the gravel drive in his official car, typical of his attractively modest style. It was 10.30 in the morning, but Baldwin was nervous and restless. On the way down he had been 'praying and planning'.[16] On arrival, to Edward's surprise, he asked for a drink. As the Prime Minister poured himself a stiff whisky-and-soda, he asked whether the King would care to join him. Edward refused, telling his guest primly that he never drank before seven in the evening. The two men did at least both smoke: it was about all they had in common. They lit up their pipes, started puffing and sat down to talk.

They talked for about an hour. Baldwin explained that the news of the King's relationship with Wallis Simpson was causing immense embarrassment abroad, where it was the subject of scandalous reports in the popular press. The monarchy was in danger. At last he came to the nub of the question: Wallis Simpson's divorce. 'Must the case really go on?' he asked. The King, somewhat priggishly and certainly disingenuously, responded that it would be wrong for him to interfere in the affairs of private individuals. The meeting ended with Baldwin begging the King 'to think the matter over'. Both men had skirted round the central question: the possibility of the King's marriage to Wallis Simpson after her divorce.[17]

Those who stood behind Baldwin were furious that he had not confronted the issue. A cabal formed, intent on forcing him into action. Its members were predictable. Most formidable was Neville Chamberlain. With him were: Geoffrey Dawson, pro-appeasement editor of *The Times*, an establishmentarian who detested the new King; the unctuous Cosmo Lang, shaking his head in despair at the prospect of consecrating an adulterer at the coronation, praying for

change; and the lynchpin, Alec Hardinge, febrile and uncompromis-
ing. Both Dawson and Lang were frequent visitors to Hardinge at
Buckingham Palace. Alec Hardinge was their bridge to Prince Albert,
the King-in-waiting, keeping him informed of developments. On
the day that Wallis Simpson's divorce petition was heard, 27 October,
he dined with the Duke of York once more. No doubt he informed
the Duke that, like it or not, powerful forces were gathering to hand
him the crown if the King were to marry Wallis Simpson.

The case of Simpson vs. Simpson was heard outside London, at
Ipswich Assizes, to avoid unwanted publicity. Wallis Simpson was
cross-questioned by her barrister, and evidence was presented of
Ernest Simpson's adultery with 'Buttercup' Raffray in the Hotel de
Paris at Bray the preceding July. The suit was not contested. The
judge, Mr Justice Hawke, awarded Wallis a decree nisi, which, when
made absolute the following April, would leave her free to marry
again. *The Times* gave the story no more than twelve lines; the
Morning Post ran a small paragraph; the *Daily Telegraph* devoted
twenty-two lines to the case on the inner pages, sandwiched between
'Colonel Accused in Private' and 'Boy with Mania for Silk
Stockings'.[18]

The self-imposed silence of the press did not mean that the entire
public was unaware of the significance of the case. It seemed that just
about anybody in the establishment, or with connections to it, was in
the know. The diarist Harold Nicolson heard rumours that Edward
was about to make Wallis Duchess of Edinburgh and marry her.[19]
The socialite photographer Cecil Beaton commented on the King
and Mrs Simpson: 'American newspapers have already announced
the engagement . . . it is said that Queen Mary weeps continuously.
I am taking bets that the marriage will not happen this year.'[20]

The silence was kept at this stage not so much to prevent the
public knowing as to spare the King's blushes. His behaviour offended
people of all backgrounds and classes, at a time when a rigid code of
public morality still held sway. During the Jarrow Crusade Ellen
Wilkinson and Ritchie Calder, marching at the front of the men,
gossiped about the King and Mrs Simpson. At the midday break,
Calder remembered,

we saw mutiny in the ranks and finally a deputation. 'What's all this about the King and that woman?' We tried to pass it off lightly but they were furious with us for repeating the story, and then furious with him . . . the people of Jarrow had nothing other than the family, and this symbolically came as a threat to the family.[21]

The revelations in the USA, coming hard on the heels of the divorce hearings, prompted the King's enemies to fire their first salvo. The editor of *The Times*, Geoffrey Dawson, visited Alec Hardinge at Buckingham Palace. He brought with him an anonymous letter written by a British expatriate in the USA. The writer, who signed himself 'Britannicus in Partibus Infidelium' (literally 'a Briton in the lands of the infidel'), spoke of the shame and humiliation that the King's affair was bringing on his country. He concluded: 'Nothing would please me more than to hear that Edward VIII had abdicated his rights in favour of the Heir Presumptive.'[22] The letter, with its suggestion of abdication and its tone of moral disapproval, may have mirrored Dawson and Hardinge's feelings, but it did not reflect the attitude of the American press at all. The coverage in the infidel USA, while sensational, was universally friendly; the possibility of a US citizen becoming Queen of England was one that was warmly welcomed. The 'Britannicus' letter was so much at variance with the real American attitude that a conspiracy theorist might think that Dawson himself had concocted it. With its claim that 'the foundations of the British throne are undermined, its moral authority, its honour, its dignity cast into the dustbin', it certainly reflected Dawson and Hardinge's views, and they seized on it as an opportunity to confront the King.

Hardinge, having discussed the idea with Dawson, used the 'Britannicus' letter as the excuse to compose his own letter to the King. What he wrote, however, was not his work alone. As the historian Susan Williams has discovered, it was the product of several hands – what she called a 'conspiracy of strategic thinking and planning'.[23] Hardinge consulted Chamberlain; he received advice from the head of the Civil Service and government law officers. Several drafts were written and passed round government before the document was considered good enough to send. Geoffrey Dawson had one last look at it when he visited the Palace that Friday.[24]

The letter itself was intended to be part of a three-pronged attack designed to force Baldwin into taking immediate and firm action against the King. Neville Chamberlain was furious at what he perceived to be Baldwin's pusillanimity at his last meeting with Edward. He was in bed suffering from an acute attack of gout in the big toe of his right foot, which did nothing for his temper. He told his sister Hilda, in one of his intimate weekly letters, that his doctor believed the gout to be the result of overwork. He feared his illness might impede his taking over from Baldwin, as he remarked ruefully: 'I wonder if by the time S. B. makes up his mind that his King & Country can do without him there will be anything left of me except an enormous toe!'[25]

Unwell or not, he saw the crisis as an opportunity to assert his authority and out-manoeuvre the Prime Minister, hastening his departure as well as the King's. Chamberlain told Hilda that he had, 'without telling' Baldwin, made inquiries about the constitutional and legal processes necessary to remove a king. He admitted to her that 'I have even drafted certain communications which I consider should be made'. Chamberlain then 'induced the PM to call a few colleagues together' for a meeting to discuss the situation.

At the meeting Chamberlain revealed his plans to this Cabinet inner circle, which included Ramsay MacDonald, the former Prime Minister, Sir John Simon, the Home Secretary, and Walter Runciman, the scourge of Jarrow. Chamberlain showed Baldwin the draft of the ultimatum, called 'a memorandum of censure',[26] which he wanted to present to the King, in conjunction with Hardinge's letter. It was an unprecedented attack on a British monarch, deploring his conduct and ordering him to end his relationship with Wallis Simpson immediately or to abdicate. The plan was for the Private Secretary's letter to be sent first, followed by the 'memorandum of censure'.[27] The memorandum also contained an implicit threat: if the King did not heed his government's call to end his affair with Mrs Simpson, the press silence would cease. Geoffrey Dawson had drafted a leader to this end.[28] With the press in full cry and without the support of the government, Edward's situation would be impossible.

With characteristic guile Chamberlain had prepared his coup

well, showing his colleagues his draft and getting their backing in advance of the meeting. But Baldwin would have none of it. He too was well briefed. As he told Thomas Jones after the crisis, an ultimatum at that stage would have risked disaster, with the King refusing point-blank. 'It would send him sky-high',[29] Baldwin said, and could force the government's resignation and a general election on the issue. If a government could not be formed after an election, the King would have to govern on his own, as a dictator (a prospect that some Fascists, led by the eccentric Lady Houston, had suggested at the start of his reign). To precipitate such a crisis would be the height of irresponsibility.

To Chamberlain's intense irritation, Baldwin foiled his plan and persuaded the others at the meeting to step back into line. The Chancellor's coup attempt had failed because he was wrong and the Prime Minister was right. The affair needed to be handled with more grace and delicacy than Chamberlain possessed – a sign, perhaps, of the fundamental lack of judgement that would come to haunt him in future as Prime Minister. He retired hurt, consoling himself that, 'the machine has been started and, provided I am not confined to bed, I will see that it continues to move in the hope (now getting very thin) of averting a catastrophe'.[30]

The machine had indeed begun to move, but the driving force was no longer Chamberlain and his fellow conspirators. Although many have accused them of plotting to bring down the King, their role in the affair at this point was effectively over. From now they would be bit-players in the drama, egging on the Prime Minster from the sidelines. Baldwin, roused into action by their conspiracy and sensing political advantage, became the central figure. He would handle the crisis on his own, reporting to the Cabinet frequently to discuss the issues and to secure the backing of colleagues for his action but making all the moves himself. He took command and on Friday 13 November instructed that Alec Hardinge's letter be sent to the King.

The letter warned that the silence of the British press could not be maintained indefinitely and that when the story broke the effect would be 'calamitous'. He told the King that the government's resignation over the issue of his relationship was a real possibility, resulting in 'Your Majesty having to find someone capable of forming a government' that would have the support of the House of Commons. Given the current feeling of the House, there was little chance of this. The only alternative was, Hardinge told the King, for 'Mrs Simpson to go abroad without further delay'.

The King was away on a two-day visit to the Home Fleet, anchored off Portland. This tour of the Fleet brought out all that was best in Edward, away from the disapproval of Court and Cabinet. He had arrived at four in the morning in the middle of a storm, exhausted after the wreath-laying at the Cenotaph, followed by the Festival of Remembrance at the Albert Hall the previous day. He made no complaint, plunging into his duties with all the energy and charm of which he was capable and which had made him so popular. He refused to wear a raincoat while inspecting the men in a downpour, unlike Sir Samuel Hoare, the First Lord of the Admiralty, who accompanied him on the tour. As one of those present observed, 'a small thing, but sailors take note of small things, and in this they saw the real difference between the Politician and the Monarch'.[31]

Edward loved the Royal Navy, the service in which he had trained and served as a young man. Sir Samuel Hoare noted his ability to make each sailor to whom he spoke feel as if he knew him personally. On board the aircraft carrier HMS *Courageous* he attended a packed concert held in the ship's cavernous hangar beneath the flight deck. Hoare remembered how he plunged into the crowd of sailors, elbowed his way through to the back and started a sing-song, to the accompaniment of a sailor's mouth-organ. When he came back to the platform, he made an impromptu speech 'that brought the house down. Then, a seaman in the crowd proposed three cheers for him, and there followed an unforgettable scene of the wildest and most spontaneous enthusiasm.'[32]

When Edward returned to the Fort, Hardinge's letter was waiting for him. It was not a relaxing start to the weekend. He was outraged by what he read, suspecting – rightly – that his Private Secretary had not been 'straight' with him. The letter was a turning-point. The King ceased to seek the advice of Hardinge and to use him as a channel to the Prime Minister.

The atmosphere at Buckingham Palace became ever more poison-ous, with cliques forming and hushed voices in corridors. The King turned for advice to those whom he trusted. There were not many of these. He used Sir Walter Monckton, an old friend and a barrister, as an alternative to his Private Secretary, and he sought out Max Beaverbrook. To his dismay, Beaverbrook was at sea, on board the German liner *Bremen,* bound for America seeking a cure for his asthma in the arid deserts of Arizona.[33] Edward ordered him back. If the ship could not turn around mid-ocean, he was to remain on board and come back on its return. Beaverbrook obeyed.

Having discussed the situation with Wallis over the weekend, on Monday 16 November Edward summoned Baldwin to the Fort for a second meeting. It took place at 6.30 p.m. This time the two men were more frank with each other, speaking openly of the relation-ship. As Baldwin spoke, Edward noticed that he had a disconcerting nervous habit of emphasizing what he said by 'cracking his fingers with a quick flip of the hand past his right ear'.[34] For his part, Baldwin described seeing Edward come into the room after he had spoken to Wallis on the telephone 'with the most beautiful look I have ever seen on his face, like a young knight who has just seen the Holy Grail'.[35]

Baldwin told the King that he believed he had an instinct for public opinion. He knew that the British people would not tolerate their monarch's marriage to a twice-divorced woman.

> I pointed out to him that the position of the King's wife was different from the position of any other citizen in the country . . . His wife becomes Queen; the Queen becomes the Queen of the country; and, therefore, in the choice of a Queen, the voice of the people must be heard.[36]

Edward would have none of it. Wallis was for him, as his great-nephew was to say of the divorced woman he wished to wed sixty years later, 'non-negotiable'. 'I want you to be the first to know,' he told the startled Prime Minister, 'I have made up my mind and noth-ing will alter it – I have looked at it from all sides – and I mean to abdicate and marry Mrs Simpson.'[37] Baldwin responded: 'Sir, this is most grievous news, and it is impossible for me to make any comment on it today.'[38] He needed time to consult his colleagues.

The Prime Minister then departed in the same 'undersized little black box' (actually a Rolls-Royce) that was his official car. Edward remembered, 'As the box with its portly occupant shot away into the dark, it began to take on the guise of a sinister and purposeful little black beetle. Where was it off to now?'[39] It was off to Westminster. Far from being downcast by the news of the King's intentions, Baldwin was relieved. It appeared that Edward was prepared to go without being pushed. The threats and ultimatums that Chamberlain had proposed were unnecessary. When he arrived at the House of Commons, Baldwin bumped into Ramsay MacDonald, who noted in his diary: '7.30 met PM ebullient. Put his arm in mine . . . the King was determined to marry Mrs S and was prepared to abdicate. Nice kettle of fish.'[40] Baldwin also spoke to the King's one Cabinet ally, Duff Cooper. He informed him of Edward's intentions and said, tellingly, that his brother Prince Albert was better suited to the job, and 'would be just like his father'.[41]

While the Prime Minister was at Westminster, the King changed into white tie and tails and went quickly to Marlborough House, the residence of his mother, Queen Mary, for dinner. It was a tense affair. His sister Princess Mary, the Princess Royal, was there with his new sister-in-law, the Duchess of Gloucester, to lend moral support to the elderly Queen, who had guessed the purpose of her son's visit. After a painful dinner, where Edward did his best to keep the conversation flowing, the Duchess tactfully retired to bed, leaving the three family members to the privacy of the Queen's boudoir. Out of hearing of the servants, the King was at last able to tell them what they knew but dreaded to hear: that he intended to marry Wallis, and that his Prime Minister and government were opposed to the union. If necessary, he informed his stunned and horrified mother, he would abdicate. Nothing, not even the throne itself, would stand between him and his love.[42]

Twenty-four hours later the King boarded a special train at Paddington and set off on a tour of the distressed areas of south Wales. The two-day visit to the Rhondda and Monmouth valleys had been planned for some time. Its purpose was to show the King's continuing commitment to the plight of the unemployed. At 5.35 a.m. on Wednesday 18 November the train pulled into Llantwit Major, a small town on the coast of Glamorgan. After breakfast the royal party set off on the first of a series of visits to the desolate mining towns and villages of the area.

The King started his visit in good humour. The sun was shining on a sunny and cool autumnal day; he was dressed in a grey overcoat and suit, which contrasted with the formal black attire and wing collars of those who accompanied him. His party included Ernest Brown, the Minister of Labour, an unpopular politician in an area that had seen riots against the hated Means Test, and the health minister, Sir Kingsley Wood. To counterbalance these figures from the Conservative establishment, the King commanded that Malcolm Stewart, the Commissioner for the Special Areas, dine with him that evening on the special train. Stewart had just resigned in frustration at the government's failure to give him the backing he needed to do his job. Shortly before his resignation, he published a damning report on the feebleness of measures to tackle unemployment.[43] Edward was walking into an area of acute political sensitivity.

The King's party made its way to Boverton, in the Vale of Glamorgan, for the first visit of the day. It was here that the Welsh Land Settlement Society ran a co-operative farm for seventy unemployed miners, many of them veterans of the First World War. The idea was to retrain them as smallholders. It turned out a failure, a mere palliative, like many of the schemes to help the unemployed that Edward inspected on this tour.

The troubles of the co-operative were put aside, however, when Edward arrived. The apprentice farmers had built an archway of leeks, through which the King walked on arrival, joking with Mr Bean, the manager, that he was partial to the Welsh national vegetable, 'you can send me some of these to London. I am fond of them'.[44] The tone became serious when Edward asked one of the ex-miners whether he preferred his new life: 'No, I would rather be a miner, Sir,' was the answer, 'but we are lucky indeed to have anything to do, and we always think of our pals in the Valleys, who are just sitting and looking at the empty mines.' The King responded with words that were to become the leitmotif of the tour: 'Yes, it is a great pity that something more can't be done about it.'[45]

There was a minor kerfuffle when one of the land workers darted from the crowd, grasped the King's arm and started speaking to him. The police grabbed him and hustled him away. He was an ex-serviceman who had been one of the King's honour guard when, as Prince of Wales, he had landed in France during the war. This was another theme of the tour. Just as 60 per cent of the Jarrow marchers had served in the conflict, so many of the miners had done their duty in the trenches and proudly sported their medals for the royal visit.

The King's party then made its way to the Government Junior Training Centre at Llandough. The boys on the scheme lined his route, banging the tools of the trades that they were learning: shovels, saws and dustpans and brushes. Prominent among the places on this royal visit were training centres for domestic staff – both male and female. The idea was to train the young unemployed in the distressed areas before sending them to work 'in service' in the houses of the middle classes, to help make up the shortage of servants. One report asserted that most of the fourteen-year-old girls in the Rhondda that year 'are trained by the local Council and fitted out with uniforms to go away into domestic service'.[46] This 'transference' of labour led to dislocation and loneliness for thousands of youngsters.

The tour continued, past disused collieries turned into recreation centres, through maternity and child welfare clinics, into local housing estates and along lines of the ex-servicemen of the British Legion, standing to attention with their colours flying. Wherever he went, Edward could be seen doffing his black bowler hat to the cheering crowds, a diminutive figure standing out from the crowd in his light-coloured coat. Always his tone was informal and sympathetic, 'I am the King, may I come in?' Always the same request was made of him: tell Whitehall to do something to bring jobs to the valleys.

A cartoon, 'The Slackers' Dilemma', in the South Wales Echo, summed up the political symbolism of the visit. Three builders, Chamberlain, Ernest Brown and Baldwin, are seated on a bench in a tumbledown house doing nothing. They turn round in shocked surprise as the King approaches. Baldwin, the foreman, comments: 'Gosh, lads! Here comes the chief inspector, and we can't even pretend to do anything.' But the King could offer no practical solutions. The significance of his visit lay in the feeling that someone of importance actually cared, as John Meredith, a local schoolboy at the time, later remembered: 'We were all looking for a ray of hope out of the darkness that we were in and this was the only ray of hope that we had seen for years. We felt at last we have got somebody who is going to speak for us in the corridors of power.'

From Merthyr Tydfil the King's party made a detour to the Bessemer Steel Works of Dowlais, shut down six years earlier. Just as the closure of Palmer's shipyards at Jarrow had blighted a town, so the ending of steelmaking in this part of south Wales had brought ruin to a region. Nine thousand men had worked making steel; now there was nothing remaining but the wreckage of the old works, and no other industry to take them on. In 1936 three-quarters of the men of Dowlais were unemployed. But this bleak statistic did not dampen the welcome they gave to the King. John Meredith was one of the 2,000 who had come out to greet him: 'everybody flocked along, packed the pavements and jumped from one place to the other . . . It was a spontaneous reaction.' Schoolchildren waved Union Jacks, and the Dowlais Aged Comrades choir sang 'God Save the King'.[47] Vera and Elsie, two schoolgirls, joined the crowd: 'His face was pink and his hair was brushed back, and he was so good looking. He looked so lovely, and people really loved him.' Not all who came waved flags or sang the national anthem, however. Iorweth Williams, a Dowlais schoolboy, stood silently with his fist held up in the clenched salute. Iorweth came from a radical family. His father, Jack, an unemployed miner, was an NUWM activist who had organized sit-ins, strikes and hunger marches and was soon to leave with fifteen local men to fight Fascism in Spain. 'My father was basically a republican at heart and had no time for the monarchy. There was a tradition of radicalism in south Wales in those days.'[48]

Radical or not, most of Dowlais had come out to see the King. He walked forward through an arch made of coal, into the ruined steelworks. The ragged men who had once worked there surrounded him, raising their caps. Some had clambered up on to the twisted gantries and rusting walkways of the derelict works, from where they looked down on him. He stood by the defunct blast furnace surveying the scene, his face drawn and grave, his hat removed as a mark of respect. As he looked on, some of the men started to sing the Welsh hymn 'Crugybar'.[49] The King, visibly moved, turned to those next to him and said 'These steelworks brought the men hope. Something must be done to see that they stay here – working.'

The four words 'something must be done' echoed around the country. They became a refrain taken up by those of all political persuasions who felt that the government had done too little to alleviate the suffering of the poor and unemployed. The King's words, as the Jarrow march had done, gained a significance that transcended the immediacy of the plight to which they referred. His intervention chimed with the growing consensus that something had to be done to create a more just and fair society. Edward, in expressing the national mood, was fulfilling the role that destiny had set out for him. He had started the tour certain that he was about to reject that destiny. Now, buoyed up by the success of his visit, he began to think that he should put up a fight for the throne and the woman he loved.

19

The Cornwall plan

THE KING RETURNED to London in high spirits. The visit to
south Wales had demonstrated his immense popularity and his
great ability to empathize with the sufferings of his people. When
combined with the politics of long-term unemployment, it made
for a heady brew. The King's opponents became concerned. 'These
escapades should be limited', Ramsay MacDonald commented
sternly in his diary. 'They are an invasion into the field of politics
and should be watched constitutionally.'[1] Geoffrey Dawson, in *The
Times*, agreed, calling the King's comment that 'something must be
done' 'monstrous'. He penned a leader in which he dismissed it as a
'a constitutionally dangerous proceeding that would threaten, if
continued, to entangle the Throne in politics'.[2]

Dawson was right. The King had entered a political minefield.
The *Daily Mail* was quick to make political capital out of the King's
comment, with an article under the headline 'The King Edward
Touch', praising his visit. 'Never has the magic of personal leadership
been better shown than by the King's visit to south Wales', the *Mail*
trumpeted, contrasting his care for the plight of the unemployed with
the indifference of his government: 'As few Ministers have done, the
Sovereign examined their plight and drew from them the tale of their
trouble.'[3]

Edward later reflected that the words to the people of Dowlais
were 'the minimum humanitarian response' that he could have made
to the suffering he had seen. The episode made him all too aware,
however, that the modern world had made it 'almost impossible for a
monarch to continue to play the role of the Good King, free to move
unhindered among his subjects, and speak what is in his mind'.[4]

His subjects in south Wales certainly did not object to the political tone of his comment. The Royal Archives at Windsor are the repository of thousands of letters addressed to the King during this crucial period, the vast majority of which are positive.[5] 'You could profess concern and interest and yet stay away,' wrote one correspondent, expressing the feelings of many, 'but that you do not do, and may God bless you for it.' Another emphasized the King's willingness to stoop to the level of the poorest, another common sentiment: 'We like you for the concern you have for the welfare of the poorest and most unfortunate of your subjects. No other King has gone among them as you have done, or shown signs of appreciating their distress in the way you do.'[6]

The success of the visit to south Wales certainly seems to have encouraged Edward sufficiently to make him wish to remain King, and not to go without a fight. Full of confidence, he telephoned his brother, the Duke of Kent, on the evening of his return and apparently told him that it was his intention to marry Wallis, and make her Queen of England and Empress of India, 'the whole bag of tricks'.[7]

This confidence was not solely the result of his visit to south Wales. Behind the scenes a new and powerful ally had sprung to his defence. Winston Churchill's motives for supporting Edward were a mixture of the personal and political. Since his rejection by Baldwin in the spring, his disdain for what he regarded as the Prime Minister's criminal sloth in the face of the German danger had grown. That autumn it reached a peak of contempt. On Thursday 12 November, Baldwin had spoken in the defence debate with self-confessed 'appalling frankness', admitting that his reluctance to seek a popular mandate for rearmament had arisen from political calculation. The country, in its pacifist mood, Baldwin told a startled House of Commons, would not have elected a party on a rearmament ticket.

To Churchill this was immoral: a clear admission of a Prime Minister putting the interests of his party before those of the country. Later in the debate he made his feelings plain in a characteristically florid attack on the government's vacillation: 'decided only to be undecided, resolved to be irresolute, adamant for drift, solid for fluidity, all powerful to be impotent. So we go on preparing more months and years – precious, perhaps vital, to the greatness of Britain – for the locusts to eat.'[8] It was a marvellous put-down, but its political impact at the time was marginal. Neville Chamberlain told his sister that 'in spite of the House's enjoyment of Winston's sarcasm, it did not seem to me that they were accepting his conclusions'.[9]

Churchill was looking for opportunities to revive his flagging political career as well as to do down Baldwin. His adoption of the cause of the League of Nations with a campaign for 'Arms and the Covenant' earlier in the year had seemed cynical and out of character and did not catch fire. He had resigned his position on the government defence committee after the expulsion of his friend Lindemann. He remained a big beast, certainly, but a big beast still tramping around, bellowing in the wilderness. To back the King in a popular cause presented an opening. It would add to Baldwin's discomfort and, if successful, might lead to his defeat, and the formation of a new government with Churchill at its heart. There was something unquestionably expedient about his coming out for the King. Only a few weeks earlier, as Lord Salisbury, Churchill's ally in most matters, sternly pointed out to him in a letter, Churchill had argued that Edward should be ready to sacrifice Wallis, just as 'others had made every sacrifice in the War'. Now he seemed to have made a sudden volte-face and to be making the opposite case. 'I am watching your attitude with great anxiety', Salisbury warned.[10]

But Churchill's reasons for changing his position and supporting Edward were not entirely cynical. He held romantic views about the power of love, as he told the trade union leader Walter Citrine when he encountered him at a League of Nations meeting on 3 December, with quiet intensity: 'I will defend him. I think it is my duty.' Citrine asked him why. 'Winston looked grave, and putting his hand on his breast, he said with emotion, "He feels it here".'[11] Churchill was also romantic about royalty, having long harboured an antiquated reverence for the chivalry of monarchy. For twenty-five years, Churchill argued, as Prince of Wales and now King, Edward had done his duty. It had been exhausting, demanding, and – trapped in the world of royalty – unreal. 'One must have something real somewhere. Otherwise far better die.'[12] The law affirmed the right to remarry:

why should the King not benefit from the right of every subject? It was a persuasive and personal argument, and one that convinced him, with all the other factors, to come to the aid of his monarch.

When Edward was visiting south Wales, Churchill came up with a plan that would enable him to marry Wallis and remain on the throne: a morganatic marriage. This would deny Wallis the royal title of Queen and preclude Edward's heirs from taking the throne. The crown would pass on his death instead to the Duke of York's eldest daughter, Princess Elizabeth. In this way the unsuitability of Mrs Simpson, Churchill believed, would be neutralized.

Rather than putting this plan directly to the King, he used an intermediary, Esmond Harmsworth, Lord Rothermere's son. By using the press baron as a go-between, Churchill must have hoped to avoid any accusations of political meddling. Lord Harmsworth took Wallis Simpson to lunch at Claridge's and suggested the scheme to her. He told her, as Churchill had instructed, that if on marriage she became the King's consort but not his Queen, she might be created 'Duchess of Lancaster' or 'Duchess of Cornwall'. Wallis was taken with the idea. She telephoned the King on his special train that afternoon and told him of the conversation.[13] The fact that Wallis was informed of the idea before Edward was significant. All knew that she was the dominant partner in the relationship, faster of mind and more astute. Nothing could be done without her backing. Edward returned to London not only buoyed up by the stunning success of his tour but also convinced that the morganatic marriage was the answer to his problem. Over the weekend at the Fort he discussed Churchill's proposal further with Wallis. Both agreed it was the way forward. Edward requested Esmond Harmsworth to go to Downing Street on Monday to propose the idea, which Churchill called 'the Cornwall plan', to Baldwin.

The Prime Minister was utterly opposed to the plan the moment he heard of it from Harmsworth, whom he considered 'a disgustingly conceited fellow'. He told him that it would require an act of Parliament and that MPs would never pass it. Harmsworth retorted, 'Oh, I'm sure they would! The whole standard of morals is so much more broad-minded since the war.' Baldwin agreed with him that 'the ideal of morality and duty and self-sacrifice and decency certainly has gone down since the War', but surely this was all the more reason for the King to be seen as a model of propriety. 'The idea of kingship has gone up', he told the press baron.[14] It was the Prime Minister's constant refrain that at a time of decline the monarchy was expected more than ever to uphold standards and that the country would never accept Wallis Simpson, whatever her constitutional position. The next day he talked the morganatic idea over with Neville Chamberlain, who also opposed it, seeing it as the thin end of the wedge that would inevitably lead to Mrs Simpson becoming Queen. Despite Churchill's best efforts to remain out of the picture, they both suspected that he was up to no good, cynically using the King's affair to further his own career.

The prospect of Winston Churchill forming a 'King's Party' to push the 'Cornwall Plan' prompted Baldwin to act. On Tuesday 24 November he summoned Churchill, together with the Labour Leader of the Opposition, Clement Attlee, and the Liberal leader, Sir Archibald Sinclair, and told them that the government would resign if Edward pressed on with his plans to marry. He demanded a pledge that they would not form an alternative government. Both Attlee and Sinclair fell into line, putting pressure on Churchill to do the same.[15] He was not to be boxed in, however. He equivocated, saying that, although his attitude was a little different, he would certainly support the government.[16] Baldwin did not trust Churchill for a moment. He remained suspicious that he would challenge the government on the issue.

The fevered gossips of Westminster had spread word of Churchill's machinations around Parliament and beyond. Baldwin's plans for a smooth transition from one monarch to another were now in jeopardy. Leo Amery, the Birmingham MP, shared the general distaste: 'It is clear Winston has thought this a wonderful opportunity of scuppering B. by the help of Harmsworth and Beaverbrook', he wrote in his diary. 'What a fool he is when it comes to questions of political judgment!'[17] Chips Channon, by contrast, revelled in the excitement of it all. 'A bombshell', he exclaimed, after bumping in to the transport minister, 'Leslie Hore-Belisha thinks that the Conservatives will resign, and that the premiership will be hawked about to anyone who will take it, and that Winston Churchill will summon a party meeting, create a new party and rule the country.'[18] Chips was not exaggerating the mood in the smoking-rooms and bars when he wrote of 'the Conservative Party divided, the country divided, mental civil war and schism in the Royal Family'.[19]

Still the press remained silent. While the King's affair was the subject of endless discussion in Westminster, across the drawing-rooms and dinner tables of London's élite the fiction was maintained that the world of court and politics was continuing as normal. There was something implicitly snobbish and archaic about this assumption. Helen Hardinge decided to write her diary in French, to prevent the servants reading it. She advised her mother-in-law, Violet Milner, to do the same. Violet was in the thick of things, having frequent conversations with her friend Geoffrey Dawson and inviting him, Alec Hardinge and the Chamberlains to lunch on the day that Churchill was confronted at Downing Street. 'Le roi est archifou', she exclaimed in her diary, 'Great confabulation between Alec & Neville & Alec & Geoffrey. Le roi continue à croire qu'il va épouser sa maitresse.'[20]

The following morning, Wednesday 25 November, the King commanded Stanley Baldwin to attend an audience at Buckingham Palace. It was a short meeting. This time Edward put forward to him directly the idea of a morganatic marriage. Baldwin side-stepped the issue with a suggestion that, as he later said to his daughter, 'I don't expect your Reverend Mother would have approved of. I said to him, was it absolutely necessary that he should marry her? In their peculiar circumstances, certain things are sometimes permitted to Royalty which are not allowed to the ordinary man.' Edward rejected this suggestion that Wallis become his Mrs Keppel (the long-term mistress of his grandfather Edward VII) out of hand. It was the essence of the hypocritical old morality he so hated. 'Oh, there's no question of that,' he replied straight away, 'I am going to marry her.'[21]

Baldwin told him that he did not believe that Parliament would support the morganatic proposal, but that – if the King wished – he could consult the Cabinet and the Prime Ministers of the Dominions on the question.[22] The King agreed. The Prime Minister asked him once more with emphasis: 'Do you really wish that, Sir?' Edward confirmed that he did. This was a decisive moment. By handing his Prime Minister the initiative, Edward was constitutionally bound to follow his 'advice'. If he did not do so, his options as King were to try to form a new government under Winston Churchill – a very un-realistic scenario – or he could try to rule the country on his own as a dictator – an even more unlikely state of affairs.[23] The only realistic option, if he wished to marry Wallis in opposition to his ministers, would be to abdicate in favour of his brother.

Baldwin hurried back to Downing Street in his 'little black box' and set to work. The morganatic proposal was a challenge that required all his political skills to overcome. The crisis was, he later recalled, 'an unforgettable period'. He had nine secretaries on call, staying in the office, working night and day, with 'private cables whizzing backwards and forwards between the Dominions and myself, Cabinet meetings, and all the time I had to be going between Fort Belvedere and Buckingham Palace and Downing Street.'[24] The King was ringing him at all hours, according to Geoffrey Dawson, 'shouting orders at him, orders which were wholly unconstitutional. He thought he could be Hitler!!'[25] Baldwin was a man transformed. From the depressed, lethargic, broken-down figure of the summer he had turned into a man of energy, initiative and action. He called a Cabinet. He dispatched suitably phrased telegrams to the Prime Ministers of Australia, Canada, New Zealand, South Africa and Ireland. When he met with his colleagues on Friday 27 November, the King's marriage was discussed in open Cabinet for the first time.[26] There was, as expected, no support for the morganatic proposal. Edward's sole friend and supporter, Duff Cooper, pleaded for the question of his marriage to be delayed until after the coronation, but he gave no backing for morganatic marriage.

Baldwin also privately told his colleagues of Churchill's intrigues, warning them that he believed Winston might be prepared to form an alternative government which would back the King's marriage. This would divide the country into two camps and 'would be fraught with danger of the most formidable kind'. Lord Zetland, the Secretary of State for India, reported the Cabinet meeting in a

fevered letter to the Viceroy in Delhi. The possible consequences of
the Churchill plan were almost too awful to contemplate: 'On this
issue it might well be that the Empire would disintegrate, since the
throne is the magnet which at present keeps it together.' At home,
he warned, the situation might arise 'which would not be far short
of civil strife'. Zetland shared a feeling widespread at the time of
unreality: that it was not possible for a constitutional crisis of this
kind to arise in the twentieth century. 'I sometimes ask myself if
these things are really happening, or if they are made of the stuff that
dreams are made of, the insubstantial phantasmagoria of some incred-
ible mass hallucination.'[27]

When Lord Beaverbrook learned of the King's position, he was
aghast. He had arrived on the *Bremen* on Thursday and driven straight
to the Fort from Southampton. Over lunch the King told him of his
conversation with Baldwin. Beaverbrook understood immediately
that Edward had sold the pass. It was too late for any bold strategy.
He told the King bluntly: 'Sir, you have put your head on the execu-
tion block. All that Baldwin has to do now is swing the axe.' Privately
he reflected that the King was no match for Baldwin, an accom-
plished and experienced politician: 'He had mixed more freely with
the people than any Heir Apparent had ever done before, but he had
hardly mixed at all with the politicians . . . he had friends in the coalmines, but not in the Cabinet.'[28] It was the truth. Edward was an
innocent, quite out of his depth.

Meanwhile, Churchill continued to threaten rebellion. He had
been ruminating on the King's position while shooting over the
weekend with the Duke of Westminster. His daughter Mary Soames
remembered her parents having 'heated arguments' about the issue;
her father – always the romantic – told Clementine that 'if the young
were in love, then let them be in love'.[29] On Monday 30 November,
Churchill buttonholed Duff Cooper in the lobby of the House of
Commons, announcing that he wished to brief the King's sole supporter in Cabinet on 'the direction of his thinking'. He spoke with
passion, as Cooper related in his diary, bursting out: 'What crime, he
asked, had the King committed? Had we not sworn allegiance to
him? Were we not bound by oath?' Churchill then raised the ques-

tion of the King's human rights. 'Was he to be condemned unheard? Was he seeking to do anything that was not permitted to the meanest of his subjects. For his own part he would need satisfaction on a great many points before he would consider himself absolved from his oath of allegiance.'[30]

The King's stoutest supporter could huff and puff, but there was little that he could do. Baldwin held all the cards in his hands; he was playing them with all the guile and cunning of the grizzled political fox that he was. In the evening of Wednesday 2 December the Prime Minister went once more to the Palace. It was his fourth meeting with the King. He carried with him news of the initial response of the Dominion premiers. Even before he was announced, Edward could see from his demeanour that the news was not favourable. As he expected, Baldwin told him that the Dominions were unanimous. They would not support a morganatic marriage. Without the full backing of the self-governing countries of the British Empire, Edward would be unable to proceed with the Cornwall plan.

But Baldwin was not telling the full truth. A 'most secret' Annex to the Cabinet Minutes, scheduled to be opened only in 2037[31] but released to the National Archives in 2003, reveals that the Prime Minister presented the King with only a selective account of the views of his overseas realms. Baldwin relied on the Australian Prime Minister's response, which was dead-set against the marriage. The view from New Zealand was quite different: the Prime Minister, Michael Savage, backed the morganatic marriage. In a telegram received that very afternoon Savage said that the morganatic marriage 'would no doubt be acceptable to the vast majority of the people of New Zealand' because of 'the great affection felt in New Zealand for His Majesty'.[32] Lord Galway, the Governor-General, added for good measure that Edward was 'much more inspiring' than his younger brother, Prince Albert. The Canadian premier, Mackenzie King, shared this outlook, saying that the abdication would only be supported in his country if it were not forced on the King. He added that there was widespread sympathy for the King's determination to marry the woman of his choice. Baldwin took care to see that these contrary views were not put to Edward or mentioned formally to the

Cabinet. The official record was changed by the Cabinet Secretary, Maurice Hankey, to weaken the New Zealand Prime Minister's statement.[33] Baldwin's economy with the truth was a sign of his determination to prevent the morganatic marriage and to ensure that the abdication went ahead.

Edward, unaware (as he would be for the rest of his life) of the true measure of support for his plan in the Dominions, was crestfallen. Over the years, as Prince of Wales, he had made many arduous tours of the Empire, travelling millions of miles to shore up Britain's tenuous hold over the declining institution. With his charm and intense magnetism he had built up a personal following. Now Baldwin had led him to believe that the unanimous response of the Dominions was against him. In desperation, he asked his Prime Minister whether, at the very least, the Parliament of the United Kingdom might be consulted formally. After the success of his tour of south Wales, he was well aware of his abiding popularity at home. Baldwin, brutally correct, refused. He told the King that he had taken soundings among MPs and knew that opinion was against him. The meeting ended with Edward reiterating his desire to marry the woman of his choice and confirming that, if necessary, he would abdicate in order to do so.[34] 'He seemed *bewitched*', Baldwin told his niece, '"I can't do my job without her – I am going to marry her, and I will *go*." There was simply no moral struggle and it appalled me.'

That same evening London's diarists had one subject for their journals. Chips Channon excitedly wrote 'the storm has burst . . . the fat is now properly in the fire'. Harold Nicolson reported 'a blowing of the whole gaff'. Duff Cooper, a little more prosaically, entered in his diary, 'the hunt was up'.[35] They were all commenting on the words of the Bishop of Bradford, Alfred Blunt, who had innocently given an address on Sunday at his diocesan conference attacking the King's lack of Christian commitment. In Belfast, David Strain read a short report in the evening paper of the Bishop's speech: 'He said one would wish that the King would give a little more evidence of his regard for religious duties; rather Blunt.'[36] The *Yorkshire Post* reported his criticism more fully and lit the touchpaper. On Thursday 3 December the front pages of the national press were ablaze with the story.

The Duke of York, waiting in the background with mounting dread, had been visiting Scotland on official business. A shy and retiring man who had fought valiantly to overcome a debilitating stammer, he was prone to sudden outbursts of bad temper. He had no desire for the job that seemed to be approaching with awful inevitability. He arrived that Thursday morning at Euston Station, where he saw to his surprise and horror 'that the posters of the daily press had the following as their headlines in black letters "The King's Marriage". He hurried off to warn his mother. She and her daughter-in-law were dead set against the morganatic proposal. As Elizabeth, Duchess of York, put it: 'if she is not fit to be Queen, she is not fit to be the King's morganatic wife.'[37]

The newspapers, pent up for so long, now filled their pages with the story. There were queues at newspaper vendors' stalls, and 'not a man or woman in the street who was not either carrying a copy or trying to buy one', Duff Cooper reported.[38] Violet Milner complained that the headlines 'have been screaming, their placards have made London hideous'.[39] There were biographies of Wallis Simpson, photographs of her previous husbands, reports of the *Nahlin* cruise, pictures of the couple together and – of course – columns of comment. Chips Channon revelled in the excitement of the story: 'The Country and the Empire now know that their Monarch, their young Emperor, their adored Apollo, is in love with an American twice divorced, whom they believe to be an adventuress. The whole world recoils from the shock.'[40] Hensley Henson, the Bishop of Durham, found 'the whole business deplorable . . . the mouth-filling sensation of the King's projected marriage with a twice-divorced American woman of forty'.[41]

The Times came out with a leader written by Geoffrey Dawson attacking the King's proposed marriage. Dawson had prepared his comments in consultation with the Prime Minister, and had gone to 10 Downing Street to discuss it on Wednesday evening. He had met Baldwin in his study, where he found him 'worn out' sitting with his head in his hands, 'but quite clear about his course'.[42] Dawson hurried off to Printing House Square to write his piece. When completed, he rang the Prime Minister to check it over. Baldwin told him that the King had been on the telephone twice before midnight, 'v jumpy', pleading with him to stop publication. Edward, with some justice, regarded Dawson as his arch-enemy and suspected him of closely working with the Archbishop of Canterbury to do him down.

While the King faced the hostility of the quality press, the *Daily Mail* and the *Daily Express* backed him, reflecting the views of their owners. So too did the *Daily Mirror*. Surprisingly, the nonconformist and Liberal *News Chronicle* also came out in favour of the morganatic marriage. It was some seventy years ahead of its time: 'the public would, we think, wish that he should marry the woman of his choice, but that he should do so in his capacity as Duke of Cornwall . . . His wife's position would then be that of King's Consort.' If the newspapers were representative of the views of their readers, popular feeling would have been heavily weighted in favour of the King. While 80,000 or so read the heavyweight broadsheets, the combined circulation of those supporting his marriage was close to 9 million.[43] But many ordinary readers, however fascinated they were, were also horrified by what they regarded as an intrusion into the private affairs of the monarchy, a modern development that damaged a great institution. David Strain was outraged: 'All respect for the throne seems to have been discarded', he fulminated in his diary, 'the King they loved so much is nothing more than an extra "tit-bit" for the hungry blood-sucking sensational press.'

A possible indicator of the King's popular support was his postbag. As soon as the newspapers gave coverage to the affair, he started to receive hundreds of letters. The majority were in support.[44] But there were many against him and – more especially – against Wallis Simpson. Lady Londonderry explained this with all the frankness of a practised political hostess, when she met Wallis at a function in London. She told her straight that the 'English people would never tolerate her marriage to the King', given that she was American and had two husbands living. Later Wallis thanked her for her directness, writing disingenuously: 'I have come to the conclusion that no one has been really frank with a certain person in telling him how the country feels about his friendship with me . . . I feel that he should know however and therefore I am going to tell him the things you told me.'[45] It is not known whether Wallis did tell Edward of her conversation with Edie Londonderry. It would have made no difference to the King. He truly believed that once the British people and his own close family came to know Wallis Simpson they would see in her all the qualities that he loved so much. In this he was utterly misguided.

Wallis herself was not entirely the disinterested party in the affair that she made out. Throughout the early part of the crisis she acted as the King's principal adviser, calling on him to stand up to Baldwin and to take up Churchill's proposal of morganatic marriage. She urged the King to broadcast an appeal to his subjects over the heads of the politicians, in which he could use his great popularity to argue his case directly.[46] He would then leave the country, travel to Switzerland and wait to see if public acclaim would force the government's hand. Two aircraft were prepared to take him and his party to Zurich, where a hotel was booked.[47]

Edward agreed with the idea. Urged on by Wallis, he had summoned the Prime Minister to a secret meeting at Buckingham Palace at 9 p.m. on 3 December. Baldwin told the Cabinet the next morning that he had driven to the palace 'and had been taken in by a back entrance' in order to avoid the waiting press photographers, and was then 'introduced through a window' to a downstairs room where he met the King (surely the only time a Prime Minister has been forced to climb through a window for an audience with the monarch). Edward 'was frantically keen' to speak directly to his subjects over the radio and to read a draft of the proposed broadcast to the Prime Minister. Baldwin responded by saying that he would consult the Cabinet but that he felt certain that they would agree that it would be 'thoroughly unconstitutional'.[48] At this the King cried, 'You want me to go, don't you?' Baldwin responded, 'What I want, Sir, is what you told me you wanted: to go with dignity, not dividing the country, and making things as smooth as possible for your successor.'[49] There was little warmth now between the two men, but Baldwin always covered his steel in a carapace of kindliness. Once, during their talks late in the night, he said to the King, 'the missus and I would like to tell you how sorry we are for you', at which – according to the diarist Robert Bernays – 'the King burst into tears and so did Baldwin'.[50]

The bizarre comings-and-goings of the Prime Minister were the most extreme representation of the paradox at the heart of the British constitution. As King, Edward could command Baldwin literally to jump through windows for him. But on the matter of substance, his marriage, he could do nothing without the say-so of his government.

When the Cabinet heard of Baldwin's late night cloak-and-dagger visit to the Palace, there was consternation. All were against the idea of a royal broadcast to the nation. Neville Chamberlain left the Cabinet meeting for a moment and returned to tell his colleagues that the Chief Whip had informed him that 'Mr Winston Churchill and Lord Beaverbrook were in close consultation and were working together on the lines adopted by the *Daily Mail*, the *Daily Express* and the *News Chronicle*'. He urged Baldwin to bring the King 'sharply up to the point' and make his decision to abdicate that very day. There was a sense of panic among the politicians. They knew full well the popularity of the King. If he were to broadcast, they feared that public opinion could move irrevocably in his favour. The transport minister, Leslie Hore-Belisha, warned of the 'terrible possible consequences . . . Mr Churchill might be sent for and might form a Government and then demand a General Election.' Baldwin calmed the situation. It was agreed that the King's broadcast was out of the question and that the Prime Minister would make a statement to Parliament the following Monday ruling out any such possibility.[51]

Wallis was furious when she learned that Edward had been prevented from broadcasting. 'You must speak', she urged Edward, in the mistaken belief that he could overrule his ministers; 'don't be silenced and leave under a cloud I beseech you.'[52] She was under intense nervous strain, close to a breakdown. As fears for her safety grew, on Wednesday 2 December she agreed to go to France, to stay with her friends Katherine and Herman Rogers at their villa in Cannes. She had only a day to get ready, before departing on

Thursday by car, carrying with her a small amount of luggage and £100,000 (£3.7 million today) worth of jewels – some of the booty that the King had showered on her.

Edward arranged for one of his lords-in-waiting, Lord Brownlow, to travel with her. Perry Brownlow arrived at the Fort at dusk to find the King 'looking rather pathetic, tired, overwrought, and evidently dreading Wallis's departure'. Like Wallis, Edward was under intense nervous and emotional strain. Before departure the threesome dined. Brownlow noticed that the King, always a fidget, could not keep still. He buzzed around his guests, mixing drinks, fetching ice, even insisting on getting up to toss the salad. The time soon came for Wallis and Brownlow to leave. The King ushered them to the waiting car; once inside, he leaned across to Wallis 'to get one last touch of her hand – there were tears in his eyes and on his cheeks, and his voice was shaking – "Wherever you reach tonight, no matter what time, telephone me. Bless you my darling."'[53]

To elude the press photographers waiting outside, Brownlow used his own Rolls-Royce to spirit Wallis away from the Fort. After she had said her last goodbye to the King, she lay on the limousine's floor. Brownlow piled blankets on top of her and then, with a smart tap on the dividing window, ordered the chauffeur to drive off. They made fast progress that freezing foggy evening, catching the cross-Channel steamer (on to which Wallis's own car, a Buick, had been loaded) and early the next morning reaching the hotel in Rouen where they planned to get some rest.

As promised, before she went to bed, Wallis telephoned the King, who had been staying up in the small hours, worrying about her safety. She and Perry Brownlow, travelling under assumed identities, had been given adjoining rooms. After some time Brownlow heard a knock on his door. It was Wallis. 'Will you please leave the door open between your room and mine', she begged, 'I am so frightened. I'm so nervous.' A little later Brownlow heard her plaintive voice once more through the open door: 'Perry, will you please sleep in the bed next to me? I cannot be alone.' Brownlow was acutely embarrassed. Nevertheless, he obliged. Wallis broke down completely: 'Sounds came out of her that were absolutely without top, bottom . . . that were primeval. There was nothing that I could do but lie down beside her, hold her hand, and make her feel that she was not alone.'[54]

On Friday 4 December, in Wallis's absence, Churchill hurried down to the Fort for his first face-to-face meeting with the King over dinner. He was shocked by what he found. At first Edward was 'gay and debonair', but soon his insouciant front collapsed. He became incoherent, twice losing the thread of what he was saying, seized with 'mental anaesthesia'.[55] He was chain-smoking and fidgeting. Churchill diagnosed that Edward was being 'driven to the last extremity of endurance' and advised him to see Lord Dawson, the royal doctor, as soon as possible. He was also alarmed by his isolation, his 'appalling loneliness', without, as he put it 'one real friend to lean on in this frightful emergency'.[56]

Churchill left Fort Belvedere a whirlwind of energy and immediately set to work. He wrote to Baldwin alerting him to the King's nervous condition and asking for delay. 'The combination of public and private stresses is the hardest of all to endure . . . it would be most cruel and wrong to extort a decision from him in his present state.'[57] (Baldwin was not impressed, and told colleagues when he was handed Churchill's note during the weekend's emergency Cabinet that he believed the King to be perfectly sane.[58]) On Saturday morning Churchill issued a press statement calling for a period of reflection, urging 'time and patience', and criticizing the constitutional propriety of Baldwin's approach: 'No Ministry has the authority to advise the abdication of the Sovereign.' He questioned the Prime Minister's behind-the-scenes deal with the leader of the opposition, 'thus confronting the King with an ultimatum. Again there is cause for time and patience', and ended with a typical flourish: 'If an abdication were to be hastily extorted the outrage so committed would cast its shadow forward across many chapters of the British Empire.'[59]

Churchill's press release added to the sense of fevered unreality. Forty Conservative MPs, the whips told Baldwin, were known to be ready to back a King's party. It was rumoured that Lord Londonderry was ready, along with other has-beens, malcontents and habitual rebels, to join in the bid to oust the Prime Minister. Chamberlain was informed that Churchill had gone a long way in selecting his own

Cabinet and was already planning his first actions as Prime Minister. Winston had, Chamberlain snidely told his sister, 'gorgeous visions of a clash between the Sovereign and his Cabinet, the resignation of Ministers, general consternation and then in a flash of glory a champion stepping forth to defend his King in shining armour'.[60]

Such rumours exacerbated the already febrile mood inside the Cabinet. Malcolm MacDonald drew attention to 'the extraordinary clash of public opinion on this question'. He said, 'There was a strong party that were [sic] supporting the King at any cost'. Lord Zetland agreed: 'The possibility of a morganatic marriage might be dead but not the feeling in favour of it. There was still a strong driving force in favour of the plan.'[61]

The Archbishop of Canterbury shared the politicians' sense of alarm. He had learned from ecclesiastical colleagues that a large proportion, especially of the young, to whom the King was a popular hero, 'felt a strong sympathy with him'.[62] To make matters worse, the Beaverbrook and Rothermere press were in full cry. The *Daily Express* urged Baldwin to allow Edward to speak directly to the public, as he had wished: 'Let the King give his decision to the people and let him give the reasons for it too.' The *Daily Mail* declared that 'abdication is out of the question'. Crowds formed outside Downing Street and Buckingham Palace, where they sang 'God Save the King – from Stanley Baldwin' and 'For He's a Jolly Good Fellow'.[63] Some demonstrators held placards with slogans 'Cheer your King at the Palace' and 'After South Wales You Can't Let Him Down'.[64]

Liberal intellectual opinion was generally behind the King too, with support expressed by the playwright George Bernard Shaw in a humorous article in the *Evening Standard* that placed the crisis in a fantasy world, 'the Kingdom of the Half Mad'. Shaw's Prime Minister accused the King of being insane, to which he replied: 'To a little London clique some two or three centuries behind the times I no doubt seem so . . . The modern world knows better.'[65] John Maynard Keynes agreed: 'Won't sympathy gradually increase for the King against the Archbishop's oozing humbug? If the government offered him a morganatic marriage, that would be all right. But apparently – I don't know why – they refuse this.'[66] The trouble with this support was that it counted for little. Liberal opinion, as represented by Shaw's 'modern world', was by nature not greatly supportive of the monarchy. It was certainly not ready to join with the reactionary Beaverbrook and Rothermere press to engage actively on behalf of the King.

But to almost everyone during that extraordinary period, wherever they stood on the matter, the subject was a source of overwhelming and intense interest. Neville Chamberlain complained to the Cabinet that the crisis was having a bad effect on the Christmas trade. Vera Brittain blamed it for the poor sales of her new novel *Honourable Estate* (unlikely, as sales of another new novel, *Gone with the Wind*, were booming). Republicans, however, were delighted, as the novelist Geoffrey Wells wrote in his diary: 'To give up marrying Mrs S or abdicate, either way the monarchy gets a kick in the guts, which is all to the good. In principle, anyway!'[67] Not all took the affair seriously. Evelyn Waugh expressed the feeling of many, that in a world where the menace of war loomed this crisis at least was 'a great delight to everyone'. He wrote in his diary: 'At Maudie's nursing home they report a pronounced turn for the better in all adult patients. There can seldom have been an event that has caused so much general delight and so little pain.'[68]

What may have raised spirits at 'Maudie's nursing home' was causing continuing dyspepsia in Downing Street. The focus of irritation that weekend was not the King, who was proving naïve and malleable, but Winston Churchill. Neville Chamberlain complained: 'As you can imagine this has been a most anxious and worrying weekend, and we are contending with Winston's intrigues in addition to all our other troubles.'[69] Churchill spent Saturday at his flat in Westminster. Judging by the tone of his advice to the King that day, he did not remain sober.

For the last eleven months he had kept to his pledge given to Lord Rothermere in Morocco at the New Year not to touch spirits until his sixty-second birthday, on 30 November, and won the bet of £600. Although he had given up brandy, his favourite tipple, he had not been entirely abstemious since January. The diarist Robert Bruce Lockhart reported that earlier in the year, at a lunch with a Foreign Office official, he had drunk quantities of beer with the meal and

finished it off 'with five large glasses of port'.[70] Although port is a
wine fortified with brandy, Rothermere did not baulk at paying the
£600, 'which you have so bravely earned. I have never with more
pleasure paid money to anyone.'[71]

Perhaps over-fortified by a generous indulgence in the brandy he
had kept off for so long, he tried to put some steel into the King's
backbone. He fired off a letter to him as though written from the
scene of battle: 'Sir, News from all fronts! No pistol to be held at the
King's head. No doubt that this request for time will be granted.'
This was an over-optimistic view of the prospects for delay. The very
next day Baldwin insisted to the Cabinet that the matter be settled by
Christmas. Churchill, however, was aware that the King was on the
brink of giving up the fight. Beaverbrook had visited Edward that
morning and reported that 'Our cock won't fight'. He no longer
wanted the press baron's advice or support and was considering
departing from Britain. '*On no account must the King leave the country*',
Churchill expostulated in his letter to Edward, speaking of him in
the third person. 'Windsor Castle is his battle station (poste de commandment). When so much is at stake no minor inclination can be
indulged.'[72]

Becoming desperate, he advised Edward to meet Lord Craigavon,
the Prime Minister of Northern Ireland and a loyal supporter, on
Sunday. 'He shares my hopes such as they are of an ultimate happy
ending. It's a long way to Tipperary.' He ended the outburst with a
plea to the King to reinstate Beaverbrook as his adviser, and a final
morale-boosting rallying call: 'Good advances on all parts giving
prospects of gaining good positions and assembling large forces
behind them. Your majesty's faithful and devoted servant & subject,
WSC.'[73] It was a marvellous piece of braggadocio, an over-the-top
rumbustious letter, a last florid plea, but it was hopeless.

King Edward's mind was made up. On Friday night, 'a night of
soul searching', he decided finally and irrevocably to abdicate. In the
absence of Wallis he had neither the heart nor – to borrow Churchill's
military metaphor – the forces to challenge Baldwin. He had no
desire to be King of a divided nation and Empire: 'A civil war is the
worst of all wars', he concluded. 'Its passions soar highest, its hatreds

last longest. And a civil war is not less a war when it is fought in words and not blood.'[74] He had, he realized, reached the limits of his power to shape events and 'fend off catastrophe'. His attempt to reshape the monarchy, to make it more informal and – as he saw it – in tune with the changing times had utterly failed. So too had his rejection of the morality of the older generation. He believed in the supremacy of love. It was a modern belief, but, as he had discovered, modernity and monarchy do not mix.

On Sunday 6 December he summoned Sir Walter Monckton to his room (Monckton was staying at the Fort so as to be on hand at all times, such is the importance of lawyers at moments of crisis) and told him of his final decision. It was a decision motivated by love, clearly, but also by an ingrained respect for the constitution. Edward may have been 'the most modernistic man in England', but he was one, as the historian A. J. P. Taylor argued, not 'to shatter the Establishment, [but] at best only to niggle at it'. Since his earliest youth the idea of service and duty had been drilled into him. He had served in the First World War, where duty was paramount. Afterwards he had travelled millions of miles in service to the Empire. He, of all men, was aware of the mighty edifice he had fleetingly threatened. He had no wish to be the Hamlet of a drama that could, if he chose, play out to its better end. He chose to become an attendant lord and to go quietly. But if Edward regarded doing his duty as doing the decent thing and going without a fuss, most regarded his readiness to quit for a woman as precisely the opposite. John Prichard's father had served on the Western Front in the First World War and had been badly wounded. His idea of a King's role was 'to perform his duties and not to fail in his task in favour of a somewhat unsavoury American woman'.[75]

Stanley Baldwin had asked MPs, before they left for the weekend, to return to their constituencies to take the temperature of public feeling on the King's proposed marriage. In the days before polling, this was Baldwin's preferred method of gauging opinion: 'I have always believed in the weekend', he said.[76] Honourable Members duly fanned out across the country, where they consulted their constituents – as Baldwin had instructed – in the pubs, golf and working men's clubs, after church and over the Sunday roast. The weekend was a watershed in the crisis – a watershed of which Winston Churchill was quite unaware.

The response was clear. Just as the King had looked into the abyss and seen a country divided, an Empire crumbling and a tottering throne, so the British people it seemed – while sympathetic to the King's personal plight – had no taste for a 'King's Party' or for the whiff of revolution that went with it. However much they liked Edward – and there was no doubting his popularity – a clear majority view appeared to have formed across every class and region, which echoed the outrage of the Jarrow marchers when they learned of the affair some weeks earlier. The Bishop of Durham received a letter from one of his priests working in a poor parish. 'I am profoundly struck', the vicar wrote, 'with the intense personal sadness with which our own poor folk have taken their disillusionment about His Majesty.'[77]

John Prichard remembered his parents discussing the matter: 'they were shocked. "Surely he will never go with this woman – a divorcee, an American!"' Marguerite Patten's mother, a teacher, shared the widespread view that duty came before love and told her daughter, '"This was his job, and this was what he was bred to do, he's known about it from the very moment he was born and he should realise his responsibilities." My mother was very adamant about that.'[78]

There was also a feeling that, at a time of growing public concern about the international situation, a constitutional crisis was the last thing that was needed, as John Prichard recalled. 'People thought, if the monarchy goes what is to stop the whole country falling apart? People were particularly anxious because of the increasing threat from outside, the occupation of the Rhineland and the resurrection of German military power.' It seemed that a solid consensus had emerged. The journalist Robert Bruce Lockhart considered that 'ninety per cent of intelligent public regard the Beaverbrook–Rothermere campaign on the King's behalf as mischievous and irresponsible anti-Baldwinism'.[79] Harold Nicolson noted how unanimous feeling in the House of Commons had become: 'no hysteria and no party politics . . . What a *solid* people we are under all our sentimentality.'[80]

On Monday no formal announcement was made of the King's decision. At Prime Minister's Questions, Stanley Baldwin told the House that he had nothing to say for the moment on the question of the King. Churchill then rose from his seat beneath the gangway, asking 'that no irrevocable step would be taken before the House has received a full statement'. He tried to develop the question into a short oration in favour of the King. It was a personal and political disaster. All sides of the House howled him down as one, with a rage rarely seen in the Chamber. Churchill battled on: 'I am not afraid of this House. When I see my duty I speak out clearly.' There were cries of 'Twister', in reference to his inconsistency on the matter, 'No! No!' and 'Sit down'.[81] Churchill appeared shocked and stunned, 'completely staggered by the unanimous hostility', as the Speaker, calling the House to order, told him to take his seat.[82] Since he first entered the House of Commons in 1900, he had never experienced such a tidal wave of hostility. He had completely misjudged the mood of the House. Baffy Dugdale, herself a niece of a former Prime Minister, wrote in her diary: 'I think he is done for. In three minutes his hopes of a return to power and influence are shattered. But God is once more behind his servant Stanley Baldwin.'

As the crisis approached resolution under his management, Baldwin came to relish his role. Only a few weeks earlier he had reached the nadir of his career, with the confession to Parliament that he had done little about defence because public opinion was pacifist. As Leo Amery commented: 'it seemed clear that the sooner he was got rid of the better. And yet for this particular crisis he was ideally fitted.'[83] At the height of the affair Baldwin told his Private Secretary, Tommy Dugdale, 'this is making history. This is what I like.'[84]

The King did not much like it and found Baldwin's company increasingly wearing. On Tuesday 8 December the unlikely couple met for the last time. Baldwin was driven down to Fort Belvedere from Downing Street in his small black car, accompanied by Dugdale and Walter Monckton. The passengers, cramped in the back, sat impatiently as the chauffeur, limited by Baldwin to a maximum speed of 25 miles an hour, made his way through the suburbs of Sunningdale and Virginia Water. Impatient motorists hooted at the prime ministerial car, unaware of the occupant, who sat unruffled, humming to himself, puffing on his pipe and occasionally clicking his fingers. To Edward's horror, when he greeted his guests, he noticed that Baldwin, prepared for lengthy negotiations, had brought a suitcase. The thought of the Prime Minister staying the night at the Fort was too much for this normally most attentive of hosts. He took an official aside and instructed him that under no circumstances was the Prime Minister to remain after dinner.

The King's brothers Prince Albert, Duke of York (soon to take the crown), and his closest sibling, Prince George, Duke of Kent, were also at dinner. He had deliberately kept both at arm's length during the crisis, refusing to meet them or take their repeated telephone calls so that they would not be tainted, he argued, by the affair. Now, with the crisis on the point of resolution, he welcomed them warmly. During the meal he appeared, according to Baldwin, 'happy and gay, as if he were looking forward to his honeymoon',[85] keeping the conversation going, never allowing it to stray into the one subject that had brought all the guests together. Later that evening he told Baldwin privately, 'I quite understand the reason you and Mrs Baldwin don't approve of my action. It is the view of another generation. My generation don't feel like that about it.'[86] When Wallis was mentioned, Baldwin recollected, all he would say was, 'this is the most wonderful woman in the world'. The Duke of York looked on with astonishment as his brother, 'the life and soul of the party', told Baldwin things 'I am sure he had never heard before' about unemployment in south Wales. He turned to his neighbour, Walter Monckton, and whispered, 'and this is the man we are going to lose'. It seemed impossible. Baldwin needed reassurance. As he left Edward for the last time, he asked 'Can I take it for certain, Sir, that if an Archangel came down from heaven and asked you to change your mind, it would have no effect on you?' The King replied, 'Not the slightest.'[87]

Baldwin had been secretly preparing the Duke of York for the role that the Prince was so reluctant to assume. Several times during the crisis the Duke had slipped into Downing Street through the garden entrance for talks with the Prime Minister. He was under enormous strain and felt ill suited for the position in which his brother was placing him. He had none of Edward's charisma, and he felt the lack acutely. He came close to complete breakdown. To make matters worse, his wife was absent. Elizabeth, who had suffered pneumonia when her father-in-law died at the beginning of the year, was ill once more, having taken to her bed with influenza. She did struggle from her sick-bed to write a letter to her brother-in-law, which she kept secret from her husband, begging him to treat her husband with extreme care and kindness, given his mental state.[88]

Under the expert guidance of Stanley Baldwin events were moving inexorably to their close. There was a brief hiccup when Wallis Simpson, stuck with Lord Brownlow in Cannes, issued a surprise statement. Taking the advice of Brownlow, who, in turn, was acting on Beaverbrook's instructions,[89] she announced on 7 December that she was willing 'to withdraw from the situation'. The *Daily Express* then trumpeted this, as ordered by their proprietor, as the 'End of the Crisis'.

For a moment the government took the statement seriously. Stanley Baldwin summoned Mrs Simpson's solicitor, Theodore Goddard, and ordered him to go by special government chartered plane to the south of France. His task was to find out whether she was being sincere and was actually prepared to give up any relationship with Edward. Goddard was a workaday solicitor, a bit-part player quite out of his depth in the unfolding drama, likened to 'an uneasy bull having walked into the farmer's sitting room instead of his own stable'.[90] He had a weak heart, had never flown before and insisted on taking a doctor with him. To Brownlow's fury, the newspapers immediately reported that he was taking a gynaecologist to test whether Wallis Simpson was pregnant.

Such rumours were a sign of the contempt in which many held Wallis. While the King remained a popular figure, as was shown by the thousands of letters of support he received,[91] there were many messages of hatred directed against her and some threats. A brick had been thrown through her window. A statement of renunciation, Beaverbrook hoped – and the King agreed – would improve her public image. Although Goddard returned from Cannes with a document signed by Wallis Simpson, confirming that she was willing to renounce her hold on Edward, few believed her to be sincere. Whatever Wallis said, everybody knew that Edward was so besotted with her that he would follow her to the ends of the earth. The statement was seen for what it was: a move to curry favour with the public, engineered by Beaverbrook. Baldwin sent a telegram to the Dominion governments saying that he doubted its '*bona fides*' and that he believed it to be 'no more than an attempt to swing public opinion in her favour and thereby give her less reason to be uneasy as to her personal safety'.[92]

The statement was consigned to the waste-paper basket. When Wallis telephoned Edward on Wednesday 9 December to tell him that she was willing to give him up if it meant saving his crown, he replied: 'it's too late . . . the Abdication documents are being drawn up – You can go wherever you want – to China, Labrador or the South Seas. But wherever you go, I will follow you.'[93]

At ten o'clock in the morning on Thursday 10 December, King Edward VIII signed the Instrument of Abdication, renouncing for ever all claim to the throne:

> I, Edward the Eighth of Great Britain, Ireland and the British Dominions beyond the Seas, King Emperor of India, do hereby declare my irrevocable determination to renounce the Throne for Myself and My descendants, and My desire that effect should be given to this instrument of Abdication immediately.

His three brothers acted as witnesses. In the days leading up to the signature there had been frenetic and sometimes acrimonious argument about the terms of the financial settlement. Edward had claimed, wrongly, that he faced a life of penury, and – egged on by Wallis – had lied about his financial situation in order to gain a huge pay-off. When he departed the throne he was, in fact, one of the richest men in Europe, with a private fortune of well over £1 million (worth about £37 million today).

Money is often at the heart of a family breach, but it was not the main cause in this case: Wallis Simpson bore that responsibility. But money was certainly the source of lasting bitterness. As the true picture of Edward's wealth became clear in the months that followed, his apparent dishonesty poisoned relations with his brother the King and contributed to a bitter family split that was never healed in his lifetime. It also led to a damaging falling out with his great ally and friend Winston Churchill.

Before signing the Instrument of Abdication Edward had seen his mother at Royal Lodge, in Windsor Great Park, to tell her of his final decision.[94] On the surface, relations were cordial. Queen Mary, Edward remembered fondly, sympathized with his enforced absence from Wallis: 'her heart went out to her hard-pressed son.' So besotted was he that he failed completely to understand the position from her point of view. The truth was that she was utterly horrified by his action. She could not understand, as she later told him,[95] how when more than a million men of the British Empire had done their duty during the First World War and made the ultimate sacrifice, he could not have made a far smaller sacrifice and given up a woman whom she believed so manifestly unsuitable. There was another cause of her anger: the intolerable burden that Edward was placing on his brother Albert's shoulders. 'It is a terrible blow for us all and particularly to poor Bertie', she wrote in her diary.[96] Worst of all, as she told the Prime Minister, after all that her husband had done, her son had brought shame on the family, 'in not carrying out the duties and responsibilities of the Sovereign of our great Empire'.

That afternoon Stanley Baldwin made the official announcement of the King's abdication to the House of Commons. Every seat was taken in the crowded Chamber. Members squatted in the gangways or perched on the steps of the Speaker's chair. Winston Churchill sat in his usual place, 'doubled up in grief', Harold Nicolson noticed, a picture of despondency. From the packed galleries above, the press and public looked down. Peers crowded into their allotted places; ambassadors filled the Distinguished Strangers' Gallery. The Liberal MP Robert Bernays, surveying the scene, felt 'a tremendous sense in everyone that we were on a great stage and the world was taking account of how we were comporting ourselves'.[97]

Baldwin entered and made his way to the dispatch box, from where he bowed to the Speaker and handed him the Instrument of Abdication, declaring: 'A message from the King signed by His

Majesty's own hand'. The Speaker took the note and began in a quavering voice to read. Chips Channon was watching: 'At the words "renounce the Throne" his voice broke, and there were stifled sobs in the House.' This formal announcement of abdication led to a banging of doors and wild stampede above the Chamber in the press gallery as reporters scuttled out to telephone the news to their papers.[98]

After the Speaker's statement the Prime Minister rose to speak. It was a classic piece of Baldwin theatre – bumbling, ordinary, seemingly incompetent but brilliantly effective. Baldwin spoke for an hour, referring only briefly to his notes. He resisted all rhetorical flourish, and his speech was all the more effective for its simplicity. He was heard in dead silence, 'the silence of Gettysburg', as Harold Nicolson called it, 'Sophoclean and almost unbearable'.[99] Lucy Baldwin felt that she 'was at a memorial service'.[100] Baldwin's speech was one of reconciliation. He praised the man who was now 'the former King' for his behaviour during the crisis with, according to Channon, 'tribute after tribute', singling out his constitutional rectitude and above all his refusal to countenance a King's Party and his determination to 'go with dignity'.

Edward had written a note in which he requested that Baldwin make special mention of Wallis Simpson's attempts to dissuade him from abdicating. 'Mrs Simpson has consistantly [sic] attempted to withdraw',[101] he wrote plaintively, but – to his lasting bitterness – the Prime Minister made no mention of it. Baldwin spoke of his own handling of the crisis, just before the end of the speech: 'I am convinced that where I have failed no one else could have succeeded.' He allowed himself one passing reference to the stubborn character of the man whom he had defeated: 'His mind was made up and those who know His Majesty know what that means.'[102] When the speech was over, the House remained silent. The leader of the opposition, Clement Attlee, rose and asked that the sitting be adjourned. Harold Nicolson was moved to hyperbole: 'We file out broken in body and soul, conscious that we have heard the best speech that we shall ever hear in our lives. There was no question of applause.'[103]

After the speech Nicolson retreated to the Commons library to sign some letters. As he was leaving he bumped into the Prime Minister and congratulated him on the speech. Stanley Baldwin took his arm. 'Yes,' he said, 'it was a success. I know it. It was almost wholly unprepared. I had a success, my dear Nicolson, at the moment I most needed it.'[104] The abdication was Baldwin's triumph. It called on all the qualities of stage management and quiet but determined action that he possessed. He could now take his bow from the political stage at the time of his choosing.

Baldwin's triumph was Churchill's failure. Churchill the romantic, the vainglorious, had stumbled badly. He detested Baldwin's speech; immediately it was over, the Prime Minister told Nicolson, Churchill had been in touch with his Private Secretary to complain that, in praising the King for his refusal to be side-tracked by external advice, the Prime Minister had made a coded attack on him.

To thank Churchill for his loyal support Edward invited him on the next day, 11 December, to come through the icy fog for a farewell luncheon at the Fort, before his final broadcast and departure from Britain for Austria. Over lunch Churchill helped Edward write the script. He added one or two flourishes, and the sentence that went to the heart of the issue: that, as King, Edward could not share 'one matchless blessing, enjoyed by so many of you and not bestowed on me – a happy home with wife and children'. When lunch was over, Edward saw him off. It was an emotional moment. Churchill stood in the gravel drive and, 'tapping out the solemn measure with his walking-stick', he began to recite, as though to himself: 'He nothing common did or mean / Upon that memorable scene.' The words were from Andrew Marvell's description of the beheading of Charles I. Edward felt that 'his resonant voice seemed to give an especial poignancy to these lines'. Churchill then got into his car, with tears flowing, and was driven home to Chartwell.[105]

While Churchill and Edward were having lunch, at 1.52 p.m. exactly, as agreed by the lawyers who drew up the terms of the abdication, Prince Albert, Duke of York, became King. He took the title of George VI, in honour of his father, and as a deliberate sign of continuity with the tradition and style of kingship that his brother had wished to change. Bill Deedes, then a young reporter with the *Morning Post*, was sent to the new King's home in Piccadilly to witness his departure to his new official residence, Buckingham Palace. He saw him, accompanied by his wife, Elizabeth, as he emerged from his house looking tense and pale: 'there was something in his face that has lasted. It was a portrait you never forget. I can best describe it as the look of a soldier going into battle. Very set . . . very set.'[106]

That evening Edward joined the royal family at Royal Lodge at Windsor for a farewell dinner, before going to the Castle to make his final broadcast. His mother urged him not to speak on the radio but he insisted on having his final say. There had been some discussion as to how he should be announced to listeners. Sir John Reith, the puritanical Director-General of the BBC, had intended to introduce him insultingly as plain 'Mr Edward Windsor' but the new King put a stop to that. As 'Mr Windsor', he pointed out, he could stand for Parliament, and that would never do. Given his popularity, the prospect of Mr Windsor MP leading a new party seemed a frightening possibility. Instead, King George, in his first act as monarch, ordered that he should be made a royal duke, with the title Duke of Windsor. Edward was happy with the new name, the seventh title of his life.[107]

The BBC had rigged up a temporary studio in Edward's old rooms in Windsor's Augusta Tower. When the time came for the live transmission, Reith introduced the ex-King to listeners in his deep Scottish voice as 'His Royal Highness, Prince Edward' before creeping out of the room and – accidentally – banging the door. Edward launched into his speech, declamatory at first, before settling into a more conversational style. His voice, with its unmistakable and idiosyncratic accent, was heard by millions across the nation. All human activity appeared to cease; 'there was complete emptiness everywhere', Virginia Woolf noted, as people crowded around their radio sets in rapt attention to the short royal message. Many were moved to tears as they listened to his justification for his abdication. 'You must believe me when I tell you that I have found it impossible to carry the heavy burden of responsibility and to discharge my duties as King as I would wish to do without the help and support of the woman I love.'[108] In the south of France, Wallis Simpson broke down, lay on a sofa and covered her face with her hands to try to hide her tears, as she moaned and sobbed.[109] Edward emphasized how he had behaved with constitutional propriety throughout – 'very correct and rather moving', Geoffrey Dawson, the editor of *The Times*, was generous enough to concede. Churchill, listening in Chartwell, wept as Edward concluded: 'I now quit altogether public affairs, and I lay down my burden. It may be some time before I return to my native land.' He wished his brother and his former subjects well, ending with a rousing 'God Save the King'. When the speech was over, Chips Channon 'murmured a prayer for he who had once been Edward VIII'.[110]

John Prichard, at school in Bexleyheath at the time, was marched with his class down to the 'Great Hall' to sit in rows, form by form, to listen to the broadcast of the speech on the wireless. Before Edward spoke, the children were warned by their teacher to be suitably solemn: 'this is a great crisis for our country, you must concentrate and behave.'[111] In Merthyr, in south Wales, another schoolboy, John Meredith, also listened. Only a few weeks before crowds had come out to greet their beloved King; now there was a sense of loss and betrayal. 'The effect of his abdication speech was shattering. All hopes just faded. We in Merthyr lost someone who we thought would have done something for us. So we felt slightly differently from the national response.'[112] Even die-hard republicans were moved. Geoffrey Wells found it to be a 'wholly dignified, moving utterance of a self-possessed, confident *man*. Listening, one feels him to be the one real *man* in the affair. I'd like to know what Baldwin and the rest thought as they listened!'[113]

After the broadcast Edward returned to Royal Lodge. The tension had eased somewhat as a result of the warm things he had said about his family in the broadcast. He first took leave of his mother, formal and unyielding as ever. 'The dreadful goodbye', Queen Mary called their parting, 'the whole thing was too pathetic for words.'[114] Edward next kissed his brother, before bowing to him as his King and shaking his hand as a Freemason. After parting from his family he stepped out into the cold, clambered into the waiting Buick and was driven in the freezing, clear night to Portsmouth, where the destroyer HMS *Fury* was waiting to take him to France, from where he would travel to Austria and exile. 'From being the beloved Prince Charming and the real democrat who could and did understand the people', Sibyl Colefax wrote with oracular foresight, 'he goes to live out a life which must become a tragedy among the gad-abouts of the Riviera and Rio de Janeiro.'[115] At two o'clock in the morning of 12 December *Fury* slipped its moorings and, unwatched and unescorted, headed out to the murky sea. Down below, the hyperactive former King stayed awake, firing off telegrams of thanks to his supporters, writing letters and thinking always of the woman for whom he had given up the throne. He had ruled for 326 days.

20

The year the music stopped

THE BLOOD-ORANGE LIGHT of the great conflagration, reful-
gent against the night sky, was seen as far afield as Brighton. It
was visible to pilots crossing the channel at Margate. Spectators in
south London could feel the intense heat of the blaze on their faces
half a mile away. The flames, leaping 500 feet into the air, bathed the
capital in an eerie glow. John Prichard watched from his back garden
in Bexleyheath. 'Everyone was saying there's a big fire down there,
then gradually the news passed from door to door, you know it's the
Crystal Palace alight.'[1]

The blaze in the massive Victorian glass conservatory had started at
6.30 p.m. on 30 November, during an orchestral rehearsal in the
lobby. At first, managers dismissed it as a minor fire, which could
easily be put out. The orchestra played on. But the flames, fanned by
a strong north-westerly wind, spread quickly and the musicians had
to be evacuated. They were lucky to escape alive. The central transept collapsed minutes after they got out.[2] Soon the entire structure
was ablaze, a volcano of flaming wood, molten iron and streams of
liquid glass. The noise of the crashing roof could be heard five miles
away.

Thousands of Londoners came to Sydenham to watch the spectacle, climbing trees and perching on the tops of walls to get a better
sight. The police had to hold them back, as ninety fire tenders from all
over the capital converged on the scene. Planes chartered by the press
and the wealthy keen to get a good view circled overhead, some of
them so low that they were buffeted by the powerful updraft from the
heat as the flames erupted from the blazing crater. For the less well-off,
enterprising pedlars rented out binoculars for 'twopence a look'.[3] The

Duke of Kent arrived on the scene to boost the morale of the men attacking the blaze, donned a firefighter's helmet and stayed until 2.30 a.m.

The next morning all that remained of Joseph Paxton's immense glass structure, built to house the Great Exhibition in 1851, were the two 300 foot water towers, like 'two vast and trunkless legs of stone'.[4] They stood desolate at either end of the colossal wreck, a tangle of twisted metal debris, ash and charred wood that now stretched far away on all sides. The only relics of this marvel of the Victorian age were plaster of Paris effigies of the kings of England on their tombs and the strange concrete sculptures of iguanodons and triceratops, part of a dinosaur display in the gardens.[5]

The glass exhibition hall had first stood in Hyde Park, before being moved in 1854, at great cost, to Sydenham, where it was reconstructed, enlarged and made the centre of a large pleasure park. In recent years it had fallen into decline and had become a centre for choral singing, orchestral competitions, waxworks and cat and dog shows. Mercifully, exhibitors for the National Cat Club's annual meeting, scheduled for the day after the fire, had not yet moved their pets into the building, but the waxworks had all melted away. Part of the Palace was used as a television laboratory by John Logie Baird. Much valuable equipment was destroyed. Fortunately the BBC's new TV broadcasts were unaffected.

Many saw in the spectacular destruction the pathos and tragedy of the passing of the Victorian era. Bishop Henson wrote wistfully that 'its destruction may be taken to symbolize all the generous dreams of the age which witnessed its construction'.[6] Others saw the fire as an almost divine judgement on the King's attempted rejection of traditional values. Queen Mary was deeply affected by the fire. She and the King had reopened the restored Palace in 1924 as the first home of the Imperial War Museum, before it moved to Lambeth. In horror she watched the smoke rising in the distance as she stood at the windows of Marlborough House. Three days later she summoned her green Daimler and went to Sydenham to inspect the still smoking ruins. There her stately figure could be seen, still dressed in black, surveying the melancholy scene. Queen Mary's presence, it was hoped, would calm the country's frayed nerves. The *Yorkshire Post* reported that her visit was 'widely appreciated for its sedative effect upon an excited country'.[7]

A year that had started with some optimism was now ending in a morass of gloom and destruction. At home the monarchy, which to many underpinned the established order of things, seemed on the verge of collapse. Abroad the warlike turn of events had destroyed Chamberlain's hopes of economic recovery and further social reform. The nation's resources had to be diverted to rearmament. As he himself said, 'no man hesitates to set his fire-fighting appliances in readiness when already he can feel the heat of flames on his face. Our safety is more important to us than our comfort.'[8] The peace movement's hopes for a lasting change in world affairs had, in the process, been shattered. The public mood was deeply pessimistic. Nineteen thirty-six had indeed been the last dance of the Thirties. Now the music had stopped, the guests were leaving and the staff were turning out the lights.

Crystal Palace's mass of debris and piles of ashes, and the remains of steel and glass swinging precariously in the breeze, seemed to symbolize it all. Many were reminded of a bomb site. For *The Times* it 'irresistibly recalled Madrid'.[9] Images of the bombing of the Spanish capital had filled the newsreels and newspapers over recent weeks. German planes of Hitler's Condor Legion had participated in the raids, demonstrating the power and effectiveness of the Luftwaffe. On the day *The Times* reported the Crystal Palace fire, the newspaper carried a photograph of a number of families taking shelter from the German bombers in an underground station in Madrid. The picture of the huddled men and women crowded on a platform, many comforting children and holding babies, was a terrible premonition of things to come. So too were the constant reports of the atrocities carried out by both sides against civilians.

While the Spanish Civil War had at first divided the country on party lines, with the right generally supporting Franco and the left the Republican government, the reports of the Nazi-supported bombing were beginning to shift opinion in Britain. Winston Churchill's views changed from cautious support for the non-intervention agreement to hostility to the Fascists. Others went much further. Katharine, Duchess of Atholl, a Conservative MP, shocked her party when she delivered a fulminating attack on the Franco regime in November.[10] She became known as 'The Red Duchess' and 'Red Kitty' as she campaigned for the Republican cause.

In Spain itself more British volunteers were arriving by the day to join the newly formed International Brigades. James Albrighton, a medical student from Salisbury, joined the Brigades in October and fought on the outskirts of Madrid. It was there that he witnessed a horror 'that will live for ever in my memory': the bombing of a play-ground. He described in his diary how 'the children stood as if spellbound by some irresistible power that these strange machines held over them'. But fascination soon turned to fear 'as the sounds of explosions shattered the silence of the sunny morning . . . The screams of little children, many of them under nursery school age, rent the air screaming for their parents.'[11] Albrighton raced forward to help and found a scene 'of wholesale carnage'. He reeled in horror, 'the wounded some limbless, all mutilated, many dying in our arms as we attempted to comfort them . . . I realised that there was no longer the sounds of the planes or of screams. The silence caused by shock had taken hold.' It was for him a kind of terrible epiphany: 'this is indeed the modern version of the slaughtering of the innocents.' What James Albrighton had witnessed was just one event among many of similar horror, but it was sufficient in itself, he believed, 'to show the free world what the future holds in store for all humanity under the Fascist regime'.[12]

While Franco could count on the support of Hitler and Mussolini, the Republicans were prevented by the non-intervention agreement from buying arms on the world market. They became increasingly reliant on Russian aid albeit on a much smaller scale than the Fascist aid to the rebels. This led to a growth in Communist influence and added to the pressure for Stalinist conformity, with all its grim ap-paratus of show trials, purges and executions. In December, Albrighton and his men were prepared for a new role as shock troops of the revolution. He was told that his unit was being assigned to 'special duties'. They had to obey every order without questioning. 'Some of the duties we shall be called upon to perform may not be to our liking. These duties may include being called to act as firing squads. We have to execute traitors, and other enemies that the courts have, after proper judicial trial, sentenced to death.'[13] In return for their 'special duties' the men were to receive extra pay, leave and special privileges – and extra cigarettes. It was a sinister development.

Meanwhile in London, on 8 December, George Orwell was issued with a passport. Having just finished writing *The Road to Wigan Pier*, he had decided to join the fight in Spain. During the autumn he had watched Franco's advance on Madrid with mounting alarm, and now his mind was made up. 'This fascism,' he said with typical direct simplicity, 'somebody's got to stop it.'[14] Unlike John Cornford or James Albrighton, Orwell was not a Communist and did not go to Spain sponsored by the Party; he was a leftist supporter of the Spanish Republican government, who believed that a Fascist victory would be calamitous to European civilization. He was ready to fight with any group that was taking up arms against Fascism and joined the anti-Moscow Marxist militia POUM when he arrived in Barcelona at the end of the month. But what he would find in Spain in the following year was not the simple conflict against the forces of Fascism that he expected. It was to be a journey of discovery that would end with him fleeing the very same Communist militias with 'special duties' that James Albrighton had joined. Orwell's disillusionment with Soviet-style Communism grew out of his experience of the Civil War. The conflict would release his full genius and inspire his masterpiece *Animal Farm*.

Orwell must have been relieved to depart from a damp and foggy Britain, still reeling from the crisis he dismissed as 'the glutinous humbug of the abdication'.[15] The affair had been the sole focus of attention for two weeks, and it took some time for a sense of normality to return. As after a car crash, there was a sense of stunned disbelief and fuzzy silence as people recovered their wits. Violet Milner indulged in a Turkish bath. 'I felt I must wash off the dirt of this horrible crisis.'[16] The House of Commons was listless, waiting for the Christmas recess, as the Liberal MP Robert Bernays told his sister Lucy: 'Nothing indeed seems to have happened since the King's abdication and nothing seems likely to happen again. The nation has sunk back into a sort of coma . . . the newspapers are empty of everything except the test matches.'[17] Geoffrey Dawson, freed from his duty as the King's thunderous opponent in the press, went home after seeing the Garter King of Arms proclaim George VI, and retired satisfied to bed, where he 'slept for 10–11 hours without opening an eye'.[18]

Part of the feeling of unreality arose from the nature of the monarchy itself. A moment of extreme significance had just passed, yet the world appeared exactly the same. It was a striking example of the symbolic role of royalty and the elastic nature of the British constitution. While people were fighting and dying in a bitter internecine conflict in Spain over the destiny of the nation, in Britain a palace coup had taken place with all the superficial courtesies and fudging of a system that had evolved since its own Civil War 300 years earlier, precisely to avoid a repeat of the experience the Spanish were now suffering. But the abdication was not only significant to the destiny of Britain, but also to that of Europe and the world.

For the royal family, battered and damaged by the crisis, a period of retrenchment was called for. The new King, George VI, with his wife and daughters, retired to Sandringham, where they could rest and take stock over a quiet Christmas. Stanley Baldwin had said that George would be 'the dead spit of his father', and he was right.[19] The monarchy now returned, under the steely guidance of Queen Elizabeth and her willing husband, to the unchanging routines and rituals of George V. Geoffrey Dawson crowed in his diary: 'everything was rapidly being restored to the conditions prevailing under George V – Sandringham, racing, reappointment of Clive Wigram and Alec Hardinge'.[20] Edward's 'Ritz bar set' were cast into outer darkness. His cocktail parties and cabarets in clubs were replaced by cordials with picnics and cocoa by the fire. The annual massacre of pheasants at Sandringham and the stalking of stags at Balmoral were reinstated.

The change in style could not have happened more quickly. Many in society who had been travelling happily in convoy with Edward and Wallis had quickly to make a handbrake turn, ditch their Buicks and Cadillacs and set off in the opposite direction in Rovers and

Daimlers. They rightly feared ostracism, or worse, by the new court. Nancy Astor hissed at Chips Channon, 'people who have been licking Mrs Simpson's boots should be shot'.[21] The prospect of social death led to skidmarks everywhere on the carpets of Belgravia and Mayfair.[22] The Mountbattens quickly declared their new loyalties; Emerald Cunard announced she had never heard of Wallis and Edward; even Sibyl Colefax was thought to have been disloyal and had to make amends.[23] 'What do they say, that jolly crew, who must make even Judas queasy?' the Elizabethan loyalist Osbert Sitwell commented in his satirical poem 'Rat Week'. Queen Mary was delighted when she read it.[24]

For some there was no turning back. Perry Brownlow, who had with such chivalry escorted Wallis to the Riviera, was devastated to find that he was sent to Coventry at White's and that friends snubbed him in the street. 'I am completely, *totally* alone', he lamented.[25] In desperation he appealed to the Prime Minister, visiting him on a rainy December day at Chequers. 'Lord Brownlow came to see Stan,' Lucy Baldwin wrote, 'harried and very worried at the odium he has incurred by looking after Mrs Simpson for Edward.'[26] But it was too late. He had already been dismissed as Lord-in-Waiting, as he was to discover by reading the court circular.

The accession of King George to the throne, with the companionship of his consort Elizabeth and two daughters, showed that cherished family values had been placed once more on their pedestal. As the Victorian sage of the British constitution, Walter Bagehot, had written: 'We have come to regard the Crown as the head of our *morality*. We have come to believe that it is natural to have a virtuous sovereign.'[27] Edward's belief that the public role of the monarch should be separated from his or her private life had been rejected. The monarch and the man were one again. His short-lived jive with modernity was over and the monarchy returned, to the general relief of a broadly conservative-minded country on matters royal, to a stately march down the red carpet of tradition.

This wholesale return to Victorian virtues was an attempt, endorsed by Stanley Baldwin and his allies, to reverse what they regarded as the decline in moral values that was afflicting the nation. It was, in some ways, successful. The new King and his wife stabilized the rocking throne and, when he died, his daughter Elizabeth II faithfully followed her father's path of virtue. In society at large the liberalization in public attitudes to sex and marriage did not take place until the 1960s. But the pretence that members of the royal family could continue as exemplars of a way of life, however moral, that no longer had much relevance to modern Britain, was maintained at immense personal cost until it broke down, finally, in the wreckage of a car crash in an underpass in Paris. The irony remains that the Prince of Wales is now married to Camilla, the divorced woman who was his mistress and whose title is 'Duchess of Cornwall'.

Stanley Baldwin reaped the political reward, 'the highest pinnacle of his career', as Chamberlain called it.[28] He could choose the time of his departure; there was no more talk of forcing him out before the coronation. He and Lucy retreated to Chequers to rest after the exertions of the crisis. Lucy wrote in her diary of the many congratulatory messages he received, 'tellies began to pour in from all over England in appreciation of Stanley's wonderful work of the past weeks'.[29] But not everybody was appreciative. Lloyd George, resting in Jamaica, complained that the Conservatives now had 'just the sort of King which suits them', and, he harrumphed, George VI 'will not pry into any inconvenient questions: he will always sign on the dotted line and he will always do exactly what he is told'.[30] The novelist Geoffrey Wells was disgusted by 'the sheer hypocrisy of the British press and public, the sheer unqualified immorality, which makes a loving woman of Queen Mary and a bloody adulteress of Mrs Simpson, when it knows nothing. After Queen Mary, I could have done with a little Mrs Simpson!'[31]

The idea took hold that there had been an establishment plot to remove the King. Edward himself, encouraged by Wallis, came to believe it almost to the point of paranoia, and his feelings were widely shared in leftish circles. Vera Brittain, sickened by the hypocrisy of the affair, expressed the views of many liberal-minded intellectuals. 'Mrs Simpson . . . had merely been made a convenient excuse for removing a monarch whose informality, dislike of ancient tradition, and determination to see things for himself had affronted the "old gang" from the beginning.'[32] Certainly, the removal of Edward was a satisfactory outcome for Baldwin and the 'old gang' which, if not willed in secret conspiracy, was at the very least nudged along by an establishment that found him quite unsuitable. It was, indeed, 'a very British coup'.[33]

The satisfaction that Edward had gone was expressed openly by the Prime Minister. Robert Bernays bumped into him in the House of Commons shortly after his parliamentary triumph. Baldwin was in mellow mood, reflecting that 'when he retired to the shades of Worcestershire he would go there very much more happily than if the late King had remained'. Most tellingly, Baldwin told Bernays that 'a crisis was bound to come and that it might have come on a far more difficult issue'.[34] The abdication of the King for reasons of the heart did not profoundly affect the welfare of the state. But a possible future confrontation with his ministers over a range of issues from unemployment to relations with Nazi Germany would be a matter of the gravest importance. If a clash were to take place at a time of national peril, Baldwin had the foresight to understand, it might be catastrophic. Far better that Edward go sooner rather than later.

Other than Baldwin, few politicians came out particularly well from the affair. Neville Chamberlain wrote bitterly to his sister that 'S. B. as I anticipated has reaped a rich harvest of credit'.[35] As usual, he complained, Baldwin had taken 'the kudos' while he had been up 'night after night' drafting papers and briefing the press 'long after S. B. had gone to bed'. This was the moment of glory, when the Prime Minister should retire but, Chamberlain fumed, 'He could gain nothing & might lose much by waiting over till after the Coronation of King George VI, but I doubt he is capable of adapting himself quickly enough to a new situation and I expect him therefore to stick on'.[36] He was right and resigned himself to Baldwin's staying on, disingenuously telling his sisters that he would like to be 'spared' the duties of Prime Minister during the ceremonies of the coronation. There was, of course, nothing he would have liked more than being centre-stage at the crowning of George VI.

Chamberlain also wanted to get his hands on the levers of foreign policy so that he could pursue the policy of appeasement with greater energy than his slothful neighbour at Number 10. This was denied him by Baldwin's success. Had he been able to oust the Prime Minister in 1936, as he had wished, it is likely that he would have set in train the meeting with Hitler that Ribbentrop had wanted to arrange that year and that Baldwin had refused. The outcome of such a summit is a matter for ultimately fruitless but nonetheless fascinating speculation. Chamberlain's eagerness to appease Hitler might have pre-empted the Munich settlement of 1938, allowing the Führer to take the first steps to the mastery of Europe he desired and lulling Britain into a false sense of security that would have had appalling consequences in years to come.[37]

Winston Churchill was another casualty of the abdication. His intervention had damaged his career, some felt irrevocably. Lord Tweedsmuir (the novelist John Buchan) was one of the many to congratulate Baldwin, telling him gleefully that 'the power for mischief in Winston and his like has now been killed'.[38] Churchill himself admitted that he was 'deeply distressed' by the turn of events, 'much battered' and 'profoundly grieved'.[39] He continued to argue that the crisis could have been avoided by the simple expedient of delay. Although he never said so openly, he was certain that Edward's infatuation for Wallis, like so many other passions in his life, would have passed. There had been no need, in his view, to force the issue. Now that the crisis was over, he retired to Chartwell for Christmas, suffering from an 'almost fatalistic depression'.[40] For the time being he remained loyal to the former King,[41] sending him letters with news of events in England, arranging hospitality for him and lobbying Baldwin to ensure the Simpsons' divorce went through uncontested.[42] He cancelled plans for a holiday in Florida and went back once more to the great issue that concerned him: the rearmament of Britain.

Churchill's intemperate support of Edward kept him in the wilderness, untainted by participation in the appeasing governments of Baldwin or Chamberlain, until the outbreak of war. It is one of the ironies of history that his failure in the winter of 1936 preserved him for greatness four years later. Here too Baldwin was prophetic. Much as he disliked Churchill, and much as he dismissed his judgement, he did see in him the potential that was to make him the saviour of the nation. When, earlier in the year, his friend and confidant J. C. C. Davidson asked him why he was not including Churchill in his government, Baldwin is reported to have replied: 'As for Winston I feel we should not give him a post at this stage. Anything he undertakes he puts his heart and soul into. If there is going to be a war – and no one can say that there is not – we must keep him fresh to be our war Prime Minister.'[43]

Cosmo Gordon Lang was one of the 'old gang' victors in the battle of the abdication, but his triumph went to his head. On Sunday 13 December the Archbishop broadcast a sanctimonious homily in which he compared Edward to James II fleeing into exile ('in darkness he left these shores'), attacked him for putting his 'craving for private happiness' before duty and condemned his morals. He also put down Edward's friends as 'a social circle whose standards are alien to all the best instincts and traditions of his people'.[44]

Hensley Henson excoriated his colleague after listening to the radio sermon: 'His Grace of Canterbury surpassed himself in unctuous and egotistic eloquence, "painting the lily" and pointing the moral. Am I wholly wrong in regarding all this moralising as unwise, generous and unfair?' He was not wrong. The broadcast caused what Churchill called 'a perfect storm of protest'. Middle England's sense of fair play was offended. The prelate had given a man who was down a kicking. There were letters to the *Daily Telegraph* condemning Lang's words as 'unnecessary and needlessly unkind'.[45] The Archbishop's mailbag was mostly abusive; H. G. Wells called the sermon 'a libellous outburst'.[46] Lang was lampooned in a verse that became justly famous:

> My Lord Archbishop, what a scold you are!
> And when your man is down, how bold you are!
> Of Christian charity how scant you are!
> And, auld Lang swine, how full of cant you are![47]

Perry Brownlow was so incensed that he went to Lambeth Palace and confronted the prelate. Lang, he told Chips Channon afterwards, was 'unctuous, adamant, tearful and angry'. Brownlow demanded an apology, but the Archbishop refused: 'his tiny eyes screwed up, "the innocent must suffer with the guilty" he remarked.' The frank exchange of views ended with Lang, in slight panic, admitting that he found the job of Archbishop 'a most disgusting post'.[48]

Perhaps his greatest mistake was to patronize the new King in the broadcast, thus alienating friend as well as foe. He tactlessly referred to George's long battle to overcome his speech defect. 'When his people listen to him', he pontificated, 'they will note an occasional and momentary hesitation in his speech. But he has brought it into full control, and to those who hear it need cause no sort of embarrassment, for it causes none to him who speaks.'[49] For years King George had struggled heroically with his stammer, under the guidance of his speech therapist Lionel Logue. To draw attention to it at this stage could only make matters worse, as Logue complained.[50] It was unpleasant, embarrassing and uncalled for. It also damaged the standing of the Church.

Henson was disgusted. 'There was an assumption of patronising familiarity with the new King and his family which was offensive',[51] he noted, before condemning the Archbishop and his colleagues for their readiness to speak out. 'They simply can't resist the temptation of talking where they can count on an audience, & provide copy for the papers.'[52] This, though true, coming from a man who revelled in controversy himself, was more than a bit rich.

On Christmas Eve Henson received an urgent circular from Lang imposing a period of ecclesiastical silence. Piling Pelion on Ossa, the Archbishop of York had joined the prelatical offensive against the former King with a condemnatory letter to his diocese. Lang was forced into action. 'I think enough has been said on this painful matter and the time has come for reticence', he told his colleagues, fearful that they might take to their pulpits with yet more homiletic fusillades on Christmas Day. Henson mischievously concluded: 'It is difficult not to perceive that His Grace has received what is commonly called "a wigging" from our new Defender of the Faith.' He was right. Lord Wigram had rung Lambeth Palace late the previous night and told the Archbishop that King George 'was put out' and urged him 'to exhort the leaders of religion to reticence'.[53]

The *brouhaha* died down, the dogs ceased to bark and the caravan moved on. But for some there remained a lingering sense of dissatisfaction that the views of the people themselves about the abdication had not been properly taken into account, and there had been a democratic failure in the press and Parliament. Without the evidence of polling, the range of feeling over an issue that split the nation will never be fully known. Baldwin, always convinced he had his finger on the pulse, was certain that public opinion had been expressed through the views of MPs in Parliament. But this confidence was challenged by the many letters of support the King received.[54] Edward did indeed have a degree of popular support that was never able to express itself. 'There is a vast body of the English Public inarticulate . . . who were unable to have any influence on the outcome of the crisis', one supporter wrote to him.[55] Another complained to Churchill that 'no means existed for ascertaining the guidance and extent of the "public opinion" to which the newspapers so glibly referred'.[56]

Nonetheless, it does seem that the majority was supportive of Baldwin and the abdication. There was undoubtedly a widespread sense of disappointment in Edward and a feeling that a much-loved monarch had betrayed his people. John Prichard remembered his parents' view, shared by many ordinary people, that 'he was undoubtedly popular because he was not a distant toff, but someone who identified with the people. But there was a feeling of having been let down, that he had feet of clay.'

The lack of exact knowledge of popular feeling about the abdication revealed a glaring failure in the British political system. It was 'a triumph for dictatorship', as Churchill's correspondent put it. This democratic deficit so incensed Tom Harrisson, a young man in Lancashire, that he set up an organization to gauge public opinion. He called it Mass Observation. With his friends the poet Charles Madge and the documentary-maker Humphrey Jennings he sought to find out and publish ordinary people's views of the burning issues of the time, from Spain and Germany to pacifism and unemployment.

Within a month, in January 1937, Mass Observation had enlisted 500 volunteers. Harrisson and his colleagues instructed them to keep diaries, fill in questionnaires and in this way get the feel of the popular mood. The Mass Observers fanned out across the country, going to shops, pubs, churches and sporting events, both asking questions and listening in (some thought snooping) on other people's conversations. The début subject was, appropriately, the coronation of George VI. Mass Observation was the first attempt to measure opinion; the more scientific approach (although perhaps less rich in content) of George Gallup's surveys followed soon afterwards from the USA. Never again would politicians be able to bandy about public opinion to such effect without any real evidence to support their confident assertions.

One man above all totally misjudged British public opinion and misread the abdication with calamitous consequences. He was, inevitably, Joachim von Ribbentrop. From the beginning he had asserted confidently 'the whole affair will go up in smoke'. 'You'll see,' he told his staff, 'the King will marry Wally and the two will tell Baldwin and his whole gang to go to the devil.'[57] He went on to pronounce that, far from being Baldwin's triumph, the abdication was his nemesis. 'This was the end of Baldwin', he told a startled lunch guest, and predicted 'there would be shooting in the streets, and the King's Party would eventually restore Edward VIII to the throne'.[58] The situation was so grave, he believed, that he was 'extremely nervous' walking the streets of London.

His misreading would have been laughable, had its effects not been so grave. The hapless diplomat had built up the King as a man of destiny, capable of forging a new alliance with Nazi Germany. He had convinced Hitler that the monarchy held the key to Germany's future in Europe. Now Edward was sacrificing all for love. It was a humiliating blow that felt like a personal betrayal and made Ribbentrop look a fool. Instead of accepting his error, however, he presented the abdication to Hitler as an anti-German conspiracy of Jews, Freemasons and plutocrats. Hitler readily accepted his Ambassador's explanation.

Von Ribbentrop's mission to London, which had begun with such high hopes on all sides, was now heading for disaster. The debonair diplomat became ever more morose and ill-tempered, turning into a brooding bore, laughed at behind his back, insulted to his face and lampooned in the newspapers. The diplomatic dance was over. Like a spurned lover, his feelings of affection for Britain switched to loathing. He briefed Hitler that the departure of the well-disposed King had ended for ever all hopes of an alliance between the two countries.[59] Henceforth, he warned the Führer, Britain and her Empire must be regarded as Germany's most dangerous enemy. He spent little further time in London, preferring to advance his cause in Berlin, which he did with such success that Hitler appointed him Foreign Minister within the year.

Once in charge of Nazi foreign policy under the Führer, Ribbentrop did everything he could to isolate the British. He forged a global alliance with Italy and Japan. He urged Hitler to strike against Britain at the earliest opportunity, doing everything he could to obstruct Chamberlain's overtures. So great was his hostility that he pulled off his master-stroke, a pact with the arch-enemy, Bolshevik Russia, completing the encirclement of the British Empire and making war inevitable. With some justice, the Second World War has been called 'Ribbentrop's war'.[60]

The dark shadow of war was casting its gloom that year ever more widely over the country as Christmas approached. The front pages of the newspapers continued to carry news from Spain, highlighting the effectiveness of Hitler's bombers in the increasingly bitter conflict. Marguerite Patten heard the Spanish Civil War described as Germany's rehearsal for a future war. It added to her sense of anxiety. 'There were so many good things, pleasant things, like the Ideal Home and the Olympics but running underneath we all felt a feeling of not being secure. We had wonderful things to take our minds off it for five minutes, but only for five minutes.'[61]

Some of those things were turning out be rather less wonderful than expected. The great ocean liner the *Queen Mary* had entered scheduled service in the summer months, steaming her way back and forth across the Atlantic. The maiden voyage had been 'a long festival, a joyful cruise experience', according to Edwin Praine, a young waiter on board.[62] With her average speed of nearly 30 knots, the crossing took only four and a half days. In August she won the Blue Riband for the fastest trans-Atlantic time, beating her French rival the *Normandie* by a couple of hours. By December thousands, including many film stars, bankers and industrialists, had made the journey. All were seduced by the individual luxury of the state rooms, the fine dining and the beauty of the contemporary decorations and art works in the public areas. Henry Hall and his celebrated Dance Band had broadcast live fourteen times from the Ballroom during the first crossing. His passenger dance concerts were relayed by the ship's powerful wireless transmitter to fans all over the world.

But in December, as the winter gales took hold and the seas became stormy, a design fault in the 81,000 ton liner became apparent.[63] There would be no dancing during the winter crossings. When the seas became rough, the *Queen Mary* began a terrifying dance of her own: the ship's roll. Experiments with models during the construction of the ship had not shown that this alarming trait would be a problem. The designers had considered precautions unnecessary. No handrails were fitted on the main passenger alleyways, which were several hundred feet long, nor were the liner's heavy furnishings anchored to the floor. It turned out to be a hubristic error. In rough seas the ship's low centre of gravity made her roll to one side, pause, roll further – sometimes by as much as 45 degrees – then hold and return to an upright position before rolling in the same way to the other side. To those unused to the experience the pause at the furthest point of the roll was disquieting. For a few haunting seconds it seemed as though the ship might not recover. For all aboard it was uncomfortable and dangerous.[64]

Ron Winter served in the *Queen Mary* during her early voyages as a junior electrical engineer. 'Brother could she roll!' he remembered, 'this was her besetting sin.'[65] He witnessed the effect of the design fault in the Cabin Class Lounge, where carpets lay on a floor that was highly polished for dances. On top of them stood 'some very expensive and beautiful furniture, heavy settees and easy chairs, large and solidly constructed occasional tables'. A disaster was waiting to happen. During the first great storm in December the carpets began to slide across the room as the rolling increased, followed by the furniture, hurtling and crashing 70 feet each way. The crew attempted at first to lash it down, 'but this was a very dangerous exercise and only partially successful, and for a couple of days and nights the furniture had to be left to its own devices, as it was too dangerous to go into the room. The devastation can be imagined.'[66] For the passengers movement about the ship was severely restricted. Those who left their cabins 'ricocheted from side to side' of the passageways. If they reached the wide open spaces, Ron Winter observed with horror, 'it was impossible to remain standing, and you were just rolled from one side to the other gathering speed on the way.'[67]

The crew rigged ropes across all the open spaces for people to grab hold of, which allowed some movement. Those with courage enough and their sea legs ventured out in search of entertainment. They were not disappointed. The prima donna Lily Pons gamely gave a recital, clutching a rope that had been rigged across the stage as she sung. Most passengers remained below, many suffering from seasickness. At the height of the storm telephone calls to the bridge had to be cut off as the Captain was 'besieged with requests to slow down, to stop, to turn back, to do anything that would lessen the misery'. When the ship docked at Southampton, twenty-seven ambulances were waiting for the casualties.[68] During subsequent voyages handrails were fitted and furniture screwed to the floors. The owners, Cunard, were forced to correct the fundamental problem of rolling. Before the invention of stabilizers, however, it could never be fully solved.

The Queen Mary's flaws were kept from the public, who continued to revere the ship as one of the symbols of Britain's enduring greatness. The country prided itself that winter on another demonstration of its engineering prowess and technological lead: the first scheduled television broadcasts. Transmissions had begun from Alexandra Palace in November for two hours every day. The audience was small; it was estimated that the opening ceremony was seen on no more than 400 receivers.[69] The early televisions were enormous, expensive contraptions with tiny, flickering screens, some with the picture reflected into a mirror in the lid. They cost £100 each, the price of a small car, and were beyond the reach of most people. Nonetheless, the early transmissions were the first step in a communications revolution that would change the world.

The opening schedules offered a fairly bland diet of topical magazine programmes, concerts with the BBC Dance Orchestra (led by the ubiquitous and ever-popular Henry Hall) and scenes from theatre and the news, supplied by the newsreel company British Movietone. Gaps in the schedule were filled by craftsmen demonstrating their skills and parades of wild animals. There were also short documentaries. The most popular programme was *Picture Page*, a chat show. Joan Miller, a Canadian actress, acted out the nation's Freudian obsession with telephone switchboard girls by sitting at a mock-up of a switchboard and 'putting you through' to people of interest and celebrities.

At first the BBC's Director-General, Sir John Reith, was dismissive of the new medium. He wrote in his diary of the inauguration, 'To Alexandra Palace for the television opening. I have declined to be televised or to take any part.'[70] But, like so many after him who affected lofty disdain of the new box in the corner, he was soon drawn to watching its flickering effervescence. 'Television is an awful snare', he complained.[71] Others, as always happens when a rival technology appears, thought it a threat to existing media. Graham Greene, writing as film critic for *The Spectator*, warned of the end of cinema.[72] But almost all acknowledged the immense potential both for good and ill of the world-changing technology. The BBC had earlier prophesied that, 'if the control fell into the wrong hands', television entertainment might be 'debased to the level of international millions or used for the vilest propaganda'.[73] Both warnings would prove true. But if the puritanical Scots pathfinders, John Grierson and John Reith, were to watch the BBC today, they would no doubt detest a great deal but would also find in the countless documentaries and dramas many programmes that still live up to, or surpass, their values and expectations.

For the time being, radio remained the dominant medium. The BBC geared up for Christmas offering festive concerts and sacred reflections. George V had started the Christmas Day broadcasts from Sandringham four years earlier (with messages written for him, ironically, by Cosmo Lang), and there was some speculation as to whether George VI would continue the tradition. In the event Alec Hardinge, acting on the advice of Lionel Logue, decided that he should not.[74] The King was in a nervous state. The Archbishop's tactless remarks about his stammer would only make him more self-conscious and the public more aware of it; there was a feeling that a period of silence from a monarchy that had disgraced itself would be in order. The royal family remained closeted in Sandringham, spending the holiday break in quiet and reflective seclusion.

At the other great English country houses there was no call for self-imposed restraint. Joyce Grenfell spent Christmas with her aunt Nancy Astor at palatial Cliveden, where the day was celebrated in the style that might be expected of such a wealthy dynasty. It was the opportunity for a gathering of more than two dozen of the powerful Astor clan in Charles Barry's glorious Thameside setting.[75] Nancy's six children, including William the future 3rd Viscount and David, who would later edit *The Observer* and befriend George Orwell, were there, as well as assorted cousins, close friends and lonely hearts, such as Baldwin's confidant Thomas Jones.

Joyce Grenfell, who stayed in a cottage in the grounds loaned to her by her aunt, went up to the big house on Christmas Eve. She played carols after tea with the children: 'we all roared them.' Aunt Nancy retired to her boudoir to wrap her presents. 'We were yelled at if we approached the sacred precincts. Very exciting and Christmassy.'[76] On Christmas Day everybody assembled once again for breakfast before presents and church in the low-ceilinged but large oak-panelled hall. Gifts were piled on every available chair, stool and sofa; a Christmas tree glowed at the foot of the stairs; holly, ivy and yew tangled round the banisters and over the portraits. 'Soon we all began undoing red ribbon and tissue paper,' Joyce told her mother, 'there was a series of exclamations, thank-yous and excited squeaks.'

After lunch in the Rococo dining-room (only one plate for every course, to reduce the servants' workload[77]) the party went outside, descended the double staircase from the parterre and played games on the terrace enclosed by the celebrated Borghese balustrade. After tea there was hide-and-seek for the children all over the great house, 'an endless game'. Dinner at 7.30 was fancy dress, with the huge chest on the French landing unlocked, revealing a treasure trove of 'old velvet cloaks, Aunt N.'s old hats, a pierrot costume and any number of mismatched shoes'. Most of the adults cheated by wearing masks, but Nancy Astor dressed as a very wealthy old woman of the type found in the Ritz in those days 'in any country'. She wore 'false teeth and her hair in a frizz on top . . . uncanny and terribly funny'. During Christmas dinner of turkey and plum pudding the men sat opposite the women, and Aunt Nancy amused everyone by making the 'awful face of a woman who has had a stroke. I thought we'd be sick we laughed so and when you think of a room full of people roaring at something that in real life is a terrible tragedy one wonders what humour is!' To round off a glorious day there were party games, songs and sketches, with David Astor and a cousin performing as soldiers on the North-West Frontier.

In Belfast, David Strain spent the Christmas holiday with his mother in their home in Upper Galwally. On Christmas Eve he posted a gift of a tie to John, the Catholic office boy for whom he felt such affection, and sent presents and cards to others who worked in his draper's shop. After tea he cleaned the house with his new vacuum cleaner and then decorated the morning room and tree. The next day his Uncle Sam and two brothers with their children arrived after church for lunch. 'We had our dinner at half two: roast beef, sprouts, turnip, mashed potatoes.'[78] David and his uncle did not eat meat, so were given 'vegetarian patties and apple sauce', then all enjoyed 'plum pudding, tea and shortbread'. In the afternoon he went down to check on the shop. His uncle 'went to his office for a little also'.

The family reassembled for tea and presents at 6.30. David, used to keeping accounts for the shop, made a meticulous list of gifts. Compared with the cornucopia of today's Christmas exchange, 1936 was, for the vast majority, a much more frugal time. To his mother David gave a scarf, and from her he received two pairs of pyjamas, sweets and a pen wiper; to one brother and sister-in-law he gave sheets and pillow cases (not very imaginative for a draper) and was given 4 oz of tobacco; to the other couple he gave 10s. each, and received from them sweets. To the children he gave shoes, books and a clown doll. At half-past ten in the evening 'I tidied up the place and got to bed about half twelve – a really good Christmas Day'.

John Prichard spent Christmas in Colchester, having taken the train with his family from their bungalow in Bexleyheath to be with his grandparents. They represented a direct link to the Victorian era, when Christmas had been celebrated very differently, if at all. Many poorer families of the older generation still did not have Christmas trees, nor did they exchange presents. John's grandparents, born in the 1860s, had not moved with the times. 'Trees had not spread to all the lower classes. There wasn't a tradition of handing round. My parents smuggled in a large pillow case stuffed with presents while we slept in our bedrooms and we opened them on our own.'[79] John had won a scholarship to Erith County Grammar, which paid for the fees but not the extras. While he received gifts of Meccano and Hornby models, there was also a useful geometry set for school.

For the better-off, winter sports were becoming increasingly fashionable. Many of the moneyed upper-middle classes preferred to spend Christmas in the Alps. Geoffrey Dawson headed with his family for Kitzbuehl, where his children promptly fell ill with flu on arrival. Before departing he learned to his horror that the former King was in Austria, staying with the Rothschilds, and had taken a house in the resort for some skiing during the break. The thought of bumping into him on the slopes was a ghastly prospect. He had already been forced to defend himself against attacks from Churchill for the cruelty with which he had treated Edward during the crisis. Fortunately for him, however, Edward remained near Vienna. In Kitzbuehl, Dawson bumped into the Duchess of Saxe-Coburg, like her husband a fervent pro-Nazi, and learned from her that the ex-King 'moved in the worst rich Jew set in the Austrian capital'.[80]

The year moved to its close. Nineteen thirty-six had been the hinge of the decade, a pivotal year on which much turned and in which much changed. Optimism swung to pessimism, as conflict emerged abroad and the hopes of pacifism were dashed at home. Rearmament, rather than social and economic reform, became the priority. As they prepared for war once more, the British longed for peace. Neville Chamberlain's policy of appeasement grew directly out of a sense that in the coming of war all would be lost. Wilson Harris, editor of *The Spectator*, expressed the fear that all felt as the prospect of a second Armageddon overshadowed the country.

> Life goes on; trade slowly but consistently expands; stock exchange values mount; unemployment diminishes; slums are cleared and houses built. But through it all penetrates ceaselessly the recurrent thought that all our building is for destruction, all our wealth is being amassed only to be destroyed in the work of destroying, all the wise expenditure of the nation on the education and health of its children and the support of its unemployed, its sick and aged will be checked or disastrously contracted by the need for laying on ourselves and future generations insupportable burdens in preparation for a new war.[81]

There was one glimmer of hope on the dark horizon. Rearmament, in the short term, would in the next few years bring an end at last to the suffering of the distressed areas. But in the longer term the dreams of many were to come to an abrupt end just as Harris foretold.

It was not until after the war that many of the hopes that were born in 1936 and grew out of the work of writers such as Orwell and economists such as Keynes, or out of the dignified protests of the Jarrow marchers, could be given full expression. And if the attempts of Edward VIII to modernize and to challenge the values of the older generation failed that year, his informal style and more tolerant values were to prevail in the years after the Second World War.

New Year's Eve was a quieter affair than the previous year. There were no half-naked bacchanals at the Craven Lodge ball. The Scots did not compete with Londoners to outdo each other with singing outside St Paul's. The pacifist Dick Sheppard spent a desultory New Year with his family, coping with marital breakdown, in a hotel in wintry Cannes. The royal family rested in retreat at Sandringham, as the new King came to terms with his unwanted destiny. From his Schloss the Duke of Windsor fretted on the phone to Wallis, who in turn suspected him of adultery with Baroness Rothschild. Hensley Henson surveyed the scene from Durham with customary pessimism:

'I end the year in perplexity and depression', he wrote in his diary.[82] Winston Churchill told a friend that he had no regrets: 'as you know in politics I always prefer to accept the guidance of my heart to calculations of public feeling.'[83] Lucy Baldwin, more sanguine and less prone to introspection, concluded with a customary flourish: 'Good night old year with your faults & fears & triumphs – and for all, Praise God.'[84]

There was no break for those battling Fascism in Spain as 1937 dawned. John Cornford, now a battle-hardened warrior, had returned to Spain in October and taken part in the defence of Madrid. He was no longer fighting with the suspect Trotskyist militia but had joined the International Brigades with six clean-shaven, idealistic and innocent young men whom he had recruited during his brief stay in England. He led them to the slaughter. By Christmas he was the only remaining member of the group who survived to fight.[85] Enthusiasm for the cause counted for little when facing the superior arms and experience of Franco's Moorish troops. Poorly led, barely trained and fighting with obsolescent weapons, the British volunteers were too often sitting targets. During the fighting in Madrid, Cornford himself had been wounded in the head by a rogue anti-aircraft shell and he now sported a large white bandage.

In late December, Cornford joined a newly formed British company made up of a few survivors, like him, and some fresh volunteers. They were ordered south from Madrid to join up with a French battalion. The plan was that they should take part in a diversionary attack on the Córdoba front, against a small town, Lopera, thus relieving the pressure on Madrid.[86] The British contingent arrived on the front, 30 miles or so west of Córdoba, on Christmas Eve. Many had never handled a weapon before in their lives.[87] They were issued with antique guns that dated from the turn of the century and ordered into battle on Christmas Day.

From the first they were outnumbered and out-manoeuvred. Forced to bivouac in the cold on Christmas night, they came under intense enemy fire the next day, when the Fascists attacked them in their exposed position on the brow of a hill. Later they were strafed by enemy planes. There was panic and in the confusion the men's

English commander ordered them to withdraw. Two days later, on 28 December, they attacked once more, again without success. John Cornford, wearing his white bandage, was seen climbing up the brow of a hill to reconnoitre. He was an easy target for a sniper. He was shot through the head. It was just one day after his twenty-first birthday. His body was not recovered.

The death of the young poet reminded many of the loss of a previous generation's *jeunesse dorée* in the trenches. It presaged more to come. One undergraduate at Oxford at the time recalled, 'we knew then that another major war was inevitable'.[88]

Discussion points

1. To what extent did the general mood of pacifism following the First World War contribute to appeasement? How realistic were the aims of pacifist leaders such as Dick Sheppard and his followers?

2. Orwell and Grierson are championed as heroes of the working class, however Orwell's *The Road to Wigan Pier* is often criticized for painting an unfair picture of the town, and many considered Grierson's representation of the workers in *Night Mail* unrealistic and patronising. Did they in fact deny those who they endeavoured to give a voice to?

3. What was the public appeal of the Jarrow marchers?

4. Why did Mosley fail to mobilize significant support in 1936?

5. If Winston Churchill had died at the end of 1936 would his manifest failings have been remembered and his many virtues forgotten?

6. Rates of maternal mortality were extremely high in the 1930s, and Lucy Baldwin was instrumental in the passage of the 1936 Midwives Act. Would Mrs Baldwin be regarded today as exerting improper political influence over her husband, the prime minister?

7. Why did Hitler and his cronies believe the British aristocracy to have influence over policy? What was the impact of their misperception?

8. Why did young intellectuals such as John Cornford become so radicalized? Why is there no equivalent radicalism today?

9. Was the Spanish Civil War the key turning point of the year? Or has the abdication had more lasting impact on British consciousness?

10. Was Wallis Simpson unfairly vilified as a femme fatale? Have hostile attitudes persisted because of her sex and background as an American?

11. Can King Edward's decision to abdicate be considered as a direct consequence of Baldwin's manipulation?

Acknowledgements

A year packed with events, personalities and drama, 1936 offers a vast field for an author to explore. I have been fortunate to have been able to draw on the work of many biographers and historians whose work has covered different aspects of the time. In particular, I would like to thank Dr Susan Williams for her kind help and guidance with my researches, and for her suggestions and comments on the text. I am indebted to her for sharing her great knowledge of the abdication and her expertise on the wider period, without which my task would have been far harder. I am also grateful to Professor Robert Self for his generosity and for his comments and corrections. Professor Self's unrivalled knowledge of Neville Chamberlain, in particular, has informed my portrayal of this fascinating and often misunderstood figure. I must also thank Dr Tom Buchanan for his assistance with my chapter on the Spanish Civil War. I am grateful to Professor Richard Overy for his advice during the research for this book at a time when he was finishing his masterly work on the 1930s, and to Professor Peter Scott for his many useful suggestions of sources and facts and figures. I would also like to thank Dr James Thomas for his PhD thesis on the Special Areas, and Hugo Vickers for kindly helping with information about Queen Elizabeth The Queen Mother.

I am grateful to the staff and librarians at the Bodleian Library, the British Library, the British Library Newspapers, the British Library Sound Archive, the British Film Institute National Library, the Syndics of Cambridge University Library, Durham Cathedral Library and Archives, the Imperial War Museum Sound Archive, the Marx Memorial Library, Merthyr Tydfil Public Library, The National Archives, Newbury Public Library, the Deputy Keeper of Records,

Public Record Office of Northern Ireland, the Robinson Library, University of Newcastle upon Tyne, the Royal Television Society, South Shields Reference Library, South Tyneside Public Libraries and the Wellcome Library.

I have been helped enormously by the assistance of Rachel Harris, whose research in the archives has shown both great organizational skills and initiative. I am also grateful to Oliver Gregory, who explored the archives in Newcastle and Durham on my behalf. Thanks too to Carolyn Jacob at Merthyr Tydfil Public Library, who put me in touch with witnesses who remembered South Wales in 1936, and to Paul Burton for his work in the Public Record Office of Northern Ireland.

My colleagues at Blakeway Productions have shown great forbearance during my absences while writing. Alex Connock, chief executive of Ten Alps, offered much encouragement and I am grateful to him and Nitil Patel for their understanding of the demands of authorship. Rebecca Burrell enthusiastically helped me to contact several of those whom I interviewed about their memories of 1936. She also assisted with great efficiency with the picture research and numerous other queries about material from the 1930s. Alex Leith, the producer of the documentary *A Tale of Two Britains*, provided me with much useful information. Peter Scott, whose knowledge of the film archives is second to none, helped me to track down relevant archival programmes. I am indebted to Bella Barr for her patience in handling the many book requests from the London Library, to Selina Mehta for juggling the competing demands of a busy schedule and to Fiona Stourton for her understanding of the pressures of writing a book.

I am grateful to a number of individuals for their kind assistance. Steve Humphries provided me with much interesting testimony from his excellent BBC series *Forbidden Britain*. Nicholas Moss and Clare Colvin, of the Royal Television Society's History and Archives Group, helped me with the history of the BBC's first television broadcasts. Earl Baldwin of Bewdley and Miles Huntington-Whiteley shared with me memories of their grandparents, Stanley and Lucy Baldwin. Robert Harris gave me thoughtful advice and generously loaned books from his library. Martina Hall and Alexandra Lowe Richardson put me in touch with Dorothy Tyler. John Prichard patiently answered my frequent questions about life in the 1930s and attitudes to particular events of 1936, with astonishing recall and compelling authority. Robert Conquest, an undergraduate at Oxford with my late father in 1936, gave me many useful insights. I am grateful also to all those whose memories of 1936 I have used in the book. Their generation experienced extraordinary dangers, challenges and change. All those whom I have spoken to in the course of writing this book have left me awestruck and humbled by their wisdom, courtesy, humility and strength.

I would never have written this book were it not for my agent, Gill Coleridge. I am extremely grateful to her for putting me in touch with Kate Parkin, my excellent, patient and understanding editor at John Murray. I am also indebted to Kate's team, in particular to Caroline Westmore for her painstaking and meticulous work on the book's production, Matthew Taylor for copy-editing and Douglas Matthews for his skilful indexing. While I have relied on many others for the raw materials that have gone into the writing of this book, and have used my best endeavours to track down the sources of copyright material used, any errors and omissions are entirely my own.

Above all I must thank my family. My mother, Jasmine Blakeway, a member of that great generation, was a fifteen-year-old schoolgirl in 1936. She has helped me avoid numerous solecisms in the text, thanks to her prodigious memory and keen intellect, and this book is dedicated to her with my love. My beloved three daughters, Bryony, Leonie and Helena, have put up with my long absences in front of a computer when writing without a single complaint. My wife, Denny has been the source of support and encouragement from beginning to end. She has shouldered the added burden that my double life as writer and television producer has imposed; she has shown a generosity and largeness of spirit that I can never repay; she has fought my semicolons. Those who know her blue pencil are fortunate indeed.

Notes

Abbreviations

WSC Documents: Sir Martin Gilbert, *Winston S. Churchill*, vol. V, Companion Part 3, *Documents* (Heinemann, London, 1982)

NCDL: Robert Self (ed.), *The Neville Chamberlain Diary Letters*, vol. 4, *The Downing Street Years* (Ashgate, Aldershot, 2005)

Chips: Robert Rhodes James (ed.), *Chips: The Diaries of Sir Henry Channon*, rev. edn (Weidenfeld & Nicolson, London, 1996, Phoenix Paperback)

Chapter 1: The dawn of the year

1. Winston Churchill to Clementine Churchill, 26 and 30 December 1935, in Mary Soames (ed.), *Speaking for Themselves: The Personal Letters of Winston and Clementine Churchill, Edited by their Daughter* (Doubleday, London, 1998), pp. 403, 404; Celia Sandys, *Chasing Churchill* (Harper Collins, London, 2004), p. xxiv
2. *Tatler*, no. 1801 (1 January 1936)
3. *Daily Mirror* (1 January 1936)
4. Ibid.
5. *Daily Express* (1 January 1936)
6. Clementine Churchill to Winston Churchill, 7 January 1936, in Mary Soames (ed.), *Speaking for Themselves*, p. 406.
7. Winston Churchill to Clementine Churchill, 31 January 1935, ibid., p. 405
8. Ibid.
9. I have used the National Archives converter for all sterling equivalents: www.nationalarchives.gov.uk/currency.

10. Winston Churchill to Clementine Churchill, 31 January 1935, in Mary Soames (ed.), *Speaking for Themselves*, p. 405. For the average annual wage: Charles Loch Mowat, *Britain Between the Wars 1918–1940* (Methuen University Paperback, London, 1968), p. 491.

11. A term coined by Andrew Roberts in *The Holy Fox: A Biography of Lord Halifax* (Macmillan, Papermac edition, London, 1992), p.305, and taken up by David Cannadine in 'Stanley Baldwin and Francis Brett Young', *In Churchill's Shadow* (Allen Lane, London, 2002), p. 180

12. Thomas Jones report of a conversation with Stanley Baldwin, 22 May 1936, in *WSC Documents*, p. 166

13. *The Spectator* (4 December 1936)

14. Neville Chamberlain to Hilda Chamberlain, 12 January 1936, *NCDL*, p. 169

15. Ibid.

16. B. E. V. Sabine, *British Budgets in Peace and War, 1932–1945* (Allen & Unwin, London, 1970), p. 80

17. Hermione, Countess of Ranfurly, *The Ugly One: The Childhood Memoirs, 1913–1939* (Michael Joseph, London, 1998), pp. 153–4

18. Author interview with John Prichard

19. Winston Churchill to Clementine Churchill, 31 December 1935, in Mary Soames (ed.), *Speaking for Themselves*, p. 405

20. *The Spectator* (4 December 1936)

21. Martin Gilbert, *Winston Churchill: The Wilderness Years* (Heinemann, London, 1981), p. 144

22. Clementine Churchill to Winston Churchill, 7 January 1936, in Mary Soames (ed.), *Speaking for Themselves*, p. 406

23. Monica Baldwin, account of conversation with her uncle Stanley Baldwin in Monica Baldwin, diary, 7 October 1937, in Philip Williamson and Edward Baldwin (ed.), *Baldwin Papers: A Conservative Statesman* (Cambridge University Press, Cambridge, 2009), p. 420

24. Edward, Prince of Wales, to Wallis Simpson, 26 December 1935, in Michael Bloch (ed.), *Wallis and Edward: Letters 1931–7, The Intimate Correspondence of the Duke and Duchess of Windsor* (Penguin, London, 1986), p. 166

25. Wallis Simpson to Aunt Bessie Merryman, 9 January 1936, in Michael Bloch (ed.), *Wallis and Edward*, p. 167

26. *Tatler* (8 January 1936)

27. Edward, Prince of Wales, to Wallis Simpson, 1 January 1936, in Michael Bloch (ed.), *Wallis and Edward*, p. 167

Chapter 2: The King's life is being moved towards its close

1. Kenneth Rose, *King George V* (Phoenix Press, London, 2000), p. 399. I am grateful to Kenneth Rose for his detailed account of the death of King George V.
2. Ibid.
3. Helen Hardinge, *Loyal to Three Kings* (William Kimber, London, 1967), p. 48
4. Violet Milner, diary, 1 January 1936, Papers, vol. 5, Bodleian Library Special Collections, MSS Violet Milner 1–85
5. Hugh and Mirabel Cecil, *Imperial Marriage* (Sutton Publishing, Stroud, 2005), passim
6. A. Susan Williams, *Ladies of Influence: Women of the Elite in Interwar Britain* (Penguin, London, 2000), p. 63
7. Violet Milner, diary, 13 January 1936
8. David Gilmour, *The Long Recessional: The Imperial Life of Rudyard Kipling* (John Murray, London, 2002), p. 308
9. Helen Hardinge, *Loyal to Three Kings*, p. 48
10. Violet Milner, diary, 18 January 1936
11. Kenneth Rose, *King George V*, p. 400
12. The Duke of Windsor, *A King's Story: The Memoirs of HRH the Duke of Windsor* (Cassell, London, 1951), p. 261
13. Herbert Hensley Henson, diary, Durham Cathedral Library, 3 February 1936 (report of a conversation with Stanley Baldwin)
14. Kenneth Rose, *King George V*, p. 401
15. Sir Henry 'Chips' Channon, diary, 18 January 1936, *Chips*, p.53
16. Herbert Hensley Henson, diary, 18 January 1936
17. Edward, Prince of Wales, to Wallis Simpson, 18 January 1936, in Michael Bloch (ed.), *Wallis and Edward*, p. 169
18. The National Archives Special Branch file MEPO 10/35 gives details of the surveillance in 1935.
19. Thomas Jones to Lady Grigg, 24 January 1936, in Thomas Jones, *A Diary with Letters, 1931–1950* (Oxford University Press, London, 1954), p. 163

20. Herbert Hensley Henson, diary, 21 January 1936 (reporting a conversation with Serena James)

21. Author interview with Edward Baldwin, 4th Earl Baldwin of Bewdley

22. The Duke of Windsor, *A King's Story*, p. 262

23. Philip Williamson and Edward Baldwin (ed.), *Baldwin Papers*, p. 421 (quoting Monica Baldwin diary entry for 7 October 1937)

24. Thomas Jones, letter to Lady Grigg, 24 January 1936, *A Diary with Letters*, p. 164

25. Ibid.

26. Kenneth Young, *Stanley Baldwin* (Weidenfeld & Nicolson, London, 1976), p. ix

27. Thomas Jones, letter to Lady Grigg, 1 June 1936, *A Diary with Letters*, p. 150

28. Thomas Jones, letter to Lady Grigg, 24 January 1936, *A Diary with Letters*, p. 163

29. Lucy Baldwin, diary, 27 April and 18, 19 July, Lucy Baldwin Papers, Cambridge University Library

30. Neville Chamberlain, letter to Ida Chamberlain, 13 April 1936, *NCDL*, p. 497

31. Robert Self, *Neville Chamberlain: A Biography* (Ashgate, Aldershot, 2006), p. 256

32. The Duke of Windsor, *A King's Story*, p. 264

33. Lord Wigram, ennobled in 1935, assistant private secretary to George V 1910–31, private secretary 1931–6

34. Kenneth Rose, *King George V*, p. 402

35. Ibid.

36. The Duke of Windsor, *A King's Story*, p. 263

37. Joyce Grenfell, letter to her mother, Nora Langhorne, January (undated) 1936, in James Roose-Evans (ed.), *Joyce Grenfell: Darling Ma, Letters to her Mother, 1932–1944* (Hodder & Stoughton, London, 1988), p. 9

38. Vera Brittain, *Testament of Experience* (Virago, London, 1979), p. 139

39. Sarah Bradford, *King George VI* (Weidenfeld & Nicolson, London, 1989), p. 152

40. The Duke of Windsor, *A King's Story*, p. 264

41. Kenneth Rose, *King George V*, p. 408

42. Francis Watson, 'The Death of George V', *History Today*, vol. 36,

no. 12 (1986). I am grateful to Francis Watson who first revealed the King's euthanasia in his definitive account of George V's death.

43. Kenneth Rose, *King George V*, p. 408
44. Ibid.
45. Alan Lascelles, *King's Counsellor Abdication and War: The Diaries of Sir Alan Lascelles*, ed. Duff Hart-Davis (Weidenfeld & Nicolson, London, 2006), p. 107
46. The Duke of Windsor, *A King's Story*, p. 265
47. Violet Milner, diary, 20 January 1936
48. Ibid.
49. Neville Chamberlain, letter to Hilda Chamberlain, 25 January 1936, *NCDL*, pp. 171–2
50. Virginia Woolf, diary, 21 January, *The Diary of Virginia Woolf*, vol. 5, *1936–41*, ed. Anne Olivier Bell (Hogarth Press, London, 1984), p. 10
51. Neville Chamberlain, letter to Hilda Chamberlain, 25 January 1936, *NCDL*, pp. 171–2
52. David Strain, diary, 21 January 1936, Public Record Office of Northern Ireland, D2585/3/16
53. Alan Lascelles, *King's Counsellor*, p. 4
54. Ibid.

Chapter 3: Recessional

1. The Duke of Windsor, *A King's Story*, p. 264
2. Kenneth Rose, *King George V*, pp. 79, 305–6
3. A. N. Wilson, *Betjeman* (Hutchinson, London, 2006), p. 102
4. Philip Ziegler, interviewed by the author for Blakeway Productions, 2006
5. J. B. Priestley, *An English Journey* (Folio Society, London, 1997), p. 325
6. Sir Henry 'Chips' Channon, *Chips*, note on King Edward VIII, p. 50
7. Dr Henson's successor, Bishop David Jenkins, also attracted controversy in 1984 over the issue of the Resurrection.
8. Herbert Hensley Henson, diary, 21 January 1936
9. Joyce Grenfell, letter to her mother, Nora Langhorne, January (undated) 1936, *Darling Ma*, p. 9
10. Blanche Dugdale, diary, 21 January, in *Baffy: The Diaries of Blanche*

Dugdale, 1936–47, ed. N. A. Rose (Valentine Mitchell, London, 1973), p. 2

11. Neville Chamberlain, letter to Hilda Chamberlain, 25 January 1936, *NCDL*, pp. 171–2

12. The Duke of Windsor, *A King's Story* p. 265

13. Ibid.

14. Francis Watson, 'The Death of George V'

15. Duff Cooper, diary, 20 January 1936, *The Duff Cooper Diaries*, ed. John Julius Norwich (Weidenfeld & Nicolson, London, 2005), p. 227

16. Wallis Simpson to Aunt Bessie Merryman, 30 January 1936, in Michael Bloch (ed.), *Wallis and Edward*, p. 177

17. Ibid.

18. Letter to the *Daily Telegraph* (22 January 1936)

19. Andrew Lycett, *Kipling* (Phoenix, London, 2000), p. 793

20. *The Spectator* (24 January 1936)

21. Andrew Lycett, *Kipling*, p. 794

22. Malcolm Muggeridge, *Like it Was: The Diaries and Letters of Malcolm Muggeridge*, ed. John Bright-Holmes (Collins, London, 1981), p. 143

23. Ibid.

24. Herbert Hensley Henson, diary, 21 January 1936

25. Thomas Jones to Lady Grigg, 24 January 1936, Thomas Jones, *A Diary with Letters*, p. 163

26. Violet Milner, diary, 23 January 1936

27. Vera Brittain, *Testament of Experience*, p. 140

28. Andrew Lycett, *Kipling*, pp. 794–5

29. This is admirably captured in David Haig's play *My Boy Jack* (1997).

30. Andrew Lycett, *Kipling*, pp. 794–5

31. The Duke of Windsor, *A King's Story*, p. 266

32. Alan Lascelles, *King's Counsellor*, p. 5

33. Frances Donaldson, *Edward VIII: The Road to Abdication* (Omega, London, 1976), p. 97

34. Harold Nicolson, diary, 23 January 1936, Harold Nicolson, *Diaries and Letters*, ed. Nigel Nicolson (Collins, London, 1966), p. 239

35. Virginia Woolf, diary, 27 January, *Diary of Virginia Woolf*, vol. 5, *1936–41*, p. 12

36. Thomas Jones to Lady Grigg, 24 January 1936, in Thomas Jones, *A Diary with Letters*, p. 166

37. Herbert Hensley Henson, diary, 27 January 1936

38. Sir Henry 'Chips' Channon, diary, 23 January, *Chips*, p.54

39. Violet Milner, diary, 25 January 1936

40. UK population of 46 million; Charles Loch Mowat, *Britain Between the Wars 1918–1940*, p. 518, and 'The UK population: past, present and future', Julie Jefferies, www.statistics.gov.uk/downloads/theme_compendia/fom2005/01_FOPM_Population.pdf

41. Arthur Ponsonby, letter in response to complaint, January 1936, Ponsonby Papers, Bodleian Library Special Collections, MSS Eng. Hist a 20; c651-85; d.363

42. Author interview with John Prichard, 2009

43. Hermione Lee, *Virginia Woolf* (Chatto & Windus, London, 1996), p. 669

44. Geoffrey H. Wells, diary, 21 January 1936, British Library Manuscript Collections

45. Herbert Hensley Henson, diary, 26 January 1936

46. Cf. Piers Brendon, *The Dark Valley: A Panorama of the 1930s* (Jonathan Cape, London, 2000), Chapter 17, p. 353 and passim

47. Channon and others frequently remarked on his youthful appearance and his small stature (5′ 7″).

48. Author interview with Philip Ziegler for *Abdication: A Very British Coup* (Blakeway Productions, 2006)

49. Violet Milner, diary, Monday 27 January

50. *The Times* (28 January 1936)

51. Sir Henry 'Chips' Channon, diary, 25 January 1936, *Chips*, p.56

52. Ibid., 27 January 1936, p. 56

53. The Duke of Windsor, *A King's Story*, p. 269

54. Helen Hardinge, *Loyal to Three Kings*, p. 62

55. Philip Ziegler, *King Edward VIII: The Official Biography* (Collins, London, 1990), p. 246

56. Rupert Godfrey (ed.), *Letters from a Prince: Edward Prince of Wales to Mrs Freda Dudley Ward, March 1918–January 1921* (Little, Brown & Co., London, 1998), p. 190 and passim

57. Thomas Jones, *A Diary with Letters*, p. 167

58. Robert Graves and Alan Hodge, *The Long Weekend: A Social History of Great Britain, 1918–1939* (Hutchinson, London, 1985), p. 321

59. Sir Henry 'Chips' Channon, diary, 28 January 1936, *Chips*, p. 56

60. James Pope-Hennessy, *Queen Mary* (Phoenix Press, London, 2000), p. 562

61. Neville Chamberlain to Ida Chamberlain, 1 February 1936, *NCDL*, p.173
62. J. G. Lockhart, *Cosmo Gordon Lang* (Hodder and Stoughton, London, 1949), p. 394

Chapter 4: Orwell's sordid imagination

1. George Orwell, *The Road to Wigan Pier* (Penguin, London, 2001), p. 91
2. Ibid.
3. Ibid., p. 113
4. J. B. Priestley, *English Journey*, passim
5. James Thomas, 'The Work of the Special Areas Commission: Schemes for Social Improvement, 1934–1939', Institute of Education, University of London PhD thesis, 2005, p. 62
6. Peter Scott, *The Triumph of the South* (Ashgate, Aldershot, 2007), Introduction, passim
7. South Wales, north-east England, Cumberland and central Scotland. This was extended in 1936 to include Orwell's destination: Wigan and surrounding areas.
8. James Thomas 'The Work of the Special Areas Commission', passim
9. Robert Skidelsky, *The Return of the Master* (Allen Lane, London, 2009), Preface
10. Robert Skidelsky, *John Maynard Keynes*, vol. 2, *The Economist as Saviour* (Macmillan, London, 1992), p. 537
11. Ibid, p. 539
12. Robert Self, *Neville Chamberlain: A Biography*, p. 208
13. W. R. Garside, *British Unemployment, 1919–1939* (Cambridge University Press, Cambridge, 2002), p. 17
14. Robert Self and Martin Pugh, interviews for *A Tale of Two Britains*, BBC4 (Blakeway Productions, 2009)
15. Richard Hoggart, Introduction, George Orwell, *The Road to Wigan Pier*, p. xi
16. George Orwell, 'The Road to Wigan Pier Diary', in *The Collected Essays, Journalism and Letters of George Orwell*, vol. 1, *An Age Like This, 1920–1940*, ed. Sonia Orwell and Ian Angus (Penguin, London, 1971), p. 194
17. George Orwell, *The Road to Wigan Pier*, part II, p. 113

18. Ibid., p. 119
19. George Orwell, 'The Road to Wigan Pier Diary', p. 196
20. Richard Rees, in Audrey Coppard and Bernard Crick, *Orwell Remembered* (BBC Ariel Books, London, 1984), p. 115
21. Joe 'Jerry' Kennan, in Audrey Coppard and Bernard Crick, *Orwell Remembered*, p. 130
22. Ibid.
23. George Orwell, 'The Road to Wigan Pier Diary', p. 199
24. I am grateful to D. J. Taylor, *Orwell: The Life* (Vintage, London, 2004), Chapter 9, 'English Journeys', for his account of Orwell's time in Wigan; I have followed his research on the names of the people with whom Orwell stayed.
25. W. R. Garside, *British Unemployment, 1919–1939* (Cambridge University Press, Cambridge, 2002) p. 5, and Charles Loch Mowat, *Britain Between the Wars 1918–1940*, p. 433.
26. James Thomas, 'The Work of the Special Areas Commission', p. 28
27. Jack Common (ed.), *Seven Shifts* (Victor Gollancz, London, 1938), Introduction
28. James Thomas, 'The Work of the Special Areas Commission', p. 75
29. G. C. M. M'Gonigle and J. Kirby, *Poverty and Public Health* (Victor Gollancz, London, 1936)
30. John Boyd Orr, *As I Recall* (MacGibbon & Kee, London, 1966), p. 115
31. Interview with Marguerite Patten
32. John Boyd Orr, 'The Nation and its Food', *The Listener* (18 March 1936)
33. Interview with Dorothy 'Dorrie' Cooper
34. Ted Willis, interview, *The Road to War: Britain* (BBC TV, 1989)
35. D. John Shaw, *Sir Hans Singer: The Life and Work of a Development Economist* (Palgrave Macmillan, Basingstoke, 2002), p. 9
36. Thomas Jones, diary, 27 February 1932, in Thomas Jones, *A Diary with Letters*, p. 28
37. Figures from Richard Overy, *The Morbid Age* (Penguin, London, 2009), p. 267
38. George Orwell, 'The Road to Wigan Pier Diary', p. 201
39. Joe 'Jerry Kennan', in Audrey Coppard and Bernard Crick, *Orwell Remembered*, p. 130
40. George Orwell, 'The Road to Wigan Pier Diary', p. 202
41. George Orwell, *The Road to Wigan Pier*, p. 15

42. D. John Shaw, *Sir Hans Singer*, p. 21
43. Ibid.
44. Bernard Crick, *George Orwell: A Life*, pp. 281–2
45. There is some disagreement among Orwell's biographers about the location of the tripe shop.
46. D. J. Taylor, *Orwell: The Life*, p. 178
47. George Orwell, *The Road to Wigan Pier*, p. 4
48. Kay Ekevall, in Audrey Coppard and Bernard Crick, *Orwell Remembered*, p. 105
49. George Orwell, *The Road to Wigan Pier*, p. 14
50. Ibid., p. 13
51. Sidney Smith, in Audrey Coppard and Bernard Crick, *Orwell Remembered*, p. 138
52. Humphrey Dakin, in Audrey Coppard and Bernard Crick, *Orwell Remembered*, p. 128
53. Joe 'Jerry' Kennan, in Audrey Coppard and Bernard Crick, *Orwell Remembered*, p. 131
54. George Orwell, 'The Road to Wigan Pier Diary', p. 212
55. Ibid., p. 213
56. Joe 'Jerry' Kennan, in Audrey Coppard and Bernard Crick, *Orwell Remembered*, p. 131
57. George Orwell, 'The Road to Wigan Pier Diary', p. 209
58. Ibid.
59. Ibid., p. 54
60. Pilgrim Trust, *Men without Work*, with an Introduction by the Archbishop of York (Cambridge University Press, Cambridge, 1938), p. 141
61. Ibid., p. 139
62. George Orwell, *The Road to Wigan Pier*, p. 14
63. Joe 'Jerry' Kennan, in Audrey Coppard and Bernard Crick, *Orwell Remembered*, p.131

Chapter 5: A meeting with Herr Hitler

1. Viscount Castlereagh Memorandum (note of *c*. February 1936 conversation, written August 1936), Philip Williamson and Edward Baldwin (ed.), *Baldwin Papers*, p. 367
2. Ibid.

3. Sir Ian Kershaw, *Making Friends with Hitler. Lord Londonderry and Britain's Road to War* (Penguin, London, 2005), p. 20. I am grateful to Sir Ian Kershaw and Anne de Courcy for their accounts of the Londonderrys in 1936.

4. Harold Nicolson, diary, 20 February 1936, *Diaries and Letters*, p.245

5. Anne de Courcy, *Circe: The Life of Edith, Marchioness of Londonderry* (Sinclair-Stevenson, London, 1992), p. 245

6. John Charmley, *Churchill: The End of Glory* (Hodder & Stoughton, London, 1993), p. 302

7. The Marquess of Londonderry, *Ourselves and Germany* (Penguin, London, 1938)

8. Ibid., p. 19

9. A. Susan Williams, *The People's King: The True Story of the Abdication* (Penguin Books, London, 2004), p. 4

10. Sir Henry 'Chips' Channon, diaries, 29 May 1936, *Chips*, p. 62

11. A. Susan Williams, *Ladies of Influence*, p. 16

12. David Marquand, *Ramsay MacDonald* (Cape, London, 1977), pp. 406–7

13. A. Susan Williams, *Ladies of Influence*, p. 16

14. Castlereagh Memorandum, Philip Williamson and Edward Baldwin (ed.), *Baldwin Papers*, p. 370

15. Herbert Hensley Henson, diary, 29 January 1936

16. Owen Chadwick, *Hensley Henson: A Study in Friction between Church and State* (The Canterbury Press, Norwich, 1998), p. 286

17. Herbert Hensley Henson, diary, 5 May 1936

18. Sir Ian Kershaw, *Making Friends with Hitler*, p. 157 and passim

19. Geoffrey T. Waddington, 'Aspects of the Operation of the Dienstelle Ribbentrop, 1934–1938', *History*, vol. 265, no. 1 (January 1997)

20. Quoted in Geoffrey T. Waddington, 'Aspects of the Operation of the Dienstelle Ribbentrop, 1934–1938'

21. Ribbentrop was widely disdained; with regard to Londonderry see, for example, Cuthbert Headlam, quoted in Sir Ian Kershaw, *Making Friends with Hitler*, p. 21.

22. Reinhard Spitzy, Ribbentrop's assistant, 1936, interviewed for *The Road to War* (BBC TV, 1989)

23. Joachim von Ribbentrop, *The Ribbentrop Memoirs* (Weidenfeld & Nicolson, London, 1954), p. 8

24. Sir Henry 'Chips' Channon, diary, 29 May 1936, *Chips*, p. 62

25. Joachim von Ribbentrop, *The Ribbentrop Memoirs*, pp. 8–9, 27–9,

describes his first experiences of London and his conversations with Hitler.

26. The Marquess of Londonderry, *Ourselves and Germany*, p. 74
27. Ibid., p. 75
28. This should not obscure the fact that Chamberlain was one of the leading forces in instigating the rearmament programme when he served as the driving force behind the ministerial committee examining the Defence Requirements Committee report in 1934.
29. Quoted in Geoffrey Waddington, 'Aspects of the Operation of the Dienstelle Ribbentrop, 1934–1938'
30. Anne de Courcy, *Circe*, p. 269 (note 244)
31. Sir Ian Kershaw, *Making Friends with Hitler*, p. 135
32. Ibid., note to p. 135
33. Anne de Courcy, *Circe*, p. 270
34. Sir Ian Kershaw, *Making Friends with Hitler*, p. 135
35. Ibid., p. 136
36. The Marquess of Londonderry, *Ourselves and Germany*, p. 80
37. Ibid., p. 79
38. The Marquess of Londonderry, *Wings of Destiny* (Macmillan, London, 1943), p. 156
39. Sir Ian Kershaw, *Making Friends with Hitler*, p. 137
40. The Marquess of Londonderry, *Ourselves and Germany*, p. 84
41. Sir Ian Kershaw, *Making Friends with Hitler*, p. 141
42. The Marquess of Londonderry, *Ourselves and Germany*, p. 87
43. Ibid., p. 91
44. Ambassador Phipps, quoted in Geoffrey Waddington, 'Aspects of the Operation of the Dienstelle Ribbentrop, 1934–1939'
45. The Marquess of Londonderry, *Ourselves and Germany*, p. 72
46. Sir Ian Kershaw, *Making Friends with Hitler*, p. 118
47. Anne de Courcy, *Circe*, p. 272
48. Keynes called Jews who had fled Germany 'refujews' (Robert Skidelsky, *John Maynard Keynes*, vol. 2, *The Economist as Saviour*, p. 513).
49. Herbert Hensley Henson, diary, 7 and 8 February 1936
50. Ibid.
51. Letter to *The Times* (13 February 1936)
52. Anne de Courcy, *Circe*, p. 271
53. Winston Churchill to Lord Londonderry in *WSC Documents*, pp. 142–3, and Sir Ian Kershaw, *Making Friends with Hitler*, p. 144

54. Harold Nicolson to Vita Sackville-West, 20 February 1936, Harold Nicolson, *Diaries and Letters*, p. 245

55. Unity Mitford to Diana Guinness 8 February 1936, Charlotte Mosley (ed.), *The Mitfords: Letters between Six Sisters* (Harper Perennial, London, 2008), p. 69

56. Herbert Hensley Henson, diary, 15 November 1936 (evidently an old copy of the paper, as Sir Ian Kershaw dates it as May; *Making Friends with Hitler*, p. 155)

57. Sir Ian Kershaw, *Making Friends with Hitler*, p. 140

Chapter 6: Night Mail

1. Robert Skidelsky, *John Maynard Keynes*, vol. 2, *The Economist as Saviour*, p. 628

2. Blake Morrison, *Night Mail,* introductory essay, British Film Institute BFIVD833, p. 1

3. Ibid.

4. Forsyth Hardy, *Grierson on Documentary* (Collins, London, 1946), p. 11

5. James Beveridge, *John Grierson* (Macmillan, New York, 1978), p. 66

6. Ibid., p. 15

7. Forsyth Hardy, *John Grierson: A Documentary Biography* (Faber & Faber, London, 1979), p. 73

8. Grierson quoted by Graham Greene, *The Spectator* (24 January 1936)

9. Forsyth Hardy, *Grierson on Documentary*, p. 15

10. Scott Anthony, Introduction, Scott Anthony et al., *We Live in Two Worlds*, introductory booklet to British Film Institute video disc (2008)

11. Forsyth Hardy, *Grierson on Documentary*, p. 11

12. Miguel Mera, 'Benjamin Britten and the GPO Film Unit', in Blake Morrison et al., *Night Mail*, introductory essays, British Film Institute BFIVD833, p. 10

13. Interview with documentary maker Robert Coldstream, son of William Coldstream

14. *The Spectator* (24 January 1936)

15. James Beveridge, *John Grierson*, p. 49

16. Ibid.

17. Benjamin Britten, diary, 1 January 1936, reproduced in Blake

Morrison et al., *Night Mail,* introductory essays, British Film Institute BFIVD833

18. Harry Watt, *Don't Look at the Camera,* quoted in Blake Morrison et al., *Night Mail,* introductory essays, British Film Institute BFIVD833, p. 9

19. James Beveridge, *John Grierson,* p. 85

20. Esmond Romilly, *Boadilla* (Macdonald, London, 1971), p. 27

21. Ibid.

22. Harry Watt, interviewed in James Beveridge, *John Grierson,* p. 85

23. Ibid.

24. BFI Information Department, *Night Mail* undated factsheet, BFI Library

25. Forsyth Hardy, *John Grierson,* p. 76

26. *The Spectator* (24 January 1936)

27. Harry Watt, quoted in James Beveridge, *John Grierson,* p. 83

28. Harry Watt in Blake Morrison et al., *Night Mail,* introductory essays, British Film Institute BFIVD833, p. 5

29. Blake Morrison, *Night Mail,* p. 1

30. Arthur Calder-Marshall, *The Changing Scene,* quoted by Scott Anthony, *Guardian* (24 August 2007)

31. Forsyth Hardy, *Grierson on Documentary,* p. 11

32. Harry Watt in Blake Morrison et al., *Night Mail,* introductory essays, British Film Institute BFIVD833, p. 7

33. Blake Morrison, *Night Mail,* BFIVD833, p. 3

34. Ibid.

35. Richard Davenport-Hines, *Auden* (Heinemann, London, 1995), p. 144

36. Harry Watt, Blake Morrison et al., *Night Mail,* introductory essays, British Film Institute BFIVD833, p. 8

37. Richard Davenport-Hines, *Auden,* p. 144

38. Harry Watt, Blake Morrison et al, *Night Mail,* introductory essay, *Night Mail,* introductory essays, British Film Institute, BFIVD833, p. 9

39. Harry Watt, ibid.

40. Benjamin Britten, diary, 15 January 1936 reproduced in Blake Morrison et al., *Night Mail,* BFIVD833

41. Scott Anthony, An Introduction to the GPO Film Unit in Scott Anthony et al., *We Live in Two Worlds,* BFIVD759, p. 4

42. BFI Information Department undated note, British Film Institute Library

43. *Sight and Sound*, vol. 5, no. 17 (April 1936)

44. Richard Davenport-Hines, *Auden*, p. 145

45. Ibid.

46. Scott Anthony et al., *We Live in Two Worlds*

47. *The Spectator* (24 January 1936)

48. I am grateful to the authority on Benjamin Britten, author and television producer John Bridcut, for this information.

49. Interview with Harry Watt, in James Beveridge, *John Grierson*, p. 86

50. For example, *Target for Tonight, Listen to Britain, Coastal Command, Fires Were Started*

51. *The Spectator* (24 January 1936)

Chapter 7: The gathering storm

1. Victor Cazalet, diary, 13 February 1936, quoted in Martin Gilbert, *Winston Churchill: The Wilderness Years*, p.146

2. Blanche Dugdale, *Baffy*, p. 38

3. In collaboration with Jeanne de Casalis

4. R. C. Sherriff, *No Leading Lady* (Victor Gollancz, London, 1968), p. 302

5. Martin Gilbert, *Winston Churchill: The Wilderness Years*, p. 145. An MP's salary in 1936 was £400 p.a. (equivalent to £14,792.00 today); House of Commons Information Office, Members' pay, pensions and allowances, Factsheet M5 Members Series, revised May 2009, Appendix A, p. 12

6. For a breakdown of Churchill's income in 1936 from literary contracts see *WSC Documents*, p. 517

7. Adrian Fort, *Prof: The Life of Frederick Lindemann* (Jonathan Cape, London, 2003), p. 142; John Charmley, *The End of Glory*, p. 303, for details of the proposed air defences. I am grateful to Adrian Fort and John Charmley for details of Lindemann and Churchill and the ADRC sub-committee of the Committee of Imperial Defence and the Tizard Committee.

8. For example, Professor Lindemann to Winston Churchill, 5 March 1936, in *WSC Documents*, p. 62

9. Winston Churchill to Sir Maurice Hankey, 26 February 1936, *WSC Documents*, p. 58

10. Adrian Fort, *Prof*, passim

11. David Cannadine, *In Churchill's Shadow* (Allen Lane, London, 2002), Chapter 4, 'Language: Churchill as the Voice of Destiny', p. 94 and passim

12. Violet Pearman to T. W. Taylor of Thomas Cook, 9 February 1936, *WSC Documents*, p. 39

13. *Sunday Express* (25 March 1934), in *WSC Documents*, p. 445, n.

14. Violet Pearman to Sir James Hawkey, 27 November 1936, *WSC Documents*, pp. 443–5. In the 1930s 'groovy' meant getting stale ('caught in a groove'), rather than 'trendy' or 'with it'.

15. *WSC Documents*, p. 78, n.

16. Winston Churchill to Violet Pearman, 23 March 1936, *WSC Documents*, pp. 77–8, 78 n.

17. Quoted in Martin Gilbert, *The Wilderness Years*, p. 146

18. Winston Churchill to Clementine Churchill, 3 March 1936, *WSC Documents*, p. 60

19. Guy Walters, *Berlin Games* (John Murray, London, 2007), p. 90

20. Quoted in Charles Moore and Christopher Hawtree, *1936 As Recorded by 'The Spectator'* (Michael Joseph, London, 1986), p. 124

21. Winston Churchill, *The Gathering Storm*, vol. 1, *The Second World War* (Penguin, London, 1985), pp. 172–9; see also Roy Jenkins, *Churchill* (Macmillan, London, 2001) pp. 490–1

22. Harold Nicolson, diary, 9 March 1936, *Diaries and Letters*, p. 248

23. Martin Gilbert, *Winston Churchill: The Wilderness Years*, p. 147

24. Ben Pimlott, *Hugh Dalton* (Macmillan, London, 1985), p. 233. I am grateful to Michael Burleigh for drawing my attention to this.

25. The words of the pro-appeasement Lord Lothian

26. Letter to *The Times* (12 March 1936)

27. George Orwell, 'The Road to Wigan Pier Diary', p. 225

28. Blanche Dugdale, diary, 12 March 1936, *Baffy*, p. 8

29. Violet Milner, diary, 9 March 1936

30. Edward Grigg (later Lord Altrincham), colonialist and politician, was an ally of Lloyd George.

31. Virginia Woolf, diary, 13 March 1936, *The Diary of Virginia Woolf*, vol. 5, *1936–41*, ed. Anne Olivier Bell

32. Herbert Hensley Henson, diary, 7 March 1936

33. *WSC Documents*, 10 March 1936, p. 66, quoting Neville Chamberlain's diary

34. Hugh Greene, in 'Dear Mumma', *1936 As Recorded by The Spectator*, p. 126

35. Winston Churchill to Clementine Churchill, 3 March 1936, in *WSC Documents*, p. 62

36. Martin Gilbert, *Winston Churchill: The Wilderness Years*, p. 150

37. For example, Desmond Morton's comments to Winston Churchill, 14 March 1936, *WSC Documents*, p. 72

38. Quoted in Adrian Fort, *The Prof*, p. 144

39. Quoted in Martin Gilbert, *Winston Churchill: The Wilderness Years*, p. 150

40. Speech to the Birmingham Jewellers' and Silversmiths' Association, 14 March 1936, *WSC Documents*, p. 77; Robert Self writes in *Neville Chamberlain: A Biography*, p. 3: 'By common consent, had Chamberlain retired or died in 1937 instead of just three years later, he would have gone down in history as a great peacetime minister – a radical but realistic social reformer, a supremely talented administrator and the driving force behind many of the National Government's under-estimated successes of the early and middle-1930s. Instead, at the age of 68, he became Prime Minister, to be dismissed by posterity as "an outstanding example of the leader whom the current of world events carried out of his depth".'

41. Neville Chamberlain to Ida Chamberlain, 28 March 1936, *NCDL*, pp. 182–3

42. Sir Henry 'Chips' Channon, diary, 15 May 1936, in *Chips*, p. 60

43. Pathe Budget, April 1936, ITN Archives

44. Robert Self, *Neville Chamberlain: A Biography*, p. 271

45. Speech to the Birmingham Jewellers' and Silversmiths' Association, 14 March 1936

46. Neville Chamberlain to Hilda Chamberlain, 14 November 1936, *NCDL*, pp. 218–21

Chapter 8: The house of things to come

1. Descriptions of the Ideal Home Exhibition, *Daily Mail* (24 March 1936), p. 6

2. Interview with Betty Clark

3. 'How London is Moving Out', *Daily Mail* (23 March 1936); London

Regional Council for Juvenile Employment annual report, March 1936

4. Ibid. See also Peter Scott, 'The State, Internal Migration, and the Growth of New Industrial Communities in Inter-War Britain', *English Historical Review*, vol. CXV, no. 461 (April 2000).

5. 'Artist's "Ideal Home" from Old Boxes', *Daily Mail* (16 March 1936)

6. Peter Scott, 'The Twilight World of Interwar British Hire Purchase', *Past & Present*, no. 177 (November 2002)

7. Interview with Professor Peter Scott; lending was running at an equivalent today of £4bn per annum (*A Tale of Two Britains*, BBC TV, September 2009); see also Professor Peter Scott, 'The Twilight World of Interwar Hire Purchase', *Past & Present*, no. 177 (November 2002)

8. *Daily Mail* (27 March 1936), p. 17

9. Ibid.

10. Interview with Professor Peter Scott, Reading University

11. The phrase was coined by Anthony Eden ten years later, in 1946

12. James Thomas, 'The Work of the Special Areas Commission', p. 175

13. Interview with John Prichard

14. Ibid.

15. Ibid.

16. Paul Vaughan, *Something in Linoleum* (Sinclair-Stevenson, London, 1984), p. 113

17. Ibid., p. 94

18. Interview with Paul Vaughan

19. Interview with Betty Clark

20. Peter Scott, 'Marketing mass home ownership and the creation of the modern working-class consumer in inter-war Britain', *Business History*, vol. 50, no. 1 (January 2008), pp. 4–25

21. Interview with Betty Clark

22. Peter Scott, 'Marketing mass home ownership . . .'

23. Interview with John Prichard

24. David F. Hutchings, *RMS Queen Mary: 50 Years of Splendour* (Kingfisher Railway Productions, Southampton, 1988), pp. 8–9

25. Interview with Dorothy 'Dorrie' Cooper

26. Deborah S. Ryan, *The Ideal Home Through The 20th Century* (Hazar, London, 1997), p. 61

27. Violet Milner, diary, 8 and 10 July 1936

28. David Strain, diary (referring to the Ideal Home Exhibition's travelling show in Belfast), 11 February 1936
29. Interview with Paul Vaughan
30. Charles Loch Mowat, *Britain between the Wars, 1918–1940* (Methuen & Co., London, 1955), pp. 443, 465; see also Peter Scott, 'Managing Door-to-Door Sales of Vacuum Cleaners in Interwar Britain', *Business History Review*, no. 82 (Winter 2008), pp. 761–88, for a fascinating account of the hard sell and sharp practices of vacuum-cleaner salesmen
31. Interview with Marguerite Patten
32. *The Shape of Things to Come* is the full title of H. G. Wells's 1933 novel.
33. *Daily Mail* (16 March 1936)
34. Deborah S. Ryan, *The Ideal Home through the 20th Century*, p. 84
35. Charles Loch Mowat, *Britain between the Wars 1918–1940*, p. 501
36. Interview with John Prichard
37. *Daily Mail* (17 March 1936)
38. *Daily Mail* (26 March 1936)
39. For example, *Daily Mail* (27 March 1936)
40. *Daily Mail* (20 March 1936)
41. Interview with John Prichard
42. Reported in the *Daily Mail* (21 March 1936)
43. Ibid., and obituary in *TIME* (29 April 1945)
44. W. H. Auden and Christopher Isherwood, *The Ascent of F6* (Faber & Faber, London, 1986), pp. 16, 17
45. Paul Vaughan, *Something in Linoleum*, p. 114

Chapter 9: The new King struggles to modernize

1. Fritz Hesse, *Hitler and the English* (Allan Wingate, London, 1954), p. 22
2. Sir Henry 'Chips' Channon, diary, 3 August 1936, *Chips*, p. 74
3. Quoted in Sarah Bradford, *King George VI*, p. 165
4. Philip Ziegler, the official biographer of Edward VIII, dismisses him as an unreliable witness, *King Edward VIII*, p. 267.
5. Lord Brownlow was a lord-in-waiting to the King who was later ostracized for his loyalty; Sir Henry 'Chips' Channon, diary, 12 February 1936, *Chips*, p. 58.

6. Sir Robert Bruce Lockhart, diary, 27 October 1936, in *The Diaries of Sir Robert Bruce Lockhart*, vol. 1, *1915–1938*, ed. Kenneth Young (Macmillan, London, 1973), p. 356

7. Referred to in Philip Ziegler, *King Edward VIII*, p. 236

8. Michael Bloch describes her stay with a lesbian party in Biarritz, in *Wallis and Edward*, p. 55.

9. Sarah Bradford, *King George VI*, p. 147

10. Edith Marchioness of Londonderry, *Retrospect* (F. Muller, London, 1938), p. 252

11. Quoted in Monica Baldwin, diary, 7 October 1937, Philip Williamson and Edward Baldwin (ed.), *Baldwin Papers,* p. 425

12. The King's Proctor, accounts of interviews with servants, The National Archives (TNA), TS22/1

13. Wallis Simpson to Aunt Bessie Merryman, 9 February 1936, Michael Bloch (ed.), *Wallis and Edward* p.181

14. Sir Henry 'Chips' Channon, diary, 11 June 1936, *Chips*, p. 65

15. Harold Nicolson to Vita Sackville-West, 19 February 1936, *Diaries and Letters*, ed. Nigel Nicolson, p. 244

16. Sarah Bradford, *King George VI*, p. 156

17. Quoted in A. Susan Williams, *The People's King*, p. 46

18. Sarah Bradford, *King George VI*, p. 156

19. Sir Henry 'Chips' Channon, diary, 17 November 1936, *Chips*, p. 80

20. John Weitz, *Hitler's Diplomat* (Weidenfeld & Nicolson, London, 1992), p. 88

21. Harold Nicolson, diaries, 10 April 1939, *Diaries and Letters*, ed. Nigel Nicolson, p. 396

22. John Weitz, *Hitler's Diplomat*, p. 93

23. Stanley Baldwin conversation with Osbert Sitwell, quoted in Philip Ziegler, *King Edward VIII*, p. 269

24. Edward, Prince of Wales, to Freda Dudley Ward, 27 April 1920, in Rupert Godfrey (ed.), *Letters from a Prince*, p. 289

25. Interview with John Prichard

26. Helen Hardinge, *Loyal to Three Kings*, p. 76

27. Quoted in Philip Ziegler, *King Edward VIII*, p. 258

28. Alan Lascelles, diary, 5 March 1943, *King's Counsellor*, pp. 104–13

29. Ibid.

30. Ibid.

31. The Duke of Windsor, *A King's Story*, p. 280

32. Philip Ziegler, *King Edward VIII*, p. 261; The Duke of Windsor, *A King's Story*, p. 292

33. Michael Bloch, *The Reign and Abdication of King Edward VIII* (Bantam, London, 1990), p. 36

34. Ibid.

35. Sarah Bradford, *King George VI*, p. 160

36. Ibid.

37. Frances Donaldson, *The Road to Abdication*, p. 48

38. The Duke of Windsor, *A King's Story*, p. 292

39. Ibid.

40. Ibid., p. 281

41. Helen Hardinge, *Loyal to Three Kings*, p. 82

42. The Duke of Windsor, *A King's Story*, p. 288

43. Robert Bernays, diary, 26 February 1936, *The Diaries and Letters of Robert Bernays, 1932–1939: An Insider's Account of the House of Commons*, ed. Nick Smart (Edwin Mellen Press, Lampeter, 1996), p. 243

44. The Duke of Windsor, *A King's Story*, p. 288

45. Sarah Bradford, *King George VI*, p. 161

46. Philip Ziegler, *King Edward VIII*, p. 274

47. Sarah Bradford, *King George VI*, p. 161

48. Michael Bloch, *The Reign and Abdication of Edward VIII*, p. 45, quoting Sir Walter Monckton

49. Helen Hardinge, *Loyal to Three Kings*, p. 90

50. Ibid., p. 92

51. Philip Ziegler, *King Edward VIII*, p. 279

52. Wallis Simpson to Aunt Bessie Merryman, 16 March 1936, Michael Bloch, *Wallis and Edward*, p. 191

53. Wallis Simpson to Aunt Bessie Merryman, 14 April 1936, Ibid., p. 194

54. Wallis Simpson to Aunt Bessie Merryman, 11 May 1936, Ibid., pp. 200–1

55. Ibid.

56. Ibid.

57. Edward VIII to Wallis Simpson, n.d., Ibid., p. 193

Chapter 10: The height of hypocrisy

1. The Duke of Windsor, *A King's Story*, p. 293

2. Duff Cooper, diary, 20 January 1936, *The Duff Cooper Diaries*, p. 230

3. Martin Pugh, *We Danced All Night* (Bodley Head, London, 2008), p. 145

4. *The Spectator* (31 July 1936)

5. Baldwin said this to the King directly, as he later told Cabinet colleagues. Cabinet Minutes, 27 November 1936, PRO, CAB 23/86 vol. LIII 69(36).

6. Duff Cooper, diary, 20 January 1936, *The Duff Cooper Diaries*, p. 226

7. Duff Cooper's account of the abdication, *The Duff Cooper Diaries*, p. 230

8. Ibid.

9. Wallis Simpson to Aunt Bessie Merryman, 24 February 1936, Michael Bloch (ed.), *Wallis and Edward*, p. 184

10. Thomas Jones, *A Diary with Letters*, Introduction, p. xxxiv

11. Andrew Lycett, *Rudyard Kipling*, p. 706

12. Ibid.

13. Martin Pugh, *We Danced All Night*, p. 159

14. Ibid.

15. H. Montgomery Hyde, *The Other Love: An Historical and Contemporary Survey of Homosexuality in Britain* (Heinemann, London, 1970), p. 197

16. Noel Annan, *Our Age* (Weidenfeld & Nicolson, London, 1990), p. 113

17. H. Montgomery Hyde, *The Other Love*, p. 200

18. Ibid. (Hyde calls the restaurant 'The Charles'.)

19. Noel Annan, *Our Age*, p. 113

20. Ibid.

21. *The Spectator* (31 July 1936)

22. David Strain, diary, 12 April 1936

23. Martin Pugh, *We Danced All Night*, p. 156 (Martin Pugh gives an excellent survey of attitudes to sex in the 1930s.)

24. David Strain, diary, 1 February 1936

25. The youth reminded him of a previous young man whom he had worshipped from afar.

26. David Strain, diary, 30 May and 7 December 1936

27. Jane Mulvagh, *Madresfield: One Home, One Family, One Thousand Years* (Doubleday, London, 2008), p. 305

Chapter 11: Mrs Baldwin delivers

1. Winifred Holtby, *South Riding* (Virago, London, 2007), p. 113
2. A. Susan Williams, *Women and Childbirth in the 20th Century*, p. 2
3. For a full discussion of maternal mortality see, for example, A. Susan Williams, *Women and Childbirth in the 20th Century: A History of the National Birthday Trust Fund, 1928–93* (Sutton, Stroud, 1997), and *Maternal Care*, Witnesses to 20th-Century Medicine, 12 (Wellcome Trust, London, 2001) http://www.ucl.ac.uk/silva/histmed/downloads/c20th_group/wit12.pdf.
4. Pilgrim Trust, *Men without Work*, p. 140
5. A. Susan Williams, *Women and Childbirth in the 20th Century*, Chapter 3, 'The 1936 Midwives Act', passim
6. The maternal death rate in the Rhondda in 1933 was almost 7 in 1,000. See A. Susan Williams, *Women and Childbirth in the 20th Century*, p. 74, and Keith Laybourn, *Britain on the Breadline: A Social and Political History of Britain 1918–1939* (Sutton, Stroud, 1990), p. 63.
7. Martin Pugh, *We Danced All Night*, pp. 146, 165–70
8. Ibid., p. 150
9. For a full discussion of eugenics and Marie Stopes see Richard Overy, *The Morbid Age*, Chapter 3, 'A Sickness in the Racial Body', p. 93.
10. Margery Spring Rice, *Working-Class Wives* (Virago, London, 1989), passim
11. Ibid., New Introduction by Barbara Wooton, p. iv. Out of 1,000 babies born in 1936, 56 were dead before they were a year old, Charles Loch Mowat, *Britain Between the Wars 1918–1940*, p. 515, n.; the Department of Health gives an overall rate of 4.8 deaths per 1,000 live births in England and Wales for the period 2006–8 (Department of Health, 3 December 2009, Mortality Target Monitoring (infant mortality, inequalities update) (www.dh.gov.uk/en/Publicationsandstatistics/Publications/PublicationsStatistics)).
12. Margery Spring Rice, *Working-Class Wives*, Notes, p. xi. 'One half of Social Class III women at risk used some form of birth control and one in four used any appliance (which would normally have been a condom).'
13. Lucy Thomas's memories are taken from Sean James Cameron, *Rhondda Voices*, part of the Tempus Oral History series (Sutton, Stroud, 2002), Chapter 8, pp. 93–107

14. Ibid., p. 94
15. Interview with Margaret Lloyd
16. Interview with Margaret Lloyd, with the comments that follow
17. Sean James Cameron, *Rhondda Voices*, p. 103
18. A. Susan Williams, *Women and Childbirth in the 20th Century*, p. 55
19. As Hans Singer discovered during his visit to south Wales (cf. Chapter 4, pp. 70–1)
20. Wellcome Trust, *Maternal Care*, p. 5
21. Kenneth Young, *Stanley Baldwin*, p. 80
22. A. Susan Williams, *Ladies of Influence*, p. 39
23. Ibid, p.57
24. Sean James Cameron, *Rhondda Voices*, p. 103
25. *Reports on Public Health and Medical Subjects* (HMSO, London, 1924), p. 5, quoted in Margery Spring Rice, *Working-Class Wives*, p.19
26. Thomas Jones to Lady Grigg, 1 June 1935, in Thomas Jones, *A Diary with Letters*, p. 150
27. A. Susan Williams, *Ladies of Influence*, p. 41
28. Wellcome Trust, *Maternal Care*, p. 5
29. A. Susan Williams, *Women and Childbirth in the 20th Century*, p. 59; see also Wellcome Trust, *Maternal Care*, p. 19
30. Wellcome Trust, *Maternal Care*, p. 19
31. Dame Janet Campbell, quoted from 1924, in Margery Spring Rice, *Working-Class Wives*, p. 18
32. Ibid., p. 35
33. A. Susan Williams, *Women and Childbirth in the 20th Century*, p. 99
34. James Thomas and A. Susan Williams, 'Women and Abortion in the 1930s', *Social History of Medicine*, vol. 11, no. 2 (1998), p. 284
35. Interview with Margaret Lloyd
36. James Thomas and A. Susan Williams, 'Women and Abortion in the 1930s', p. 284
37. A. Susan Williams, *Women and Childbirth in the 20th Century*, pp. 45–6
38. Robert Self, *Neville Chamberlain: A Biography*, p. 105
39. For example, widows' and orphans' pensions, abolition of the poor law, local government finance, educational provision and health provision by local authorities
40. Robert Self, *Neville Chamberlain: A Biography*, p. 133
41. Ibid., p. 62
42. A. Susan Williams, *Women and Childbirth in the 20th Century*, p. 64

43. Ibid., p. 63
44. In 1936 the National Government's other major reform was raising the school-leaving age from fourteen to fifteen, to start from 1939; but this did not come into effect because of the war.
45. Robert Self, *Neville Chamberlain: A Biography*, p. 133
46. Irvine Loudon, *Death in Childbirth* (Clarendon Press, Oxford, 1992), pp. 542–4
47. Irvine Loudon, *Death in Childbirth*, pp. 254–62, argues that the decline was also the result of raised standards of care as a consequence of the Midwives Act.
48. A. Susan Williams, *Women and Childbirth in the 20th Century*, p. 71

Chapter 12: The awful weight of war

1. Vera Brittain, *Testament of Experience*, p. 165
2. Sybille Bedford, *Aldous Huxley: A Biography*, vol. 1, *1894–1939* (Chatto & Windus, London, 1974), p. 308
3. R. Ellis Roberts, *H. R. L. Sheppard: Life and Letters* (John Murray, London, 1942), p. 106
4. Carolyn Scott, *Dick Sheppard* (Hodder & Stoughton, London, 1977), p. 214
5. R. Ellis Roberts, *Dick Sheppard: Life and Letters*, p. 246
6. Robert Bernays, diary, 28 May 1936, *The Diaries and Letters of Robert Bernays, 1932–1939*, p. 264
7. *Manchester Guardian* (16 October 1934)
8. Carolyn Scott, *Dick Sheppard*, p. 202
9. Sybille Bedford, *Aldous Huxley: A Biography*, vol. 1, p. 309
10. Richard Overy, *The Morbid Age*, p. 221
11. Ibid. Britain's population in 1936 was 46 million.
12. Pathe Gazette newsreel broadcast, October 1935
13. Margery Smith to Arthur Ponsonby, 6 June 1936, Ponsonby Papers, Bodleian Special Collections
14. Kenneth Young, *Stanley Baldwin*, p. 20
15. Information from Edward Baldwin, Lord Baldwin of Bewdley
16. For example, Philip Noel Baker, Lord Robert Cecil, both of the League of Nations Union, through the Focus Group; cf. Roy Jenkins, *Churchill*, pp. 493–500

17. Edward VIII, speech on the Presentation of the Colours to the three senior regiments of the Brigade of Guards, 16 July 1936
18. Carolyn Scott, *Dick Sheppard*, p. 62
19. *The Times* (3 April 1936)
20. Anthony Mockler, *Haile Selassie's War* (Signal Books, London, 1984), p. 82, and Thomas M. Coffey, *Lion by the Tail: The Story of the Italian Ethiopian War* (Hamish Hamilton, London, 1974), p. 263
21. *The Spectator* (10 April 1936)
22. Carolyn Scott, *Dick Sheppard*, p. 196
23. R. Ellis Roberts, *H. R. L. Sheppard*, p. 266
24. Jane Emery, *Rose Macaulay: A Writer's Life* (John Murray, London, 1991), p. 249. Chamberlain's words were 'Peace with honour', echoing Disraeli's words after the conference of Berlin in 1878.
25. Philip Ziegler, *King Edward VIII*, p. 271
26. Herbert Hensley Henson, diary, 3 June 1936
27. Stanley Baldwin speaking in the House of Commons, 10 November 1932
28. Stanley Baldwin speech, 4 April 1936, quoted in Keith Middlemas and John Barnes, *Baldwin: A Biography* (Weidenfeld & Nicolson, London, 1969), p. 937
29. Interview with Paul Vaughan
30. Ibid.
31. Nick Cooper, *'Things to Come' Viewing Notes* (Granada Ventures, London, 2007)
32. Interview with John Prichard
33. Richard Overy, *The Morbid Age*, p. 316
34. George Orwell, *Keep the Aspidistra Flying* (Penguin, London, 2000), p. 22
35. Herbert Hensley Henson, diary, 11 November 1936
36. Richard Overy, *The Morbid Age*, p. 225
37. Carolyn Scott, *Dick Sheppard*, p. 215
38. George Bernard Shaw et al., *St Martin's Review* special issue, 'H. R. L. Sheppard, Himself and His Work' (December 1937)
39. Dick Sheppard to Arthur Ponsonby, 31 August 1938, Ponsonby Papers, Bodleian Special Collections
40. Richard Overy, *The Morbid Age*, p. 215
41. Dick Sheppard to Arthur Ponsonby, 14 May 1936, Ponsonby Papers
42. Dick Sheppard to Arthur Ponsonby, 15 September 1936, Ponsonby Papers

43. Sir Ian Kershaw, *Making Friends with Hitler*, p. 64
44. Jane Emery, *Rose Macaulay*, p. 216
45. R. Ellis Roberts, *H. R. L. Sheppard*, p. 277
46. Ibid., p. 285
47. Ibid., p. 36
48. Sybille Bedford, *Aldous Huxley*, p. 312
49. Ibid.
50. Richard Overy, *The Morbid Age*, p. 248
51. Peace Pledge Union, www.ppu.org.uk/e_publications/huxleycase4.html
52. Margery South to Arthur Ponsonby, 28 December 1936, Ponsonby Papers; also in Richard Overy, *The Morbid Age*, p. 253
53. Richard Overy, *The Morbid Age*, p. 252
54. For example, the Communist poet Cecil Day-Lewis
55. Carolyn Scott, *Dick Sheppard*, p. 218
56. Paul Berry and Mark Bostridge, *Vera Brittain: A Life* (Virago, London, 2008), p. 349. I am grateful to Paul Berry and Mark Bostridge for detail of Vera Brittain's encounter with Dick Sheppard.
57. Vera Brittain, *Testament of Experience*, p. 165
58. Ibid.
59. Ibid., p. 167
60. Paul Berry and Mark Bostridge, *Vera Brittain: A Life*, p. 356
61. Vera Brittain, *Testament of Experience*, p. 170
62. Paul Berry and Mark Bostridge, *Vera Brittain: A Life*, p. 355
63. Ibid.
64. Vera Brittain, *Testament of Experience*, p. 171
65. Carolyn Scott, *Dick Sheppard*, p. 220
66. Paul Berry and Mark Bostridge, *Vera Brittain: A Life*, p. 354
67. R. Ellis Roberts, *H. R. L. Sheppard: Life and Letters*, pp. 292–5
68. Ibid., p. 287

Chapter 13: History forming in our hands

1. Mark Amory, *Lord Berners: The Last Eccentric* (Pimlico, London, 1999), p. 160
2. Gavin Bryars, 'The Berners Case', gavinbryars.com/Pages/writing_Lord_Berners.html

3. Mark Amory, *Lord Berners: The Last Eccentric*, p. 160
4. Salvador Dalí, *My Secret Life*, quoted at daliplanet.blogsome.com
5. Herbert Read, 'Why the English Have No Taste', *Minotaure* (7 June 1935), p. 67, quoted at http://revolutionaryboredom.wordpress.com
6. *Daily Mirror* (20 June 1936)
7. *Daily Express* and *Daily Mirror* (15 June 1936)
8. *The Listener* (17 June 1936)
9. *The Spectator* (19 June 1936)
10. Richard Davenport-Hines, *W. H. Auden*, p. 146
11. Herbert Read, *Introduction to Surrealism* (Faber and Faber, London, 1936), quoted at http://revolutionaryboredom.wordpress.com
12. Richard Baxell, *British Volunteers in the Spanish Civil War* (RKP, London, 2004), p. 7. I am grateful to Richard Baxell for his meticulous study of the British volunteers who fought in Spain.
13. Interview with John Prichard
14. Jason Gurney, *Crusade in Spain* (Readers' Union, London, 1974), p. 17
15. David Gascoyne, *Journal 1936–7* (Enitharmon Press, London, 1980), p. 24
16. Quoted in Tom Buchanan, *The Impact of the Spanish Civil War on Britain,* Sussex Studies in Spanish History (Sussex Academic Press, Brighton, 2007)
17. James Albrighton, diary, Marx Memorial Library (Box 50, L), Introduction, fol. 4
18. Jason Gurney, *Crusade in Spain*, p. 18
19. David Marshall, memories recorded for the Imperial War Museum Sound Archive, 9330/1/2
20. Peter Stansky and William Abrahams, *Journey to the Frontier: Julian Bell and John Cornford: Their Lives in the 1930s* (Constable, London, 1966), p. 132. I am grateful to the authors for their account of the life of John Cornford.
21. Noel Annan, *Our Age*, p. 185
22. Stanley Baldwin thought Winston Churchill lacked 'judgement and wisdom'; see Martin Gilbert, quoting Thomas Jones, diary, 22 May 1936, *WSC Documents*, p. 166.
23. A. L. Rowse, *The Spectator* (31 July 1936)
24. Esmond Romilly, *Boadilla*, p. 88
25. Ibid., p. 186

26. John Cornford, *Understand the Weapon*, ed. Jonathan Galassi (Carcanet New Press, Manchester, 1976), p. 160

27. I am grateful to Tom Buchanan of Oxford University for information about Felicia Browne. His essay 'The Lost Art of Felicia Browne', in Tom Buchanan, *The Impact of the Spanish Civil War on Britain* (Sussex Academic Press, Brighton, 2007), first drew attention to this enigmatic figure.

28. L. Susan Stebbing, 'In Memoriam', *Kingsley School Magazine*, no. 21 (October 1936)

29. Quoted in Tom Buchanan, 'The Lost Art of Felicia Browne', in *The Impact of the Spanish Civil War on Britain*, p. 65

30. Ibid.

31. Information from Revd Peter Marshall, Felicia Browne's nephew

32. L. Susan Stebbing, 'In Memoriam'

33. 'Felicia Browne An Appreciation', in *Drawings by Felicia Browne*, (Lawrence and Wishart, London, 1936)

34. Ibid.

35. Tom Buchanan, *The Impact of the Spanish Civil War on Britain*, p. 72

36. Ibid., p. 73

37. Noel Annan, *Our Age*, p. 184

38. Miranda Carter, *Anthony Blunt: His Lives* (Macmillan, London, 2001), p. 121

39. For example, Michael Straight, the American member of the Whitney family, son of the founder of Dartington Hall, Dorothy Elmhirst; Miranda Carter, *Anthony Blunt: His Lives*, p. 182

40. Peter Stansky and William Abrahams, *Journey to the Frontier*, p. 242

41. Ibid., p. 239

42. Ibid.

43. The photograph – one of the great photo-portraits of the 1930s – is in the National Portrait Gallery.

44. John Cornford's poems in John Cornford, *Understand the Weapon*: 'Sad Poem', p. 36; 'Sergei Mironovitch Kirov', p. 35

45. Noel Annan, *Our Age*, p. 185

46. Peter Stansky and William Abrahams, *Journey to the Frontier*, p. 246

47. David Marshall, IWM Sound Archive 9330/1/2

48. I am grateful to Revd Peter Marshall, Felicia Browne's nephew, for this information.

49. Felicia Browne to Elizabeth Watson, 12 July 1936 (mistakenly dated

June); I am grateful to Tom Buchanan for providing me with the Felicia Browne letters.

50. The National Archives Special Branch report 300/NM/204, 11 July 1936

51. Felicia Browne to Elizabeth Watson, undated August 1936

52. Ibid.

52. Ibid.

53. Ibid.

54. Ibid.

55. Ibid.

56. *Daily Express* (2 August 1936)

57. John Cornford, *Understand the Weapon*, p. 181

58. Ibid., p. 171

59. Peter Stansky and William Abrahams, *Journey to the Frontier*, p. 359

60. Ibid., p. 326

61. John Cornford diary letter to Margot Heinemann, 16–30 August 1936, *Understand the Weapon*, p. 171

62. Peter Stansky and William Abrahams, *Journey to the Frontier*, p. 328

63. Felicia Browne to Elizabeth Watson, August 1936

64. Georges Brinkman typescript, 30 August 1936, Marx Memorial Library, Box 21/B/1a

65. Ibid.

66. *Daily Worker* (4 September 1936)

67. 'Felicia Browne An Appreciation', in *Drawings by Felicia Browne*

68. Ibid.

69. John Cornford, *Understand the Weapon*, p. 171

70. Ibid., p. 175

71. Peter Stansky and William Abrahams, *Journey to the Frontier*, p. 338

72. Ibid., p. 341

73. Ibid.

74. Ibid., p. 345

75. Ibid., p. 347

76. John Cornford, *Understand the Weapon*, p. 38

77. Peter Stansky and William Abrahams, *Journey to the Frontier*, p. 344

78. Ibid., p. 346

79. John Cornford, *Understand the Weapon*, p. 41

80. It is difficult to establish exact numbers of casualties. These figures come from Peter Stansky and William Abrahams, *Journey to the Frontier*,

p. 365; Richard Baxell estimates that roughly 2,500 British volunteers fought in the Spanish Civil War and explains that record-keeping of casualties was haphazard (Richard Baxell, *British Volunteers in the Spanish Civil War*, Chapter 1, 'Who Were the British Volunteers?', passim).

81. Quoted in Peter Stansky and William Abrahams, *Journey to the Frontier*, p. 360

Chapter 14: Eternal gossip around the situation

1. I am grateful to Lady Sophy Cavendish for this information.
2. Robert Bernays, diary, 28 May 1936, *The Diaries and Letters of Robert Bernays, 1932–1939*, p. 264
3. *Tatler* (3 June 1936)
4. Hermione, Countess of Ranfurly, *The Ugly One*, p. 159
5. Ibid.
6. Joyce Grenfell to her mother, Nora Langhorne, 15 June 1936, *Darling Ma*, p. 12
7. *Tatler* (3 June 1936) gives the typical ball dinner menu.
8. Joyce Grenfell to her mother, Nora Langhorne, 15 June, 1936, *Darling Ma*, p. 12
9. *Cavalcade* (15 August 1936), p. 9
10. Sibyl Colefax to Bernard Berenson, undated June 1936, Bodleian Library, Special Collections, Sibyl Colefax Papers Ms. Eng. C.3176
11. Ibid.
12. Mark Amory, *Lord Berners: The Last Eccentric*, p. 160; see also Kirsty McLeod, *A Passion for Friendship: Sibyl Colefax and Her Circle* (Michael Joseph, London, 1991), p. 98
13. Sir Robert Bruce Lockhart, diary, 10 June 1936, *The Diaries of Sir Robert Bruce Lockhart*, p. 345
14. Harold Nicolson to Vita Sackville-West, 11 June 1936, Harold Nicolson, *Diaries and Letters*, p. 263
15. Ibid.
16. Ibid.
17. Kenneth Clark, *Another Part of the Wood* (John Murray, London, 1974), p. 214
18. Mark Amory, *Lord Berners: The Last Eccentric*, p. 161

19. Kenneth Clark, *Another Part of the Wood*, p. 215
20. Sir Robert Bruce Lockhart, diary, 10 June 1936, *The Diaries of Sir Robert Bruce Lockhart*, p.345
21. Rubinstein denied that the King was either bored or offended. Cf. Philip Ziegler, *King Edward VIII*, p. 204.
22. Interview with Marguerite Patten
23. Francis Watson, *Dawson of Penn: A Biography* (Chatto & Windus, London, 1951), p. 285
24. Sir Henry 'Chips' Channon, diary, 16 July 1936, *Chips*, p. 70
25. The Duke of Windsor, *A King's Story*, p. 298
26. Philip Ziegler, *King Edward VIII*, p. 264
27. Anne de Courcy, *1939: The Last Season* (Thames and Hudson, London, 1989), p. 36
28. *Tatler* (23 July 1936)
29. *Daily Express* (22 July 1936)
30. Sir Henry 'Chips' Channon, diary, 6 July 1936, *Chips*, p. 68
31. Ibid.
32. To R. A. Butler when he was Parliamentary Under-Secretary at the Foreign Office
33. Sir Henry 'Chips' Channon, diary 7 July 1936, *Chips*, p. 68
34. Sir Henry 'Chips' Channon, diary, 2 July 1936, Ibid.
35. Sir Henry 'Chips' Channon, diary, 8 July 1936, Ibid., p.69
36. Anne De Courcy, *1939: The Last Season*, p. 132
37. Quoted by Robert Rhodes James in *Chips*, Introduction, p.7
38. Sir Henry 'Chips' Channon, diary, 1 August 1936, *Chips*, p. 73
39. Ibid.
40. Ibid.
41. Ibid.
42. Helen Hardinge, *Loyal to Three Kings*, p. 106
43. *Cavalcade* (15 August 1936)
44. The Duke of Windsor, *A King's Story*, p. 306
45. Duff Cooper, *The Duff Copper Diaries*, illustration opposite p. 179
46. *Cavalcade* (22 August 1936), p. 7
47. Frances Donaldson, *Edward VIII: The Road to Abdication*, p. 106
48. *Daily Mirror* (12 August 1936), p. 3
49. The Duke of Windsor, *A King's Story*, p. 307
50. Philip Ziegler, *King Edward VIII*, p. 285
51. Helen Hardinge, *Loyal to Three Kings*, p. 108

Chapter 15: The Berlin Olympics

1. Interview with Dorothy Tyler
2. Guy Walters, *Berlin Games*, p. 187, and Pathe Newsreel Review of the Year (1936)
3. Joachim von Ribbentrop, *The Ribbentrop Memoirs*, p. 63
4. Sir Ian Kershaw, *Making Friends with Hitler*, p. 173
5. Reproduced in Stan Cohen, *The Games of '36: A Pictorial History of the 1936 Olympics in Germany* (Pictorial Histories Publishing Company Inc., Missoula, 1996), p. 68
6. Ibid.
7. *The Spectator* (7 August 1936)
8. Interview with Dorothy Tyler
9. Sir Ian Kershaw, *Making Friends with Hitler*, p. 163
10. Thomas Jones, diary, 17 May 1936, *A Diary with Letters*, p. 200
11. Ibid., p. 205
12. Keith Middlemas and John Barnes, *Baldwin: A Biography*, p. 956
13. Lucy Baldwin, diary, June and July 1936, passim
14. Lucy Baldwin, diary, 16, 17, 18, 19 June 1936
15. Stanley Baldwin to Joan Davidson, 3 August 1936, in Philip Williamson and Edward Baldwin (ed.), *Baldwin Papers*, p. 380
16. Ibid.
17. Details taken from Stan Cohen, *The Games of '36*, p. 63, and Guy Walters, *Berlin Games*, p. 193
18. Guy Walters, *Berlin Games*, p. 220
19. *The Spectator* (7 August 1936)
20. Guy Walters's excellent account of the Olympics explains this.
21. Martin Pugh, *We Danced All Night*, p. 292
22. Hitler's deputy flew to Britain to meet the Duke of Hamilton in May 1940.
23. Jan Dalley, *Diana Mosley: A Life* (Faber, London, 1999), p. 206
24. Guy Walters, *Berlin Games*, p. 253
25. Interview with Diana Mosley (Blakeway Productions for Channel 4 Television, 2003)
26. Ibid.
27. Ibid.
28. Ibid.
29. Vansittart MSS, The National Archives: PRO, FO 371, 800, Cabinet

Papers and minutes, quoted in *Dictionary of National Biography* (Vansittart, Robert Gilbert, Baron Vansittart)

30. Sir Henry 'Chips' Channon, diary, 11 August 1936, *Chips*, p. 109
31. Joachim von Ribbentrop, *The Ribbentrop Memoirs*, p. 63
32. James Douglas-Hamilton, *The Truth about Rudolf Hess* (Mainstream Publishing, Edinburgh, 1993), p. 66
33. Ibid., p. 64
34. Interview with Dorothy Tyler
35. Quoted in John Samuel, obituary of Godfrey Rampling, *Guardian* (8 July 2009)
36. Ibid. Abrahams was the athlete featured in the film *Chariots of Fire* (1981).
37. Stan Cohen, *The Games of '36*, p. 212
38. Description given by George Ward Price, *Daily Mail* Berlin correspondent, taken from James Douglas-Hamilton, *The Truth about Rudolf Hess*, p. 67; also in Guy Walters, *Berlin Games*, pp. 255–6.
39. Letter to *The Times* (27 August 1936)
40. Guy Walters, *Berlin Games*, p. 256
41. Martin Bormann, *Hitler's Table-Talk: Hitler's Conversations Recorded by Martin Bormann*, intro. by Hugh Trevor-Roper (Oxford University Press, Oxford, 1988), p. 15
42. Charlotte Mosley (ed.), *The Mitfords: Letters between Six Sisters*, p. 70
43. IOC website, www.olympic.org
44. Leader, *The Times* (17 August 1936)
45. It was so large that after the Second World War the building housed the British Sector HQ, British Military Government and the British Berlin Infantry Brigade; Stan Cohen, *The Games of '36*, p. 38.
46. Guy Walters, *Berlin Games*, p. 162
47. John Samuel, obituary of Godfrey Rampling, *Guardian* (8 July 2009)
48. Sir Henry 'Chips' Channon, diary, 13 August 1936, *Chips*, p. 110
49. *Schuplattling* is a Bavarian fertility folk-dance where young men slap their thighs and knees and stamp their feet.
50. Guy Walters, *Berlin Games*, p. 147
51. Before the advent of polling it is difficult be exact about this, but there is no evidence of widespread support for Hitler.
52. Harold Nicolson, *Letters and Diaries*, 20 September 1936, p. 273
53. Lord Decies letter, *The Times* (19 August 1936)

Chapter 16: They shall not pass

1. Richard Baxell, *British Volunteers*, p. 31. Richard Overy (*The Morbid Age*, p. 267), gives the figure of 22,500 for the beginning of the war, of whom 8,000 were active.
2. *Yesterday's Witness: The Battle of Cable Street* (BBC TV, 4 January 1970)
3. Interview with Nicholas Mosley, *Diana Mosley* (Blakeway Productions for Channel 4 Television, 2003)
4. George Orwell, 'The Road to Wigan Pier Diary', p. 231
5. *The Spectator* (27 March 1936)
6. *Yesterday's Witness: The Battle of Cable Street*
7. Peter Catterall (ed.), 'The Battle of Cable Street', *Contemporary Record*, vol. 8, no. 1 (summer 1994) (henceforth referred to as '*Witness* seminar'), p. 107. Robert Skidelsky gives the figure as 350,000, of whom about 230,000 lived in London, 150,000 in the East End: see Robert Skidelsky, *Oswald Mosley* (Macmillan, London, 1981), p. 393.
8. David Rosenberg, *The Cable Street Riots* (C4TV, Channel4.com)
9. *Yesterday's Witness: The Battle of Cable Street*
10. *Witness* seminar, p. 108
11. Robert Skidelsky, *Oswald Mosley*, p. 404
12. *Witness* seminar, p. 122
13. *Yesterday's Witness: The Battle of Cable Street*
14. *Witness* seminar, p. 127
15. Ibid., p. 125
16. Robert Skidelsky, *Oswald Mosley*, p. 415
17. *Witness* seminar, p. 108
18. Ibid., p. 120
19. Ibid., p. 125
20. Phil Piratin was later elected Communist MP for Mile End, Stepney.
21. Both in *Yesterdays's Witness: The Battle of Cable Street* and in *Witness* seminar, p. 114
22. *The Times* (5 October 1936)
23. *Witness* seminar, p. 125
24. *News Chronicle* (5 October 1936)
25. *Witness* seminar, p. 126
26. Charlie Goodman, interviewed by Steve Humphreys, *Forbidden Britain* (BBC TV, 1993–4), © Testimony Films (recording and typed

transcript available at British Library Sound Archive collection, ref. C590/02/35)

27. *Witness* seminar, p. 127
28. Ibid.
29. Charlie Goodman, *Forbidden Britain*
30. Ibid.
31. Ibid.
32. Figures taken from Jan Dalley, *Diana Mosley: A Life*, p. 212
33. *Witness* seminar, p. 131
34. *Yesterday's Witness: The Battle of Cable Street*
35. The National Archives (TNA) CAB/24/264, Preservation of Public Order 12/10/36
36. Ibid.
37. *Yesterday's Witness: The Battle of Cable Street*
38. *Diana Mosley* (Blakeway Productions for Channel 4, 2003)
39. Diana Mosley to Unity Mitford, 17 September 1936, Charlotte Mosley (ed.), *The Mitfords: Letters between Six Sisters*, p. 76
40. Diana Mosley to Unity Mitford, 7 October 1936, Charlotte Mosley (ed.), *The Mitfords: Letters between Six Sisters*, p. 78
41. Interview with Diana Mosley for *Diana Mosley* (Blakeway Productions for Channel 4, 2003). The photograph was confiscated by the authorities when she was imprisoned during the war
42. Interview with Diana Mosley for *Diana Mosley* (Blakeway Productions for Channel 4, 2003)

Chapter 17: The Jarrow march: tragedy and triumph

1. Ellen Wilkinson, *The Town That Was Murdered: The Life Story of Jarrow* (Victor Gollancz, London, 1939), p. 201
2. *Yesterday's Witness: The Jarrow Crusade* (BBC TV, 19 May 1971)
3. Ellen Wilkinson, *The Town That Was Murdered*, p. 191
4. Jean Clark, *Yesterday's Witness: The Jarrow Crusade*
5. J. B. Priestley, *English Journey*, p. 259
6. Matt Perry, *The Jarrow Crusade: Protest and Legend* (University of Sunderland Press, Sunderland, 2005), p.112. I am grateful to Matt Perry for his fine account of the march, its causes and consequences, and its place in history.

7. Matt Perry, *The Jarrow Crusade: Protest and Legend*, p. 86

8. Ellen Wilkinson, *The Town That Was Murdered*, p. 196

9. Ibid.

10. Ibid., p. 192

11. Matt Perry, *The Jarrow Crusade: Protest and Legend*, p. 143

12. Ellen Wilkinson, *The Town That Was Murdered*, p. 200

13. Ibid.

14. *Yesterday's Witness: The Jarrow Crusade*

15. *Manchester Guardian* (13 October 1936)

16. *Shields Gazette* (5 October 1936)

17. Quoted at www.bbc.co.uk/history, 'The Jarrow Crusade'

18. Peter Ritchie-Calder, later Baron Ritchie-Calder. He wrote under the by-line Ritchie Calder; *Yesterday's Witness: The Jarrow Crusade*.

19. *Shields Gazette* (5 October 1936)

20. Herbert Hensley Henson, diary, 6 October 1936

21. Matt Perry, *The Jarrow Crusade: Protest and Legend*, pp. 41, 45; *The Times* (9 October 1936)

22. Jean Clark, speaking on *Yesterday's Witness: The Jarrow Crusade*, remembers this puritanical viewpoint.

23. Matt Perry, *The Jarrow Crusade: Protest and Legend*, p. 34

24. *Yesterday's Witness: The Jarrow Crusade*

25. Ellen Wilkinson, *The Town That Was Murdered*, p. 203

26. Matt Perry, The *Jarrow Crusade: Protest and Legend*, p. 53

27. Ellen Wilkinson, *The Town That Was Murdered*, p. 202

28. *Yesterday's Witness: The Jarrow Crusade*

29. I am indebted to Matt Perry, *The Jarrow Crusade: Protest and Legend*, for much of this information.

30. Ibid., p. 124

31. Quoted in Ian Jack, 'Jarrow – Serious Fuel for Thought', *Independent* (9 November 2000)

32. TNA CAB/24/264, Minutes of Cabinet meeting, 14 October 1936

33. TNA CAB/24/264m March of the Unemployed on London. Memorandum by the Home Secretary; and CAB/23/85 Minutes of Cabinet meeting

34. James Thomas, 'The Work of the Special Areas Commission', passim

35. Neville Chamberlain to Ida Chamberlain, 22 November 1936, *NCDL*, pp. 222–3

36. James Thomas, 'The Work of the Special Areas Commission', p. 63
37. *North Mail* (12 November 1936)
38. Neville Chamberlin to Ida Chamberlain, 22 November 1936, *NCDL*, pp. 222–3
39. Peter Scott, 'The State of Internal Migration and the Growth of Industrial Communities in Inter–War Britain', *English Historical Review*, vol. CXV, no. 461 (April 2000)
40. Harry Stoddart and Robert Suddick to Leonard Burrows, 14 October 1936, quoted in Matt Perry, *The Jarrow Crusade: Protest and Legend*, p.78
41. Matt Perry, *The Jarrow Crusade: Protest and Legend*, p. 78
42. *Yesterday's Witness: The Jarrow Crusade*
43. Description of the day from Ellen Wilkinson, *The Town That Was Murdered*, p. 208
44. *Shields Gazette* (21 October 1936)
45. Herbert Hensley Henson, diary, 22 October 1936
46. Letter to *The Times* (24 October 1936), p. 13
47. *The Spectator* (30 October 1936)
48. Matt Perry, *The Jarrow Crusade: Protest and Legend*, p. 126
49. Ibid., pp. 134, 145
50. *The Times* (2 November 1936)
51. *Shields Gazette* (31 October 1936)
52. Ibid.
53. Matt Perry, *The Jarrow Crusade: Protest and Legend*, p. 141
54. *Shields Gazette* (3 November 1936)
55. Matt Perry, *The Jarrow Crusade: Protest and Legend*, p. 148
56. Ibid., p. 159
57. Ibid., p. 121
58. Letter to *The Times* (2 September 1936)
59. *The Times* (12 October 1936)
60. Ellen Wilkinson, *The Town That Was Murdered*, p. 211
61. *Shields Gazette* (5 November 1936)
62. Ibid.
63. Matt Perry, *The Jarrow Crusade: Protest and Legend*, p. 160
64. Ellen Wilkinson, *The Town That Was Murdered*, p. 210
65. Ibid., p. 209
66. *Shields Gazette*, special anniversary edition (1986)
67. *Shields Gazette* (6 November 1936)

68. Ibid.
69. Ibid.
70. Interview with Marguerite Patten

Chapter 18: Something must be done

1. Michael Bloch, *Ribbentrop* (Bantam Press, London, 1992), p. 111
2. Thomas Jones, diary, 5 September 1936, in *A Diary with Letters*, p. 248
3. Reinhardt Spitzy, *How We Squandered the Reich*, trans. G. T. Waddington (Michael Russell, Norwich, 1997), p. 76
4. Michael Bloch, *Ribbentrop*, p. 113
5. Reinhard Spitzy, *How We Squandered the Reich*, p. 141
6. Joachim von Ribbentrop, *The Ribbentrop Memoirs*, p. 69
7. Sarah Bradford, *King George VI*, p. 172
8. J. G. Lockhart, *Cosmo Gordon Lang*, p. 396
9. Ibid., p. 397
10. Susan Williams, *The People's King*, p. 100
11. Sarah Bradford, *King George VI*, pp. 171–2
12. The Duke of Windsor, *A King's Story*, p. 315
13. *The Spectator* (4 December 1936)
14. Winston Churchill to Bernard Baruch, 1 January 1937, Martin Gilbert, *WSC Documents*, p. 520
15. Neville Chamberlain to Hilda Chamberlain, 17 October 1936, *NCDL*, pp. 212–13
16. Quoted in Monica Baldwin, diary, 7 October 1937, in Philip Williamson and Edward Baldwin (ed.), *Baldwin Papers*, p. 419
17. Baldwin described the interview to the Cabinet, 27 November 1936, TNA CAB23/86, vol. LIII.
18. William Deedes, in Charles Moore and Christopher Hawtree, *1936 As Recorded by The Spectator*, p. 317
19. Harold Nicolson, diary, 28 October 1936, Harold Nicolson, *Diaries and Letters*, p. 276
20. Cecil Beaton, *Self-Portrait with Friends: The Selected Diaries of Cecil Beaton 1926–1974*, ed. Richard Buckle (Weidenfeld & Nicolson, London, 1972), p. 47
21. *Yesterday's Witness: The Jarrow Crusade*
22. Quoted in Helen Hardinge, *Loyal to Three Kings*, p. 123

23. Susan Williams, *The People's King*, p. 93
24. Geoffrey Dawson, diary, 13 November 1936, Bodleian Library, Special Collections, MSS Dawson 1-93
25. Neville Chamberlain to Hilda Chamberlain, 14 November 1936, *NCDL*, pp. 218–21
26. As described in conversation with Stanley Baldwin, 26 October 1937, Thomas Jones, *A Diary with Letters*, pp. 370–1
27. Ibid.
28. Geoffrey Dawson, diary, 13 November 1936
29. Thomas Jones, diary, 26 October 1937, in *A Diary with Letters*, p. 371
30. Neville Chamberlain to Hilda Chamberlain, 14 November 1936, *NCDL*, pp. 218–21
31. Frances Donaldson, *Edward VIII: The Road to Abdication*, p. 119
32. Ibid., p. 121
33. Sir Robert Bruce Lockhart, diary, 22 November 1936, *The Diaries of Sir Robert Bruce Lockhart*, p. 358
34. The Duke of Windsor, *A King's Story*, p. 331
35. Quoted in Monica Baldwin, diary, 7 October 1937, in Philip Williamson and Edward Baldwin (ed.), *Baldwin Papers*, p. 422
36. Frances Donaldson, *Edward VIII: The Road to Abdication*, p. 129, and Monica Baldwin, diary, 7 October 1937 in Philip Williamson and Edward Baldwin (ed.), *Baldwin Papers*, p. 422
37. Frances Donaldson, *Edward VIII: The Road to Abdication*, p. 129
38. The Duke of Windsor, *A King's Story*, p. 332
39. Ibid.
40. Ramsay MacDonald, diary, 16 November 1936, TNA, PRO 30/69, 1753
41. Duff Cooper, diary, 16 November 1936, in *The Duff Cooper Diaries*, p. 229
42. James Pope-Hennessy, *Queen Mary*, p. 575
43. James Thomas, 'The Work of the Special Areas Commission', passim
44. *South Wales Echo and Evening Express* (18 November 1936)
45. Ibid.
46. A. Susan Williams, *Women and Childbirth in the 20th Century*, p. 35
47. Susan Williams, *The People's King*, p. 1
48. Interview with Iorweth Williams
49. Ibid.

Chapter 19: The Cornwall plan

1. Ramsay MacDonald, diary, 21 November 1936, TNA, 30/69 1753
2. *The Times* (24 November 1936)
3. *Daily Mail* (23 November 1936)
4. The Duke of Windsor, *A King's Story*, p. 338
5. Susan Williams was granted access to the Royal Archives at Windsor Castle and has detailed many of the letters in *The People's King*.
6. Quoted in Susan Williams, *The People's King*, pp. 9–10
7. Sarah Bradford, *King George VI*, p. 238
8. Speech to House of Commons, 12 November 1936, *WSC Documents*, p. 406
9. Neville Chamberlain to Hilda Chamberlain, 14 November 1936, *NCDL*, pp. 218–21
10. Lord Salisbury to Winston Churchill, 5 December 1936, in *WSC Documents*, p. 456
11. Susan Williams, *The People's King*, p. 172
12. Winston Churchill, 'The Abdication of King Edward VIII', December 1936, in *WSC Documents*, p. 450
13. The Duke of Windsor, *The King's Story*, p. 341
14. Monica Baldwin account of conversation with her uncle Stanley Baldwin, diary, 7 October 1937, in Philip Williamson and Edward Baldwin (ed.), *Baldwin Papers*, p. 421
15. Attlee told the Prime Minister that Labour would not touch the morganatic marriage proposal 'with a bargepole'; TNA Cab23/86, vol. LIII.
16. Keith Middlemas and John Barnes, *Baldwin: A Biography*, p. 999
17. Leo Amery, diary, 4 December 1936, Leo Amery, *The Empire at Bay: The Leo Amery Diaries*, ed. John Barnes and David Nicholson, Foreword by Lord Stockton (Hutchinson, London, 1988), p. 432
18. Sir Henry 'Chips' Channon, diary, 22 November 1936, *Chips*, p. 103
19. Ibid.
20. Violet Milner, diary, 19 and 24 November 1936
21. Quoted in Monica Baldwin, diary, 7 October 1937, in Philip Williamson and Edward Baldwin (ed.), *Baldwin Papers*, p. 421
22. Minutes of the Cabinet meeting, 27 November 1936, TNA CAB 23/86, vol. LIII

23. This had been suggested in an open letter by Lady Houston on King Edward's accession to the throne.

24. Quoted in Monica Baldwin, diary, 7 October 1937, in Philip Williamson and Edward Baldwin (ed.), *Baldwin Papers*, p. 421

25. Geoffrey Dawson diary, Bodleian Library Special Collections

26. TNA CAB 23/86, vol. LIII

27. Note from Lord Zetland to Lord Linlithgow, 27 November 1936, quoted in *WSC Documents*, p. 440

28. Lord Beaverbrook, *The Abdication of Edward VIII*, quoted in A. Susan Williams, *The People's King*, p. 118

29. Interview with Mary Soames, *Abdication: A Very British Coup*, Blakeway Productions (BBC TV, 2006/7); Mary Soames, *Speaking for Themselves*, p. 418

30. Duff Cooper, *The Duff Cooper Diaries*, 30 November 1936, p. 234

31. TNA CAB 23/86, vol. LIII, Confidential Annex, opened to the public in 2003 as part of the Open Government initiative

32. TNA CAB 127/156, 2 December 1936

33. The change to the typewritten document in Hankey's handwriting can be seen on p. 1 of the Confidential Annex, TNA CAB 23/86, vol. III.

34. The Duke of Windsor, *A King's Story*, p. 355

35. Diary entries 2/3 December 1936: Sir Henry 'Chips' Channon, *Chips*, pp. 88–9; Harold Nicolson, *Harold Nicolson Diaries and Letters*, p. 281; Duff Cooper, *The Duff Cooper Diaries*, p. 235.

36. David Strain, diary, 1 December 1936

37. Quoted in William Shawcross, *The Queen Mother: The Official Biography* (Macmillan, London, 2009), p. 380

38. Duff Cooper, *The Duff Cooper Diaries*, 2 December 1936, p. 236

39. Violet Milner, diary, 3 December 1936

40. Sir Henry 'Chips' Channon, diary, 3 December 1936, *Chips*, p. 89

41. Herbert Hensley Henson, diary, 3 and 4 December 1936

42. Geoffrey Dawson, diary, 2 December 1936

43. Susan Williams, *The People's King*, p. 136

44. Ibid.

45. H. Montgomery Hyde, *The Londonderrys: A Family Portrait* (Hamish Hamilton, London, 1979), p. 238

46. The Duke of Windsor, *A King's Story*, p. 356

47. Philip Ziegler, *King Edward VIII*, p. 315

48. TNA CAB 2/86, vol. LIII, minutes of Cabinet meeting, 4 December 1936

49. Kenneth Young, *Baldwin*, p. 138, and TNA CAB 2/86, vol. LIII, minutes of Cabinet meeting, 4 December 1936

50. Robert Bernays, diary, 15 December 1936, *The Diaries and Letters of Robert Bernays, 1932–1939*, p. 280

51. TNA CAB 23/86, vol. LIII, minutes of Cabinet meeting, 4 December 1936, p. 18

52. Wallis Simpson to Edward VIII, 6 December 1936, in Michael Bloch (ed.), *Wallis and Edward*, p. 243

53. Notebook kept by Lord Brownlow, Brownlow Papers, BNLW 4/4/9/1, and quoted in Susan Williams, *The People's King*

54. Susan Williams, *The People's King*, p. 152

55. As Churchill described it to Robert Bernays, *The Diaries and Letters of Robert Bernays, 1932–1939*, p. 277

56. Churchill notes on abdication, December 1936, *WSC Documents*, p. 450

57. Winston Churchill to Prime Minister, 5 December 1936, *WSC Documents*, p. 455

58. TNA CAB 23/86, vol. III, notes of a meeting of Ministers, 6 December 1936, p .1

59. Winston Churchill, press statement, 5 December 1936, *WSC Documents*, p. 457

60. Neville Chamberlain to Hilda Chamberlain, 13 December 1936, *NCDL*, pp. 227–8

61. CAB 23/86, vol. LIII, minutes of Cabinet meeting, 6 December 1936

62. Robert Bruce Lockhart, diary, 4 December 1936, *The Diaries of Sir Robert Bruce Lockhart, 1915–1938*, p. 359

63. The Duke of Windsor, *A King's Story*, p. 384

64. Camera Press Photography Agency, abdication photograph of crowds in London, December 1936

65. Quoted in Susan Williams, *The People's King*, p. 167

66. Robert Skidelsky, *John Maynard Keynes*, vol. 2, *The Economist as Saviour*, p. 628

67. Geoffrey H. Wells, diary, 4 December 1936

68. Evelyn Waugh, diary, 4–8 December 1936, *The Diaries of Evelyn Waugh*, ed. Michael Davie (Weidenfeld & Nicolson, London, 1976) p. 415

69. Neville Chamberlain to Ida Chamberlain, 8 December 1936, *NCDL*, pp. 226–7

70. Robert Bruce Lockhart, diary, 17 August 1936, *The Diaries of Sir Robert Bruce Lockhart*, p. 352

71. Lord Rothermere to Winston Churchill, 17 December 1936, in *WSC Documents*, p. 438, n.

72. Winston Churchill to King Edward VIII, evening of 5 December 1936, *WSC Documents*, p. 455

73. Ibid.

74. The Duke of Windsor, *A King's Story*, p. 385

75. Interview with John Prichard

76. Philip Ziegler, *King Edward VIII*, p. 322

77. Herbert Hensley Henson, diary, 9 December 1936

78. Interviews with John Prichard and Marguerite Patten

79. Robert Bruce Lockhart, diary, 10 December 1936, *The Diaries of Sir Robert Bruce Lockhart, 1915–1938*, p. 361

80. Harold Nicolson to Vita Sackville-West, 7 December 1936, *Diaries and Letters*, p. 282

81. Harold Nicolson, diary, 8 December 1936, *Diaries and Letters*, p. 283

82. Leo Amery, diary, 7 December 1936, Leo Amery, *The Empire at Bay*, p. 433

83. Ibid.

84. Thomas Dugdale, diary, 8 December 1936, in Philip Ziegler, *King Edward VIII*, p. 322

85. The Duke of Windsor, *A King's Story*, p. 402

86. Kenneth Young, *Stanley Baldwin*, p. 138

87. TNA CAB 23/86, vol. LIII, and Robert Bernays, diary, 15 December 1936, *The Diaries and Letters of Robert Bernays, 1932–1939*, p. 280

88. Philip Ziegler, *King Edward VIII*, p. 324

89. The Duke of Windsor, *A King's Story*, p. 396

90. Philip Ziegler, *King Edward VIII*, p. 312

91. Susan Williams, *The People's King*, passim

92. Telegram, 8 December 1936, HO 144/21070/1

93. The Duke of Windsor, *A King's Story*, p. 403

94. Ibid., p. 410

95. Frances Donaldson, *King Edward VIII*, p. 130

96. Sarah Bradford, *King George VI*, p. 198; Philip Ziegler, *King Edward VIII*, p. 329

97. Robert Bernays, diary, 15 December 1936, *The Diaries and Letters of Robert Bernays, 1932–1939*, p. 280
98. Ibid., p. 279
99. Harold Nicolson, diary, 10 December 1936, *Diaries and Letters*, p. 284
100. Lucy Baldwin, diary, 10 December 1936
101. TNA Prem 1/455
102. Kenneth Young, *Stanley Baldwin*, p. 139
103. Harold Nicolson, diary, 10 December 1936, *Diaries and Letters*, p. 284
104. Ibid.
105. Recollections of Samuel Howes, chauffeur, in *WSC Documents*, p. 503
106. Interview with William Deedes, Blakeway Productions, *Reputations: King George VI* (BBC TV, 1997)
107. James Pope-Hennessy, *Queen Mary*, p. 581
108. The Duke of Windsor, *A King's Story*, p. 413
109. Perry Brownlow described to Leo Amery, diary, 28 December 1936, Leo Amery, *The Empire at Bay*, p. 435
110. Sir Henry 'Chips' Channon, diary, 11 December 1936, *Chips*, p. 99. The editor of Channon's diaries, Robert Rhodes James, appended his own words 'Then we played bridge' to Channon's diary entry for that day, giving a sense of bathos that was not in the original – as though the speech was a trifle, soon to be forgotten. In the original diary, seen by the author, the phrase does not occur.
111. Interview with John Prichard
112. Interview with John Meredith
113. Geoffrey H. Wells, diary, 11 December 1936
114. James Pope-Hennessy, *Queen Mary*, p. 581
115. Kirsty McLeod, *A Passion for Friendship*, pp. 148–9

Chapter 20: The year the music stopped

1. Interview with John Prichard
2. *Daily Express* (1 December 1936)
3. Ibid.
4. Percy Bysshe Shelley, 'Ozymandias'
5. Dan Smith, 'A Site for Saur Eyes', *New Statesman* (26 February 2001)
6. Herbert Hensley Henson, diary, 1 December 1936

NOTES

7. *Yorkshire Post* (8 December 1936), quoted in James Pope-Hennessy, *Queen Mary*, p. 578

8. B. E. V. Sabine, *British Budgets in Peace and War*, p. 80, quoting Chamberlain's budget speech of 21 April 1936

9. *The Times* (2 December 1936)

10. A. Susan Williams, *Ladies of Influence*, p. 109

11. James Albrighton, diary, 30 October 1936

12. Ibid.

13. Ibid., 19 November 1936

14. Quoted in Bernard Crick, *George Orwell: A Life*, p. 312

15. George Orwell, *The Collected Essays, Journalism and Letters of George Orwell*, vol. 1, *An Age Like This, 1920–1940*, p. 585

16. Violet Milner, diary, 9 December 1936

17. Robert Bernays to Lucy Brereton, 23 December 1936, *The Diaries and Letters of Robert Bernays, 1932–1939*, p. 281 (on 22 December England beat Australia in the second Test by an innings and 22 runs)

18. Geoffrey Dawson, diary, 12 December 1936

19. Robert Bernays, diary, 15 December 1936, *The Diaries and Letters of Robert Bernays, 1932–1939*, p. 279

20. Geoffrey Dawson, diary, 15 December 1936

21. Sir Henry 'Chips' Channon, diary, 11 December 1936, *Chips*, p. 99

22. Hugo Vickers, *Elizabeth, the Queen Mother* (Hutchinson, London, 2005), p. 149

23. Ibid.

24. Quoted in Diana Vreeland, *DV*, ed. George Plimpton and Christopher Hemphill (Knopf, New York, 1984), pp. 73–5

25. Susan Williams, *The People's King*, p. 261

26. Lucy Baldwin, diary, 18 December 1936

27. Walter Bagehot, *The English Constitution*, quoted in Sarah Bradford, *King George VI*, p. 206

28. Neville Chamberlain to Hilda Chamberlain, 13 December 1936, *NCDL*, pp. 227–8.

29. Lucy Baldwin, diary, 11 December 1936

30. Quoted in J. Graham Jones, 'Lloyd George and the Abdication of Edward VIII', *National Library of Wales Journal*, 30 (1997), p. 93

31. Geoffrey H. Wells, diary, 11 December 1936

32. Vera Brittain, *Testament of Experience*, p. 163

33. Title of a Blakeway Productions film for BBC TV, 2006

THE LAST DANCE

34. Robert Bernays, diary, 15 December 1936, *The Diaries and Letters of Robert Bernays, 1932–1939*, p. 279
35. Neville Chamberlain to Hilda Chamberlain, 13 December 1936, *NCDL*, pp. 227–8
36. Neville Chamberlain to Hilda Chamberlain, 8 December 1936, *NCDL*, pp. 226–7
37. For a historian's view, see Sir Ian Kershaw, *Making Friends with Hitler*, pp. 343–5, on the likely outcome of a settlement that Lord Londonderry desired and to which Chamberlain might have acceded.
38. Lord Tweedsmuir to Stanley Baldwin, 12 December 1936, *WSC Documents*, p. 489
39. Winston Churchill to Ian Colvin, 17 December, 1936, *WSC Documents*, p. 496; Winston Churchill to Mackenzie King, 14 December 1936, *WSC Documents*, p. 489; Winston Churchill to Bernard Baruch, 25 December 1936, *WSC Documents*, p. 516
40. Mary Soames, *Clementine Churchill* (Doubleday, London, 2002), p. 307
41. Edward was staying in Schloss Enzesfeld in Austria, as a guest of Baroness Kitty de Rothschild, chafing at his confinement and spending a fortune on phone calls to Wallis.
42. Under divorce law of the time any collusion between the divorcing couple was prohibited. There had to be an innocent party and an aggrieved party. In this case there had clearly been some collusion between Ernest and Wallis and the concern was that somebody might step forward to challenge the decree. This would have been disastrous, preventing the abdicated King from marrying. The necessary steps were taken to prevent the King's proctor (the official charged with stopping divorces where collusion could be shown) from taking any action.
43. H. Montgomery Hyde, *The Londonderrys*, p. 225
44. BBC radio broadcast, 13 December 1936, quoted in J. G. Lockhart, *Cosmo Gordon Lang*, pp. 404–6
45. *Daily Telegraph* (17 December 1936)
46. Hugo Vickers, *Elizabeth, the Queen Mother*, p. 148
47. J. G. Lockhart, *Cosmo Gordon Lang*, p. 406
48. Sir Henry 'Chips' Channon, diary, 21 December 1936, *Chips,* p. 102
49. J. G. Lockhart, *Cosmo Gordon Lang*, p. 406
50. Private information
51. Herbert Hensley Henson, diary, 18 December 1936

416

52. Ibid., 23 December 1936
53. Hugo Vickers, *Elizabeth, the Queen Mother*, p. 149
54. Held in the Royal Archives, Windsor
55. Quoted in Susan Williams, *The People's King*, p. 250
56. H. V. Evatt to Winston Churchill, 12 December 1936, quoted in *WSC Documents*, p. 487
57. Fritz Hesse, *Hitler and the English*, p. 31
58. Michael Bloch, *Ribbentrop*, p. 122, and Reinhard Spitzy, *How We Squandered the Reich*, pp. 67–8
59. In his final dispatch: Michael Bloch, *Ribbentrop*, p. 146
60. As described by Dr Geoffrey Waddington, University of Leeds, in *Ribbentrop: The Nazi Who Loved England* (BBC TV, 1999)
61. Interview with Marguerite Patten, August 2009
62. David F. Hutchings, *RMS Queen Mary – 80 Years of Splendour*, p. 24
63. Ibid., p. 8
64. C. W. R. Winter, *Queen Mary: Her Early Years Recalled* (Patrick Stephens, Wellingborough, 1986), p. 126
65. Ibid.
66. Ibid.
67. Ibid.
68. Ibid.
69. Nicholas Moss, *This is BBC Television* (BBC Network Television, London, 1996), p. 40
70. Ibid.
71. Sir John Reith, diary, 2 November 1936, in *The Reith Diaries*, ed. Charles Stuart (Collins, London, 1975)
72. Graham Greene, 'Wings over Wardour Street', *The Spectator* (24 January 1936)
73. Nicholas Moss, *This is BBC Television*, p. 39
74. Private information
75. Janie Hampton, *Joyce Grenfell* (John Murray, London, 2002), p. 33
76. Joyce Grenfell to her mother, Nora Langhorne, 29 December 1936, *Darling Ma*, p. 16
77. Janie Hampton, *Joyce Grenfell*, p. 34
78. David Strain, diary, 24 and 25 December 1936
79. Interview with John Prichard
80. Geoffrey Dawson, diary, 31 December 1936
81. Wilson Harris, *The Spectator* (18 September 1936)

82. Herbert Hensley Henson, diary, 31 December 1936
83. Winston Churchill to Bernard Baruch, 1 January 1937, *WSC Documents*, p. 520
84. Lucy Baldwin, diary, 31 December 1936
85. Peter Stansky and William Abrahams, *Journey to the Frontier*, p. 386
86. Ibid., p. 388
87. Richard Baxell, *British Volunteers in the Spanish Civil War*, p. 60
88. Quoted in A. Susan Williams, *Ladies of Influence*, p. 112

Sources

Bibliography

Amery, Leo, *The Empire at Bay: The Leo Amery Diaries,* ed. John Barnes and David Nicholson, Foreword by Lord Stockton (Hutchinson, London, 1988)

Amory, Mark, *Lord Berners: The Last Eccentric* (Pimlico, London, 1999)

Annan, Noel, *Our Age* (Weidenfeld & Nicolson, London, 1990)

Anthony, Scott, et al., *We Live in Two Worlds,* introductory booklet to British Film Institute video disc BFIVD759 (2008)

Auden, W. H., and Isherwood, Christopher, *The Ascent of F6* (Faber & Faber, London, 1986)

Baxell, Richard, *British Volunteers in the Spanish Civil War* (RKP, London, 2004)

Beaton, Cecil, *Self-Portrait with Friends: The Selected Diaries of Cecil Beaton, 1926–1974,* ed. Richard Buckle (Weidenfeld & Nicolson, London, 1972)

Bedford, Sybille, *Aldous Huxley: A Biography,* vol. 1, *1894–1939* (Chatto & Windus, London, 1974)

Bernays, Robert, *The Diaries and Letters of Robert Bernays, 1932–1939: An Insider's Account of the House of Commons,* ed. Nick Smart (Edwin Mellen Press, Lampeter, 1996)

Berry, Paul, and Bostridge, Mark, *Vera Brittain: A Life* (Virago, London, 2008)

Beveridge, James, *John Grierson* (Macmillan, New York, 1978)

Bloch, Michael (ed.), *Wallis and Edward: Letters 1931–7, The Intimate Correspondence of the Duke and Duchess of Windsor* (Penguin, London, 1986)

Bloch, Michael, *The Reign and Abdication of King Edward VIII* (Bantam, London, 1990)

Bloch, Michael, *Ribbentrop* (Bantam Press, London, 1992)

Bormann, Martin, *Hitler's Table-Talk: Hitler's Conversations Recorded by Martin Bormann*, intro. by Hugh Trevor-Roper (Oxford University Press, Oxford, 1988)

Boyd Orr, John, *As I Recall* (MacGibbon & Kee, London, 1966)

Bradford, Sarah, *King George VI* (Weidenfeld & Nicolson, London, 1989)

Brendon, Piers, *The Dark Valley: A Panorama of the 1930s* (Jonathan Cape, London, 2000)

Brittain, Vera, *Testament of Experience* (Virago, London, 1979)

Browne, Felicia, *Drawings* (Lawrence and Wishart, London, 1936)

Bruce Lockhart, Robert, *The Diaries of Sir Robert Bruce Lockhart*, vol. 1, *1915–1938*, ed. Kenneth Young (Macmillan, London, 1973)

Buchanan, Tom, *Britain and the Spanish Civil War* (Cambridge University Press, Cambridge, 1997)

Buchanan, Tom, *The Impact of the Spanish Civil War on Britain*, Sussex Studies in Spanish History (Sussex Academic Press, Brighton, 2007)

Cameron, Sean James, *Rhondda Voices* (Sutton, Stroud, 2002)

Cannadine, Sir David, *In Churchill's Shadow* (Allen Lane, London, 2002)

Carter, Miranda, *Anthony Blunt: His Lives* (Macmillan, London, 2001)

Catterall, Peter (ed.), 'The Battle of Cable Street', *Contemporary Record*, vol. 8, no. 1 (summer 1994)

Cecil, Hugh and Mirabel, *Imperial Marriage* (Sutton Publishing, Stroud, 2005)

Chadwick, Owen, *Hensley Henson: A Study in Friction between Church and State* (The Canterbury Press, Norwich, 1998)

Channon, Sir Henry, *Chips: The Diaries of Sir Henry Channon,* ed. Robert Rhodes James, rev. edn (Weidenfeld & Nicolson, London, 1996)

Charmley, John, *Churchill: The End of Glory* (Hodder & Stoughton, London, 1993)

Churchill, Winston S., *The Gathering Storm*, vol. 1, *The Second World War* (Penguin, London, 1985)

Clark, Kenneth, *Another Part of the Wood* (John Murray, London, 1974)

Coffey, Thomas M., *Lion by the Tail: The Story of the Italian Ethiopian War* (Hamish Hamilton, London, 1974)

Cohen, Stan, *The Games of '36: A Pictorial History of the 1936 Olympics in Germany* (Pictorial Histories Publishing Company Inc., Missoula, 1996)

Common, Jack (ed.), *Seven Shifts* (Victor Gollancz, London, 1938)

Cooper, Duff, *Diaries*, ed. John Julius Norwich (Weidenfeld & Nicolson, London, 2005)

Cooper, Nick, *Things to Come* Viewing Notes (Granada Ventures, London, 2007)

Coppard, Audrey, and Crick, Bernard, *Orwell Remembered* (BBC Ariel Books, London, 1984)

Cornford, John, *A Memoir*, ed. Pat Sloan (Jonathan Cape, London, 1938)

Cornford, John, *Understand the Weapon*, ed. Jonathan Galassi (Carcanet New Press, Manchester, 1976)

Crick, Bernard, *George Orwell: A Life* (Penguin, Harmondsworth, 1992)

Dalley, Jan, *Diana Mosley: A Life* (Faber, London, 1999)

Davenport-Hines, Richard, *Auden* (Heinemann, London, 1995)

Day, Barry (ed.), *The Letters of Noël Coward* (Methuen Drama, London, 2007)

De Courcy, Anne, *1939: The Last Season* (Thames and Hudson, London, 1989)

De Courcy, Anne, *Circe: The Life of Edith, Marchioness of Londonderry* (Sinclair-Stevenson, London, 1992)

Donaldson, Frances, *Edward VIII: The Road to Abdication* (Omega, London, 1976)

Douglas-Hamilton, James, *The Truth about Rudolf Hess* (Mainstream Publishing, Edinburgh, 1993)

Dugdale, Blanche, *Baffy: The Diaries of Blanche Dugdale, 1936–47*, ed. N. A. Rose (Valentine Mitchell, London, 1973)

Emery, Jane, *Rose Macaulay: A Writer's Life* (John Murray, London, 1991)

Fort, Adrian, *Prof: The Life of Frederick Lindemann* (Jonathan Cape, London, 2003)

Garside, W. R., *British Unemployment, 1919–1939* (Cambridge University Press, Cambridge, 2002)

Gascoyne, David, *Journal 1936–7* (Enitharmon Press, London, 1980)

Gilbert, Sir Martin, *Winston Churchill: The Wilderness Years* (Heinemann, London, 1981)

Gilbert, Sir Martin, *Winston S. Churchill: The Coming of War, 1936–1939* (Heinemann, London, 1982)

Gilmour, David, *The Long Recessional: The Imperial Life of Rudyard Kipling* (John Murray, London, 2002)

Godfrey, Rupert (ed.), *Letters from a Prince: Edward Prince of Wales to Mrs Freda Dudley Ward, March 1918–January 1921* (Little, Brown & Co., London, 1998)

Graves, Robert, and Hodge, Alan, *The Long Weekend: A Social History of Great Britain, 1918–1939* (Hutchinson, London, 1985)

Gurney, Jason, *Crusade in Spain* (Readers' Union, London, 1974)

Hampton, Janie, *Joyce Grenfell* (John Murray, London, 2002)

Hardinge, Helen, *Loyal to Three Kings* (William Kimber, London, 1967)

Hardy, Forsyth, *Grierson on Documentary* (Collins, London, 1946)

Hardy, Forsyth, *John Grierson: A Documentary Biography* (Faber & Faber, London, 1979)

Hesse, Fritz, *Hitler and the English* (Allan Wingate, London, 1954)

Holtby, Winifred, *South Riding* (Virago, London, 2007)

Hutchings, David F., *RMS Queen Mary: 50 Years of Splendour* (Kingfisher Railway Productions, Southampton, 1988)

Hyde, H. Montgomery, *The Other Love: An Historical and Contemporary Survey of Homosexuality in Britain* (Heinemann, London, 1970)

Hyde, H. Montgomery, *The Londonderrys: A Family Portrait* (Hamish Hamilton, London, 1979)

Jenkins, Roy, *Churchill* (Macmillan, London, 2001)

Jones, Thomas, *A Diary with Letters, 1931–1950* (Oxford University Press, London, 1954)

Kershaw, Sir Ian, *Making Friends with Hitler. Lord Londonderry and Britain's Road to War* (Penguin, London, 2005)

Lascelles, Alan, *King's Counsellor Abdication and War: The Diaries of Sir Alan Lascelles,* ed. Duff Hart-Davis (Weidenfeld & Nicolson, London, 2006)

Lee, Hermione, *Virginia Woolf* (Chatto & Windus, London, 1996)

Loch Mowat, Charles, *Britain Between the Wars 1918–1940* (Methuen University Paperback, London, 1968)

Lockhart, J. G., *Cosmo Gordon Lang* (Hodder and Stoughton, London, 1949)

Londonderry, Edith, Marchioness of, *Retrospect* (F. Muller, London, 1938)

Londonderry, The Marquess of, *Ourselves and Germany* (Penguin, London, 1938)

Londonderry, The Marquess of, *Wings of Destiny* (Macmillan, London, 1943)

Loudon, Irvine, *Death in Childbirth* (Clarendon Press, Oxford, 1992)

Lycett, Andrew, *Kipling* (Phoenix, London, 2000)

M'Gonigle, G. C. M., and Kirby, J., *Poverty and Public Health* (Victor Gollancz, London, 1936)

McLeod, Kirsty, *A Passion for Friendship: Sibyl Colefax and Her Circle* (Michael Joseph, London, 1991)

Marquand, David, *Ramsay MacDonald* (Cape, London, 1977)

Middlemas, Keith, and Barnes, John, *Baldwin: A Biography* (Weidenfeld & Nicolson, London, 1969)

Mockler, Anthony, *Haile Selassie's War* (Signal Books, London, 1984)

Moore, Charles, and Hawtree, Christopher, *1936 As Recorded by 'The Spectator'* (Michael Joseph, London, 1986)

Morrison, Blake, *Night Mail,* introductory essay, British Film Institute BFIVD833

Mosley, Charlotte (ed.), *The Mitfords: Letters between Six Sisters* (Harper Perennial, London, 2008)

Moss, Nicholas, *This is BBC Television* (BBC Network Television, London, 1996)

Muggeridge, Malcolm, *Like it Was: The Diaries and Letters of Malcolm Muggeridge*, ed. John Bright-Holmes (Collins, London, 1981)

Mulvagh, Jane, *Madresfield: One Home, One Family, One Thousand Years* (Doubleday, London, 2008)

Nicolson, Harold, *Diaries and Letters*, ed. Nigel Nicolson (Collins, London, 1966)

Orwell, George, *The Collected Essays, Journalism and Letters of George Orwell*, vol. 1, *An Age Like This, 1920–1940*, ed. Sonia Orwell and Ian Angus (Penguin, London, 1971)

Orwell, George, *Keep the Aspidistra Flying* (Penguin, London, 2000)

Orwell, George *The Road to Wigan Pier* (Penguin, London, 2001)

Overy, Richard, *The Morbid Age* (Penguin, London, 2009)

Perry, Matt, *The Jarrow Crusade: Protest and Legend* (University of Sunderland Press, Sunderland, 2005)

Pilgrim Trust, *Men without Work*, with an Introduction by the Archbishop of York (Cambridge University Press, Cambridge, 1938)

Pimlott, Ben, *Hugh Dalton* (Macmillan, London, 1985)

Pope-Hennessy, James, *Queen Mary* (Phoenix Press, London, 2000)

Priestley, J. B., *An English Journey* (Folio Society, London, 1997)

Pugh, Martin, *We Danced All Night* (Bodley Head, London, 2008)

Ranfurly, Hermione, Countess of, *The Ugly One: The Childhood Memoirs, 1913–1939* (Michael Joseph, London, 1998)

Reith, John, *The Reith Diaries*, ed. Charles Stuart (Collins, London, 1975)

Ribbentrop, Joachim von, *The Ribbentrop Memoirs* (Weidenfeld & Nicolson, London, 1954)

Roberts, Andrew, *The Holy Fox* (Macmillan, Papermac edition, London, 1992)

Roberts, R. Ellis, *H. R. L. Sheppard: Life and Letters* (John Murray, London, 1942)

Romilly, Esmond, *Boadilla* (Macdonald, London, 1971)

Roose-Evans James (ed.), *Joyce Grenfell: Darling Ma, Letters to her Mother, 1932–1944* (Hodder & Stoughton, London, 1988)

Rose, Kenneth, *King George V* (Phoenix Press, London, 2000)

Ryan, Deborah S., *The Ideal Home through the 20th Century* (Hazar, London, 1997)

Sabine, B. E. V., *British Budgets in Peace and War, 1932–1945* (Allen & Unwin, London, 1970)

St Martin's Review special issue, 'H. R. L. Sheppard, Himself and His Work' (December 1937)

Sandys, Celia, *Chasing Churchill* (Harper Collins, London, 2004)

Scott, Carolyn, *Dick Sheppard* (Hodder & Stoughton, London, 1977)

Scott, Peter, *The Triumph of the South* (Ashgate, Aldershot, 2007)

Self, Robert (ed.), *The Neville Chamberlain Diary Letters*, vol. 4, *The Downing Street Years* (Ashgate Aldershot, 2005)

Self, Robert, *Neville Chamberlain: A Biography* (Ashgate, Aldershot, 2006)

Shaw, D. John, *Sir Hans Singer: The Life and Work of a Development Economist* (Palgrave Macmillan, Basingstoke, 2002)

Shawcross, William, *The Queen Mother: The Official Biography* (Macmillan, London, 2009)

Sherriff, R. C., *No Leading Lady* (Victor Gollancz, London, 1968)

Skidelsky, Robert, *Oswald Mosley* (Macmillan, London, 1981)

Skidelsky, Robert, *John Maynard Keynes*, vol. 2, *The Economist as Saviour* (Macmillan, London, 1992)

Skidelsky, Robert, *The Return of the Master* (Allen Lane, London, 2009)

Soames, Mary (ed.), *Speaking for Themselves: The Personal Letters of Winston and Clementine Churchill, Edited by their Daughter* (Doubleday, London, 1998)

Soames, Mary, *Clementine Churchill*, revised and updated (Doubleday, London, 2002)

Spitzy, Reinhard, *How We Squandered the Reich*, trans. G. T. Waddington (Michael Russell, Norwich, 1997)

Spring Rice, Margery, *Working-Class Wives* (Virago, London, 1989)

Stansky, Peter, and Abrahams, William, *Journey to the Frontier: Julian Bell and John Cornford: Their Lives in the 1930s* (Constable, London, 1966)

Taylor, D. J., *Orwell: The Life* (Vintage, London, 2004)

Thomas, James, 'The Work of the Special Areas Commission: Schemes for

Social Improvement, 1934–1939', Institute of Education, University of London PhD thesis, 2005

Thomas, James, and Williams, A. Susan, 'Women and Abortion in the 1930s', *Social History of Medicine*, vol. 11, no. 2 (1998), pp. 283–309

Vaughan, Paul, *Something in Linoleum* (Sinclair-Stevenson, London, 1984)

Vickers, Hugo, *Elizabeth, the Queen Mother* (Hutchinson, London, 2005)

Vreeland, Diana, *DV*, ed. George Plimpton and Christopher Hemphill (Knopf, New York, 1984)

Waddington, Geoffrey T., 'Aspects of the Operation of the Dienstelle Ribbentrop, 1934–1938', *History*, vol. 265, no. 1 (January 1997)

Walters, Guy, *Berlin Games* (John Murray, London, 2007)

Watson, Francis, *Dawson of Penn: A Biography* (Chatto & Windus, London, 1951)

Watson, Francis, 'The Death of George V', *History Today*, vol. 36, no. 12 (1986), pp. 21–30

Waugh, Evelyn, *The Diaries of Evelyn Waugh*, ed. Michael Davie (Weidenfeld & Nicolson, London, 1976)

Weitz, John, *Hitler's Diplomat* (Weidenfeld & Nicolson, London, 1992)

Wilkinson, Ellen, *The Town That Was Murdered: The Life Story of Jarrow* (Victor Gollancz, London, 1939)

Williams, A. Susan, *Women and Childbirth in the 20th Century: A History of the National Birthday Trust Fund, 1928–93* (Sutton, Stroud, 1997)

Williams, A. Susan, *Ladies of Influence: Women of the Elite in Interwar Britain* (Penguin, London, 2000)

Williams, Susan, *The People's King: The True Story of the Abdication* (Penguin Books, London, 2004)

Williamson, Philip, and Baldwin, Edward (ed.), *Baldwin Papers: A Conservative Statesman,* digitally printed version (Cambridge University Press, Cambridge, 2009)

Wilson, A. N., *Betjeman* (Hutchinson, London, 2006)

Windsor, The Duke of, *A King's Story: The Memoirs of HRH the Duke of Windsor* (Cassell, London, 1951)

Winter, C. W. R., *Queen Mary: Her Early Years Recalled* (Patrick Stephens, Wellingborough, 1986)

Woolf, Virginia, *The Diary of Virginia Woolf*, vol. 5, *1936–41,* ed. Anne Olivier Bell (Hogarth Press, London, 1984)

Young, Kenneth, *Stanley Baldwin* (Weidenfeld & Nicolson, London, 1976)

Ziegler, Philip, *King Edward VIII: The Official Biography* (Collins, London, 1990)

Broadcasts and Recordings

Blakeway, Denys (with Robert Harris), *God Bless You Mr Chamberlain* (BBC TV, 1988)

Blakeway, Denys, *The Road to War* (BBC TV, 1989) (producer: Christopher Warren)

Blakeway, Denys, *Beaverbrook* (Blakeway Productions for Channel 4 Television, 1996) (producer: Leonie Jameson)

Blakeway, Denys, *Joachim von Ribbentrop, The Nazi who Loved England* (Blakeway Productions for BBC TV, 1998) (producer: Fiona Procter)

Blakeway, Denys, *Diana Mosley* (Blakeway Productions for Channel 4 Television, 2003) (producer: Leonie Jameson)

Blakeway, Denys, *Abdication: A Very British Coup* (Blakeway Productions for BBC TV, 2006) (producer: Kate Werran)

Blakeway, Denys, *Balmoral* (Blakeway Productions for BBC TV, 2009) (producer: Lucy McDowell)

Blakeway, Denys, *A Tale of Two Britains* (Blakeway Productions for BBC TV, 2009) (producer: Alexander Leith)

Humphreys, Steve, *Forbidden Britain* (BBC TV, 1993–4)

Marshall, David, Imperial War Museum, Sound Archive Recording 9330/1/2

Illustration credits

Index

Edward VIII, King (*continued*)
301–6; visits Home Fleet at Portland, 304;
tours south Wales, 306–12; criticized for
political comments, 311–12; proposed
morganatic marriage to Wallis, 314–16,
322; and Dominions' view of proposed
marriage, 317, 319–20; press coverage of
marriage crisis, 321–2; sees Geoffrey
Dawson as enemy, 322; denied broadcast
to nation, 323–4; and Wallis's departure
for France, 325; political support for,
326–7; financial settlement, 335–6; final
broadcast, 339–40; given title Duke of
Windsor, 339; leaves England for exile,
341; rumours of Establishment plot
against, 349; Lang condemns in broadcast,
352; in Austria, 362–3; Wallis suspects of
adultery with Baroness Rothschild, 363
Eisenstein, Serge, 93
Ekevall, Kay, 66
electricity: in home, 126–7
Eliot, T. S., 41
Elizabeth, Princess (*later* Queen Elizabeth
II), 223, 296, 314
Elizabeth, Queen of George VI (*formerly*
Duchess of York): opposes Edward VIII,
136; attends ceremony of Presentation of
Colours, 223; at débutante ceremony,
226; at Birkhall (Scotland), 296; relations
with Wallis Simpson, 297; denounces
Wallis Simpson as unsuitable wife for
Edward, 321; supports husband in
abdication crisis, 334; moves to
Buckingham Palace on husband's
accession, 339; as Queen, 347–9
eugenics, 159

families: size, 159–60
Fascism: in Britain, 3, 255–62, 265–6; in
Spanish Civil War, 196, 345–6; *see also*
Nazism
Faulkner, Hugh, 260–1, 263
Fellowes, Daisy, 220
films: documentary, 90–1, 93–4, 102–3; *see
also* cinema
First World War: effect, 4, 6, 124; and
pacifist movement, 174
Fishman, Bill, 257, 262
Fitzgerald, Helen, 233
Flagstad, Kirsten, 218
Forrest family (of Wigan; 'Brookers'), 65–7,
69
Fort Belvedere, Sunningdale, 145, 326, 332

Fowle, 'Chick', 96
France: and German occupation of
Rhineland, 109–10, 112; and prospective
German alliance with Britain, 240
Franco, General Francisco, 189, 194–5, 345,
364
Fritsch, General Werner von, 109
Fury, HMS, 341

Gallup, George: polls, 355
Game, Sir Philip, 263
Gandhi, Mohandas Karamchand (Mahatma),
184, 278
Garmisch-Partenkirchen: Winter Olympics
(1936), 84
Garrett, John, 121
gas (poison), 176–9
Gascoyne, David, 191, 195
General Post Office (GPO): Film Unit,
91–5, 98; displays at Ideal Home
Exhibition, 123
General Strike (1926), 29, 75
George V, King: decline and death, 2, 14,
20–2, 24–5, 29–34, 217; Jubilee (1935),
6–7; lying-in-state, 35–6, 43–7; funeral,
39–40, 49–50; popularity, 40, 45–6;
lifestyle, 143; values, 149; on
homosexuals, 152; Christmas Day
broadcasts, 359
George VI, King (*earlier* Prince Albert,
Duke of York; 'Bertie'): accession, 2, 33,
339, 347–8; and father's decline and
death, 26; opposes Edward VIII, 136; at
Hyde Park ceremony of Presentation of
Colours, 224; stammer, 224, 353, 360; at
Birkhall (Scotland), 296–7; in succession
to throne, 296–7, 314, 320; and Edward's
prospective abdication, 321; Baldwin
discusses succession with, 333–4; dines
with Edward in abdication crisis, 333;
resentment at Edward's financial
settlement and wealth, 336; style of
monarchy, 347–9; coronation, 350, 355;
rebukes Lang, 353–4
George, King of the Hellenes, 235
Germany: occupies Rhineland, 2, 109–16,
175, 254; as war threat, 4, 87–8, 111–13,
175; Londonderrys' visit to, 73–4, 77–84;
naval pact with Britain, 79, 82; strength
of Luftwaffe, 80–1, 83, 112; Britain
rejects alliance with, 81, 238, 293; British
attitudes to, 110; successes at Berlin
Olympics, 244, 251; and Nazi